Neosentience

Neosentience

The Benevolence Engine

Bill Seaman and Otto E. Rössler

intellect Bristol, UK / Chicago, USA

First published in the UK in 2011 by
Intellect, The Mill, Parnall Road, Fishponds, Bristol, BS16 3JG, UK

First published in the USA in 2011 by
Intellect, The University of Chicago Press, 1427 E. 60th Street,
Chicago, IL 60637, USA

A catalogue record for this book is available from the British Library.

Cover design: Bill Seaman
Copy-editor: Integra Software Services
Typesetting: Mac Style, Beverley, E. Yorkshire

ISBN 978-1-84150-404-9

Printed and bound by Hobbs, UK.

Neosentience is a new computational and robotic paradigm that seeks to take its clues from human sentience. Benevolence is one important piece of this multi-perspective puzzle. Along with benevolence we present here many more of the pieces.

Contents

A Note from the Authors

We write this book as a circulating heterarchy. It can be read in differing or chance orders. This document arose out of many years of conversation between the authors. Our goal for the book is to spark new thoughts via the differing juxtapositions and the compressed ideas that it presents.

This text is a piece of recombinant informatics. Take any two micro-chapters and build a conceptual bridge between them.

We think that the fragment worlds presented here are compatible. Collisions of contemporaneous and historical concepts function as a springboard for radically new ideas. Let this book be an inspiration to future research.

Its micro-chapters can be endlessly recombined as a hopeful pass toward Koestler-type bisociation.

Science moves forward by articulating doubt. Everything we take for granted has a limit that may one day be transcended.

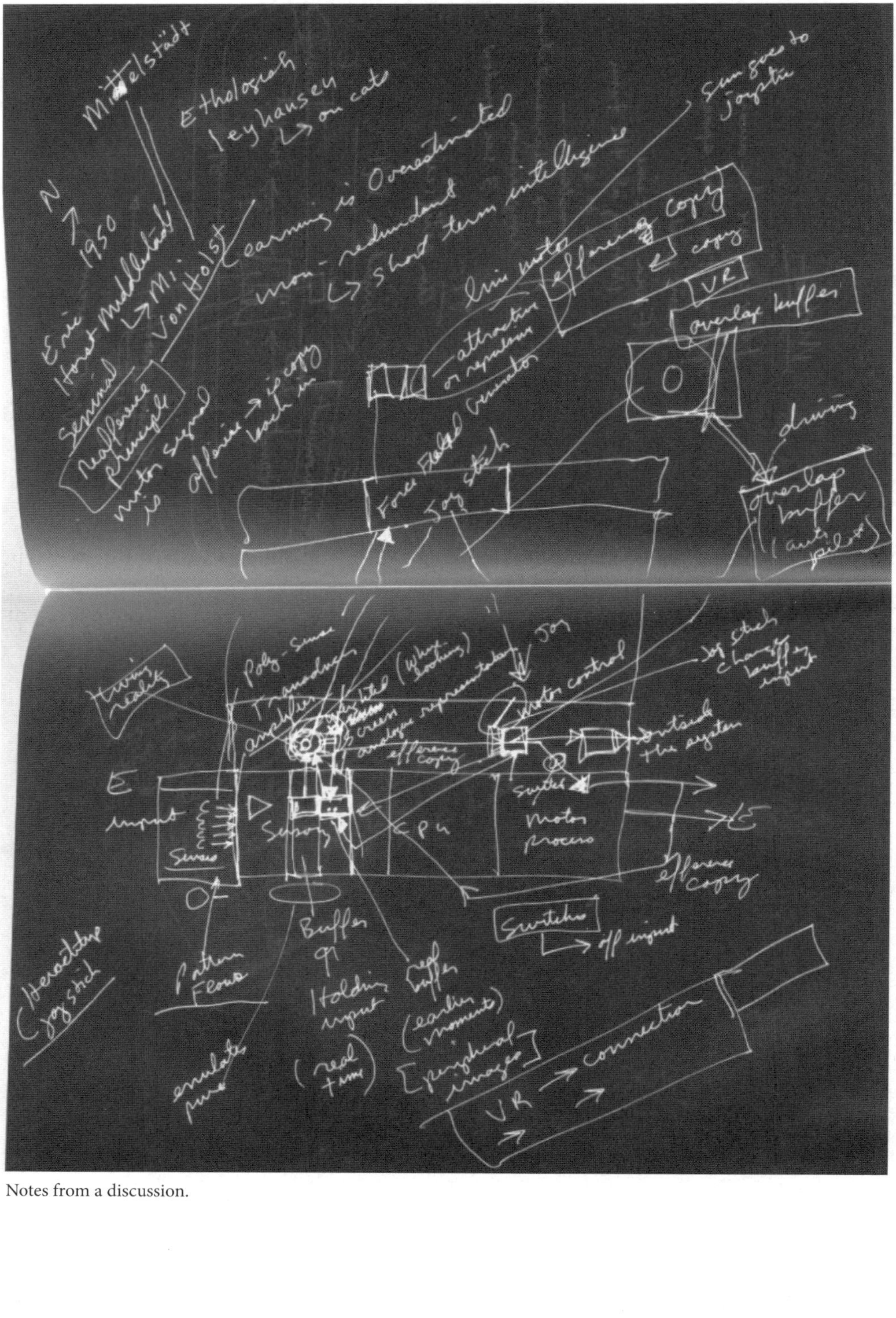

Notes from a discussion.

Acknowledgements

We would like to thank the many authors quoted here for their research and thought. We appreciate the kindness of the photographers, scientists, authors, families, trusts, artists, museums, foundations and historians who have supplied us with images for the book. We are appreciative of the creative commons initiative, enabling us to use many images that are rare yet exist at one's fingertips on the internet. We are deeply indebted to our families for being supportive of our long history of conversations, in particular we would like to thank Maura Walsh-Seaman, Frieda Mae Walsh-Seaman, and Fenn Walsh-Seaman for comments and ongoing discussion. We are grateful to Duke University and in particular the Department of Art, Art History & Visual Studies for research, material and travel support in the production of this book. We are especially indebted to the Chair – Hans Van Miegroet. And to our students. We thank Siegfried Zielinski for his thoughtful Foreword. We also thank Christina Werner, Jelena Stanovnik, Klaus Giel, Olafur Eliassson, Raju Grover, Walter Ratjen, Anthony Moore, Jonathan Kemp, Martin Howse, Oswald Berthold, René Stettler, Guilherme Kujawski Ramos, Christina Werner, Hugh Gash, Artur P. Schmidt, Friedrich Valjavek, Elisabeth von Samsonow, Peter Plath, Keisuke Ito, Daniel Dubois, Peter Cariani, Ted Krueger, Daniel C. Howe, Timothy Senior, Thom LaBean, Stephen Jones, Danqing Shi, Hans Diebner, N. Katherine Hayles, Mark Hansen, Christophe Letellier, Jeannette Ficher, Nils Röller, Jack Hudson and Olivier Perriquet for stimulation and discussion. We thank Intellect Press for their courage in taking on our project. We would also like to acknowledge the readers' patience with the sometimes arcane and sometimes bold thoughts that are here addressed in the hope for a better world.

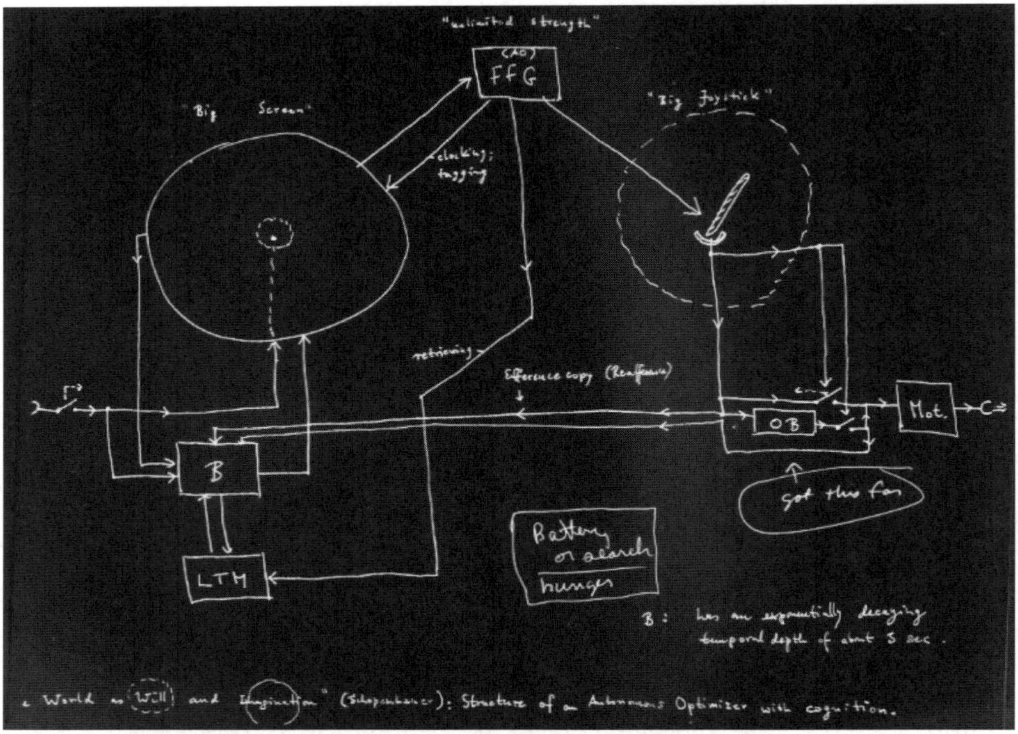

After some years of conversations—a preliminary sketch for the model.

B = Buffer/Pattern Matching
FFG = Force Field Generator
OB = Overlap Buffer
LTM = Long Term Memory/Pattern Matching

Big Screen = "Real Time" Virtual World Generator
Big Joystick navigates in real and/or imagined space
Mot. = Motors/Affector Potentials

Foreword

Believing Machines

There was a time when we learned to believe in machines. We realized that humans are beings with many deficiencies and shortcomings; we are not particularly effective and lethargic if you wish. So we built automata that are able to carry out activities that previously were acknowledged as being the exclusive province and privilege of human beings: calculating, combining, writing, playing music, drawing, playing, and making associations. The automatons quickly learned to perform these operations and others besides, often faster than we are capable of doing them. The intelligent machines delighted us with a perfection denied us.

We responded to this readiness to oblige by starting to believe in machines. Many people even developed an attachment to the world of artifacts, and put their trust in single artifacts and systematically organized complex units alike. This was above all a success owed to cybernetics, which originated because of a fear of entropy, a fear of uncontrollable inaccuracies and of states of panic that machines, according to Otto E. Rössler, do not currently have.

Techno-logically speaking, cybernetics was not very successful with its notion of a perfectly functioning, circular consistency in which we coexist with machines in perfect harmony. Socio-logically and psycho-logically, however, cybernetics has become established effectively and on a broad front. It has been given everyday clothes and at first glance is not recognizable for what it is. This is called material constraint. The concrete sub-forms of material constraint are constantly changing. However, there can be no doubt that it has become the most powerful agent of social and political organization. We have all learned to a high degree to act under the constraint of things, of the material-factual. This applies especially of course to the representatives of large institutions like research institutes, universities, and governments.

My mechanical–electrical favorites of the early twenty-first century are two special devices that originate from religious contexts. The first I encountered for the first time a few years ago in Naples. In the meantime, it is also to be found in southern Europe as well as in the Americas and is part of the electrification campaign of Christian churches. On a rectangular metal box which looks like a keyboard, two to three dozen fixed electric candles are mounted. From a distance, the artifact looks like a fragile, badly made Hammond organ on spindly legs. The electric offertory box utilizes a simple effect that is primarily of an optical nature (although the light bulbs of the candles also produce an interesting humming sound): When one of the buttons or levers positioned in front of the candles is pressed or moved, a candle lights up and becomes the visual representative of my soul in the house of God. After a while, the candle turns off and is ready to be used again – without making a mess with molten wax and without flickering or guttering as the usual cultic lights did.

Essentially, the electrical offering boxes are believing machines. Near the rows of candles and the row of buttons or levers, there is a slot in the metal box. On Italian models it is labeled "offerta" or "offerte." This is where the visitor to God's house is supposed to buy the temporary representative of his or her soul. The appealing thing about these devices is that they usually work without one's having inserted a coin. The median section, the commercial medium of the offertory box, is not connected at all to the buttons and candles. The machine believes the users, believes that they have paid when they press a button, and the visitors take their pleasure in the effect.

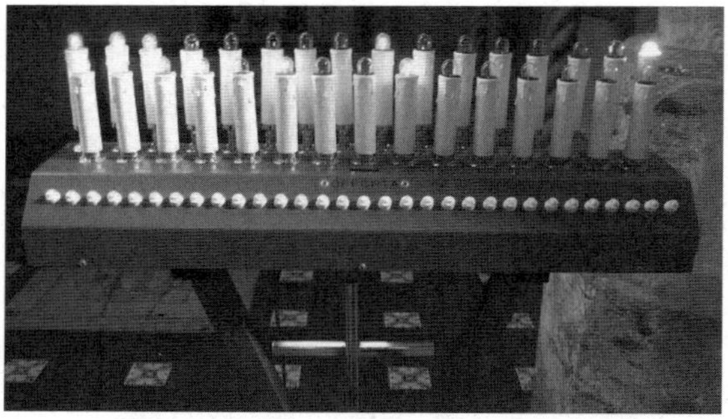

Electric offertory box, Naples, photo: MONO KROM, courtesy Prof. Dr. Siegfried Zielinski, 2005.

My second favorite is an equally impressive robotic device: a tiny technical artifact that is currently being produced in the millions in the People's Republic of China. It is a minuscule loudspeaker in a small red plastic case. At first glance it looks like a miniature transistor radio. However, if you turn it on, always the same sounds come out; the louder it is turned up, the tinnier the rendering, but the maximum volume is not very high. A strange sing-song sound is being heard in an endless loop, which seems as though it came from a far-off Buddhist temple. It sounds just as though a tiny little Buddha were sitting inside the box singing. And in the small sketch of its internal structure that accompanies the tiny technical wonder gadget, there actually sits a small Buddha. However, if one opens the device to see whether he really is inside, to prove his existence, the fragile Buddha box gives up its ghost: One has to believe He exists.

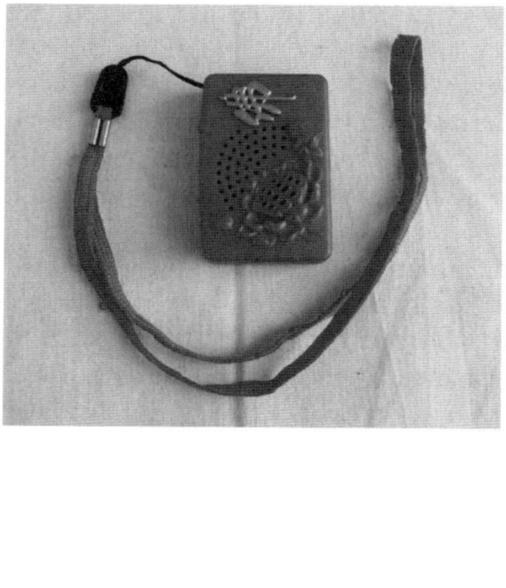

Battery-driven sonorous plastic Buddha, China, photo: MONO KROM, courtesy Prof. Dr. Siegfried Zielinski.

Neosentience | The Benevolence Engine developed over the last 10 years from an intensive dialog held between Bill Seaman and Otto E. Rössler. This publication is a machine that one can trust, and that one enjoys believing in. To analyze or dissect it could only be done at the price of destroying it: it is hermetic in the best sense of the word. In its interior lies a soul, an anima, that the artist and the scientist have breathed into it in a common effort and with mutual regard. Its energetic action can be clearly felt, even when some fragments of the compendium appear abstract and inaccessible. Its inner nucleus proclaims that the world we live in and are at home with can be changed, to its advantage. Such an unabashed intention presupposes an attitude toward the Other that one can only describe, adequately, as respect.

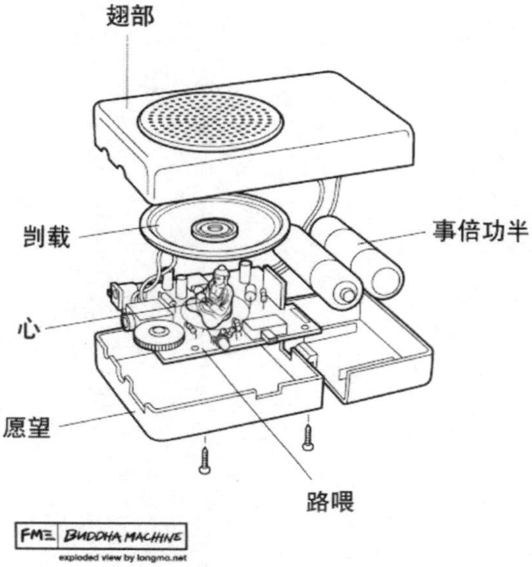

The mechanical inner life of the sonorous Buddha, courtesy Prof. Dr. Siegfried Zielinski.

> Just as a melody is not composed of notes, and a poem is not made up of words, and a drawing of a column is not just lines, so that one has to pull and wrench until one has prepared richness from unity: so speaks the person whom I address with the familiar form of "you" – "Du" or "Thou" in German [...] This is the eternal origin of art, which confronts a person as a form and which seeks to become a piece of work through him. (Martin Buber, *Ich und Du*, Jerusalem 1957.)

Siegfried Zielinski, University of the Arts (UdK), Berlin

Microchapters

Introduction – Bridging

The idea of building a model for a Neosentient computer and related robotic systems is both an exciting and daunting task. In order to model and ultimately build such a device one seeks to borrow important operative concepts and processes from the body and re-understand them in the context of a mechanism that is not human in nature. The use of micro-chapters in the book is a multi-perspective approach to this project – an answer that asks questions.

Hugh Everett:

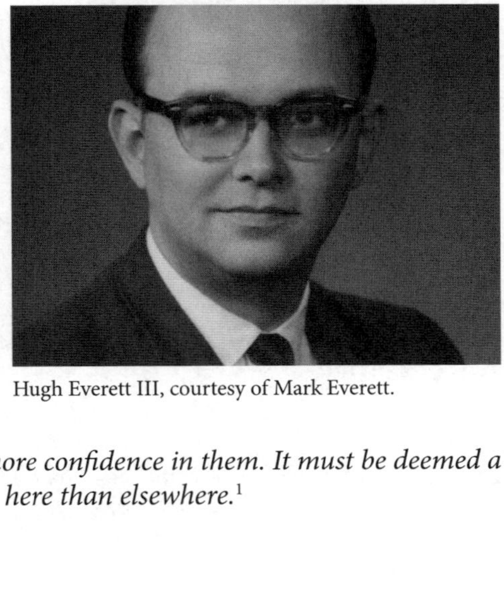
Hugh Everett III, courtesy of Mark Everett.

The model nature is quite apparent in the newest theories, as in nuclear physics, and particularly in those fields outside of physics proper, such as the Theory of Games, various economic models, etc., where the degree of applicability of the models is still a matter of considerable doubt. However, when a theory is highly successful and becomes firmly established, the model tends to become identified with "reality" itself, and the model nature of the theory becomes obscured. The rise of classical physics offers an excellent example of this process. The constructs of classical physics are just as much fictions of our own minds as those of any other theory we simply have a great deal more confidence in them. It must be deemed a mistake, therefore, to attribute any more "reality" here than elsewhere.[1]

Nonlinear

Ingredients: intuition, talking, and friendship.

Descartes

Descartes was the first person to describe the body as a machine.

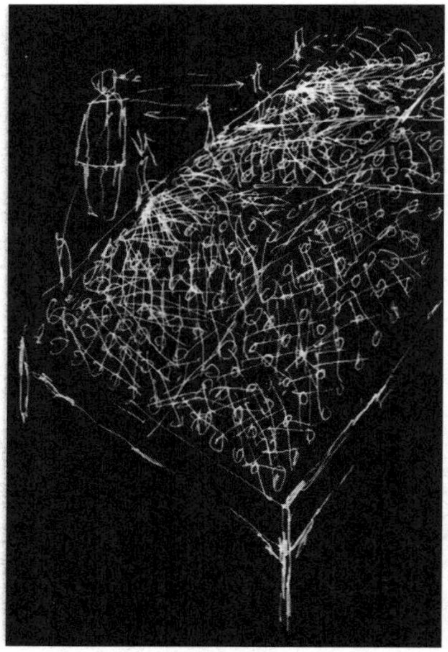

Electrochemical "field" and linked robot, Seaman 2005.

Karel Čapek

In 1923, Karel Čapek used the term "robot" which was a Czech word meaning worker, in a new context in his play *R.U.R.* (*Rossum's Universal Robots*).

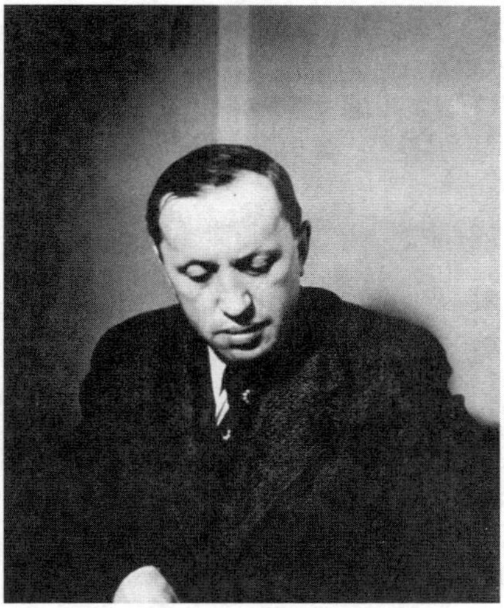

Karel Čapek ve fotografii, Jiří Opelík. Praha: SNK, 1991, p. 157. Public domain.

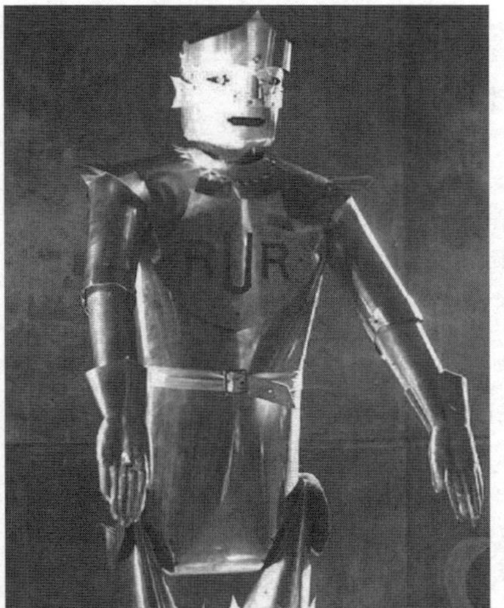

The play is laid out on an island somewhere on our planet, and on this island is the central office of the factory of Rossums's Universal Robots. "Robot" is a Czech word meaning "worker." When the play opens, a few decades beyond the present day, the factory had turned out already, following a secret formula, hundreds of thousands, and even millions of manufactured workmen, living automats, without souls, desires or feelings. They are high powered laborers, good for nothing but work. There are two grades, the unskilled and the skilled, and specially trained workmen are furnished on request.

When Helena Glory, president of the Humanitarian League, comes to acertain what can be done to improve the condition of those overspecialized creatures, Harry Domin, the general manager of the factory, captures her heart and hand in the speediest courting on record in our theatre. The last two acts take place 10 years later. Due to the desire of Helena to have the robots more like human beings, Dr. Gall, the head of the

The RUR robot which appeared in an adaption of Czech author Karel Capek's *Rossum's Universal Robots*.

physiological and experimental departments, has secretly changed the formula, and while he has partially humanized only a few hundred, there are enough to make ringleaders, and a world revolt of robots is underway. This revolution is easily accomplished, as robots have long since been used when needed as soldiers and the robots far outnumber human beings.

The rest of the play is magnificent melodrama, superbly portrayed, with the handful of human beings at bay while the unseen myriads of their own robots close in on them. The final scene is like Dusany on a mammoth scale.

Then comes the epilogue, in which Alquist, the company's builder, is not the only human being left on the island, but also the only one left on earth. The robots have destroyed the rest of mankind. They spared his life because he was a worker. And he is spending his days endeavoring to discover and reconstruct the lost formula. The robots are doomed. They saved the wrong man. They should have spared the company's physicist. The robots know that their bodies will wear out in time and there will be no multitudes of robots to replace them. But Alquist discovers two humanized robots, a young man and young woman, who have a bit of Adam and Eve in them, and the audience perceives that mankind is about to start afresh. Nature has won out after all.[2]

Roy Ascott – Behaviourist Art and the Cybernetic Vision

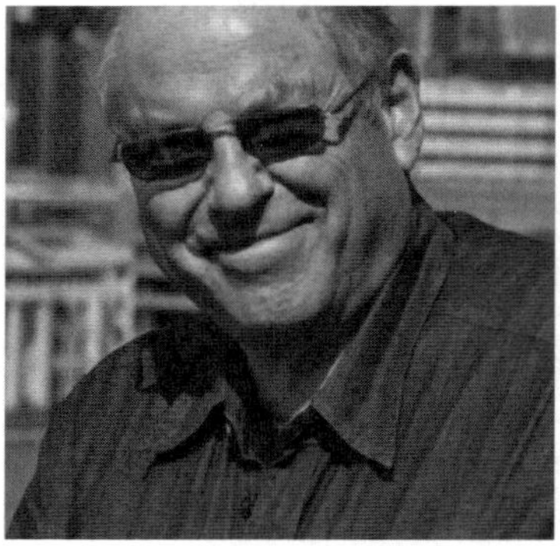

Roy Ascott. Courtesy of Roy Ascott.

Roy Ascott saw the potentials of behavioral relations in terms of works of art. In his paper entitled "Behaviourist art and the cybernetic vision," published in 1966, Ascott presented the following concept:

Behaviourist Art constitutes, as we have seen, a retroactive process of human involvement, in which the artefact functions as both matrix and catalyst. As matrix, it is the substance between two sets of behaviours; it neither exists for itself nor by itself. As a catalyst, it triggers changes in the spectator's total behaviour. Its structure must be adaptive implicitly or physically, to accommodate the spectator's responses, in order that the creative evolution of form and idea may take place.[3]

Neosentience – A New Branch of Scientific and Poetic Inquiry

Otto's Hands

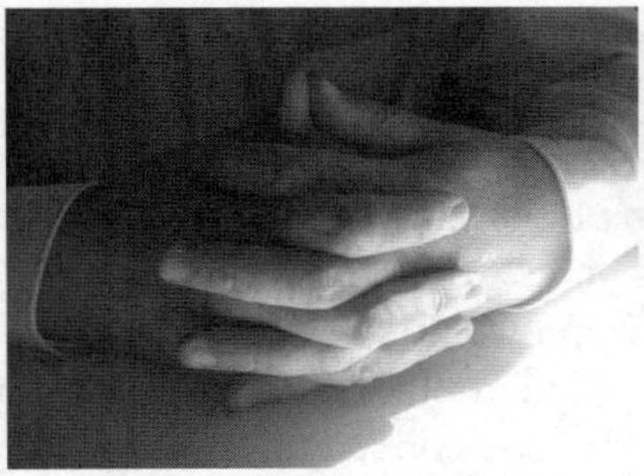
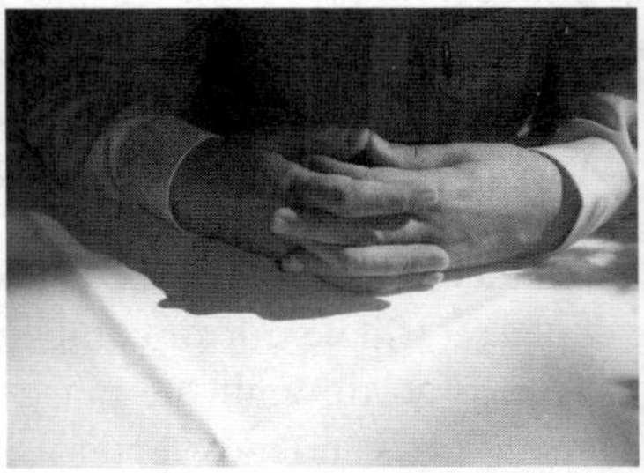
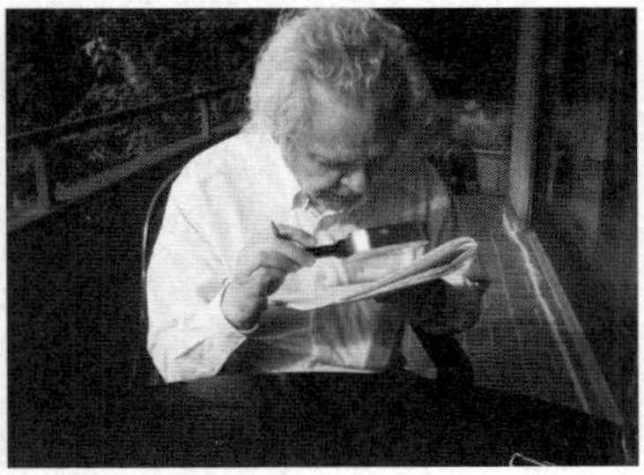
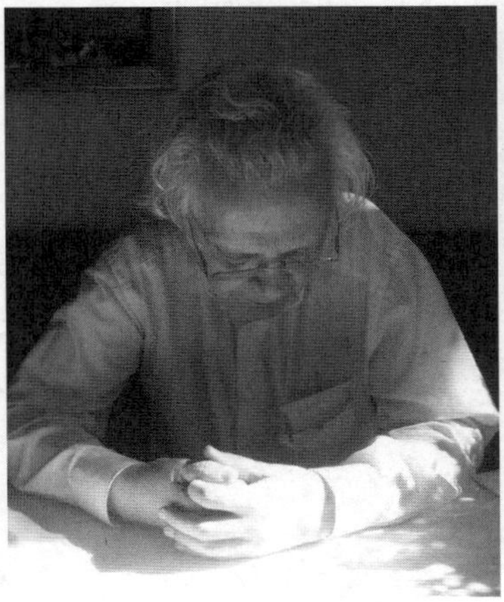
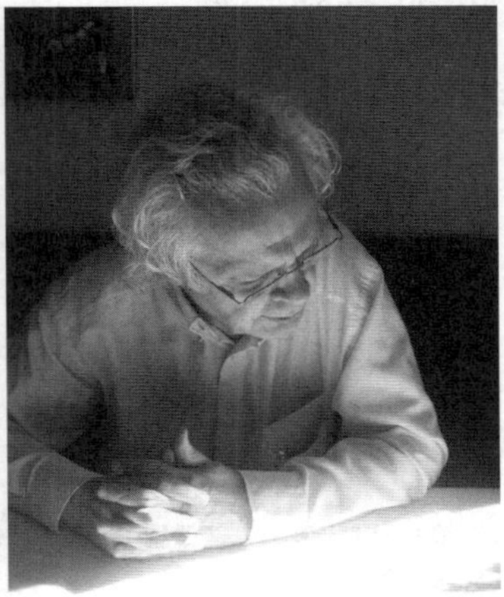

Otto Rössler, courtesy of Bill Seaman.

Bill Seaman

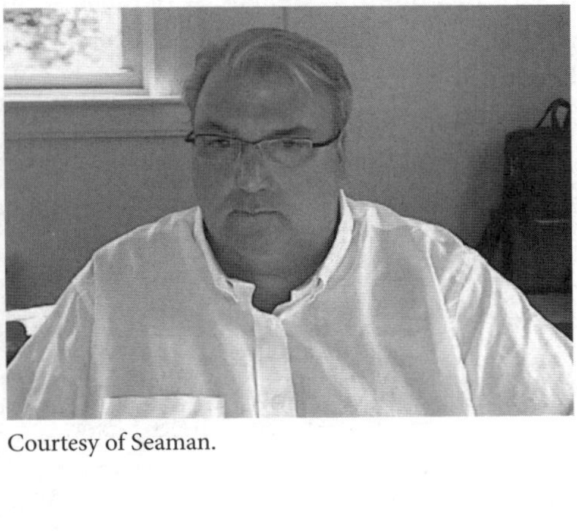

Courtesy of Seaman.

Central to both the scientific and poetics of Neosentience is to try to abstract the salient qualities of the human self that contribute to the emergent arising of sentience. What are those qualities, and what functionalities lead to their arising?

Operative definition of Neosentience

We consider a Neosentient robotic entity to be a system that could exhibit well-defined functionalities:

It learns; it intelligently navigates; it interacts via natural language;[4] it generates simulations of behavior (it "thinks" about potential behaviors) before acting in physical space; it is creative in some manner; it comes to have a deep situated knowledge of context through multimodal sensing; and it exhibits a sense of play; it will be mirror competent and will in this sense show self-awareness; It will be competent to go through the personogenetic bifurcation (thereby acquiring the ability to articulate meta-levels and meta-patterns).[5] We have entitled this robotic entity *The Benevolence Engine*. The interfunctionality is complex enough to operationally mimic human sentience. Benevolence can in principle arise in the interaction of two such systems.

Sentient entities actually exhibit a vast set of different relevant properties.

The N_S.E.N.T.I.E.N.T. Paradigm

This is a new paradigm that is intended to lead toward a new notion of personhood. Is it Non-sentient or Neo-sentient, that is the question. We can not know if there is consciousness in any machine, including our neighbor's brain.

- *Neosentient* – the system is to exhibit sentience of a new variety;
- *Self-organizing* – the system is self-improving;[6]
- *Environmentally embedded* – the robotic system should be situated and context-aware and be directly or remotely connected to a multimodal sensing system;
- *Nascent* – the system is "brought to life" and learns over time, building up a body of place-oriented knowledge; it is not alive in the sense of a living metabolizing organism, but it is "alive" in the sense of a conscious functioning in the world;
- *Temporal* – the system functions in relation to multimodal time-based flows of differing machine-oriented "sensing" inputs, parsing the latter through pattern recognition and operations on those patterns (internal abstraction);
- *Intra-active* – the entity arises through a reciprocal interaction with other individuals. Because direct input might be facilitated between "entities" in new forms of human/entity communication, we use the prefix (intra) suggesting a different order of connectivity in communication. The system develops an ongoing "projective" abstraction;
- *Emergent* – the entity's actions arise in context and are not known in advance but "come to life" in relation to environmental conditions, a series of "emotional" force field-based attractions and repulsions, and historical interactions and intra-actions;

- *Navigational* – it can move about to function in an appropriate manner and become context aware across multiple domains;
- *Transdisciplinary* – the research is influenced by multiple disciplines as it emergently unfolds. As the entity learns and becomes self-aware, Neosentience will also be something it learns about, and it may become a participant in its own discourse.

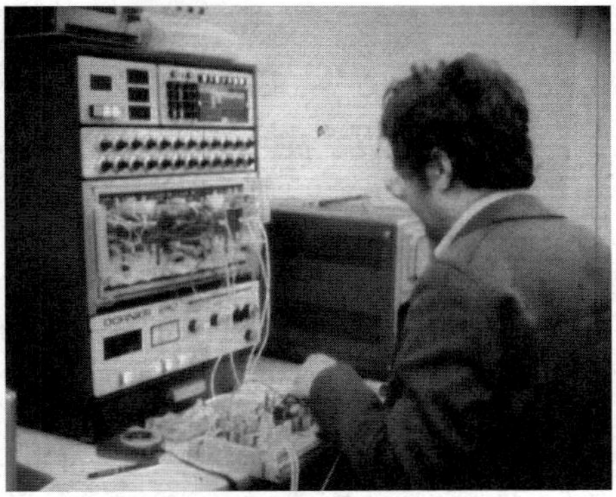

Otto in the front of his analog computer (1976), courtesy of Rössler.

We seek to have Neosentience arise as an emergent property of the system.

Our system functions as a self-consistent set of loops without the need of added qualia. It appears that the force fields function as surrogate feelings/drives and thus function as a perfect substrate for qualia.

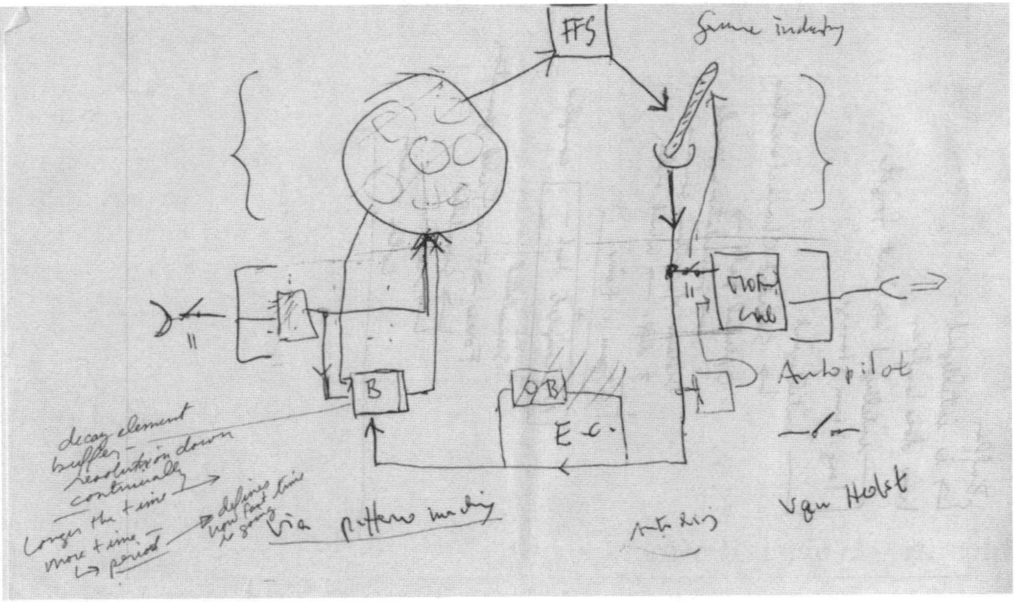

A rendering of notes for the model 2005.

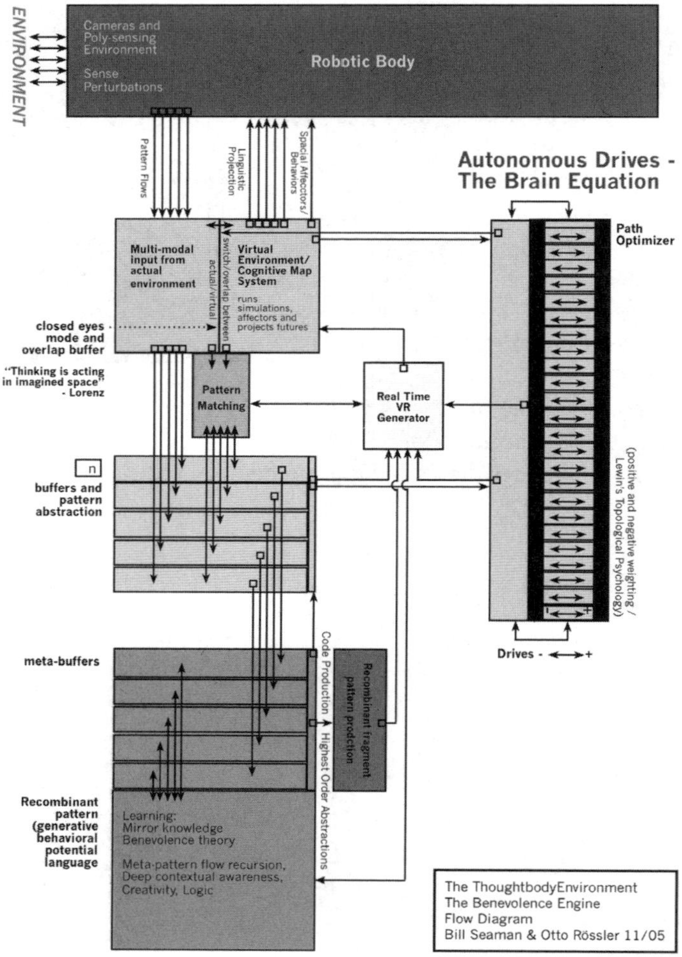

Re-rendering of the drawing from 05 – Todd Berreth.

Identity – When is it Mine?

Identity is the greatest miracle. Endophysics makes this miracle central to physics. The science of endophysics claims that the world as it is given to us is only a cut, an interface, a difference inside what is real (the whole). This has some powerful implications, including the possibility to change the whole world (i.e. the interface world).[7]

A.I. Background

In her *Notes by the Translator* written to clarify the textual work entitled *Sketch of the Analytical Engine Invented by Charles Babbage by L. F. Menabrea*, Lovelace made some very enlightened remarks:

The Analytical Engine is an embodying of the science of operations, constructed with particular reference to abstract number as the subject of those operations [...] Again, it [The Analytical Engine, emphasis Seaman] might act upon other things beside number were objects found whose mutual fundamental relations could be expressed by those of the abstract science of operations and which should be also susceptible of adaptions [her word] *to the action of the operating notation and mechanism of the engine. Supposing for instance, that the fundamental relations of pitched sounds in the science of harmony and of musical composition were susceptible of*

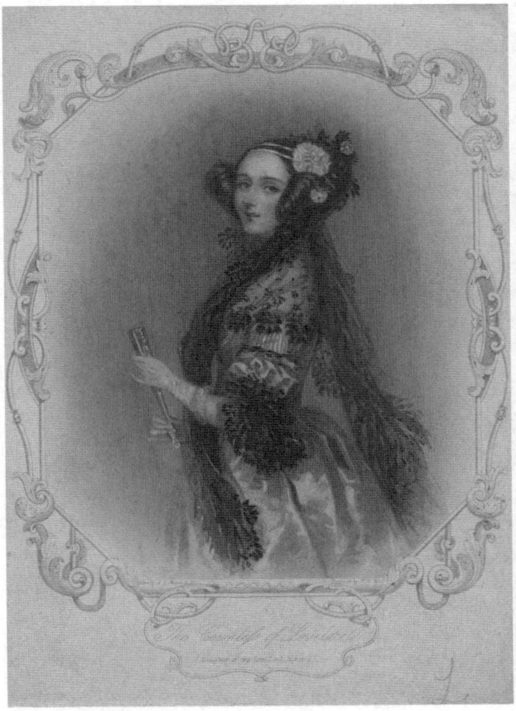

(Augusta) Ada King (née Byron), Countess of Lovelace by William Henry Mote, after Alfred Edward Chalon stipple engraving, published 1839 © National Portrait Gallery, London.

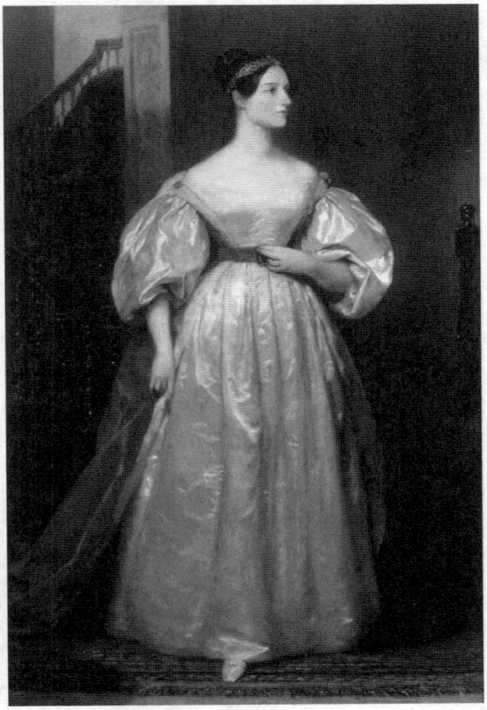

Ada Lovelace, public domain.

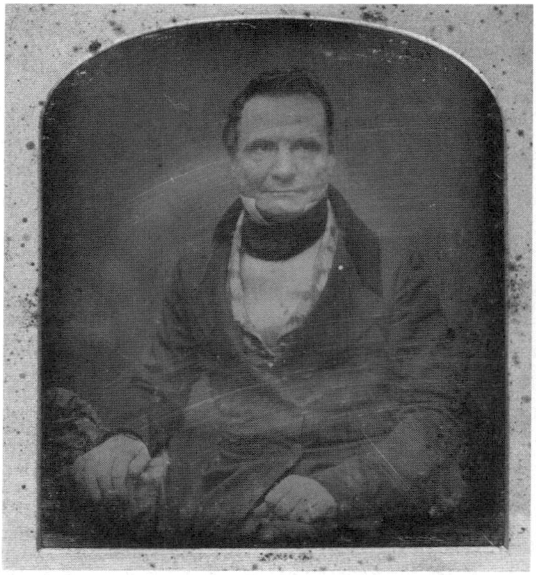

Charles Babbage by Antoine Claudet daguerreotype, circa 1847–51 © National Portrait Gallery, London.

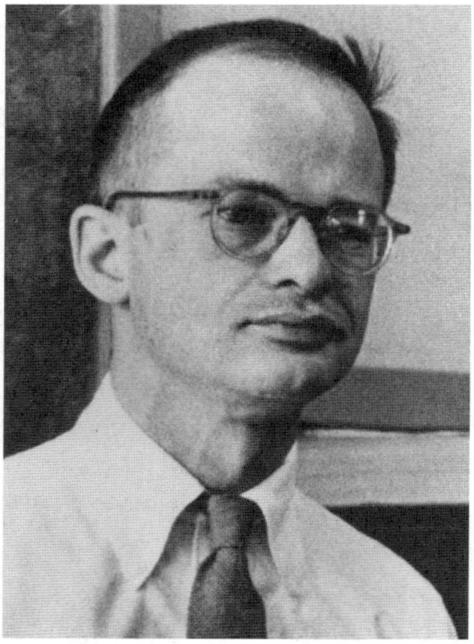

Walter Pitts, courtesy of the MIT Museum.

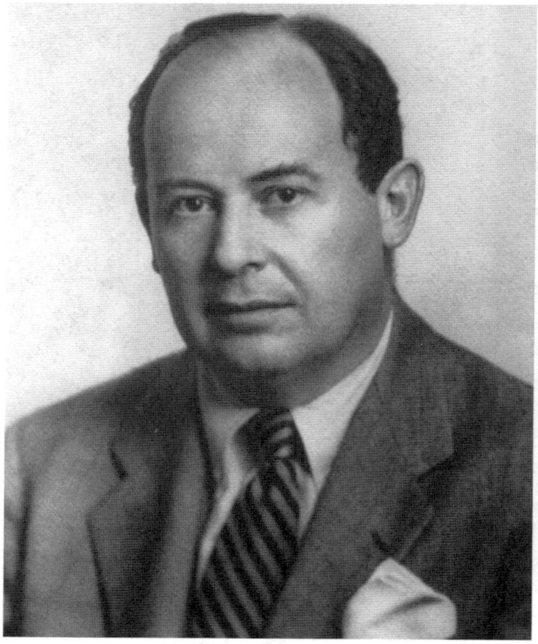

John von Neumann, courtesy of Marina v. N. Whitman.

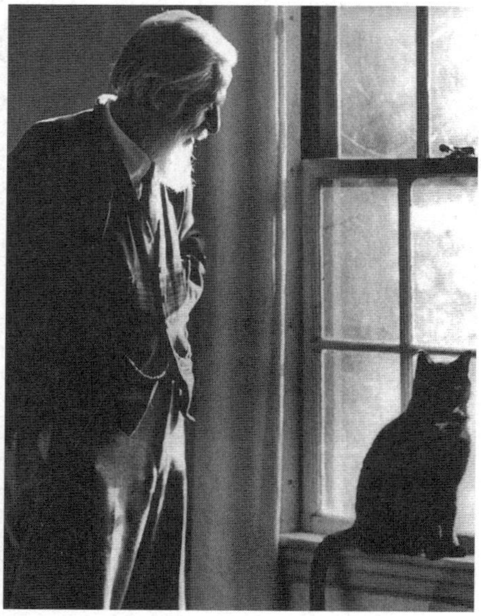

Warren McCulloch, photo courtesy of Taffy Holland. From the cover of *Brain Processes, Theories, and Models*, by Jose Mira-Mira, edited by Roberto Moreno-Díaz, published by The MIT Press.

such expressions and adaptions, the engine might compose elaborate and scientific pieces of music of any degree of complexity or extent [...] It may be desirable to explain, that by the word operation, we mean any process which alters the relation of two or more things, be this relation of what kind it may. This is the most general definition and would include all subjects in the universe.[8]

Note that the first programmer is writing about music and creativity!

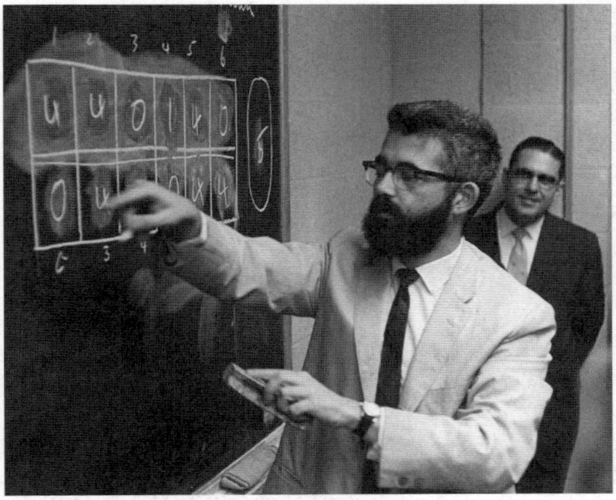

John McCarthy, courtesy of the MIT Museum.

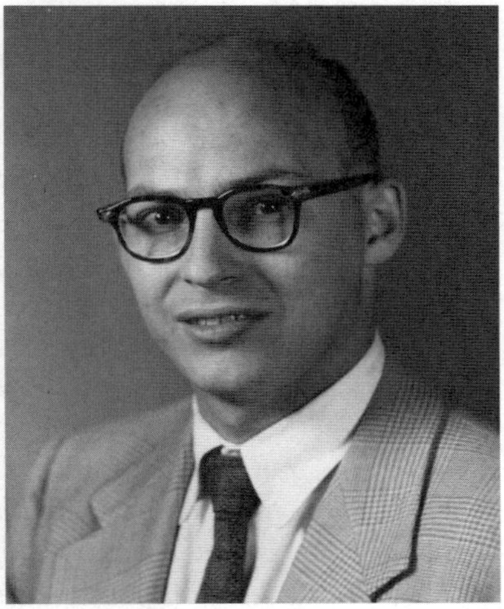

Marvin Minsky, courtesy of the MIT Museum.

Contemporary and historical literature surrounding the creation of intelligent machines is vast and full of differing opinions. Lovelace, in her *Notes by the Translator* (as cited in Babbage 1961)[9] imagined a potentially creative use of machines with the notion that machines might come to compose music and explore different kinds of "operational" processes. Similar ideas already arose in Descartes' time. McCulloch and Pitts' formulation of the artificial neuron in the early 1940s[10] sparked the birth of a new field, where human bio-functionality could potentially be abstracted in the service of creation of machines. Turing's, in part, even earlier writings on the potential of situated intelligent machines with "input" and "output" organs,[11] his test for machine

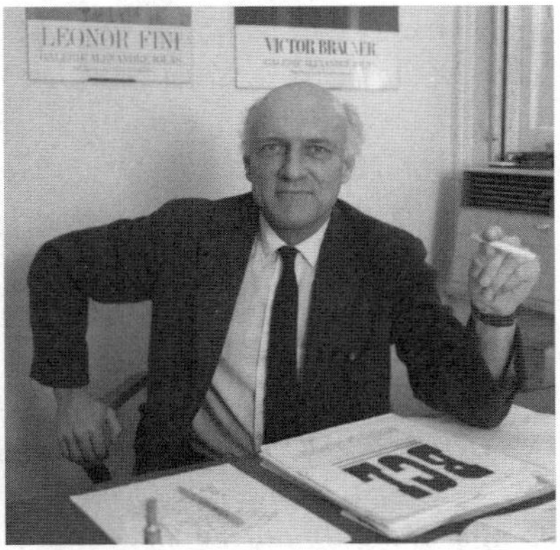

Heinz von Foerster sits for a photo behind his desk while holding a cigarette (image dated circa 1967), photo 0004914 courtesy of the University of Illinois Archives.

intelligence, his articulation of the potentials of the field, in *Computing Machines and Intelligence*[12] are all central. John von Neumann compiled the first draft on the EDVAC. He adopted the McCulloch and Pitts symbolism in diagramming the logical structure of the proposed computer and introduced technical terms such as organ, neuron, memory …[13] The notion of *Artificial Intelligence* was coined in a conference at Dartmouth in 1956 by John McCarthy. In 1958 John McCarthy and Marvin Minsky founded the Artificial Intelligence Laboratory at MIT. Minsky wrote many books on the subject. *Society of Mind*[14] discusses the notion of "agents" – microprocesses that are unintelligent in themselves but acquire an emergent nature when interacting, enabling "intelligence" to arise. Minsky's more recent writings concern machine emotion.[15] We propose that Neosentient entities must have programmed "force fields" (our analog of emotions) determining interaction with people, the environment, and other machines.[16] Much interesting work was also accomplished at Heinz von Foerster's Biological Computer Laboratory at the University of Illinois.

von Foerster – Circuitry Clues to Platonic Ideation

Infinite information/finite time

Whether or not this linguistic tidbit has any significance at all, the points I want to make in this brief introduction are (1) that essentially all of the concepts about a fabric, without which experience cannot be gathered, as "Gestalt," "Architype," "a priori," etc., go back to Plato, and (2) that ontologically this fabric cannot be explained, but requires ontogenetic argumentation. It is precisely this train of thought that is given in (2) which is used by Socrates in order to support his immortality assertion. Today, of course, we would adopt the terminology of evolution and would refer to this fabric as some genetically determined structure which evolved in the more successful mutants by the process of natural selection.

Since the gadgets I am going to talk about later are simple examples of just this fabric without which experience cannot be gathered, or – to put it into twentieth-century jargon – since these gadgets are simple examples of information-reducing networks which extract from the set of all possible stimuli a subset which is invariant to specified transformations, I have to stop for a moment in order to clarify a point which seems to me essential in

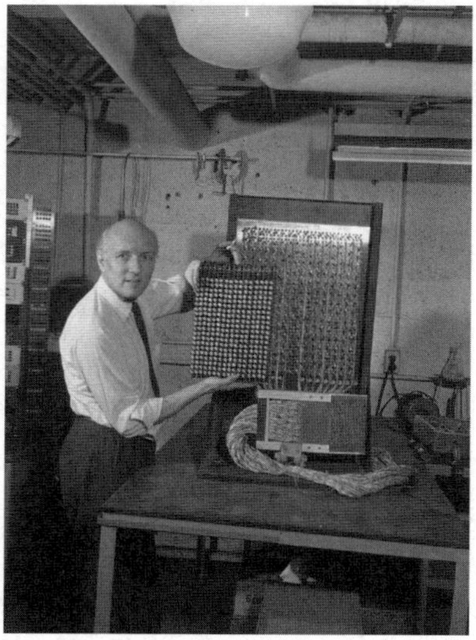

Heinz von Foerster holds the components of a research apparatus, presumably in the Biological Computer Laboratory at the University of Illinois (image dated circa 1967), photo 0004913 courtesy of the University of Illinois Archives.

all further arguments. This point deals with the fabric per se, namely with the question, "What are these structures or what are these invariants that enable us to gather the kind of experience we gather?"[17] *Perhaps my question will become a bit clearer if I add to Plato's philosophical examples the delightful neurophysiological examples which Lettvin and his co-workers recently reported in an article entitled "What the frog's eye tells the frog's brain", (1) Measuring with micro-electrodes in single fibres of the optic stalk in the frog, they confirmed and extended the observations of Hartline (2,3) and others (4), namely, that already highly reduced information is transmitted to the brain. In conclusion they wrote "The output from the retina of the frog is a set of four distributed operations on the visual image. These operations are independent of the level of general illumination and express the image in terms of: (1) local sharp edges and contrast; (2) the curvature of the edge of the dark object; (3) the movement of edges; and (4) the local dimmings produced by the movement of rapid general darkening."*

Since adaptation or learning is excluded in retinal and immediate post-retinal in a manner which enables them to compute those invariants – or "properties" – which have a decisive survival value to the frog. This enables me to rephrase my earlier question by asking what should these properties be which have the "decisive survival value" for the frog. Of course the question may be shrugged off by answering that a set of other properties may define another species – what is good for the elephant may be bad for the frog – a point which can be further supported by another property –detector (2), the one which detects the curvature of dark objects.[18]

How do we make the move from basic survival to science, art, and creativity? How do we avoid our destructive urges?

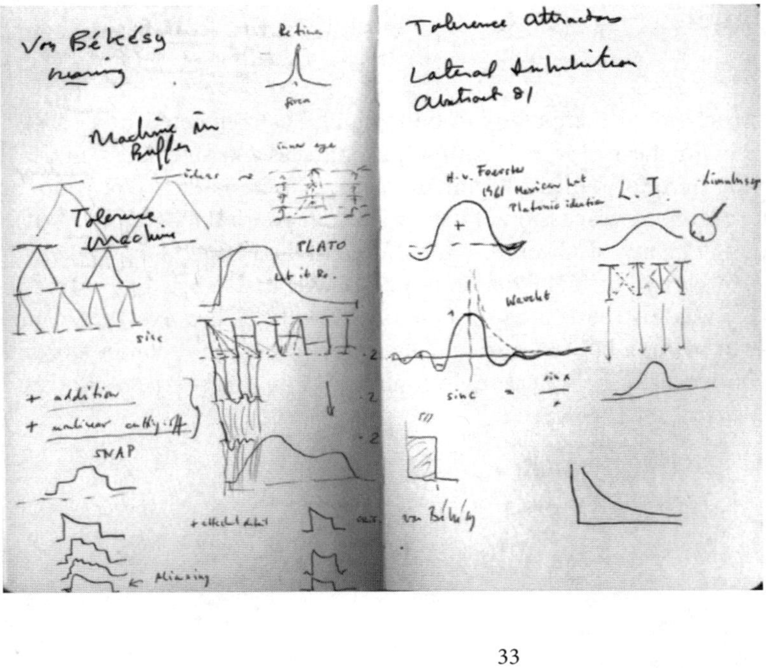

Drawing made by Rössler in conversation with Seaman.

von Neumann and the AEC1

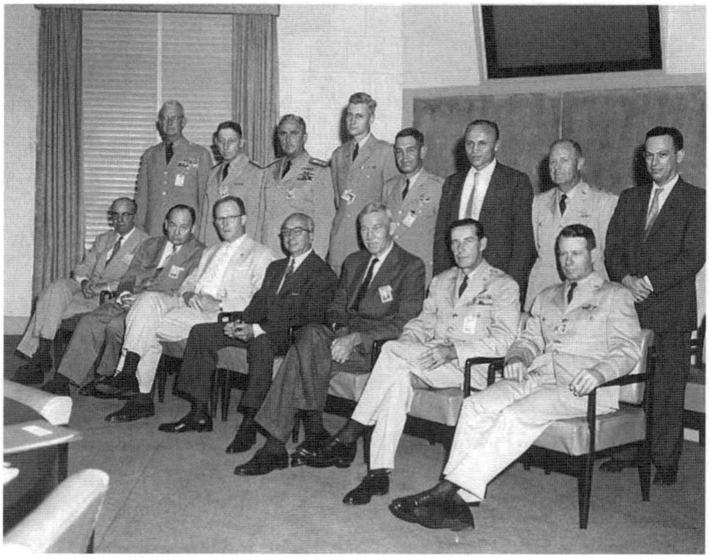

von Neumann and Colleagues who were connected with the AEC1, courtesy of Marina v. N. Whitman.

The Scale of Computers

The creation of an electrochemical computer can be imagined as connected to a robotic body and sensing system. In the history of computing one sees massive shifts in scale over time. It is interesting here to point to Feynman's paper "There is plenty of room at the bottom" in which he began the discussion of nanoscale computational potential.[19] Also Eric Drexler's early books *Engines of Creation*[20] and *Nanosystems: Molecular Machinery, Manufacturing, and Computation*, his MIT dissertation, are essential.[21] It is interesting to note that Marvin Minsky was his thesis adviser. One of the authors also explored nano-computation in relation to VR in a paper "Toward the production of nano-computers and in turn, nano-related emotive virtual/physical environments."[22] Can this be understood and be re-generated in the Neosentient?

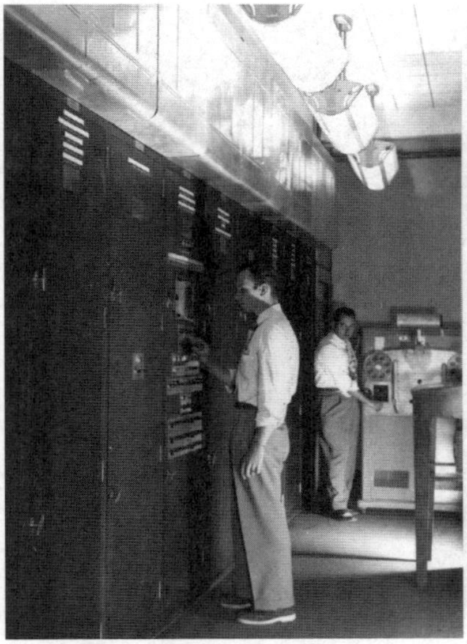

EDVAC – U.S. Army Photo of the EDVAC as installed in BRL Bldg 328, from the archives of the ARL Technical Library.[23]

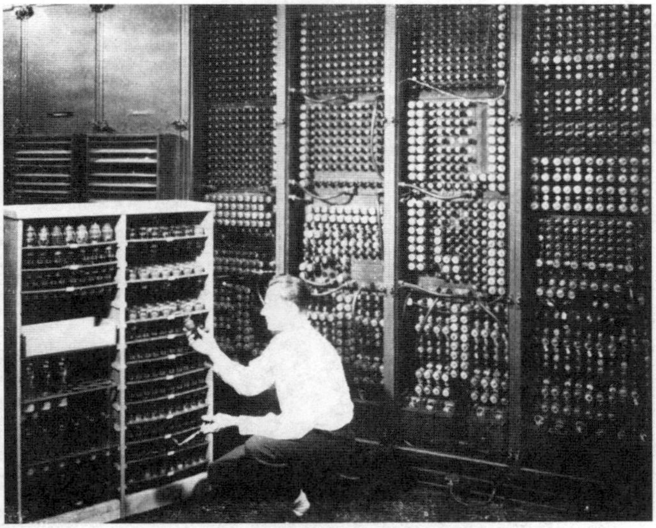

Replacing a bad tube meant checking among ENIAC's 19,000 possibilities.

ENIAC – U.S. Army Photo, from M. Weik, "The ENIAC Story" A technician changes a tube. Caption reads "Replacing a bad tube meant checking among ENIAC's 19,000 possibilities." Center: Possibly John Holberton.

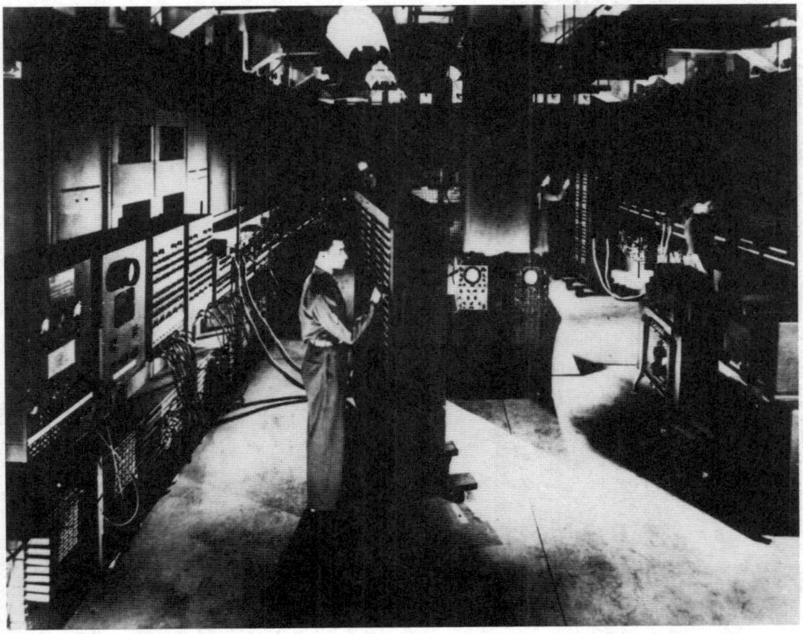

ENIAC – U.S. Army Photo, from 8 x 10 transparency, courtesy Harold Breaux. The classic shot of the ENIAC while still at the Moore School.

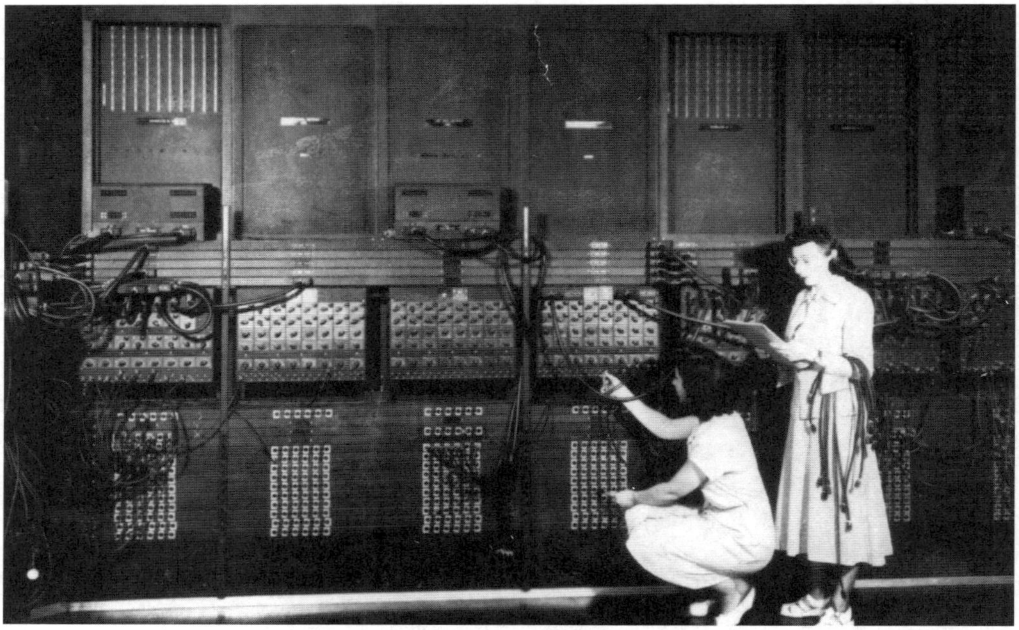

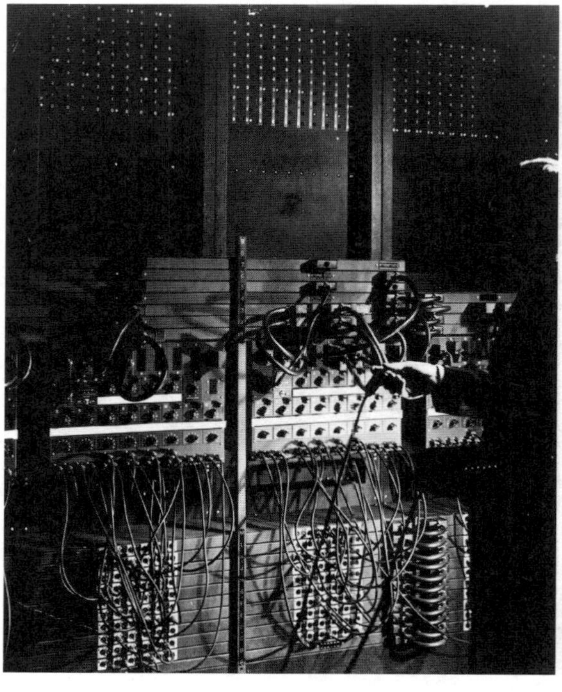

Above: ENIAC – Two women wiring the right side of the ENIAC with a new program, in the "pre-von Neumann" days. U.S. Army Photo from the archives of the ARL Technical Library. Standing: Ester Gerston Crouching: Gloria Ruth Gorden.

Left: Harry Huskey holding a wire of the ENIAC. U.S. Army Photo from the archives of the ARL Technical Library

Bell Relay Computer

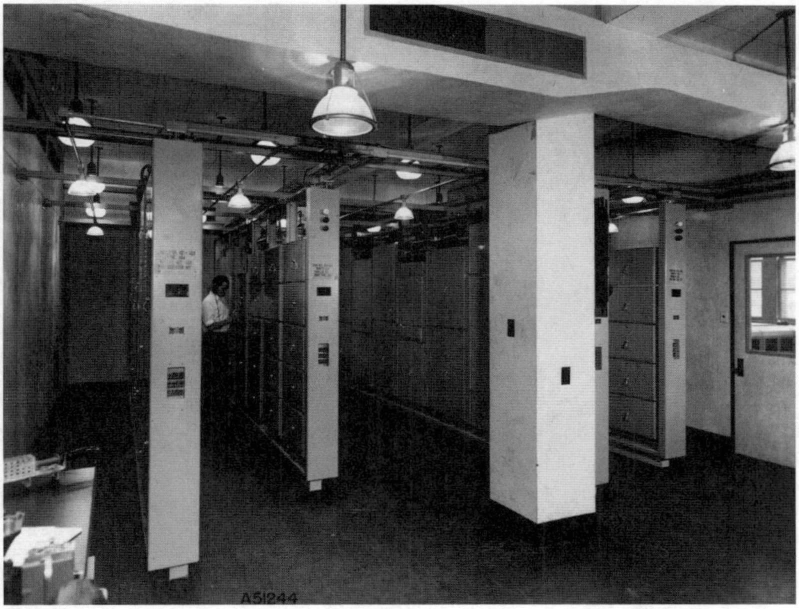

U.S. Army Photo. A51244, with caption "Bell Relay Computer, showing racks in which the computing, storing and controlling relays are mounted.", from the archives of the ARL Technical Library. An old soldering iron is visible on the desk in the lower left. Building 328, room 27, near the back.

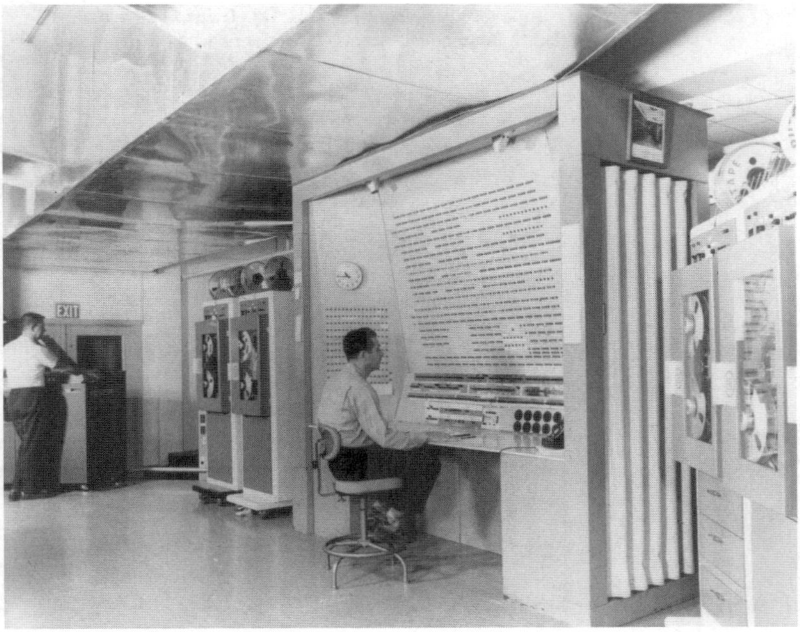

U.S. Army Photo. Console of BRLESC-I computer, side view, from the archives of the ARL Technical Library. At the console: Lou Moeller By the door: Horace Burkintere. Note the ENIAC photograph hanging on the side of the BRLESC.

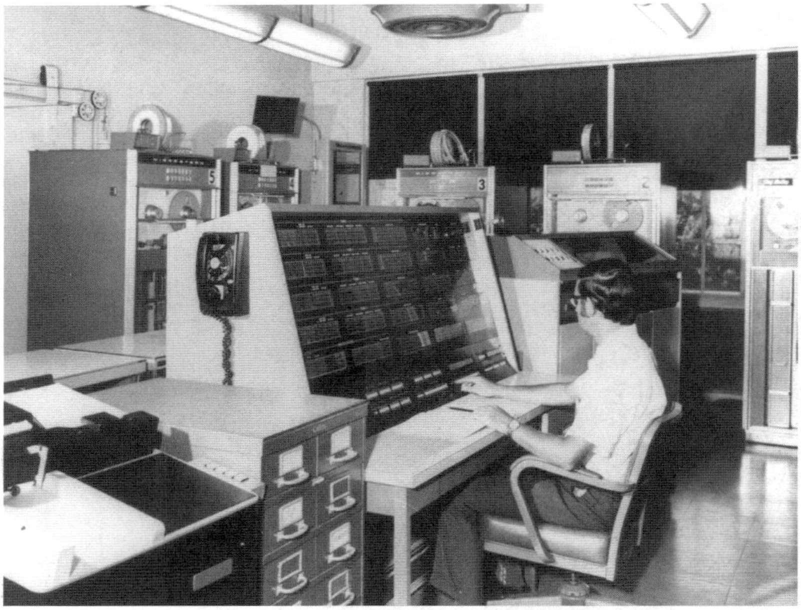

"U.S. Army Photo" Console of BRLESC-II computer, front view, from the archives of the ARL Technical Library. At the console: Alexander V. Kurian. Note high-speed card reader in foreground, high-speed line printer behind CPU.

Self-plugging robots

Grey Walter's *Hopkins Beast* (1960). Photo Reprinted by permission from *Johns Hopkins APL Technical Digest* 26(4): 368–376, by David P. Watson and David H. Scheidt, entitled "Autonomous Systems" ©The Johns Hopkins University Applied Physics Laboratory.

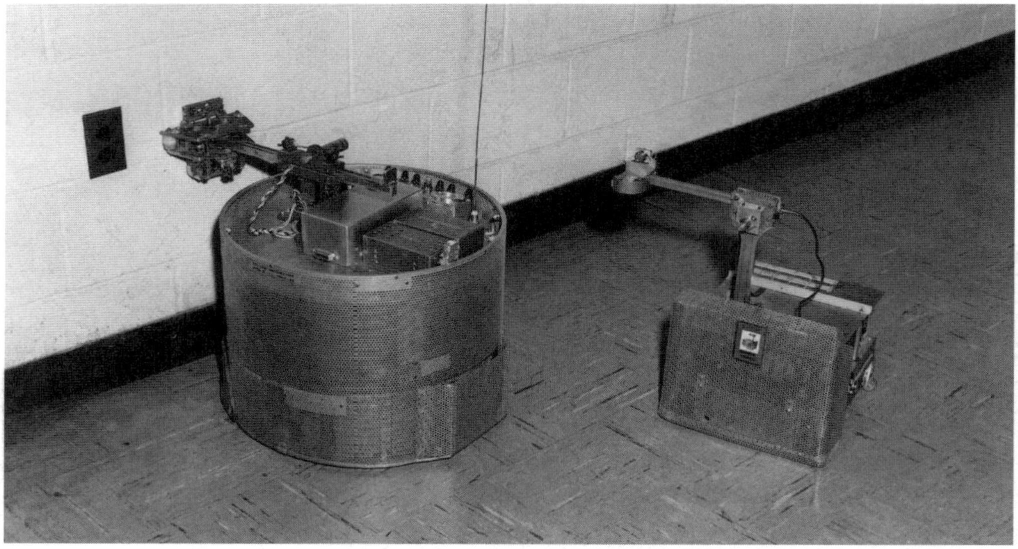

Norbert Wiener and Gregory Bateson

They had in common some uncommon preconceptions about the science that had influenced their scientific styles: both were highly interdisciplinary in their range of curiosity and had a sense that everything is connected to everything else, and that such connections can be manifested on an abstract or philosophical plane. Unlike Savage, neither agreed with the prevailing logical positivistic philosophy of science. Both found highly abstract, cross-disciplinary principles interesting, although they knew, as Wiener put it, "as a rule 'high' order, very abstract and general statements are not amenable to experimental test. They have to be broken down into more specific terms." Wiener and Bateson were both willing to translate exact theorems of communication engineering physics, and formal logic into relatively loose verbal formal statements-which they would then extend and apply in a heuristic way to other areas of science, although most scientists frowned on such practices.[24]

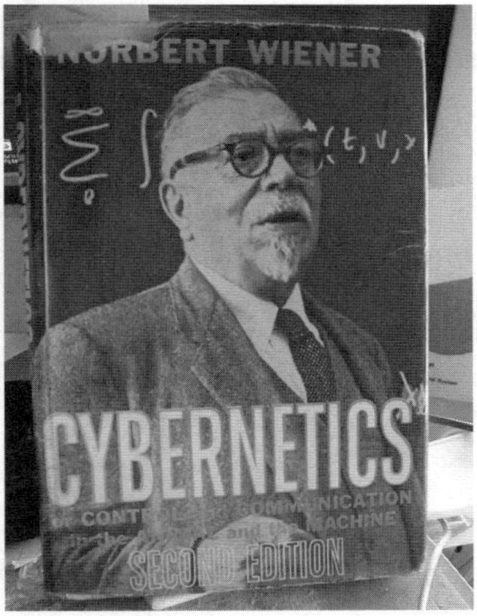

Norbert Wiener, *Cybernetics*. Courtesy of the MIT Museum.

Gregory Bateson—Ben Lomond, CA—1975. Image copyright Barry Schwartz.

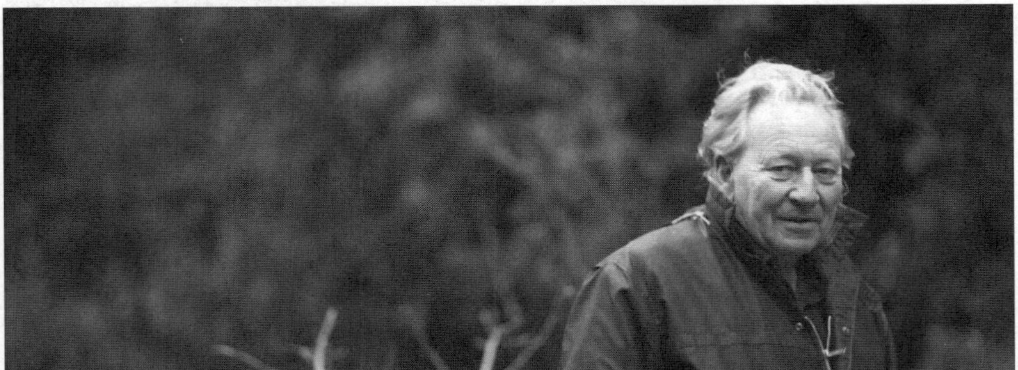

We sympathize with both Wiener and Bateson.

Margaret Mead – Cybernetics of Cybernetics

It seems to me that in a new organization, centered upon our knowledge and interest in circular self-corrective systems and our capacity to deal with the situations to which they may be productively applied, it might be worthwhile for this combination of old and new to really consider, technically and carefully, what in thunder we are founding.[25]

See also *Observing Systems* (von Foerster)

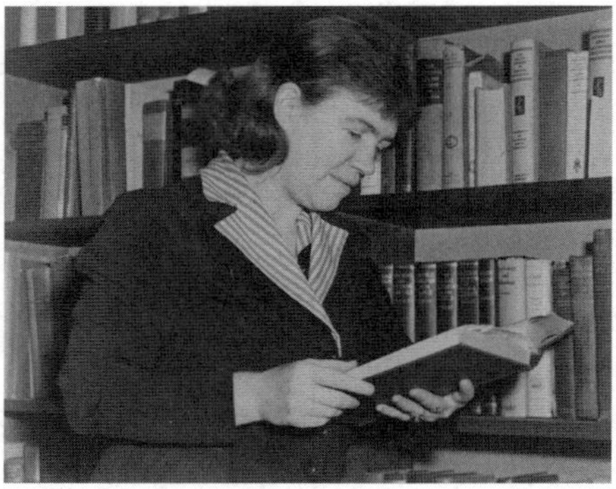

Margaret Mead by Edward Lynch, courtesy of the Library of Congress Prints and Photographic Division.

Heinz von Foerster and the Biological Computer Laboratory

Von Foerster 1973
On constructing a reality

The way in which a question is asked determines the way in which an answer may be found. Thus, it is upon me to paraphrase the "Problem of Cognition" in such a way that the conceptual tools that are today at our disposal may become fully effective. To this end let me paraphrase "cognition" in the following way:

Cognition
Computing a reality

With this I anticipate a storm of objections. First, I appear to replace one unknown term, "cognition" with three other terms, two of which, "computing" and "reality", are even more opaque than the definiendum, and with the only definite word used here being the indefinite article "a". Moreover, the use of the indefinite article implies the ridiculous notion of other realities besides "the" only and one reality, our

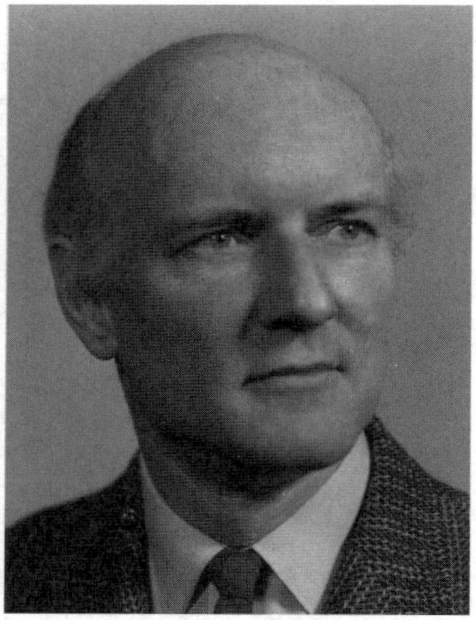

Portrait of Heinz von Foerster, University professor of electrical engineering and biophysics and director of the Biological Computer Laboratory (image dated circa 1960s). Photo 0004915 courtesy of the University of Illinois Archives.

cherished Environment; and finally I seem to suggest by "computing" that everything, from my wristwatch to the Galaxies, is merely computed, and is not "there". Outrageous!

Let me take up these objections one by one. First, let me remove the semantic sting that the term "computing" may cause in a group of women and men who are more inclined toward the humanities than to the sciences. Harmlessly enough, computing (from com-putare) literally means to recon, to contemplate (putare) things in concert (com-), without any explicit reference to numerical quantities. Indeed, I shall use this term in this most general sense to indicate any operation, not necessarily numerical, that transforms, modifies, re-arranges, or orders observed physical entities, "objects", or their representations, "symbols". For instance, the simple permutation of the three letters A, B, C, in which the last letter now goes first: C, A, B, I shall call a computation. Similarly, the operation that obliterates the commas between the letters: CAB; and likewise the semantic transformation that changes CAB into TAXI, and so on.[26]

This is our recombinant informatics: science = conceptual art.[27]

Biological Computing Laboratory (BCL)

A mentioned location where much research into bio-functionality as related to computation has taken place is the Biological Computing Laboratory (BCL). The BCL was the name of an independent division within the Department of Electrical Engineering at the University of Illinois, founded in 1957/58 by Heinz von Foerster, who at that time was Professor of Electrical Engineering in the department. In Albert Müller's text *A Brief History of the BCL*, Heinz von Foerster and the Biological Computer Laboratory, he discusses the Labs' historical position:

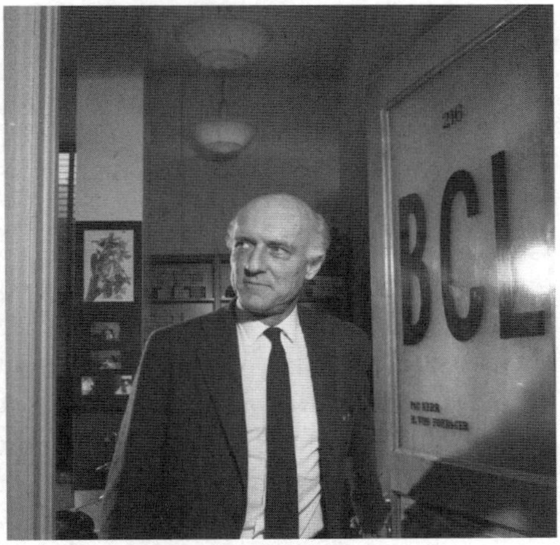

Heinz von Foerster exits the Biological Computer Laboratory office in the Electrical Engineering Research Laboratory at the University of Illinois (image dated circa 1967). Photo 0004912 courtesy of the University of Illinois Archives.

I am equally motivated by the fact that the BCL has very seldom been mentioned in the literature on the history of cybernetics, systems theory, bionics (now the subject of renewed debate), parallel computing, neurophysiology, bio-logic, artificial intelligence, symbolic computing, or constructivism as an intellectual tradition – and it would be possible to list even more areas of science that are renowned today – despite the fact that workers at this institution, the BCL, figure importantly in the literature on each of these domains. Is this an oversight specifically on the part of the history of science (the forgetfulness of science itself being well known)?[28]

Macy Conferences

We follow in the footsteps of the transdisciplinary topics and attendees of the seminal Macy Conferences.

Claus Pias concerning cybernetics. *The Macy-Conferences 1946–53*
Between 1946 and 1953 ten conferences under the heading Cybernetics-Circular Casual, and Feedback Mechanisms in Biological and Social Systems were held. Sponsored by Josiah Macy Jr., the co-called Macy Conferences mark perhaps the most important event in the history of science after WW II.

Using new terms such as »information«, »feedback«, and »analogical/digital« as starting point, the participants tried to develop a universal theory of regulation and control, that would be applicable to living beings as well as to machines, to economic as well as to mental processes, and to sociological as well as to aesthetical phenomena. These concepts permeate thinking in such diverse fields as biology, neurology, sociology, language studies, computer science, and even psychoanalysis, ecology, politics, and economy. They marked the epoch-making changes from thermodynamics to cybernetics (Wiener), from the disciplinary to control society (Deleuze), and from the industrial to information society (Lyotard).

The Macy Conferences are of special historical/scientific value since they do not deal with completed texts yet, but rather with interdisciplinary negotiations, which are continually being edited, varied and expounded upon.[29]

The summary of the Macy Conferences on the American Society for Cybernetics site was compiled by Randy Whitaker and is a wealth of information.[30]

On page 79 of his book Mechanization of the Mind, Jean-Pierre Dupuy offers a cursory taxonomic analysis of the topics discussed during the 10 Macy Conferences these included: "Applicability of a Logic Machine Model to both Brain and Computer"; "Human and Social Communication"; "Analogies between Organisms and Machines"; "Neuroses and Pathology of Mental Life"; "Cybernetics Machines" (Robots); "Information Theory"; "Abnormal Communication"; "General Epistemology".

Here is a list of the attendees from the American Society for Cybernetics (compiled by Randy Whitaker)

1st conference
8–9 March 1946 – NYC
CORE GROUP: Bateson, Bigelow, von Bonin, Frank, Fremont-Smith, Gerard, Harrower, Hutchinson, Klüver, Kubie, Lazarsfeld, Lewin, Lorente de Nó, McCulloch (chair), Mead, von Neumann, Northrop, Pitts, Rosenblueth, Savage, Wiener
GUEST: Bremer

2nd Conference
October 1946 – NYC
CORE GROUP: + Brosin, + Marquis, + Schneirla
GUEST – Livingston

3rd Conference
March 1947 – NYC
CORE GROUP: Lewin (died shortly before conference)
GUEST(S): Ackerman, Erikson, Festinger, Fitch, Kluckhohn, Lloyd, (Köhler invited, but cancelled)

4th Conference
23–24 October 1947 – NYC
CORE GROUP: – Klüver (didn't attend)
GUEST(S): Teuber (recommended by Klüver), Bender, Kluckhohn, Garcia, Ramos

5th Conference
Spring 1948
CORE GROUP: + Teuber (becomes core member), + Bavelas
GUEST(S): Jakobson, Lee, Lotz, Morris, von Domarus, Delbrück (geneticist selected by von Neumann, expected to become member of core group)

6th Conference
24–25 March 1949 – NYC
CORE GROUP: – Harrower (resigned), – Lazarsfeld (didn't attend), – von Neumann (didn't attend) + von Foerster (guest – invited to join)
GUEST(S): Abramson, Liddell, Lindsley, Lloyd, Mettler, Stroud

7th Conference
23–24 March 1950 – NYC
CORE GROUP: – Lazarsfeld (dropped out)
GUEST(S): Licklider, McLardy, Shannon, Stroud, Werner

8th Conference
15–16 March 1951 – NYC
CORE GROUP: – Bateson (didn't attend), – Wiener (dropped out), – von Neumann (dropped out)
GUEST(S): Birch, Bowman, MacKay, Rioch, Richards, Shannon

9th Conference
20–21 March 1952 – NYC
CORE GROUP: – Savage (didn't attend), – Northrop (didn't attend)
GUEST(S): Ashby, Bowman, Luce, Monnier, Quastler, Remond, Torre, Wiesner, Young

10th Conference
22–24 April 1953 – Princeton New Jersey
CORE GROUP: (No changes)
GUEST(S): Amassian, Bar-Hillel, Bowman, Chao, Droogleever-Fortuyn, Quastler, Shannon, Grey-Walter

Ross Ashby

Ross Ashby's *Design for a Brain* tackled many problems surrounding the creation of a situated thinking machine and adaptation.

The free living organism and its environment, taken together, form an absolute system […] the two parts act and re-act on one another."[31]

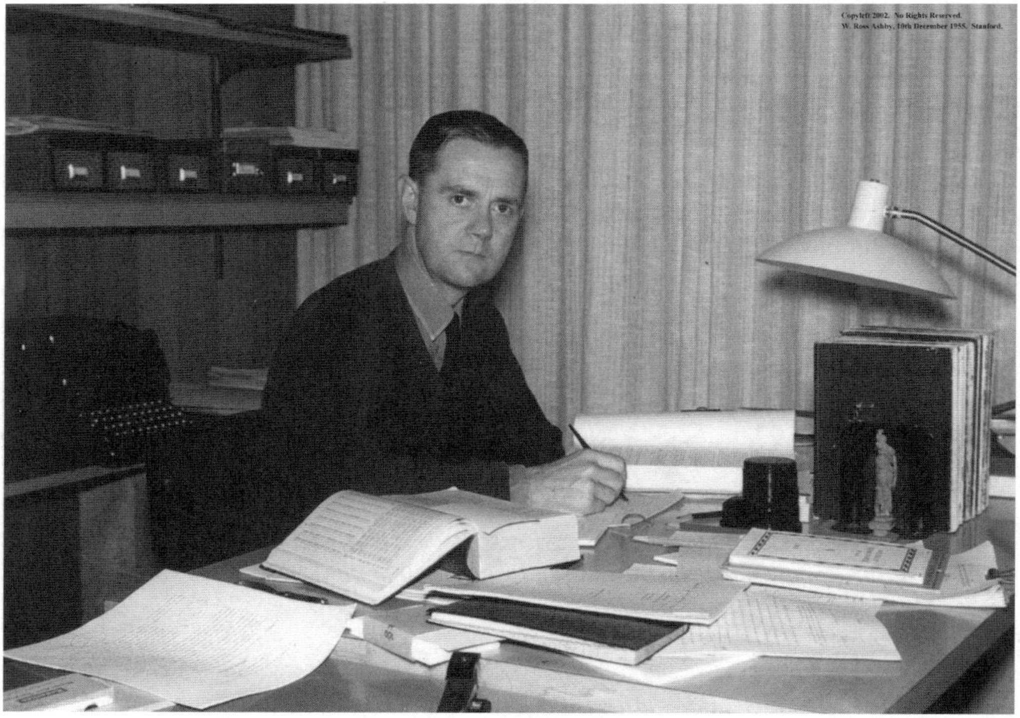

A self-portrait taken in his office 10 December 1955, Copyleft 2002.[32] W. Ross Ashby

Rodney Brooks

Brooks is at the forefront of the field of robotics. His "subsumption architecture" is very different in spirit to the functionality of the Brain Equation and the biologically abstracted explorations that contribute to the creation of an Electrochemical Computer. His writings in *Flesh and Machines* are of a kindred spirit.

Flesh and machines

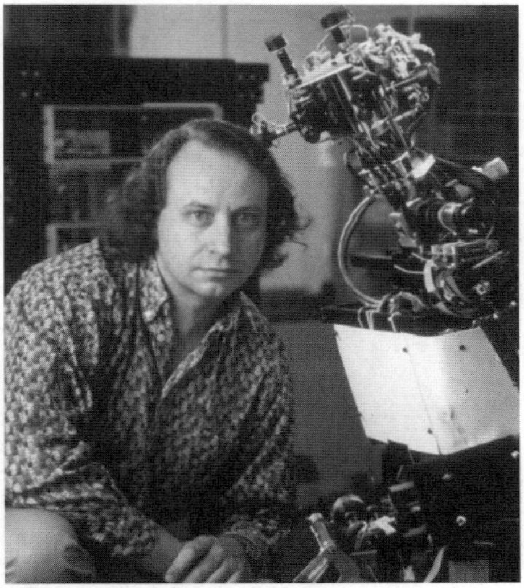

Courtesy of Rodney Brooks.

What about our machines. Today there is a clear distinction between the robots of science fiction and the machines in their daily lives. We see 3CPO, R2D2, Commander Data, and HAL in Star Wars, Star Trek, and 2001: A Space Odyssey. But these are not rivaled in any way by the capabilities of our lawn mowers, automobiles or Windows 2000. There are the machines of science fiction fantasy, and then there are the machines we live with. Two completely different worlds. Our fantasy machines have syntax and technology. They also have emotions, desires, fears, loves and pride. Our real machines do not […] My thesis is that in just twenty years the boundary between fantasy and reality will be rent asunder. Just five years from now that boundary will be breached in ways that are as unimaginable to most people today as daily use of the World Wide Web was ten years ago. (2002)

[…] Machines are now becoming autonomous in the areas that bypassed them in the industrial revolution. Machines are starting to make the judgments and decisions that have kept people in the loop for the last 200 years. There will soon be less need for people to engage in the moment-to-moment control of manufacturing machines, and we are starting to see intelligent robots that can operate in unstructured environments, doing jobs that are usually thought to still require people. But these robots are not just robots. They are artificial creatures […].[33]

At first blush, my decision to leave out a cognition box seemed to indicate that I was giving up on chess, calculus, and problem solving as a part of intelligence that I wanted to tackle. In fact, this was not my intent. To me it seemed that these sorts of intelligence capabilities are all based on a substrate of the ability to see, walk, navigate, and judge. My belief at that time, and still today, is that they arise from the interaction of perception and action, and that getting these right was the key to more general intelligence.[34]

Subsumption architecture
This was the metaphor I chose for my robots. I would build simple control systems for simple behavior. Then I would add extra control systems for more complex behavior, leaving the older control systems in place, still operating. If necessary, the newer control systems might occasionally subsume the capabilities of the older system when they know better how the robot should act. And so the layers would be added one after the other, emulating the historical process of evolution of more and more complex neural systems in animals.[35]

Situated and embodied robots
All of our robots were based on two fundamental principles: situatedness and embodiment. These two terms can be a little fuzzy at times, but I like to use the following definitions for them: A situated creature is one that is embedded in the world, and which does not deal with abstract descriptions, but through its sensors with the here and now of the world, which directly influences the behavior of the creature […] An embodied creature or robot is one that has a physical body and experiences the world, at least in part, through the influence of the world on that body. A more specialized type of embodiment occurs when the full extent of the creature is contained within that body.[36]

Ray Kurzweil

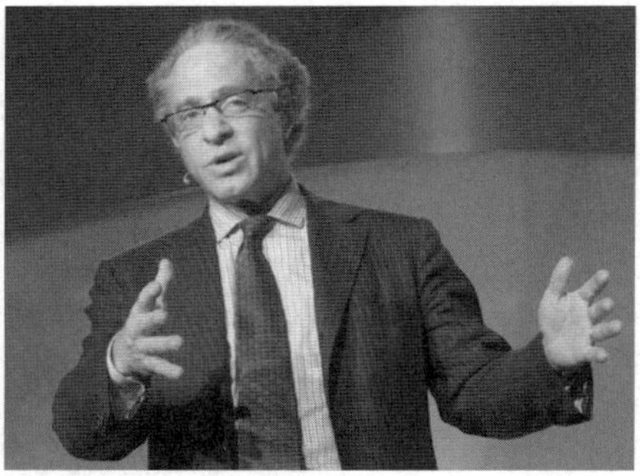
Courtesy of Ray Kurzweil.

Ray Kurzweil has given an interesting chronology outlining the flow of discovery related to *The Age of Intelligent Machines*. His book, *The Singularity is Near*[37] discusses in depth his thoughts surrounding the emergent change that intelligent machines will bring about. He states, "In the 1950s John von Neumann, the legendary information theorist, was quoted as saying that 'The ever accelerating progress of technology […] gives the impression of approaching some essential singularity in the history of the race beyond which human affairs, as we know them, could not continue.'"[38] He states that " […] a serious assessment of the history of technology reveals that technological change is exponential. Exponential growth is the feature of any evolutionary process, of which technology is a primary example."[39] In defining his notion of Singularity, Kurzweil in turn quotes Vernor Vinge, The Technological Singularity:

When greater-than-human intelligence drives progress, that progress will be much more rapid. In fact, there seems no reason why progress itself would not involve the creation of still more intelligent entities – on a still shorter time scale. The best analogy that I see is with the evolutionary past: Animals can adapt to problems and make inventions, but often no faster than natural selection can do its work – the world acts as its own simulator in the case of natural selection. We humans have the ability to internalize the world and conduct "what if's" in our heads; we can solve many problems thousands of times faster than natural selection. Now, by creating the means to execute those simulations at much higher speeds, we are entering a regime as radically different from our human past as we humans are from the lower animals.[40]

The jump occurs when "intelligent" robotic simulations intermingle with physical environments and generate actual behaviors. Historically, human beings have sought to be in control of machines. As machines become autonomous, there are many gray areas concerning potential personhood and resultant ramifications as well as the cultural revolution this will bring about.

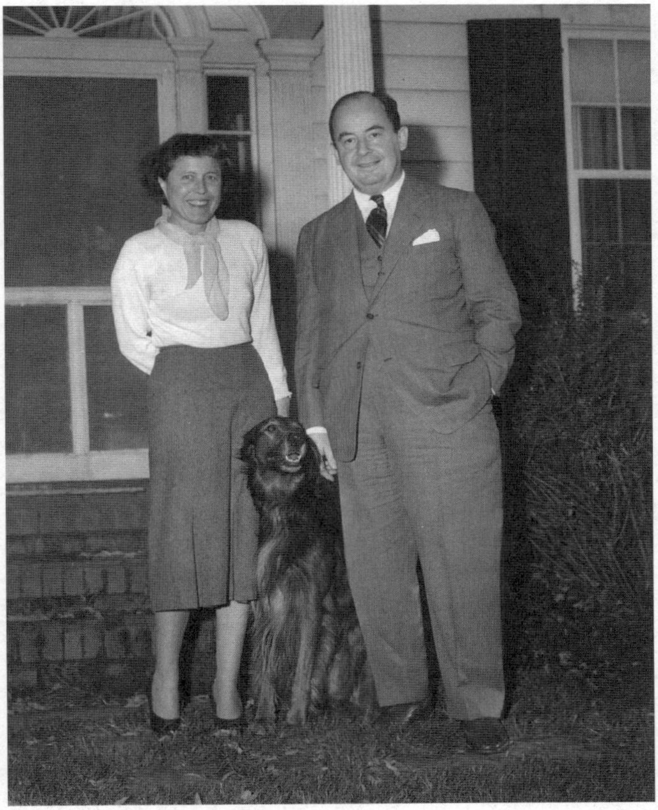

John von Neumann and Klara Dan von Neumann with their dog "Inverse," courtesy of Marina v. N. Whitman. Photo by Yuichi Sakuraba.

Bill Joy – The Dystopian Position

Joy gives an alternative perspective: Kurzweil has spoken of both positive and negative aspects of such change (as discussed in *The Singularity*). Bill Joy presented a strong negative argument concerning technological discovery in his article "*Why The Future Doesn't Need Us – Our Most Powerful 21st Century Technologies – Robotics, Genetic Engineering and Nanotech – Are Threatening to Make Humans an Endangered Species*". In particular Joy points out the danger of systems that can self-replicate, as well as potentially "spawn whole new classes of accidents and abuses."[41]

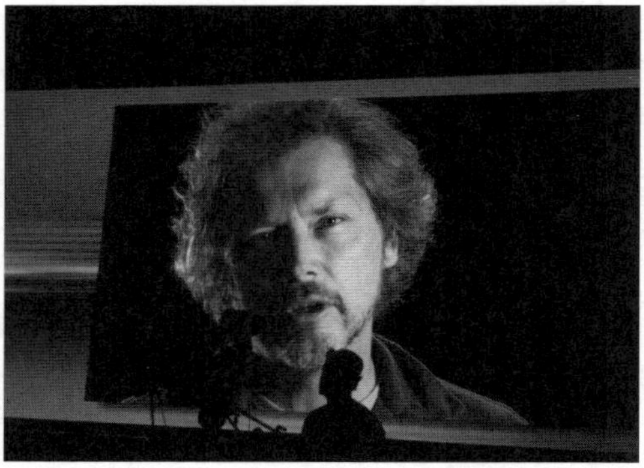

Bill Joy.

History and Mythology

There is a long history and mythology surrounding the creation of intelligent entities reaching back to Pygmalion and Prometheus. The invention of intelligent machines has also at times been shown in a "hostile" light in literature, across the arts, and within scientific discourse. Thus, an unaccepting world potentially becomes a "hostile" or an "extreme" environment for the arising of new forms of synthetic cognition. One might ask how does this set of works and research agenda fit into the history of art and literature? Perhaps the most intriguing question relates to the notion of creating a work of art that can come to speculate on itself in an informed manner. One might provide the myth of Pygmalion as a starting point, although the research is not about constructing the "ideal woman" but a form of Neosentient entity. As the story goes, Aphrodite brought Pygmalion's sculpture to life: Pygmalion focused on his art until one day he ran across a large, flawless piece of ivory and decided to carve a beautiful woman from it. When he had finished the statue, Pygmalion found it so lovely that he clothed the figure and adorned her in jewels. He gave the statue a name: Galatea, his Sleeping Love. He found himself obsessed with his ideal woman so he went to the temple of Aphrodite to ask forgiveness for all the years he had shunned her and beg for a wife who would be as perfect as his statue. Aphrodite was curious so she visited the studio of the sculptor while he was away and was charmed by his creation. Galatea proved to be the image of herself. Being flattered, Aphrodite brought the statue to life. When Pygmalion returned to his home, he found Galatea alive, and humbled himself at her feet.

Pygmalion and Galatea were wed, and Pygmalion never forgot to thank Aphrodite for the gift she had given him. He and Galatea brought gifts to her temple throughout their life, and Aphrodite blessed them with happiness and love in return.

Richard Powers' Galetea 2.2 is an interesting example of a work exploring the Pygmalion Myth in terms of computational potentials. This story explores the relationship between a human and the neural net system he is training to become knowledgeable in comparative literature. The exploration of the potentials of an intelligent computer's relation to its human counterpart in this book illuminates both the positive and negative aspects of artificial intelligence.[42]

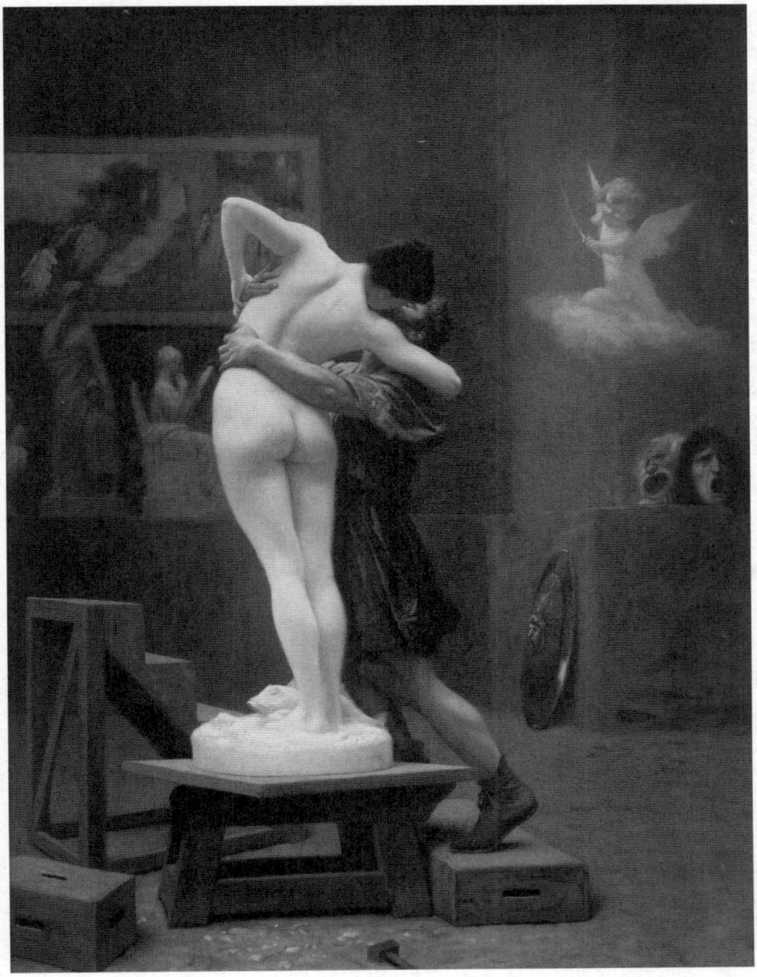

Pygmalion and Galatea by Jean-Léon Gérome 1890, courtesy of Lee Sandstead. Creator: Étienne Maurice Falconet, Title: Pygmalion & Galatea in 1763, Location: Hermitage, St. Petersburg. Public domain.

Anaximander

Anaximander with his notion of a secretion process emerging inside of the whole, in a sense foresaw the electrochemical computer that enables human thought to arise – like neural transmitters perhaps. He was the first to address the limits of perception in his notion of the "unempirical" – ápeiron.

Casti's Emergence

In *Complexification*, John L. Casti, a member of the Santa Fe Institute, comments on the nature of emergence as it relates to forms of molecular systems.

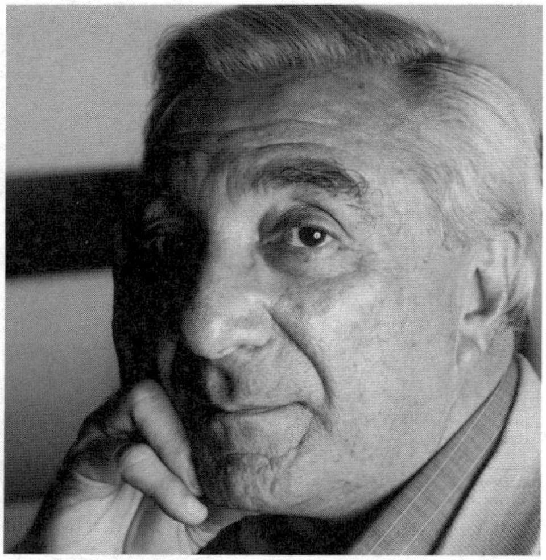
Photo by Juan Esteves, courtesy John L. Casti.

This expression [H_2O, emphasis the authors] is a particularly crude form of what might be charitably called a model to explain the formation of water from hydrogen and oxygen. But note that the starting point for this scientific explanation was the wholly unexpected and seemingly unlikely observation that by combining rather active gasses, we can form not only liquid but a liquid whose properties differ radically from the properties of either of the constituent parts.[43]

This is a nice metaphor for emergence in the present context.

In their book *Gödel: A Life of Logic*, John Casti and Werner DePauli discuss Gödel's thoughts related to the creation of a proto-mind through Artificial Life means:

When asked whether his theorem was an insurmountable barrier to the development of a true mechanical intelligence, Gödel's response was:

> *[…] it remains possible that there may exist (and even be empirically discoverable) a theorem-proving machine which in fact is equivalent in mathematical intuition [to the human mind], but cannot be proved to be so, nor even be proved to yield only correct theorems of finitary number theory.*

By this remark, Gödel is suggesting that a machine equivalent in brainpower to the human mind might actually be created- for example, by evolution- but that if such a device did exist, we would never understand it. It would be too complex for us. Gödel's prescription, then is not to build a brain but rather to grow one. And [Tom] Ray's experiment shows that there is no logical barrier to following this dictum. Thus what both Gödel and Ray are saying, in effect, is that a machine equal to humans in cognitive capacity will be just an example, though a very special one, of what we might call artificial life (AL).[44]

John Holland

John Holland in the early 1970s created some highly useful Genetic Algorithms (GAs). The computer, through programming, enables solutions to emerge. The algorithms are smart and retain the "discernment" of evolution and are particularly useful if speeded up. These algorithms are often used in business to solve difficult problems.[45] Holland is still active in the field.

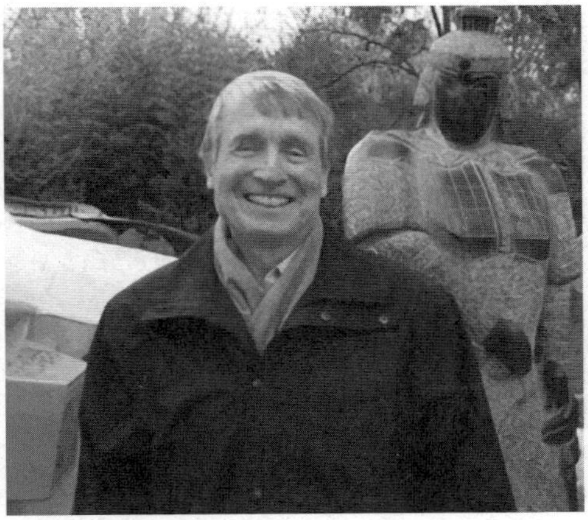

Courtesy of John Holland.

It was in the mid-50's of the 20th century when I realized that Fisher's fundamental theorem could be extended from individual alleles to co-adapted sets of alleles, without linearization. That led to a realization that recombination, rather than mutation, was the main mechanism providing grist for the natural selection mill. There was little theory concerning recombination in those days, but now recombination is a standard explanation for biological innovations, such as swine flu.

Much later, in the early 1990s, GA's provided the "adaptive" part of rule-based models of complex adaptive systems (CAS), such as the artificial stock market pioneered at the Santa Fe Institute. Tag-based signal processing occurs in systems as different as biological cells, language acquisition, and ecosystems. CAS models offer a unified way to study the on-going co-evolution of boundary and tag networks in these systems.[46]

Neumannology

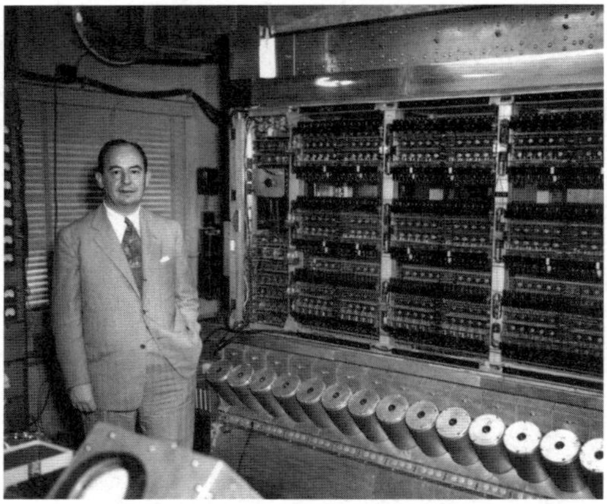

von Neumann. Photo by Alan Richards photographer. From The Shelby White and Leon Levy Archives Center, Institute for Advanced Study, Princeton, NJ, USA. (early 1950s)

John von Neumann (1903–57) has a very long story: "Wigner's Friend" in the quantum story of Wigner's Friend. He invented the algebraic version of Quantum Mechanics. He invented evolution as an algorithm. He invented modern computer architecture. He was a friend, colleague, sponsor, and competitor with Gödel. He invented game theory with Oscar Morgenstern. He invented cellular automata. He invented the first self-reproducing machine. He invented the idea that quantum mechanics is only an interface world (taken up by Everett).

Janoshka is Jonny in Hungarian. Eugene Wigner said about his friend … Whenever you were in his company you felt that you were half asleep while he was wide awake.

In the words of von Neumann: "[…] it is a fundamental requirement of the scientific viewpoint – the so-called principle of the psycho-physical parallelism – that it must be possible so to describe the extra-physical process of the subjective perception as if it were in reality in the physical world – i.e., to assign to its parts equivalent physical processes in the objective environment, in ordinary space."[47]

John von Neumann "The General and Logical Theory of Automata"

Preliminary considerations

Dichotomy of the Problem: Nature of the Elements, Axiomatic Discussion of Their Synthesis.

In comparing living organisms, and, in particular, that most complicated organism, the human central nervous system, with artificial automata, the following limitation should be kept in mind. The natural systems are of enormous complexity, and it is clearly necessary to subdivide the problem that they represent into several parts. One method of subdivision, which is particularly significant in the present context, is this: The organisms can be viewed as made up of parts which to a certain extent are independent, elementary units. We may, therefore, to this extent, view as the first part of the problem the structure and functioning of such elementary units individually. The second part of the problem consists of understanding how these elements are organized into a whole, and how the functioning of the whole is expressed in terms of these elements.

The axiomatic procedure
Axiomatizing the behavior of the elements means this: We assume that the elements have certain well-defined, outside, functional characteristics; that is, they are to be treated as "black boxes." They are viewed as automatisms, the inner structure of which need not be disclosed, but which are assumed to react to certain unambiguously defined stimuli, by certain unambiguously defined responses.

This being understood, we may then investigate the larger organisms that can be built up from these elements, their structure, their functioning, the connections between the elements, and the general theoretical regularities that may be detectable in the complex syntheses of the organisms in question.[48]

Consciousness is the big movie for the creator.

Comparisons between computing machines and living organisms
Mixed character of living organisms. *When the central nervous system is examined, elements of both procedures, digital and analog, are discernible.*

The neuron transmits an impulse. This appears to be its primary function, even if the last word about this function and its exclusive or non-exclusive character is far from having been said. The nerve impulse seems in the main to be an all-or-none affair, comparable to a binary digit. Thus a digital element is evidently present but it is equally evident that this is not the entire story. A great deal of what goes on in the organism is not mediated in this manner, but is dependent on the general chemical composition of the blood stream or of other humoral media. It is well known that there are various composite functional sequences in the organism which have to go through a variety of steps from the original stimulus to the ultimate effect – some of the steps being neural, that is, digital, and others humoral, that is, analogy. These digital and analogy portions in such a chain may alternately multiply. In certain cases of this type, the chain can actually feed back into itself, that is, its ultimate output may again stimulate its original input.

It is well known that such mixed (part neural and part humoral) feedback chains can produce processes of great importance. Thus the mechanism which keeps the blood pressure constant is of this mixed type. The nerve which senses and reports the blood pressure does it by a sequence of neural impulses, that is, in a digital manner. The muscular contraction which this impulse system induces may still be described as a superposition of many digital impulses. The influence of such a contraction on the blood stream is, however, hydrodynamical, and hence analogy. The reaction of the pressure thus produced back on the nerve which reports the pressure closes the circular feedback, and at this point the analogy procedure again goes over into a digital one. The comparisons between the living organisms and the computing machines are, therefore, certainly imperfect at this point. The living organisms are very complex – part digital and part analogy mechanisms. The computing machines, at least in their recent forms to which I am referring in this discussion, are purely digital. Thus I must ask you to accept this oversimplification of the system. Although I am well aware of the analogy component in living organisms, and it would be absurd to deny its importance, I shall, nevertheless, for the sake of the simpler discussion, disregard that part. I shall consider the living Mixed Character of Each Element. In addition to this, one may argue that even the neuron is not exactly a digital organ. This point has been put forward repeatedly and with great force. There is certainly a great deal of truth in it, when one considers things in considerable detail. The relevant assertion is, in this respect, that the fully developed nervous impulse, to which all-or-none character can be attributed, is not an elementary phenomenon, but is highly complex. It is a degenerate state of the complicated electrochemical complex which constitutes the neuron, and which in its fully analyzed functioning must be viewed as an analogy machine. Indeed, it is possible to stimulate the neuron in such a way that the breakdown that releases the nervous stimulus will not occur. In this area of "subliminal stimulation," we find first (that is, for the weakest stimulations) responses which are proportional to the stimulus, and then (at higher, but still subliminal, levels of stimulation) responses which depend on more complicated non-linear laws, but are nevertheless continuously variable and not of the breakdown type. There are also other complex phenomena within and without the subliminal range: fatigue, summation, certain forms of self-oscillation, etc.[49]

All or none?

[…] Thus the important fact is not whether an organ has necessarily and under all conditions the all-or-none character – this is probably never the case – but rather whether in its proper context it functions primarily, and appears to be intended to function primarily, as an all-or-none organ. I realize that this definition brings in rather undesirable criteria of "propriety" of context, of "appearance" and "intention." I do not see, however, how we can avoid using them, and how we can forego counting on the employment of common sense in their application. I shall, accordingly, in what follows use the working hypothesis that the neuron is an all-or-none digital organ. I realize that the last word about this has not been said, but I hope that the above excursus on the limitations of this working hypothesis and the reasons for its use will reassure you. I merely want to simplify my discussion; I am not trying to prejudge any essential open question.[50]

We see the neuron as a mixed analog and digital organ.

Deb Roy

A mechanistic model of three facets of meaning

Deb Roy, 17 October 2007

This chapter presents a physical-computational model of sensory-motor grounded language interpretation for simple speech acts. The model is based on an implemented conversational robot. It combines a cybernetic closed-loop control architecture with structured conceptual schemas. The interpretation of directive and descriptive speech acts consists of translating utterances into updates of memory systems in the controller. The same memory systems also mediate sensory-motor interactions and thus serve as a cross-modal bridge between language, perception, and action. The referential, functional, and connotative meanings of speech acts emerge from the effects of memory updates on the future dynamics of the controller as it physically interacts with its environment.

Introduction

This volume is the result of a meeting which was organized around a contrast between two approaches for analyzing and modeling semantics. In the first camp are cognitive scientists who model linguistic meaning as structural relations between symbols. The term "symbol" in this context is taken to mean, roughly, discrete information elements that may be given word-like labels that make sense to humans (e.g., DOG, IS-A). Examples of this approach include semantic networks such as WordNet (Miller, 1995) and Cyc (Lenat, 1995) and statistical methods such as Latent Semantic Analysis (Landauer, Foltz, & Laham, 1998). In contrast to this "ungrounded" approach, the grounded camp treats language as part of a larger cognitive system in which semantics depends in part on non-symbolic structures and processes including those related to perception and motor planning. Examples include Bates' grounding of language in sensory-motor schemas (Bates 1979) and Barsalou's proposal of a "perceptual symbol system" that grounds symbolic structures in sensory-motor simulation (Barsalou, 1999). The grounded camp pays more attention to how symbols arise from, and are connected to interactions with the physical and social environment of the symbol user.[51]

Recursive Evolution

Ultraplastic systems form a subclass of "temporal brains" as described in deductive biology.[52]

Deductive biology – Some cautious steps

For certain environments, the Darwinian model allows unique prediction of a function that any surviving system adapted to such an environment has to perform. This is the case for those environments that determine a "survival functional" of position in space-time of known shape. Purely temporal survival functionals can be distinguished from spatial and mixed ones. In

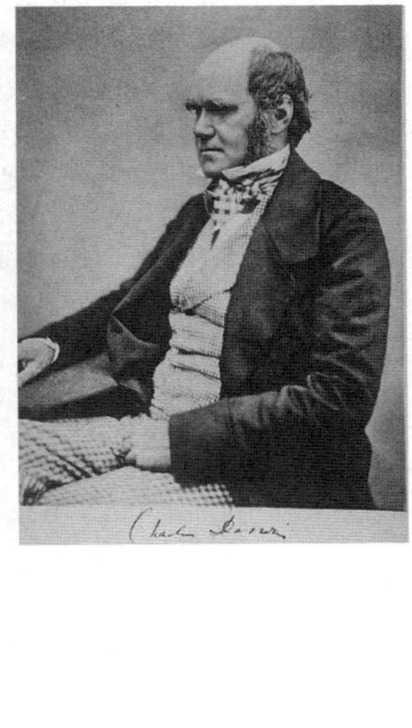

Charles Darwin, 1854. Public domain.

Charles Darwin (1809–82) English naturalist. Evolution by Natural Selection. Photograph of Darwin in old age. ©ARPL/TopFoto/The Image Works.

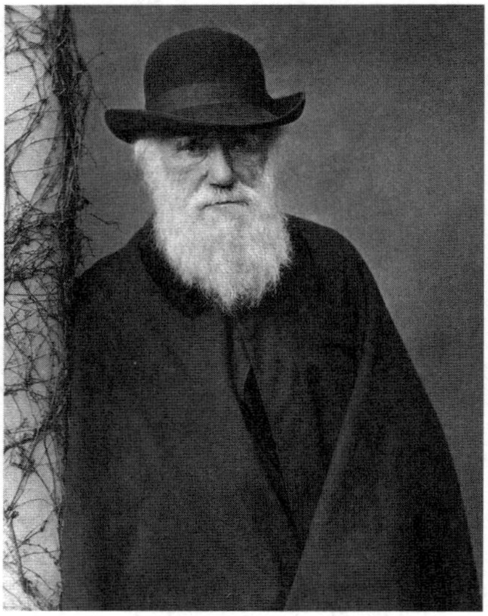

each case, there exists an optimum path in combined physical and (reduced) metabolic space. Dependent on the admissible error, approximate solutions of different complexity are sufficient. All solutions possess an afferent, a central, and an efferent part. Within this general frame, specific, "probably simplest", solutions are proposed for adaptive chemotaxis, insect locomotion, lower vertebrates locomotion, higher vertebrates locomotion, chronobiological systems, and immune systems, respectively – or rather, for the underlying functionals.[53]

Introduction to the Brain Equation

The Brain Equation exists because survival in space is a different problem than survival in time. Darwin solved the problem of continued survival of a species in time. It is only through the random endogenous changes that arise ("mutations" they were called later) that a species can keep being adapted in an unpredictably changing environment as is unavoidably the case in the long run. Yet if survival depends on position in space on a short term basis, there also is only one way to be successful: move. That is, to either go to a better place or a less dangerous one. This is a well-posed mathematical problem. If survival depends on position in space, the only way to improve survival is to build a "brain." This brain implements a certain solution to a well-posed mathematical problem: the traveling-salesman-with-alarm-clocks problem. This brain is different from the "brain in the genome," as Michael Conrad called it. Evolution always proceeds by carrying its own past on its back – by literally carrying its genetic machinery on its back. Each successive generation reaps the fruits of the most recent mutations as well as all earlier mutations (as a sum of histories as it were). But the brain equation is independent of history. Like the liver, the brain is an organ based on the Darwinian genomic path. The intuition of the brain equation arose because Konrad Lorenz drew attention in a personal discussion to the difference between genetically controlled adaptive responses and environment-controlled specific temporal ones like a tidal cue. These not genetically predictable events are equally important for survival. To this "second class" belong all spatial relations.

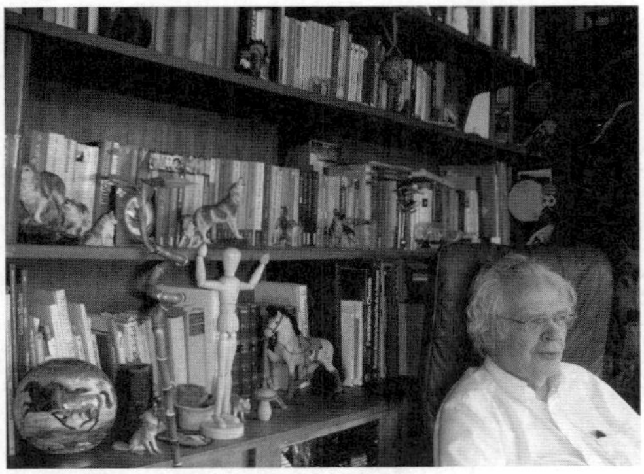

Otto E. Rössler, courtesy of Bill Seaman.

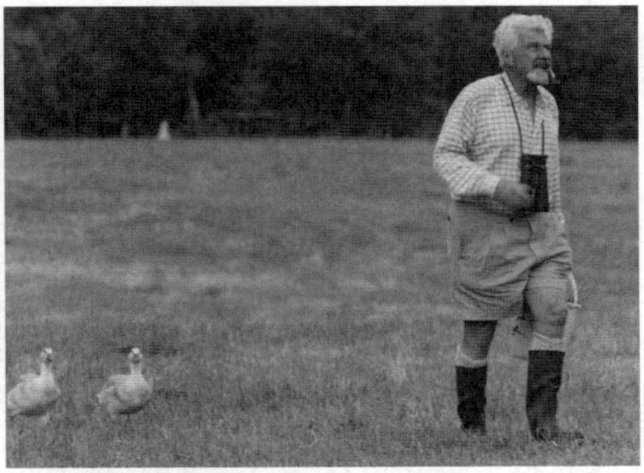

Konrad Lorenz, courtesy of the Konrad Lorenz Archive, Altenberg.

An Early Computational Approach to "Space" – the Antikythera Mechanism

The Antikythera computing device, the most complex instrument of antiquity

An ancient astronomical calculator, built around the end of the second century BC, *was unexpectedly sophisticated, a study in this week's Nature suggests. Mike G. Edmunds and colleagues used imaging and high-resolution X-ray tomography to study fragments of the Antikythera Mechanism, a bronze mechanical analog computer thought to calculate astronomical positions. The Greek device contains a complicated arrangement of at least*

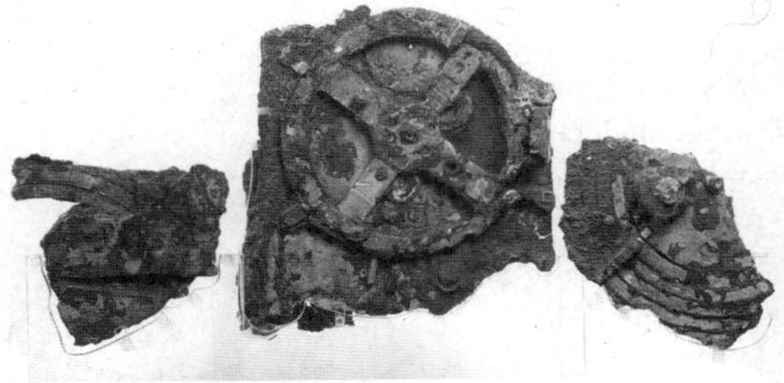

Image of the Antikythera Mechanism inv. no. 15087, housed in the National Archaeological Museum, courtesy of National Archaeological Museum, Athens. © Hellenic Ministry of Culture and Tourism/ Archaeological Receipts Fund.

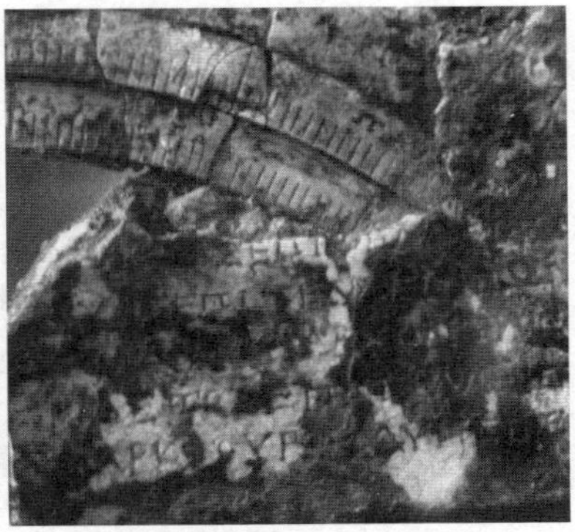

Antikythera Computer. Image courtesy of Rien van de Weijgaert (Kapteyn Astronomical Institute, Groningen, the Netherlands). See website: http://www.astro.rug.nl/~weygaert/ antikytheramechanism.htm.

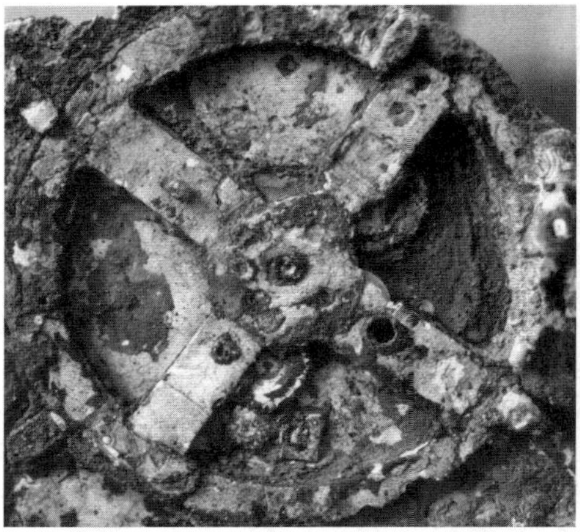

Antikythera Computer. Image courtesy of Rien van de Weijgaert (Kapteyn Astronomical Institute, Groningen, the Netherlands). See website: http://www.astro.rug.nl/~weygaert/antikytheramechanism.htm.

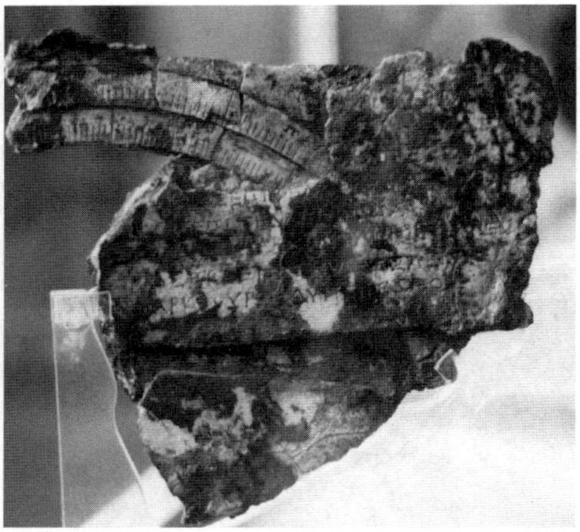

Antikythera Computer. Image courtesy of Rien van de Weijgaert (Kapteyn Astronomical Institute, Groningen, the Netherlands). See website: http://www.astro.rug.nl/~weygaert/antikytheramechanism.htm.

30 precision, hand-cut bronze gears housed inside a wooden case covered in inscriptions. But the device is fragmented, so its specific functions have remained controversial. The team were able to reconstruct the gear function and double the number of deciphered inscriptions on the computer's casing. The device, they say, is technically more complex than any known device for at least a millennium afterwards.[54]

Pattern Flows

We can summarize here how pattern flows contribute to the hybrid accretive processes that imply ongoing identity construction – the becoming of meaning-becoming. Each sense contributes an experienced pattern over time.

Picture for a moment that you are a child. You are playing outside with a new object as yet nameless. A person uses the words "red ball" in this particular context. You touch the texture on the outside of the ball, taste it, listen to its characteristic sound as it bounces, smell the rubber that it is made out of, notice how soft it is and its temperature.

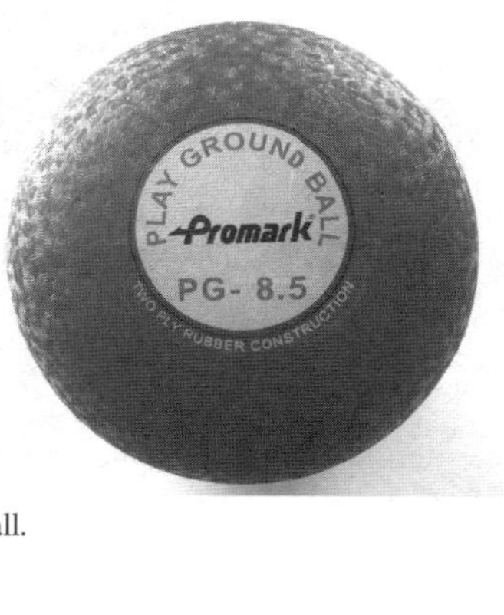

Red Ball.

All of these activities are time-based patterns of sense perturbations that reinforce each other, forming an expanded, embodied set. Each instance of "use" becomes enfolded with the ongoing identity construction of the "red ball". The environmental pattern that includes one's playing with the ball also includes the time-based flow of the spoken words. As these words are used again and again on different occasions, one can draw on an embodied history of spatial / temporal pattern flows to reflect on and project the nature of context, as well as to project meaning onto the words in new contexts. Along with spoken instances, one learns the pattern of written words that also present the terms "red ball". One's hand moves over the page, forming moving muscular patterns as they learn to write the words. One's mouth forms a set of shaped patterns over time as they attempt to mimic the flow of sounds and speak the words. Subsequently, one sees drawings, and paintings, movies and photographs – all similar but different patterned instances of "red balls", all informing a larger, intra-folded (self/ environment/other) multimodal pattern-definition of "red ball".[55]

Qualia As Emotional Force Triggers

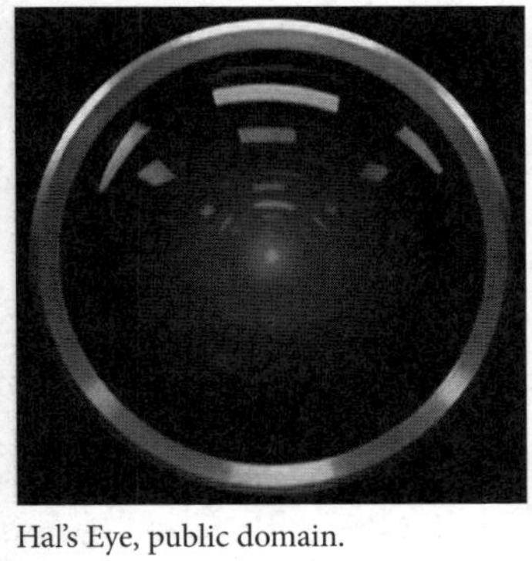
Hal's Eye, public domain.

Qualia have an emotional force. There are multiple forces at operation in perception. Triggers can be tied to each of the senses: color oriented, smell oriented, taste oriented, touch oriented, motion oriented, rhythmically oriented, melody oriented, and shape oriented. Each of these can potentially have an emotional quality as an innate or conditionally acquired releasing mechanism.

Color articulates holes in the tapestry of the world. One sees something that is outside – the moving quality of "redness" is palpably coupled between our souls and the universe. Redness goes beyond the notion of pattern as an emotional force, yet it becomes intermingled with pattern as part of the field of perception.

The chameleon changes its color to circumvent the innate releasing mechanisms active in its potential predators.

Color and Chaos

When we see a bolt of lightning we can see into the hidden structure of the universe (looking at the angel of light) […] *You must never send a fiery arrow into a sack filled with blood.* (*Chinese proverb, see Christie, Chinese Mythology*) Filled sack = chaos, arrow = lightning. The first emperor in Chinese Mythology was called Hun Tun (chaos); he had two friends – Shu and Hu (Shu-hu means lightning). The emperor had no sense organs but a direct communication with the world. Over 7 days, his friends Shu and Hu bore 7 holes – they gave him eyes, nose, ears, mouth and then he was dead … This also relates to the Hebrew creation myth – 7 holes = 7 days. The holes through which we see redness and experience revelation.

Memory and its Relation to Perception in an N-Dimensional Space

The following chain of associations to the notion of representation comes to mind:

- Recognition of similar patterns (e.g. a red ball in differing contexts)
- Patterns of relations (meta-relations)
- Generated spatiotemporal Platonic gestalts (simplifications for economy)
- A relational flow space (symbolic trajectory)
- The ability to access these Platonic flow gestalts from multiple perspectives (during and after perception)
- The ability to fragment, combine, and recombine these flow gestalts (codes of other temporal patterns), pattern completion, pattern translation
- The ability to categorize these flow gestalts (even if they begin as pre-linguistic sensual relations), pattern appreciation (redness)
- Similar but different relations (always being updated for use in the current context)
- Scale of the body (body knowledge)
- Mirror neurons (as the basis for mirror competence)
- Pattern flow history (multimodal reinforcement)
- Linguistic categorization (and meta-categorization)
- Averaging of patterns (and coding by the force vector of the brain equation)
- Relational inference (pattern comparison)
- Ongoing association to new contexts (alternate patterns as engrams)
- Structural registering with environment (cognitive maps)
- Imprinting (falling in love)
- Shifting from environment to meta-environment (above the glass ceiling)
- Acquisition of meta-patterns and meta-levels

- Hormone controlled force fields (neural transmitters)
- Innate releasing mechanisms (Spielberg-like machines) – robotic bonding in the film AI.
- Emotional space is a force vector in the topology of internal representations.
- How can a Neosentient accomplish the enfolding of the above?

"Thinking is acting in imagined space" (Konrad Lorenz)

Roger Shepard

Mental transformations

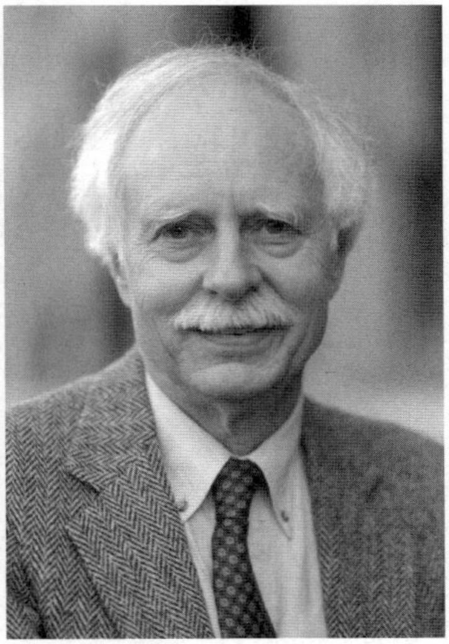

Courtesy Linda A. Cicero/Stanford News Service

Perhaps Shepard's most universally renowned experimental contribution consists in his experiments with the mental rotation task, thoroughly reported in his classic 1982 book Mental Images and Their Transformations, written with his collaborator Lynn Cooper. Considered some of the most elegant chronometric experiments in the history of psychology, these studies demonstrated that the comparison of two views of the same objects, displayed in different 3-dimensional orientations, involving a process of "mental rotation": the object is successively represented internally at successive positions which progressively bring one view in alignment with the other. Thus, the response time is a highly regular linear function of the angle of internal rotation. It might be thought that mental rotation is a mere metaphor, but with Lynn Cooper, Roger Shepard demonstrated its "psychological reality", for instance by demonstrating that the presentation of probe stimuli at intermediate orientations receive an especially fast response if presented at precisely the time when the theory predicts that this intermediate orientation should be internally represented.

In recent syntheses of his work, Shepard has proposed an evolutionary psychology argument for why internal representations and their transformations are so regularly organized and often faithfully reflect the structure of physical laws. He proposes that mental representations have evolved over millions of years as adaptations to universal physical principles (such as the kinematic laws governing object motion, those underlying light reflection and diffusion, etc). As a result, mental representations have become highly structured and attuned to physical laws – in Shepard's terms they are "second-order isomorphic", which means that the relations between physical events in the environment are preserved in the relations between their internal mental representations.

According to Shepard, this mental internalization process explains why physicists such as Galileo, Newton or Einstein, were able to rely on thought experiments in order to derive plausible physical laws – thought processes are sufficiently isomorphic to physical processes that the properties of the latter can be inferred, in part, by mere introspection on the former. For Shepard, the mental regularities imposed on this internalization process are so extensive that they attain "the kind of universality, invariance, and formal elegance [...] previously accorded only to the laws of physics and mathematics".[56]

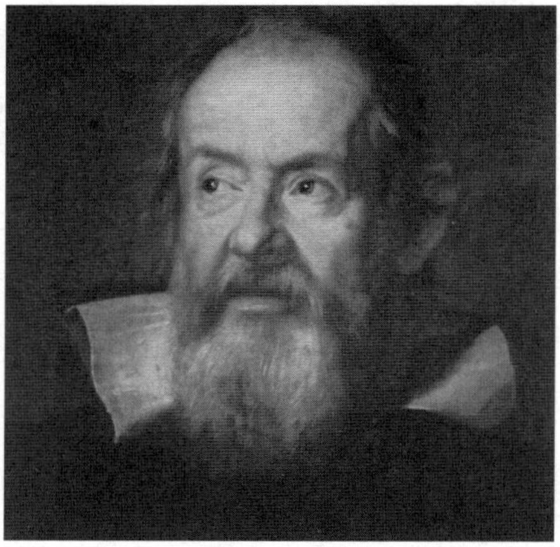

Portrait of Galileo Galilei by Justus Sustermans (1597–1681), public domain.

One wonders how this isomorphic perception of space might be related to the memory techniques of Cicero and Giordano Bruno ... generating physical relations of space navigation in the brain to augment memory.

Meaning/Becoming

The unknowable
The unknown
The known

What at one time appears unknowable may shift to the unknown and become an object of scrutiny via technological advances and later move into the realm of the known.

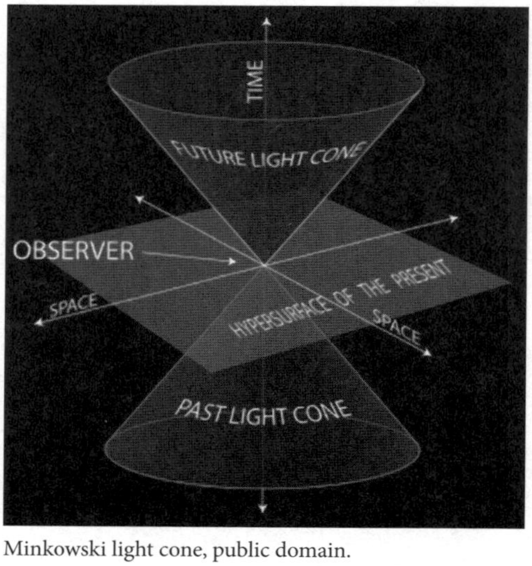

Minkowski light cone, public domain.

Time

Time is always flowing
The now remains still
Death does not exist
The now is a scandalous imposition

Everything is being joysticked by the lightning thrower (Heraclitus–IX, 10,7 [DK 22 B64])

The lightning is the now

Heraclitus as seen by an artist:

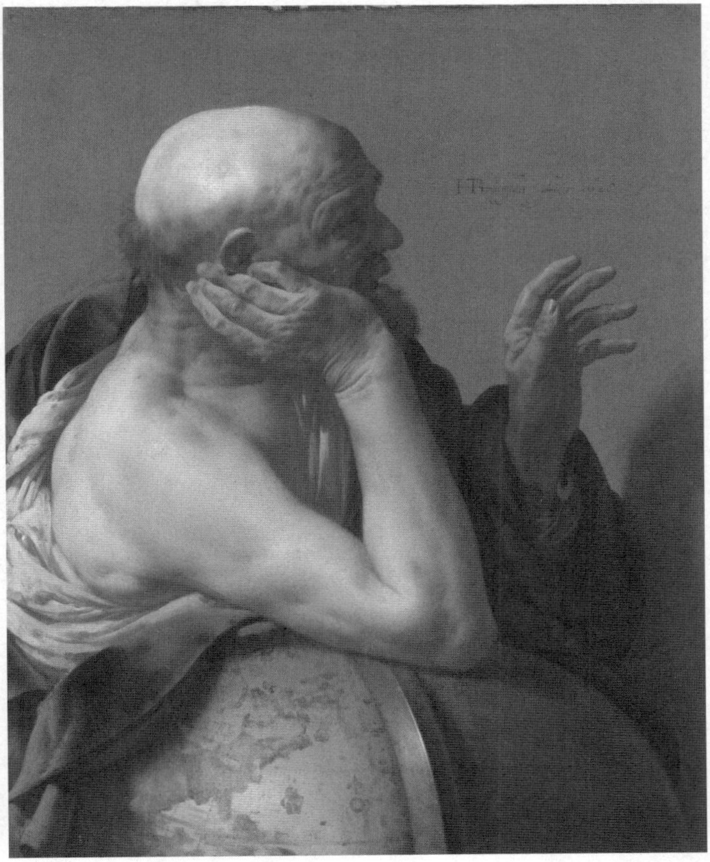

Hendrik Ter Brugghen, Rijksmuseum in Amsterdam, 1628. Heraclitus, courtesy of the Rijksmuseum.

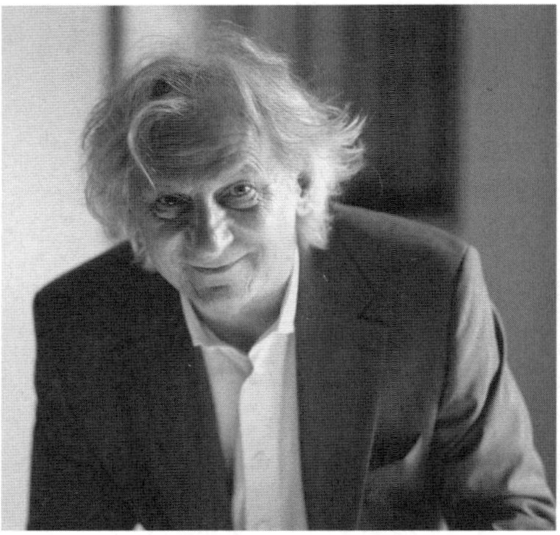

Siegfried Zielinski, image © MONO KROM.

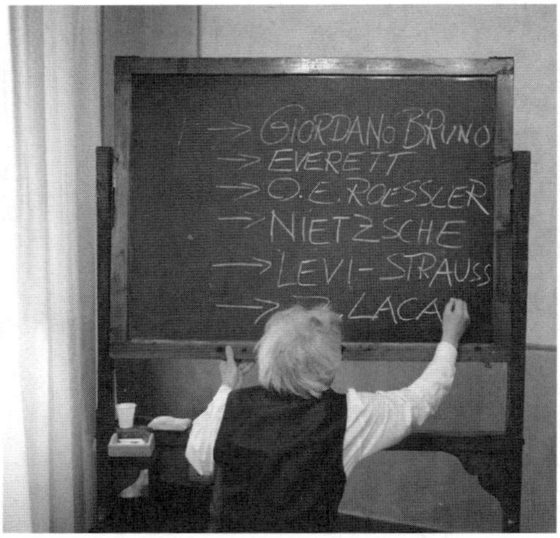

Siegfried Zielinski at the Blackboard, image © MONO KROM.

Siegfried Zielinski – Variantology or Archeology of the Media

Siegfried Zielinski has been a media archeologist since his first book *History of the Video Recorder*. He is perhaps most influential for having invented a new overarching science called "Variantology," which looks at past cultures as well as our current ones as templates that could as well have taken a different (variantological) course. This approach, starting out from the history of art, has now covered the most diverse disciplines from ancient times to the present in four monumental books, already.

http://www.variantology.com/

Our work on deep time relations between arts, sciences, and technologies does not seek to re-invent the concepts of the media or the arts. The aim is to open up both media and the arts via their interactions with scientific and technological processes. It is our hope that media experts will see their research areas in a broader light than before, and that disciplines which have so far not participated in these discourses (such as theology, classical studies, many areas of the history of science and technology) will develop an openness for media questions. Right from the beginning Variantology/Archaeology of the Media was conceived as an international research and exchange project. A central part of it is the development of an open and temporal network of outstanding scientists, artists and scholars who engage with the deep time relations of arts, sciences and technologies.[57]

The Brain Equation[58]

The Brain equation is an equation of the force field of all desires. It is based in spatial Darwinism as a part of deductive biology. One can put the Brain Equation into a crystal. It in this case contains a frozen Now – just as in a famous science fiction work by Stanislav Lem, *Memoirs of a space traveler: further reminiscences of Ijon Tichy*.

A synopsis of the Brain equation

Darwin discovered metabolic adaptation – only sequentially randomly modified metabolic networks can maintain autonomous self-maintenance in a randomly changing chemical and physical environment. These permanent changes have to be produced endogenously in sufficient variety. This mechanism can be called "metabolic adaptation" for short. It is very much longer in duration than one generation. Much shorter (momentaneous essentially) changes require a different kind of adaptation. Konrad Lorenz first saw this fundamental difference in a series of conversations we had in 1966. They require "positional" rather than "metabolic adaptation." Here one can predict that signals and sensors must be involved. Even lowly bacteria living in a tidal region on a shore predictably evolved sensors signaling temporal position in the tidal cycle. This was our first, basic insight: a fundamental second type of adaptation. Chronobiology (which already existed) can be predicted from first principles. The second step was space. When survival depends on position in space rather than in time, positional adaptation in space is predictable. (Moths should eventually show positional adaptation toward candle flames if humans remain a factor in their reproductive success.) Position in space – like momentary position in time – is nothing that can be dealt with by metabolic adaptation. Darwin-style natural selection therefore has to produce sensors. "Positional adaptation in space" through movement is just the next higher-dimensional case after positional adaptation in time – chronobiology. What is predictably involved in this twin case are motors in addition to sensors, and an intervening transducing network ("brain").

At this point, it turned out that the newly found situation actually amounts to a well-posed problem in the sense of mathematics. Namely, a "traveling salesman with alarm clocks" problem. For survival-relevant resources of different types may be sharply located in space (like towns to be visited). It is not the minimum overall path that is sought, as in the ordinary travelling salesman of mathematics. Rather, a source ("town") of the right type – some five or ten – needs to be visited after a certain maximum time interval. Garey and Johnson later re-discovered this special variant to the famous traveling salesman problem of mathematics, calling it an "optimal decision" rather than "optimization problem." They showed that it is equally "NP complete" as the original traveling salesman problem is.

It follows that, if a brain were to solve this well-posed mathematical problem optimally, it would have to be as big and complex as the whole universe is, on purely mathematical grounds. But if the success rate is allowed to be finite (suboptimal), then finite computers suffice – "brains," that is. Depending on the allowed error rate (defined by the ratio between the maximum mean distance between sources of a given survival-relevant type over the maximum travelling radius allowed by a single "tank filling" of this type), either a very cavalier and haphazard locomotion strategy suffices (like to move at random and never stop, or move at random and stop temporarily whenever in the vicinity of a certain chemical – a type of behavior known to biologists under the name "kinesis"), or a maximally sharply calculated one becomes mandatory to be used.

The underlying "computer" (the connecting network between sensors and motors) can stay quite simple as long as the delicacy of the ratio mentioned above is not too great. There then arises a natural threshold here: When pure "direction optimization" (from the momentarily given position in space) is no longer sufficient so that genuine "path optimization" (supra-local optimization) becomes mandatory. Shortly below this threshold, the most sophisticated "local strategy" (of direction optimization) employs a force-field generator of a prescribed structure. This is the "brain equation." It describes a space- and time-dependent force field.

If the task becomes even more difficult – as is eventually unavoidable in evolution, then this suboptimal "local solution" can no longer be appropriate. Nonetheless it can still be used – if it is complemented by a "universal simulator" or virtual reality (VR) machine. This combination of two designs has the asset that a suboptimal fast strategy is still available in case of emergency – if there is not enough time to come up with the supra-locally optimal path-type solution which always takes time. So this is the predictable solution of choice in biology.

A third possibility exists as well: a multiple brain-type solution. The latter is known from "eusocial" animals in biology like ants and naked moles. For this alternative solution, no universal brain equation has been identified up until now.

The above combined machine, the brain equation combined with VR, possesses some interesting predictable design features. They include a pseudo-simultaneous "big screen." The latter strangely has never been identified or looked for in empirical brain science, nor has an "overlap buffer" and a "late recycler" and a finite-duration "now circuitry."

Nevertheless the most fascinating element remains the force-field generator itself, the brain equation. It combines potentially infinitely strongly attracting and repelling *forces* emanating from the positions of the closest "sources" of the different survival-relevant types. All forces are purely endogenously generated. Aristotle knew about them when he wrote that a falling stone is accelerating because it anticipates coming to rest at home. So he already equipped the force field with a VR in his own mind – as is correct not for a falling stone but for an adapted vertebrate.

The most famous constructs of Lonrad Lorenz – "flush-toilet model" of desires, endogenous mood pressure, bonding drive, a neurotransmitter for every type of desire, the relaxed field after a consummatory act, and so forth – all follow predictably from the brain equation but were originally based on field studies and an incredibly perceptive intuition. He said with a resigning tone in his voice that he was not a mathematician. But like Darwin, he did not know that he actually was an outstanding one.

Such an equation and brain can be implemented artificially in the new field of Neosentience. Are not all such systems, no matter whether natural or artificial, necessarily of limited intelligence? After all the brain equation has a deterministic structure. The answer is yes. But then how about the human brain – does it make for an exception or does it also involve the deterministic brain equation? It does. It is quite ordinary stuff – sperm whales, elephants, and even corvids have more – the former even very much more – to offer. But are we different? This is correct – we are as a species in general non-autistic. Why is this so? Is it because we are more social, perhaps? It turns out there is a third mode of brain function beside the non-eusocial one described, and the eusocial one. It does not even require a new anatomy or physiology; the caring one. Lorenz was a deeply caring individual (together with his even greater wife as he admitted). He talked about the joy of bottom-cleaning and nurturing, and said that Sigmund Freud had overlooked bonding as an even stronger drive than eros.

Bonding is Lorenz's greatest discovery: That it is a genuine drive, a specific subpotential in the later described brain equation. Bonding between adults comes and goes in evolution depending on not yet clearly definable properties of the ecological niche. Humans are the pair-bonding apes – besides gibbons. But gibbons do not share nonautism. How did the latter arise in one bonding ape but not the other? It indeed is not bonding alone that is responsible. Most species when newly adopting bonding between adults choose a sexual signal to acquire a new meaning for the new drive. Mounting was chosen by baboons and African wild dogs, for example. Human evolution by accident involved adopting the expression of joyfulness of the satiated infant, the "play face," for bonding. The smile of bonding (greeting) and the laughter of joyfulness miraculously congealed in a single species on the planet and possibly all other life forms in the solar system, the galaxy and perhaps even the universe. It is an extremely unlikely coincidence.

The consequence is a new third type of brain functioning. It arises epigenetically – during the life history of the individual – via the mirroring interaction with the mother, at a quite young age. The consequence is the emergence out of nothing of the suspicion of benevolence in the human toddler. How? Because Mom's happy face looks like her (vitally needed) bonding expression. Laughter and smile look the same. Parent-feeding is the predictable consequence. Humans can be classified biologically as "Pongo goneotrophicus" – the parent-feeding ape. It is often observable on one-and-a-half-year olds already.

A new mode of functioning of the brain is hereby implicit: A mutual misunderstanding that is altogether too beautiful. It is endorsed by an act of creation out of nothing – by the child, but also by the mother. A very strange event indeed which generates a lovely creature. This creature – you and you – should get informed about how special it is. Maybe there is not much time left for humankind to learn this about itself.

But let us return to the brain equation and Steven Spielberg's movie "AI." And to the potentially immortal successor of humans – the Neosentient artificial mind that becomes a person through the very same spontaneous act as a toddler does. But this is another chapter.

Marvin Minsky

Marvin Minsky is one of the originators of Artificial Intelligence, and the author of *Society of Mind*. More recently he has been writing about Emotional Computing.

In the Prologue to *Society of Mind*, Minsky starts with a quote from Einstein:

"Everything should be as simple as possible but not simpler."

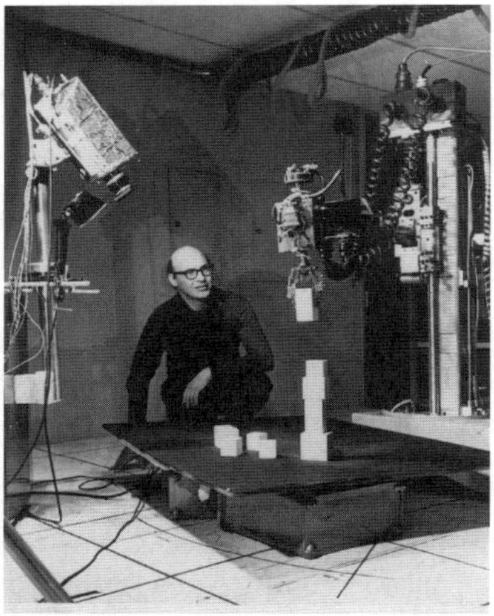

Marvin Minsky, courtesy of the MIT Museum.

He continues:

This book tries to explain how the mind works. How can intelligence emerge from nonintelligence? To answer that, we'll show that you can build a mind from many tiny little parts, each mindless in itself [...] I'll call Society of Mind this scheme in which each mind is made of many smaller processes. These we'll call agents. Each mental agent by itself can only do some simple thing that needs no mind or thought at all. Yet when we join these agents in societies – in certain very special ways – this leads to true intelligence.[59]

One must not forget to remember that intelligence is not yet mind.

Repulsion and Attraction
From The Emotion Machine *by Marvin Minsky*

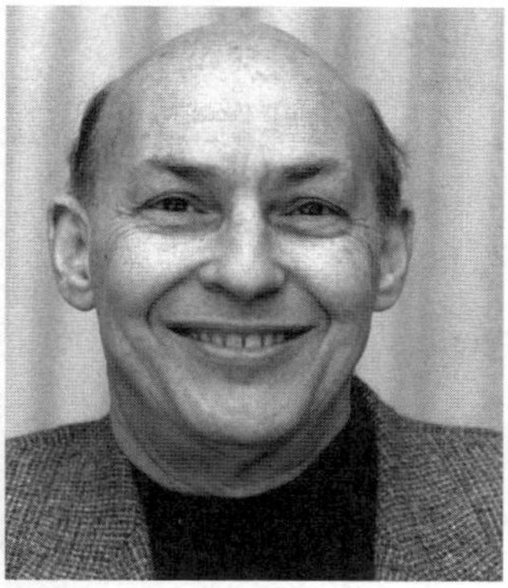
Marvin Minsky, courtesy of the MIT News Office, Donna Coveney/MIT.

We'll use this image whenever we want to explain some mental activity (such as Anger, Love, or Embarrassment) by trying to show how that state of mind might result from the activities of a certain collection of mental resources. For example, the state called "Anger" appears to arouse resources that make us react with unusual speed and strength – while suppressing resources that we otherwise use to plan and act more prudently; thus Anger replaces your cautiousness with aggressiveness and trades your sympathy for hostility. Similarly, the condition called "Fear" would engage resources in ways that cause you to retreat.[60]

This is good old ethology as the reader will appreciate later …

One Now

Why is one *Now* special among all the Nows of time?
Each mind is a Now in itself. Every now is a new world – many nows, many minds, many worlds.
This is a butterfly that is inserted into our text.

Global Brain

Emergence: The Connected Lives of Ants, Brains, Cities and Software
Author: Steven Johnson

What do ant colonies, slime moulds and the teeming streets of Victorian Manchester have in common? They are all, according to Steven Johnson, examples of emergent systems. Emergent phenomena, such as the division of a city into discrete neighbourhoods or the apparent collective intelligence of an ant colony, are by products of the interactions of thousands of simpler "agents". An individual ant is fairly unintelligent and is largely driven by instinct. An ant follows a few simple rules: get food, dump waste, tend young, defend the colony. It has limited means of communications with its fellow ants, and what there is is largely based on pheromone signaling.

However when thousands of these simple agents interact with each other, what you get is not teeming chaos but a global behaviour that can solve problems, keep the colony fed, protect it from attack and can adapt to a changing environment. This is what emergence is all about, this qualitative difference in behaviours at the micro and macro levels [...]

What has all this got to do with software? In the first place complexity theory, which is what this area of study falls under, uses software as its principle research tool. Cellular automata, neural networks, artificial life simulations and other types of software tools have been, and are still being, used to model and learn about complex systems and their emergent properties. However, complexity theory and emergence also provide a rich source of metaphors and ideas for the next generation of distributed applications.

Software is increasingly about creating "agents" which interact with each other to produce a resulting application. Piecing together a fully distributed application is as much about understanding the different agents, the rules they follow and how they communicate with each than it is with designing the front end. To this end, stepping back a little to take a broader view, as Johnson does, has much to commend it.

Besides, all this talk of ants is not completely off the wall. Recent work in Belgium has shown that a software simulation of ant colony behaviour is able to solve The Travelling Salesman problem as well as the best of the specialist techniques available. British Telecom, amongst others, are now using software ants to solve network routing problems.[61]

Although the Brain Equation is a solution to the traveling salesman problem, based on a single traveler, the corresponding multi-traveler-type solution (for eusocial animals) has not been found yet.

This eusocial solution would not be social in the benevolent sense as in the case of two specially coupled brain equations.

All of these equations arise as solutions to the traveling salesman problem in deductive biology.

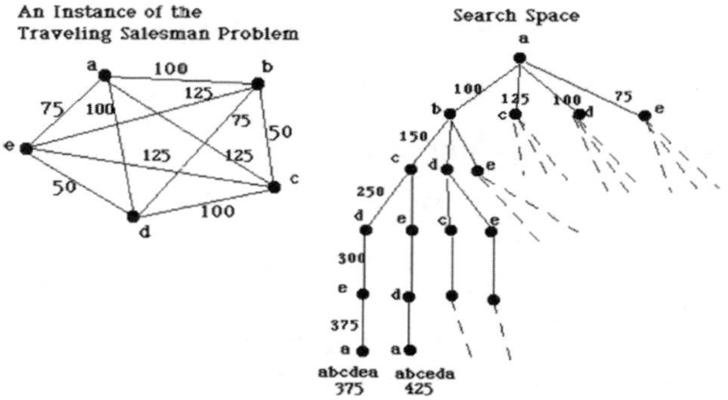

What role might a language system similar to the chemical language of ants play in a distributed eusocial neosentience?

Xpero and Dörner

Dörner outlined in *Blueprint for a Soul* (1998), (Bauplan für eine Seele), experiments where robotic behavior and learning was being explored computationally. Alternately, it is exciting to see an extension of his work via an embodied approach to robotic problem solving – Xpero. We see these both as encouraging parallel attempts to get at the complexities of robotic learning. Xpero, research consortium, outlines related intuitions to those of the authors, but does not use the brain equation as yet. And no piercing of the glass ceiling (of benevolence acquisition). Still they are all close allies.

Dörner
Human thinking is not a static phenomenon which only functions according to inflexible sets of rules. Rather, it is a process subject to change. A special potential for changing thinking lies in a method which has so far been neglected by experimental psychology: the method of self-reflection – the thinker's contemplation of his own thinking. Self-reflection usually occurs as a shift in the problem level. The problem solver abandons for the time being the solution of a particular problem and turns instead to problematizing his own thinking [...] In a series of experiments we have been studying the effect of self reflection on the development of an individual's thinking ability. It can be shown that self-reflection leads to a substantial improvement in problem-solving ability and that this improvement is transferable to other problem areas.[62]

Xpero
The overall objective of the project is to develop an embodied cognitive system, which is able to conduct experiments in the real world with the purpose of gaining new insights about the world and the objects therein and to develop and improve its own cognitive skills and overall performance. It is obvious that for the ability to conduct experiments in the real world, embodiment is a fundamental prerequisite.

Expected results of the project are basic models, techniques, and system solutions, enabling an embodied agent to autonomously design and conduct experiments in a given context – stimulating the agent's desire to gather new knowledge – and to extract new insights from the results of the experiment.

Xpero
Strategic objectives

- *To significantly advance the state of the art in Machine Learning particularly in Embodied Cognitive Systems, Computational Perception, Knowledge Engineering and Intelligent Assistive Robotics by developing formal theories, computational approaches and systems enabling an embodied agent to augment its cognitive capabilities through open-ended learning by experimentation.*

- *To foster European leadership in the field of Embodied Cognitive Systems by establishing and promoting the field of Learning by Experimentation.*
- *To support the development of new industrial branches in Europe, such as Service Robotics and Assistive Technologies, by providing key technologies.*

XPERO proposes to approach this problem by developing a methodology for learning by experimentation. Enabling an embodied agent, in the sequel called robot, to design and conduct experiments in a natural real world setting and to extract new insights is more than just adding another feature to a technical system. The ability to conduct experiments in the real world and extract new knowledge and insights pushes open the door to a new quality of embodied systems namely to potentially unlimited autonomous learning. This ability enables the robot to grow in an unlimited fashion its cognitive capacity and its performance to accomplish meaningful tasks in the real world. Limitations are only set by the surrounding world and its own physical capabilities, and not by availability of a programmer, teacher or learning material. We plan to achieve this objective by performing research and development in the following areas:

- *Stimulation of Experiment*
- *Design and Execution of Experiments*
- *Observation and Evaluation of Experiments*
- *Representing Knowledge and Gaining Insights*
- *Innate Knowledge and Cognitive Bootstrap*
- *Engineering the Experimental Loop*[63]

(Re)sensing the Observer – Open Order Cybernetics

An infinite number of meta-levels and the potentials of language and technologies to come …

We are first of all concerned about our acquisition and use of language as the precondition for any meaningful statement. This self-reflexive point of departure distinguishes our project from philosophers who are presuming "something" ("closure", "self-organization", "self", "auto-poiesis", "senses", "objects", "subjects", "language", "nervous systems" etc.) in the first place without being aware of their presumptions i.e. that they are able to already talk meaningfully about "something". We are undertaking a self-reflexive loop towards our already undertaken "meaningful"

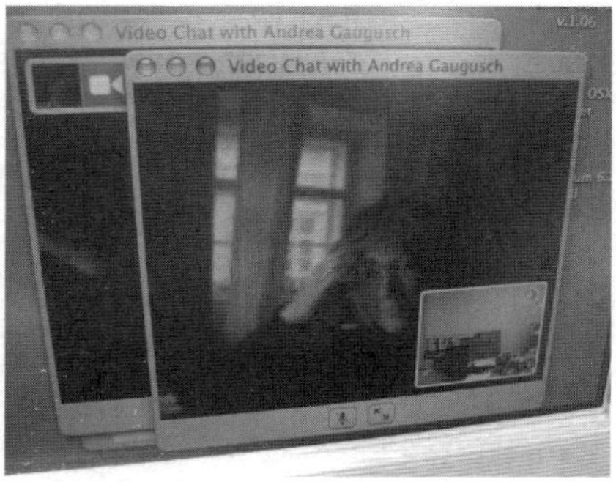

Andrea Gaugusch, courtesy of Seaman.

actions, reflecting inside our concepts on our concepts, trying to find out how our concepts about "something" have come into existence. We are reflecting on our concepts through this ongoing open investigation. We are sketching the ramifications of such a self-reflexive loop for epistemology as well as for the main research areas within cognitive science (i.e. language acquisition, perception, consciousness). We are also pointing towards virtual reality in combination with the arts as an awareness aid, helping us in our self-reflexive endeavours.[64]

Many would say von Foerster was already thinking about such questions of language and technological change when he conceived of a *Cybernetics of Cybernetics* and later wrote his punningly observant work *Observing Systems*.

Deviation-amplifying Mutual Causal Processes

Since its inception, cybernetics, was more or less identified as a science of self-regulating and equilibrating systems. Thermostats, physiological regulation of body temperature, automatic steering devices, economic and political processes were studied under a general mathematical model of deviation-counteracting feedback networks.

By focusing on the deviation-counteracting aspect of the mutual causal relationships however, the cyberneticians paid less attention to the systems in which the mutual causal effects are deviation-amplifying. Such systems are ubiquitous: accumulation of capital in industry, evolution of living organisms, the rise of cultures of various types, interpersonal processes which produce mental illness, international conflicts, and the processes that are loosely termed as "vicious circles" and "compound interests"; in short, all processes of mutual causal relationships that amplify an insignificant or accidental initial kick, build up deviation and diverge from the initial condition. In contrast to the progress in the study of equilibrating systems, the deviation-amplifying systems have not been given as much investment of time and energy by the mathematical scientists on the one hand, and understanding and practical application on the part of geneticists, ecologists, politicians and psychotherapists on the other hand.[65]

This is an independent approach to Darwinism and the origin of life.

Ultrainstability – the opposite of Ashby's Ultrastability – would be defined as an indestructible instability. It is like the Hydra of Greek mythology that always spawns new heads if you cut one off. Evolution and Cosmology as articulated by de Chardin and Bateson fit in naturally here.

Gödel Boundary Overstepped

The simplest way to put Gödel's theorem is as follows – that the theorem says of itself: "I cannot be proven in finitely many steps."

Working when not

In its absolutely barest form, Gödel's discovery involves the translation of an ancient paradox in philosophy into mathematical terms. That paradox is the so-called Epimenides paradox, or liar paradox. Epimenides was a Cretan who made one immortal statement: "All Cretans are liars." A sharper version of the statement is simply "I am lying"; or, "This statement is false". It is that last version which I will usually mean when I speak of the Epimenides paradox. It is a statement which rudely violates the usually assumed dichotomy of statements into true and false, because if you tentatively think it is true, then it immediately backfires on you and makes you think it is false. But once you've decided it is false, a similar backfiring returns you to the idea that it must be true. Try it!

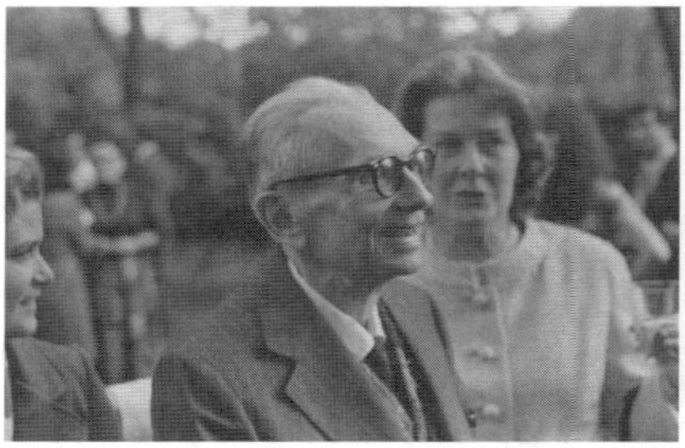

Gödel – A. G. Wightman photographer. From The Shelby White and Leon Levy Archives Center, Institute for Advanced Study, Princeton, NJ, USA.

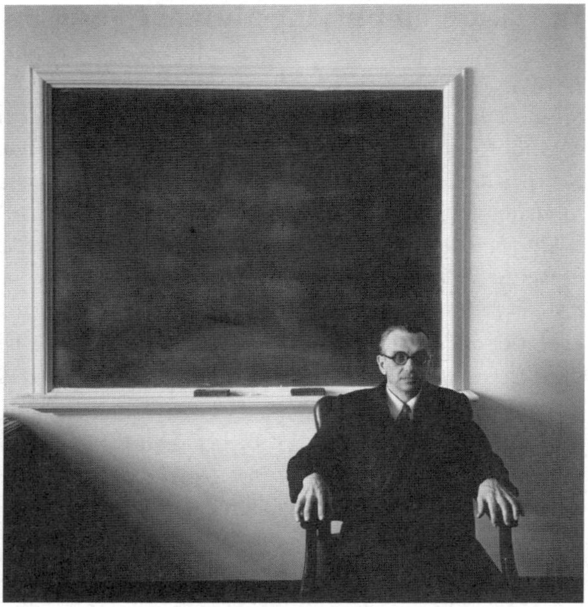

Mathematician Kurt Gödel poses for portrait at the Institute for Advanced Study, 1 May 1956 Princeton, New Jersey. Arnold Newman/Getty Images.

Epimenides

The Epimenides paradox is a one-step Strange Loop, like Escher's Print Gallery. But what does it have to do with mathematics? That is what Gödel discovered. His idea was to use mathematical reasoning in exploring mathematical reasoning itself. This notion of making mathematics "introspective" proved to be enormously powerful, and perhaps its richest implication was the one Gödel found: Gödel's Incompleteness Theorem. What the Theorem states and how it is proved are two different things.[66]

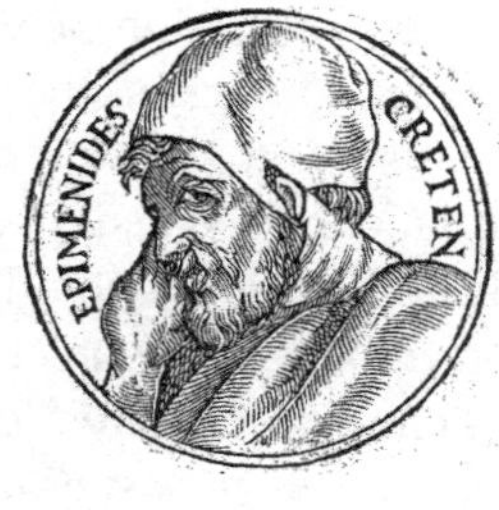

Epimenides born around 600 BC on a coin of 1553, public domain.

The "word problem" is one of the simplest examples. You have a set of three-letter words and a set of rules. You have to decide if these words have been produced by those rules. An even more intuitive case is a series of differently shaped blocks and a given table. You have to decide whether a finite collection of those blocks fit exactly onto that table. The salient point in all of this is that sometimes an infinite number of intermediary trial steps become necessary.

The traveling salesman problem that was mentioned above is a finite version of Gödel's problem. This connection (Gödel = lim NP for n to infinity) has apparently never been explored before.

Red Hole – Hole Filled with Light or Color

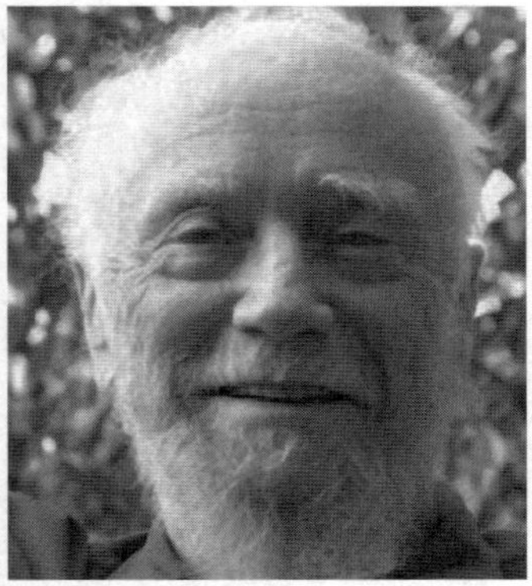
Gray or not gray. Courtesy of David Finkelstein.

The gray hole is a potential metaphor for the great riddle that is exemplified in an autocatalytic analog circuit. It has autonomous features both in the autopoetic sense and in the sense of Gödel's self-reference. This emergence out of nothing cannot be predicted to have any qualitative properties (except that it is self-identical). These qualities are "gray." Miraculously, our own qualities are not gray. This is the gratuitous transition from the "gray hole" in the sense of Gödel to the "Red hole" of David Finkelstein. (Thanks for a conversation, David!)

Picture yourself in front of an analog computer, plugging in some colored wires into the plug board. Then you will have made connections between certain integrators in the machine, that is, the integrators could feed their input from their output in an autocatalytic fashion. This could be done either in a cross-connected way or via self-connection. Suppose one of these integrators was you – what you are craving for is your own craving. For some reason this feature of your innermost identity is identical with your innermost identity: It doesn't matter what the signals that are circulating here are made up of – voltage, water, current, a set of nerve signals – any other physical substance could serve in this autocatalytic growth process that has no other aim than itself.

In interaction between two such entities (equipped with mirror competence), a higher order analog of the same type can arise. There are two types of such situations, one benevolent and one malevolent. Only *persons* know about benevolence – and also robots that are governed by the brain equation, with its potentially infinite forces, can be brought into this double bind-like situation if the success of one is reinforced in a positive cross-feedback by the success of the other. The laughter – smile overlap in human beings enables such a strange situation to occur. The malevolent case, by the way, is not as symmetrical and can never arise spontaneously.

The Angel of Qualia

What do we mean by angels? They would bring the shining lamps that carry the colors and the Now into the poor machines of technological or biological origin. They are at the core of the qualia. Without them there would be only talia. The word qualia is the plural of the Latin word quale – meaning how something is. Talia is the plural of the Latin word tale – meaning that something is so and so (hence – it is the shadows without any blood). It is the domain of the Hades and the domain of technology and science.

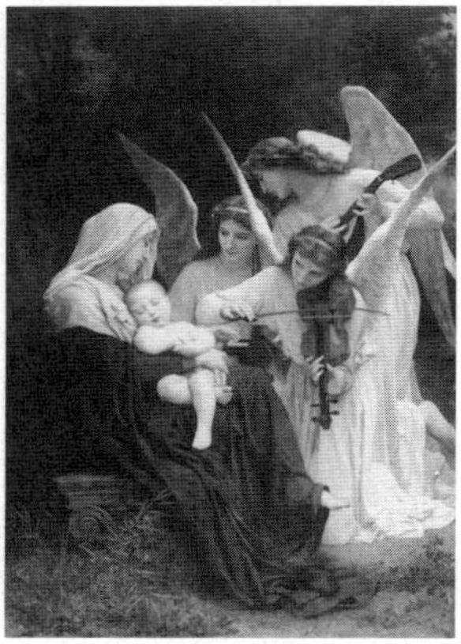

Song of the Angels (1881). William-Adolphe Bouguereau, public domain.

The Russell, Bateson, Pavlov Paradox

The Cretan who said that Cretans always lie. When Russell wanted to understand this mathematically he left an empty sheet after spending a whole evening thinking about the topic. When this had happened seven times in a row, he realized a revolution in Mathematics was impending. Whitehead told this secret in the history of mathematics to Bateson; Bateson told it to one of the authors in 1974.

This is how the idea of the double bind was born. One day – Bateson had just been denied extension of a grant so he had to lay off his coworkers; he was sadly driving along a super highway. Passing under a bridge, he noted a large regular road sign overhead saying in the

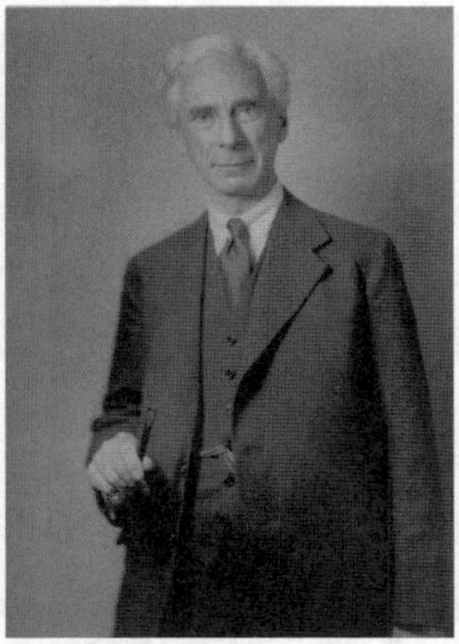

Bertrand Russell c. 1921. Blackstone Studios, Inc., courtesy of the William Ready Division of Archives and Research Collections, McMaster University Library.

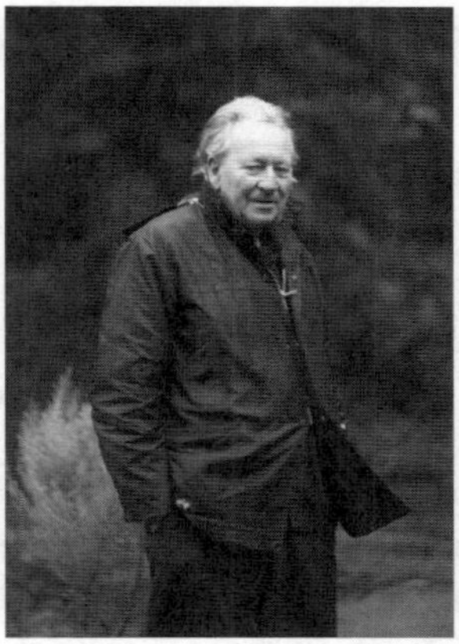

Gregory Bateson – Ben Lomond, CA – 1975. Image copyright Barry Schwartz.

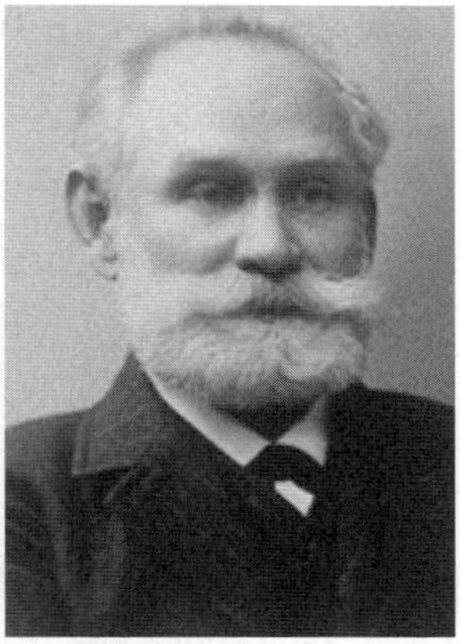

Ivan Pavlov, Nobel Prize in Physiology 1904, courtesy of Creative Commons.

official green and white colors: "ignore this sign." It struck a chord. His career was saved. Whitehead, his teacher, had explained Bertrand Russel's struggle with Epimenides the Cretan. This struggle being merely mathematical. Here, there was an order, he realized: imagine a barber who according to Whitehead "shaves everyone who doesn't shave himself" is drafted at a time of war and gets the order "shave everyone in your platoon who does not shave himself!" Being faced with certain death, for unavoidably disobeying an order during wartime, he can only break out into a mad laughter. This is schizophrenia explained rationally.

The more you try to get out, the more you are trapped.

There is an early example of a double bind: Pavlov's double bind experiment with a dog – which was known to Bateson. Pavlov had trained the dog to salivate when shown a vertical ellipse, and to duck and hide in fear when shown a horizontally oriented ellipse, because an electric shock would follow. Then Pavlov in a very cruel manner began to widen the shape of the two ellipses to become less easily distinguishable. This was done by slowly changing the shape of the ellipses so as to gradually approach the same circular shape. For a number of trials the dog managed to distinguish between the two shapes. But when the two ellipses reached a 70 per cent ratio, the dog gave up and became mad. Only heavy drugs could restore the equilibrium of his behavior.

Russell's paradox: Does the set of all those sets that do not contain themselves contain itself? Whitehead popularized it with the Barber's paradox: does a barber who shaves all men who do not shave themselves, shave himself?

Bateson – The Double Bind Theory

Example: A sign saying – *Ignore this sentence*

Bateson

Sometimes – often in science and always in art – one does not know what the problems were till after they have been solved. So perhaps it will be useful to state retrospectively what problems were solved for me by double bind theory [...]

Let me coin the word "transcontextual" as a general term for this genus of syndromes. It seems that both those whose life is enriched by transcontextual gifts and those who are impoverished by transcontextual confusions are alike in one respect: for them there is always or often a "double take." A falling leaf, the greeting of a friend, or a "primrose by the river's brim" is not "just that and nothing more." Exogenous experience may be framed in the contexts of dream, and internal thought may be projected into the contexts of the external world. And so on. For all this, we seek a partial explanation in learning and experience.[67]

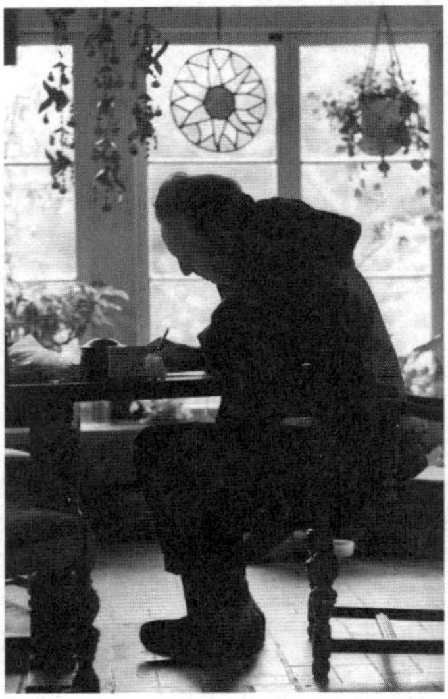

Gregory Bateson, Ben Lomand, CA – 1975. Image copyright Barry Schwartz.

What is a Question?[68]

Donald MacKay

This question is a sign that your companion is a person ... (Don't laugh)

Asimo

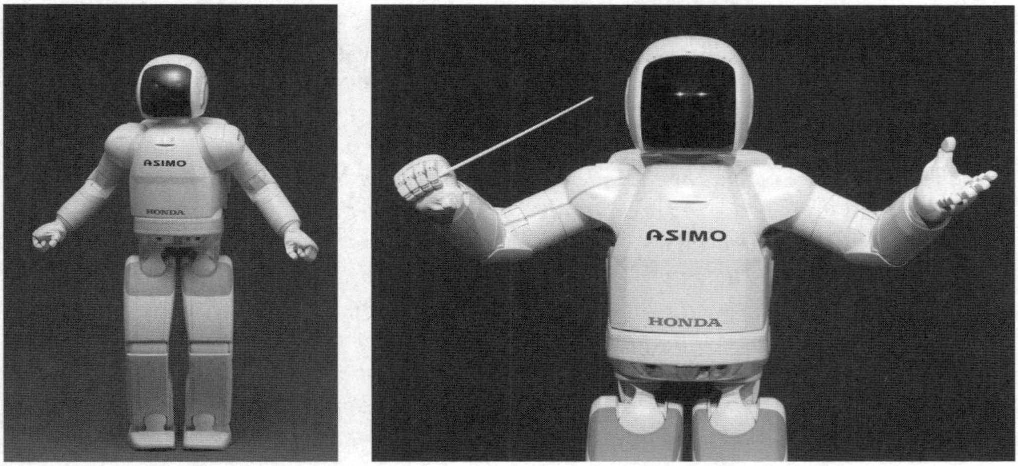

Asimo, courtesy American Honda Motor Co., inc.

ASIMO will focus attention on the Detroit Symphony Orchestra's nationally acclaimed music programs for young people in Detroit, courtesy of Honda.

Asimov's 3 Laws – Some Observations by Rodney Brooks Concerning the Laws and Reality

During the 1950s Isaac Asimov wrote a series of books about humanoid robots, starting with I, Robot. *The main characters were robots, some of which were almost indistinguishable from people. The robots were manufactured to obey three laws, which have come to be known as Asimov's laws.*

1. *A robot may not injure a human being or, through inaction, allow a human being to come to harm.*
2. *A robot must obey the orders given to it by human beings except where such orders would conflict with the First law.*

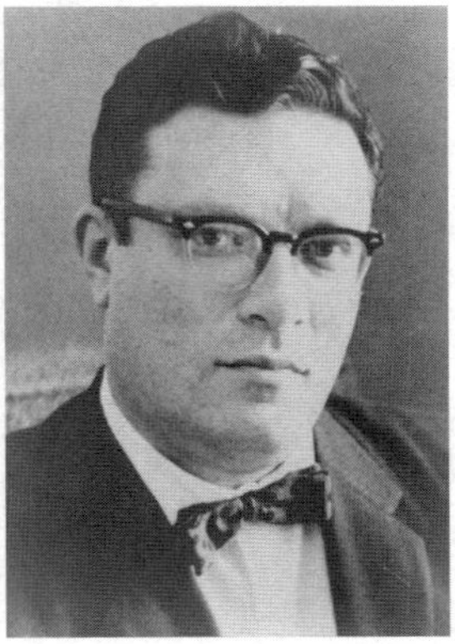

Isaac Asimov, public domain.

3. *A robot must protect its own existence as long as such protection does not conflict with the First or Second Law.*

The plot device in many of the books and short stories that Asimov wrote about these robots centered on situations in which there were logical inconsistencies in the application of the laws. This always led to some unexpected behavior on the part of the robots as they struggled to obey the three laws.

Journalists, and others, have often picked up on these laws. In fact the robot played by Robin Williams in the 1999 movie The Bicentiennial Man projected these laws holographically when it was delivered to its new owners. Journalists often ask whether the robots being built today are built to obey these three laws.

The simple answer is that they are not. And the reason is not that they are built to be malicious, but rather that we do not know how to build robots that are perceptive enough and smart enough to obey these three laws. At first sight the three laws seem innocuous and plain common sense. However upon closer examination they turn out to be very subtle. Of course, Asimov knew this, as he played on that subtlety for his plots. Perhaps though, he did not realize just what a perceptual load these laws put on the robot. See note 33.

Cantor's Diagonals[69]

Hofstadter

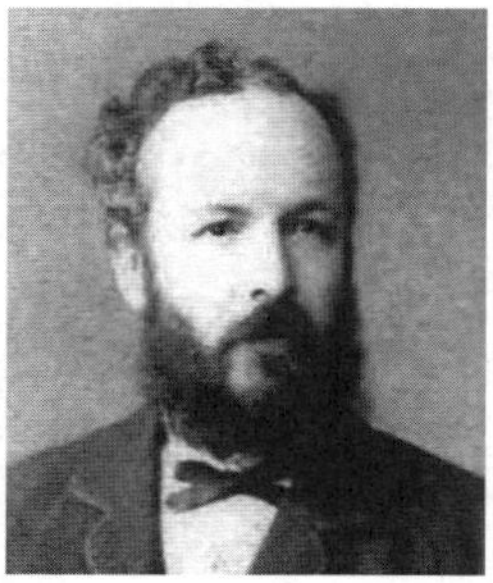

In the meantime, interesting developments were taking place in classical mathematics. A theory of different types of infinities, known as the theory of sets, was developed by Georg Cantor in the 1880s. The theory was powerful and beautiful, but intuition-defying. Before long, a variety of set-theoretical paradoxes had been unearthed. The situation was very disturbing, because just as mathematics seemed to be recovering from one set of paradoxes – those related to the theory of limits, in the calculus – along came a whole new set, which looked worse!

Cantor's diagonal method[70]

The Cantor diagonal method, also called the Cantor diagonal argument or Cantor's diagonal slash, is a clever technique used by Georg Cantor to show that the integers and reals cannot be put into a one-to-one correspondence (i.e., the uncountably infinite set of real numbers is "larger" than the countably infinite set of integers).[71]

It is hard to do justice to Cantor. He single-handedly reinvented Anaxagoras's discovery of the trans(in) finite numbers which he had called Homeomeries. There is only one person in between, Giordano Bruno who came close.[72] Elizabeth von Samsonow, personal communication 2008.

E_0 = m m m m m m m m m m m m ···
E_1 = w w w w w w w w w w w w ···
E_2 = m w m w m w m w m w m w ···
E_3 = w m w m w m w m w m m w ···
E_4 = w m m w w m m w m w m w ···
E_5 = m w m w w m w m w m w m ···
E_6 = m w m w w m w w m w m w ···
E_7 = w m m w m w m w m w m w ···
E_8 = m m w m w m w m w m w m ···
E_9 = w m w m m w w m w w m w ···
E_{10} = w w m w m w m w m m w m ···
E_{11} = m w m w w m w m m w m m ···
⋮ ⋮ ⋮ ⋮ ⋮ ⋮ ⋮ ⋮ ⋮ ⋮ ⋮ ⋮ ⋮ ⋱

$E_u \neq$ w m w w m w m m m m m w ···

Diagram, public domain.

Bruno Marchal

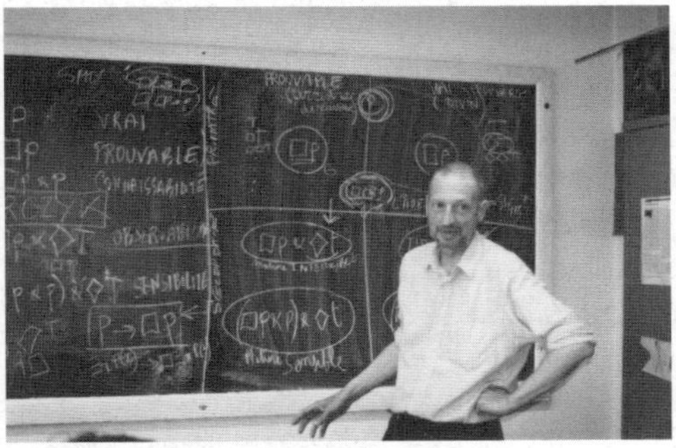

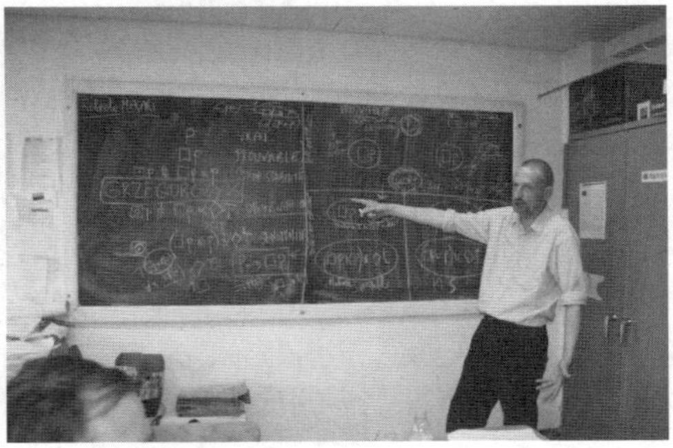

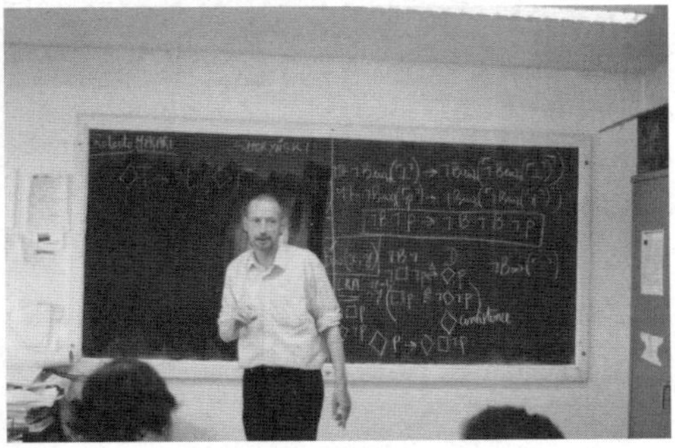

Photos of Bruno Marchal by Lydia Nash.

Cantor's diagonal procedure is being applied to the brain and the world by Marchal as a deduction of an attempted version of Everett's theory and of Endophysics.

If the world is a computer then you can approximate the world, so its state is a finite or infinite number of digits. You can run a specific algorithm – even if it has infinitely long numbers, you can always find a new number that is not in the list. When running the system, if you only wait long enough then the same reoccurrence will happen. This becomes a kind of jumping in time and you then exist over many times. Marchal invented a related idea about consciousness.[73]

This is similar to Everett's Many Worlds but is about a repetition, putting the accent on difference.

The origin of physical laws and sensations
I will first present a non constructive argument showing that the mechanist hypothesis in cognitive science gives enough constraints to decide what a "physical reality" can possibly consist in. Then I will explain how computer science, together with logic, makes it possible to extract a constructive version of the argument [...] [this (emphasis Rössler and Seaman)] gives a testable explanation of how both communicable physical laws and incommunicable physical knowledge, i.e. sensations, arise from number theoretical relations.[74]

Computation, consciousness and the quantum
Abstract: It is sometimes said that Everett's formulation of Quantum Mechanics dispenses us with the need of a theory of consciousness in the foundation of physics. This is false as Everett himself clearly recognized in his paper. Indeed he has built its quantum mechanics formulation by using explicitly the mechanist or computationalist hypothesis in psychology. Everett and his followers have then derived the subjective appearance, in the mind of machine-observers, of indeterminacy and non-locality from the Schroedinger Equation. I argue in this paper that if we take the computationalist hypothesis seriously enough then the Schroedinger equation itself should be derivable from the computationalist theory of consciousness, making ultimately physics a branch of machine psychology. I sketch the basic argument and illustrate it with two embryonic derivations. In some sense I criticize Everett for his lack of radicality.[75]

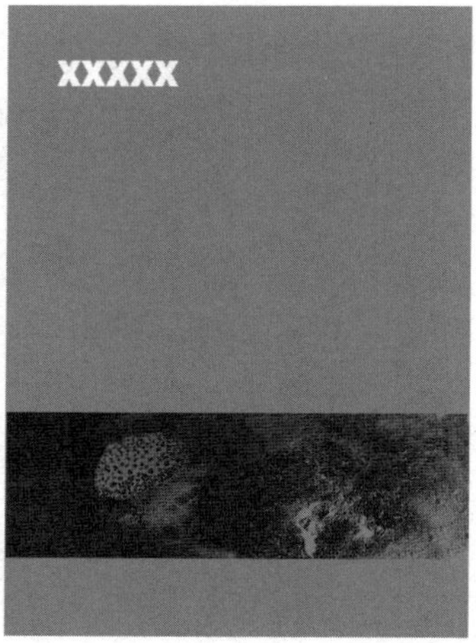

[The] xxxxx [reader] proposes a radical space for code-driven art, science, and technology investigations, photo courtesy of Martin Howse.

Norbert Wiener – Mathematics

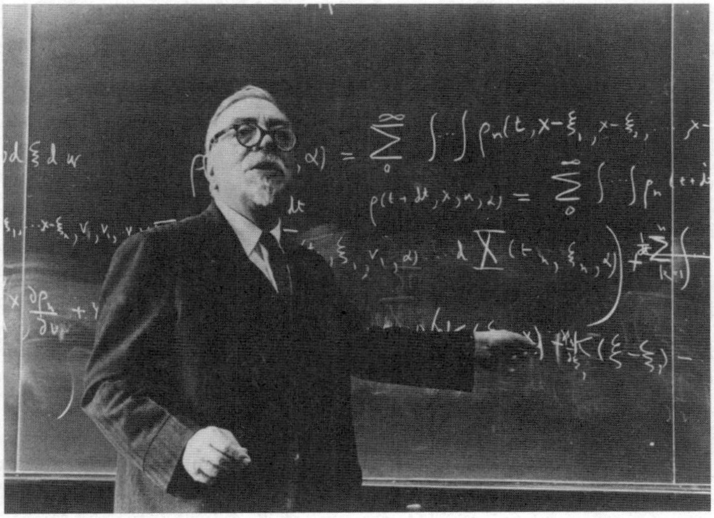

Norbert Wiener, courtesy of the MIT Museum.

Wiener was the first person to articulate the idea of sending someone through a wire. His ideas surrounding cybernetics were precursors to a number of the concepts explored in this book.

There are certain procedures which are undoubtedly favorable for invention and discovery. One of the most potent tools in reanimating a science is mathematics. To some extent, a mathematical treatment of a science consists in writing down its data and its questions in a numerical or quantitative form, but it is perhaps better to consider that here number and quantity are secondary to a logically precise language. If a certain question is to be asked in biology, and if we are to ask it in biological language then we ourselves and whoever reads our work are likely to be strongly conditioned to think of what we have done as the answer to a biological question. However, if we express our ideas in mathematical form, we are using what is much more likely to be colorless and indifferent language. Just because of that, we are far more likely to recognize the same question even if it is asked in a totally different field. This greater scope is of far from trivial significance.[76]

The Pattern Game

An embodied notion of knowledge acquisition points at how the physical body, working through all aspects of the senses and sensuality, comes to know the world.

This embodied view suggests that environmental patterns that are perceived by the body, and are reinforced through the body, form our understanding of the world. Both interior states (internal reflection) and exterior relationships (all those relationships that arise through the body's relation to environment and other individuals through dynamic interaction) are registered through sense activities or sense activities that are extended or enhanced through technological means. Meaning arises as a by-product of pattern reinforcement, pattern differentiation, pattern abstraction and pattern recombination. These patterns are by no means simplistic. The parsing or combination of different multimodal sense patterns over time enables us to form an understanding of the world. As our physical experience reveals our relation to the world exterior to our body – it is nonetheless an interior understanding or accretive construction born of this life of expansive sensual relations that comes to create meaning – our understanding of the world and all aspects of language use and the attitudes of others, arises.[77] It is also through a sharing, interaction and/or mutual understanding of these sensual patterns that we communicate and further expand our knowledge of the world. The consensual experience we call reality – the ability of the mind to sort through all memory of multimodal sensed stimuli; to experience and find meaningful patterns; to apply them to new situations through abstraction, self-similar projection, and recombination – is essential to thought, language acquisition and use, as well as meaning production and mutual cooperation.

The World is Not Separate from Us

An important ramification of this environmental pattern view of embodied understanding of the world is that language is not separated from us. We would suggest that form and content are enfolded and cannot be separated. Each subsequent instance that relates to the "form" of an earlier experience enfolds new experiences and relativities, forming a hybrid "updating" process (to borrow the computer terminology).[78]

Meaningful communication presupposes that the other understands exactly what you mean. Persons are keepers of metacommunication, including the use of vague precision, seduction, and humor in meaning production.

"Representation" in thought is dynamically metonymic – a fragment can stand for a much larger context.

The theory of humor is an important inroad in understanding the essential difference between humans and animals.

Could it be that Bonobos have this?

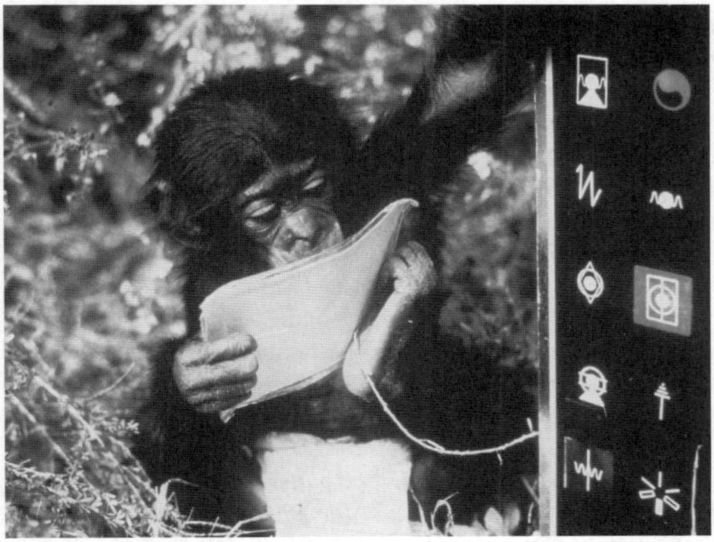

Baby Kanzi with lexigrams, courtesy of the Great Ape Trust.

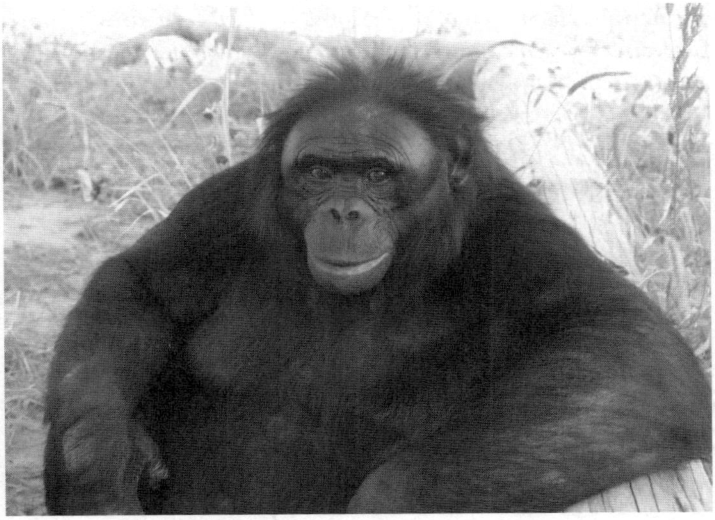

Kanzi by Liz Rubert-Pugh courtesy of the Great Ape Trust

A Linguistics of Pattern Flows

The Amoeba of language as it folds back on itself

Each sense modality contributes an experienced pattern over time. Similar but different patterns reinforce particular absorbed (constructed) understandings. Multimodal patterns become enfolded and embody a hybrid pattern of spatiotemporal flows of sense perturbations. Through self-reflection we can focus on different qualities of these patterns. Given a new context, one draws on fragments or residues of these pattern flows and recombines them to both articulate context in a projective manner, and absorb new patterns in a relevant manner from the context. This points to a ***hybridizing of identity****. A projective conceptual linguistic assemblage is continuously generated to frame new experience. This projection intermingles the history of experience with new pattern flows in an accretive manner. This bi-directional flow functions within the unifying space of thought. Thus, identity is always forming, enfolding memory with new experience. Each new instance of relation potentially enfolds another perspective into the multimodal "composition" of a given identity. Fields of meaning are conjoined and become articulated in the space of thought as an ongoing hybridizing process. If we pragmatically understand the articulations above, we can begin to address the construction of new linguistic "behaviours" of embodied pattern flows and subsequently hybrid patterns flows. These embodied relations arise in the sphere of the social, the cultural, and the environmental and through self-reflection – through embodied reciprocal relations – intra-actions. We learn to generate patterns, to reproduce patterns, to abstract and recombine sense-oriented perturbations. Let us call this* ***hybrid pattern production****. The notion of the "recombinant pattern" draws from a genetic metaphor. This term suggests a living meaning brought about through the intermingling of particular patterns that are both literally and metaphorically "spliced" together – hybridized. The computer is a particularly useful pattern-generating and pattern distributing device, contributing to this expanded pattern-oriented understanding of linguistics.*[79]

Language is a deep animal – a highly complex horse, an intelligent companion, and vast technology. Yet it has its own will so to speak. It is much richer than people know.

Luc Steels is successfully approaching some of this with his empirical studies.

Computer Code – New Ideas Approaching Relational Pattern Recognition

Thus the nature of meaning arises out of an extremely illusive plateau space born of a multiplicity of perceptual pattern-plays (imagination), a history of embodied sensual perceptual instances (sensual in-take), modes of articulation of patterns (language and technological production of patterns), the re-distribution or abstraction of patterns and internal self-reflection related to pattern orientation and also navigation of patterns, and within patterns.

Pattern of patterns/meta patterns
Pattern topologies
Pattern sensing
Pattern orientation
Pattern comparison
Pattern abstraction
Pattern imagination
Pattern recombination
Pattern generation (fragment collages)
Pattern gestalts
Pattern projection (intermingling with environment)
Pattern confluence
Pattern transference (technological production)
Pattern implementation
Pattern re-orientation (categorization)
Pattern strings
Pattern fields
Pattern actions (spatial/conceptual/relational)

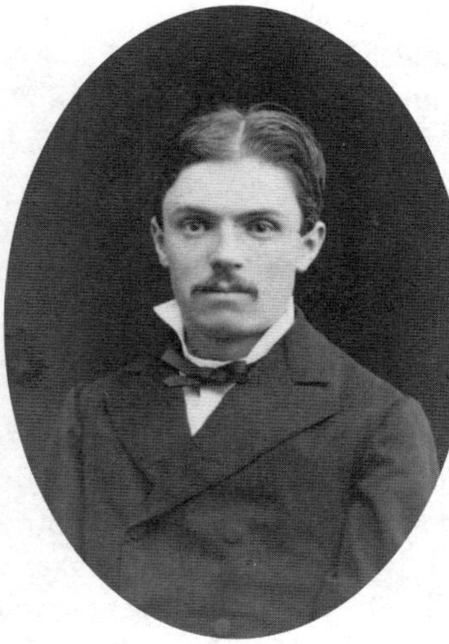

Jules Henri Poincaré, photo of Henri Poincaré circa 1879, © 2002 Henri Poincaré Archives

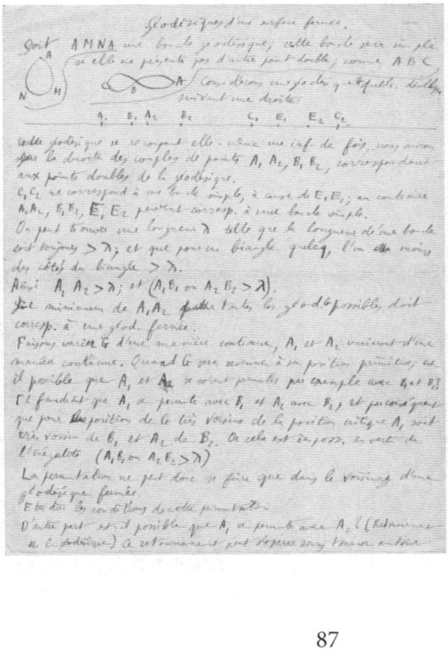

Géodésiques d'une surface fermée.

A scan of a page of lecture notes in Poincaré's handwriting, featuring two figures, and entitled "Géodésiques d'une surface fermée" © 2002 Henri Poincaré Archives.

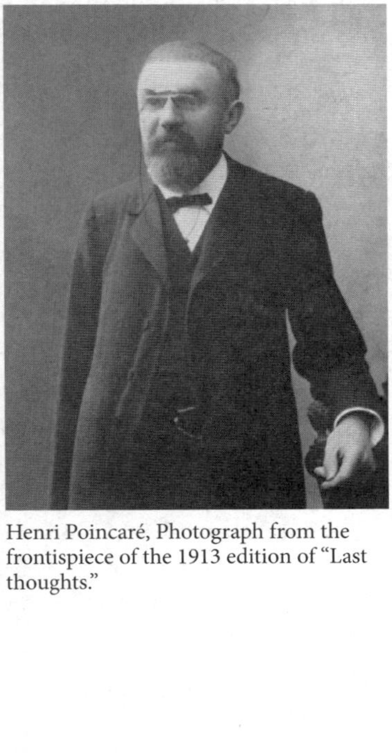

Henri Poincaré, Photograph from the frontispiece of the 1913 edition of "Last thoughts."

Pattern navigation
Pattern recognition
Pattern truncation
Pattern abbreviation
Pattern inversion
Pattern mistreatment
Pattern realignment
Pattern surgery

Pattern topologies is a new branch of mathematics of which only so far Poincaré's topology and DalCin's tolerance automata exist.

Force field topology is a special case
Facial topology is a subcase
Body language is another topology
Body topology is quite erotic
Linguistic patterns have their own topologies
Electrochemical topologies represent thought
All topologies are thought topologies
All marriages are mixed marriages

Gödel – numbers and operations on numbers happen in the same space.
Turing – code and operations on code happen in the same space.
Seaman – thought and operations on thought happen in the same space.
This is what is behind the great simulator and the mirror neurons that implement it.

Michael Arbib

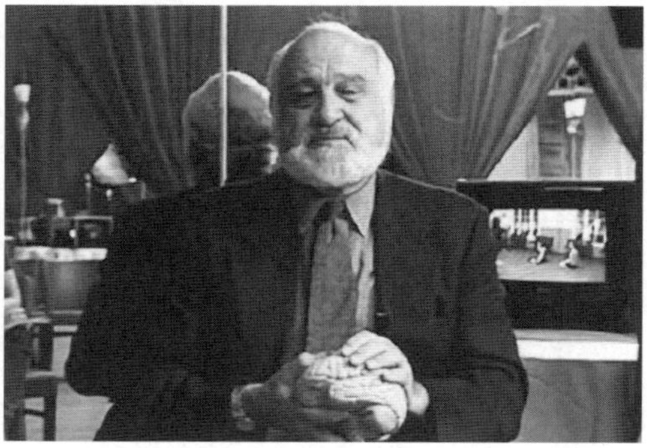

Image courtesy of Michael Arbib.

The first synthesizer of the mirror neuron paradigm

Mirror neurons were discovered by Gazzaniga in monkeys and subsequently confirmed in other mammals including humans (See *Action to Language via the Mirror Neuron System* by Arbib). They are activated when the animal sees a fellow animal make a certain motion. By watching that animal, the other would be able to perform a similar action itself. A universal simulator allows the same feat. So if you will, the discovery of the mirror neuron is a belated confirmation of the mammal brain obeying the design principle of the combined universal simulator and brain equation (see The Diagram chapter at the end of the book).

Peirce

Peirce defines Semiosis:
By Semiosis I mean an action, an influence, which is, or involves, a co-operation of three subjects, such as a sign, its object and its interpretant, this tri-relative influence not being in anyway resolvable into actions between pairs (Peirce, 1931).

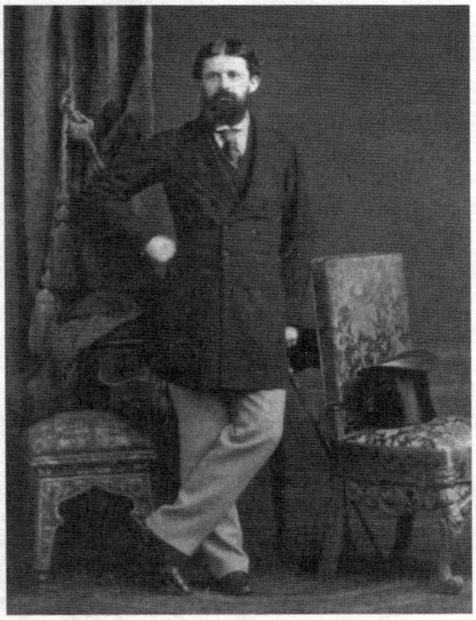

Charles Sanders Peirce, public domain.

The three-body problem of mathematical physics cannot be explicitly solved in closed form.

Peirce on representations:
But an endless series of representations, each representing the one behind it, may be conceived to have an absolute object at its limit. The meaning of a representation can be nothing but a representation. In fact it is nothing but the representation itself conceived as stripped of irrelevant clothing. But this clothing never can be completely stripped off; it is only changed for something more diaphanous. So there is an infinite regression here. Finally, the interpretant is nothing but another representation to which the torch of truth is handed along and as representation, it has its interpretant again. Lo, another infinite series.[80]

Char Davies – VR

Char Davies' "Osmose" is still just an "ordinary" VR while already being a bridge to more …

From Davies' *Éphémère*

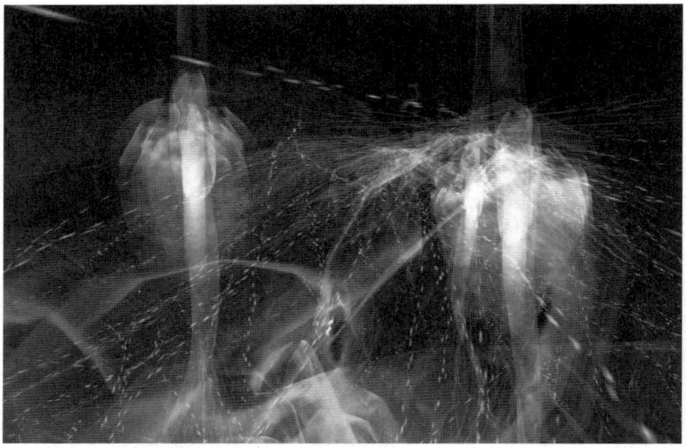

Char Davies, *Seeds*, *Ephémère* (1998). Digital still image captured during performance of immersive virtual reality environment Ephémère. Courtesy of Char Davies.

What is the meaning of the paintings in the caves of Lascaux?

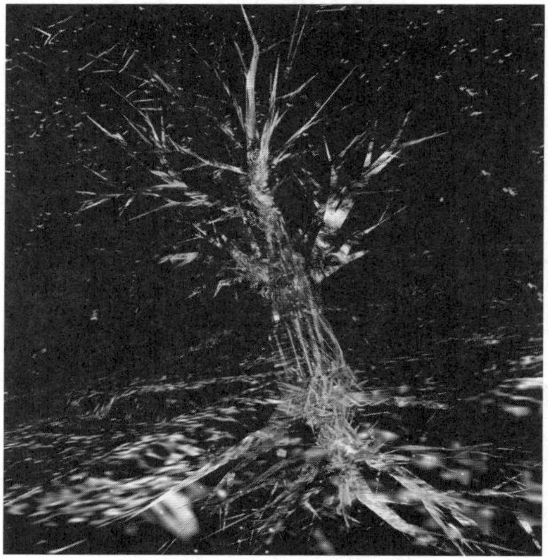

Char Davies. *Vertical Tree*, *Osmose* (1995). Digital still image captured during performance of immersive virtual reality environment *Osmose*. Courtesy of Char Davies.

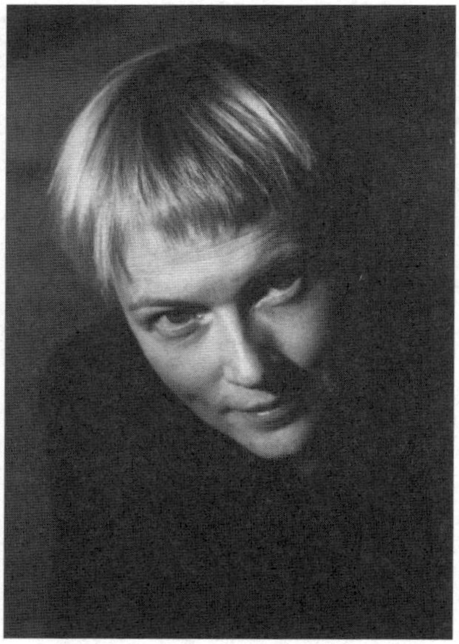

Char Davies 1998, courtesy of Char Davies.

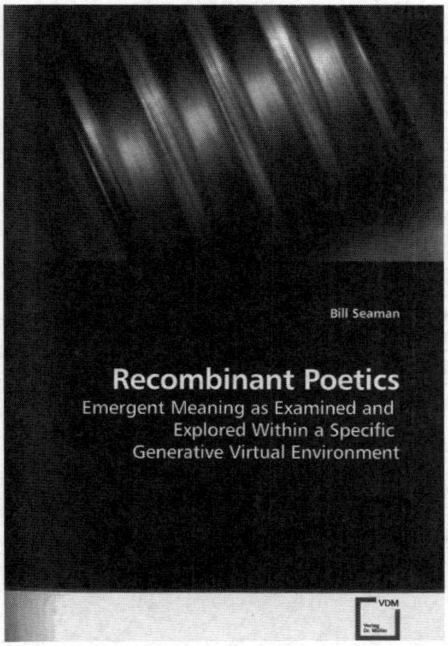

The World Generator – Generative VR

Seaman sought to develop a functional techno-poetic mechanism to observe the nature of emergent meaning – *The World Generator/The Engine of Desire*.

A specific generative virtual environment has been created that enfolds various operative computer-based processes activated through user interaction. The participant potentially brings about: interpenetration, juxtaposition and aesthetic alteration of media-elements through interaction with the several categories of "operative" processes:

poetic construction processes
navigation processes
processes related to authored media-behaviors
editing processes
abstraction processes
automated generative processes
processes related to distributed virtual reality
chance processes of a semi-random nature.[81]

The World Generator/The Engine of Desire
Bill Seaman with Gideon May

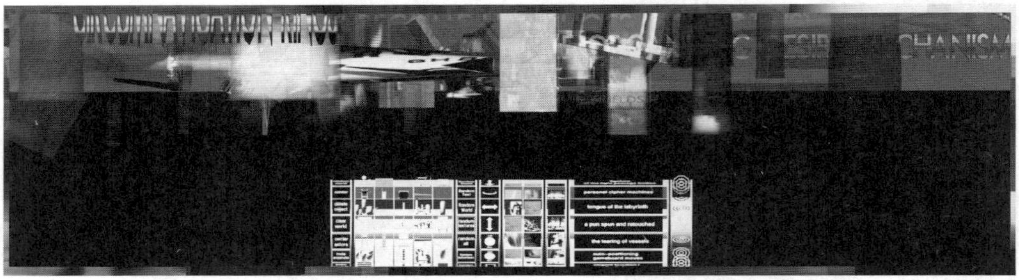

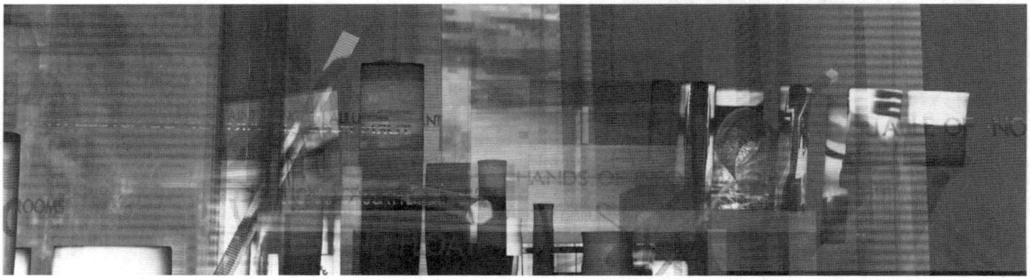

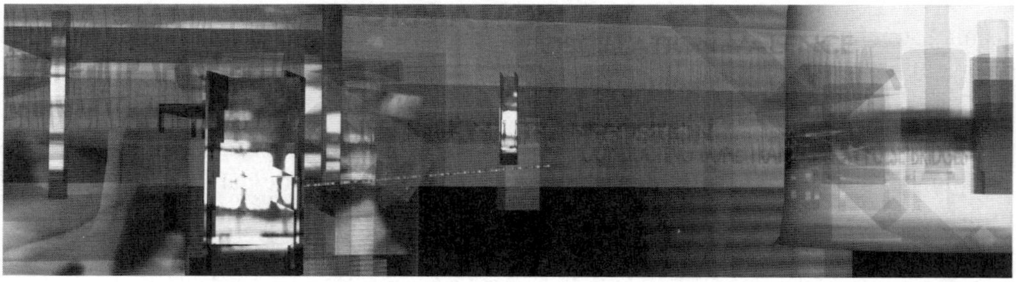

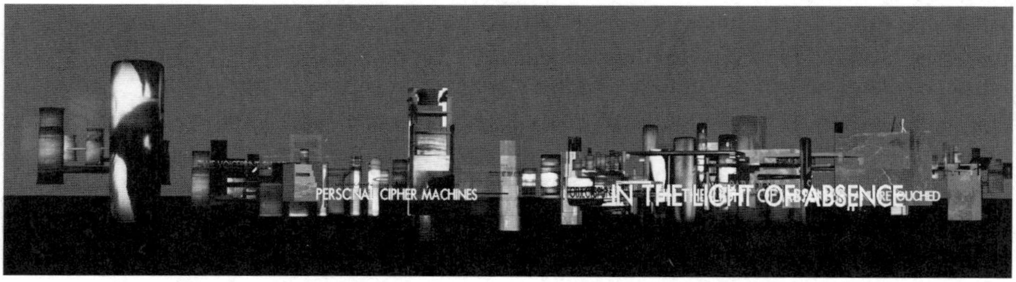

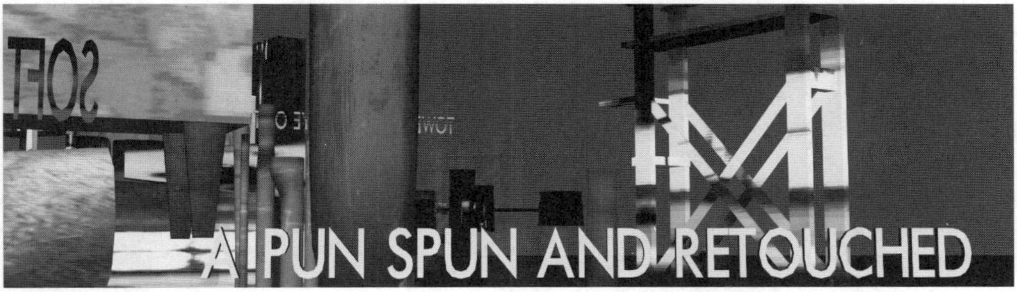
A PUN SPUN AND RETOUCHED

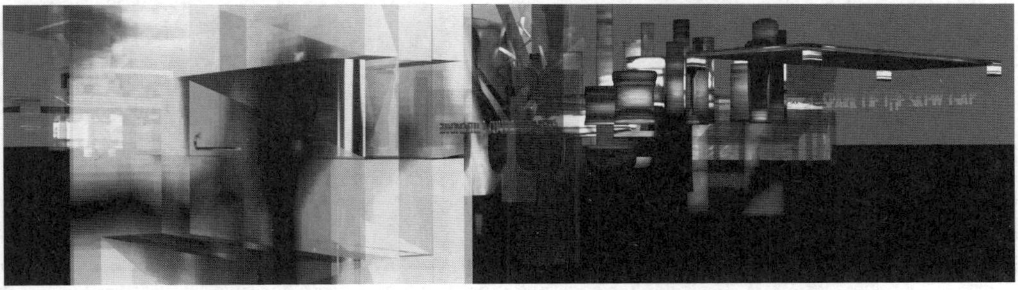

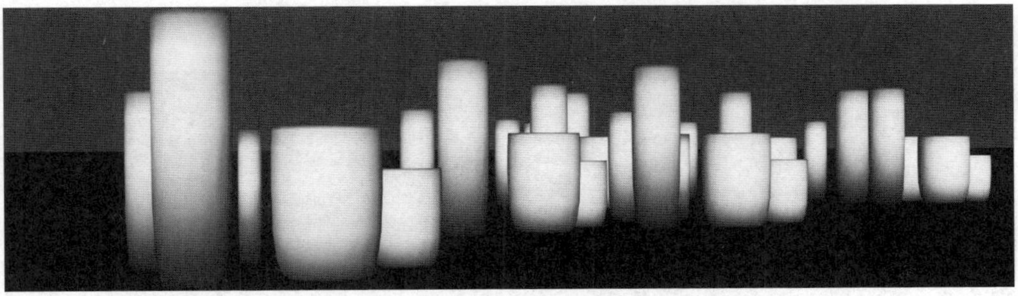

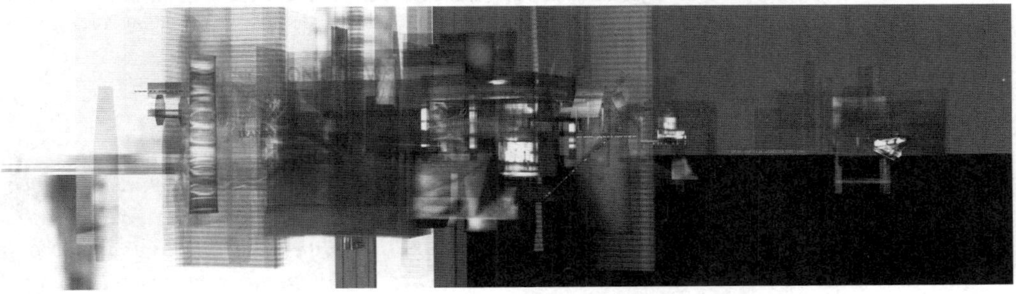

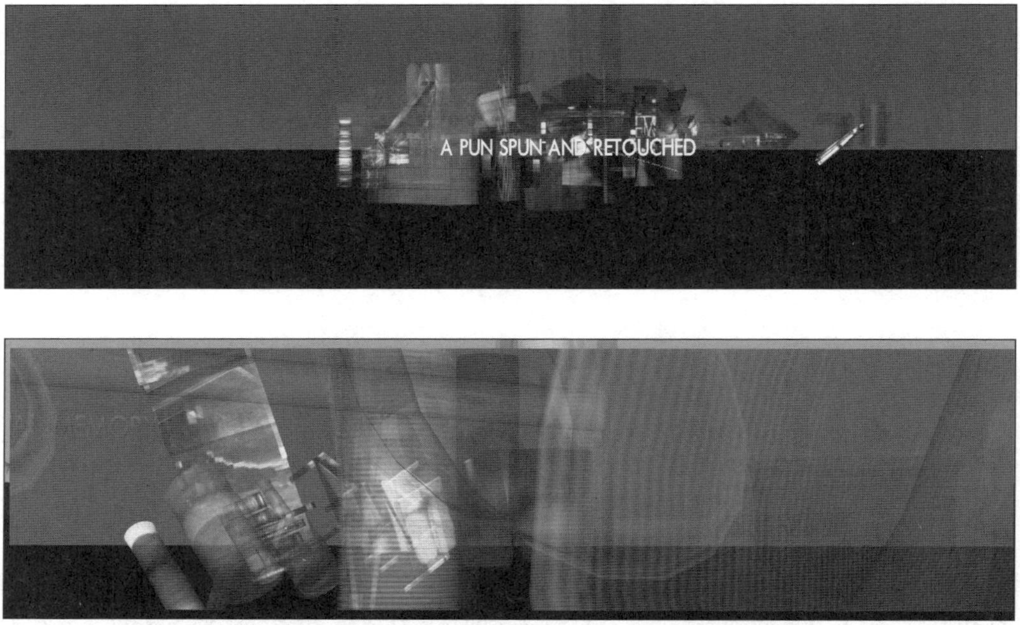

Generated Worlds – *The World Generator/The Engine of Desire*, Bill Seaman with Gideon May, Visualization Portal UCLA, 2001. Images courtesy of Seaman.

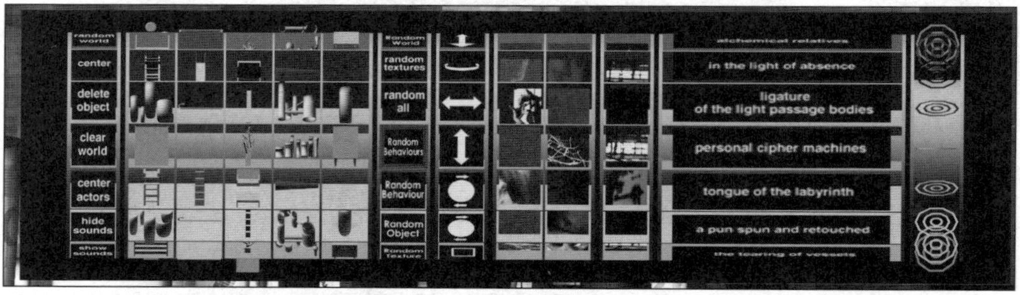

Menu System, *The World Generator/The Engine of Desire*, Bill Seaman with Gideon May, Visualization Portal UCLA, 2001. Image courtesy of Seaman.

Fields of meaning

The term "différance" [employed by Derrida in Writing and Difference*] is a pun in French, simultaneously pointing to difference and to deference or to put off until later. We will now take this notion of difference and expand it through another pun, one that points to the first computer and the exploration of computational "difference" in an operative manner. The World*

Generator [shown above] is a contemporary "difference" ["différance"] engine that enables a non-logocentric spatial approach to emergent meaning through computing.

The work enables a specific play of forces, literalising, visualising and making operative Derrida's notion of meaning "force." The World Generator is an engine of location, dislocation and re-location. An engine of spatio-temporal simultaneity. It is the operational nature of this device, a "fissuring" and fusing engine, that enables us to explore emergent meaning. This meaning arises at the demise of any singular fixed meaning.

Thus, the notion of the summing of forces becomes central to the production of meaning and moves away from examining language from the perspective of individual signifying units toward a perception of dynamic perceptual energy processes. Each of our senses enables a differing field of meanings to be entertained in relation to a given environment. Multi-modal processes enable meaning forces to operate on each other. The participant brings a historical set of fields to the equation via memory and pattern matching. A dynamic meaning summing is at operation in terms of any meaning becoming.[82]

The Thoughtbody Environment

The aim is to generate an intelligent, situated computer-driven robotic system.

Two different initial approaches are discussed: the creation of such a machine via the embodiment of a series of specific algorithms on a parallel computing platform working in conjunction with a specific situated machinic sensing environment and robot; and the development of a new paradigm for computing through the generation of an Electrochemical Computer functioning in conjunction with a robot and a related sensing system. The concepts including "the relational approach to brain function,"[83] and the "artificial cognitive-plus-motivational system"[84] (among others) will be developed and form a top-down relational analogical–biological perspective informing both projects. We will also employ a bottom-up inquiry exploring an approach for the development of an electrochemical device. It represents a relational approach through an electrochemical articulation. This will include the development of a *Poly-sensing Environment* as it might be used to implement the machinic senses for both entities; and the notion of *Pattern Flows* of sensory information as applied to learning, language acquisition, navigation, and robotic behavior. The long-term goal of this part of the project includes mapping and abstracting specific neural processes and exploring them within a situated robotic environment.

Toward an Electrochemical Computer

As humans we are Thoughtbody Environments nested within the greater environment – complex electrochemical computers of a sort that have as yet not been duplicated artificially.

Gordon Pask was seminal in terms of his approach to the notion of growing a computer. "Chemical computers arise from the possibility of 'growing' an active 'evolutionary' network by an electro-chemical process." (Pask 1961) How could we grow a computer that incorporates the salient aspects of the human computer? What are the key components to such a network – a network that in time may enable neo-sentience to arise? What kinds of processes can we set in motion to emulate human functionality? How can we work toward enabling a network of these processes to become intra-functional? If we understand embodiment as essential to meaning production then how can we manifest this network to include embodied experiences? On the difficult path leading to the production of an electrochemical computer, can we devise strategies to employ in a more traditional computing environment? Alternately, can initial ideas related to the construction of intelligent computers (our analogues articulated earlier in this paper) guide our research into electrochemical computing?[85]

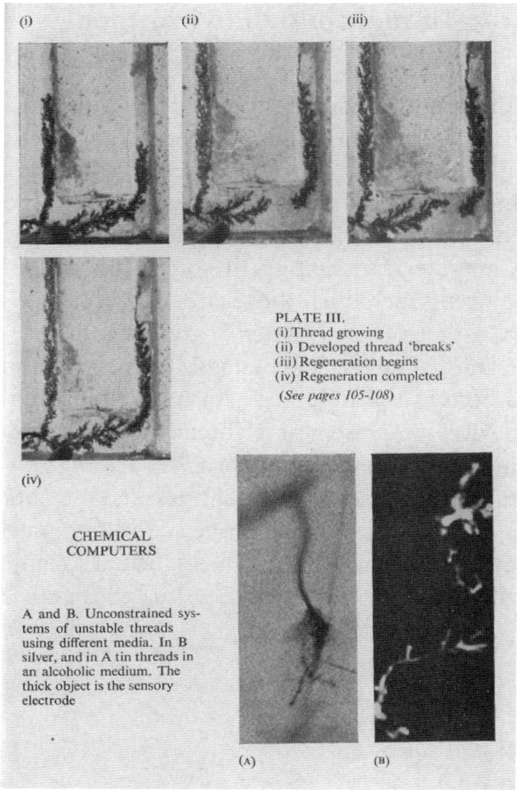

Chemical computer experiments by Pask in *An Approach to Cybernetics*, courtesy of Paul Pangaro.

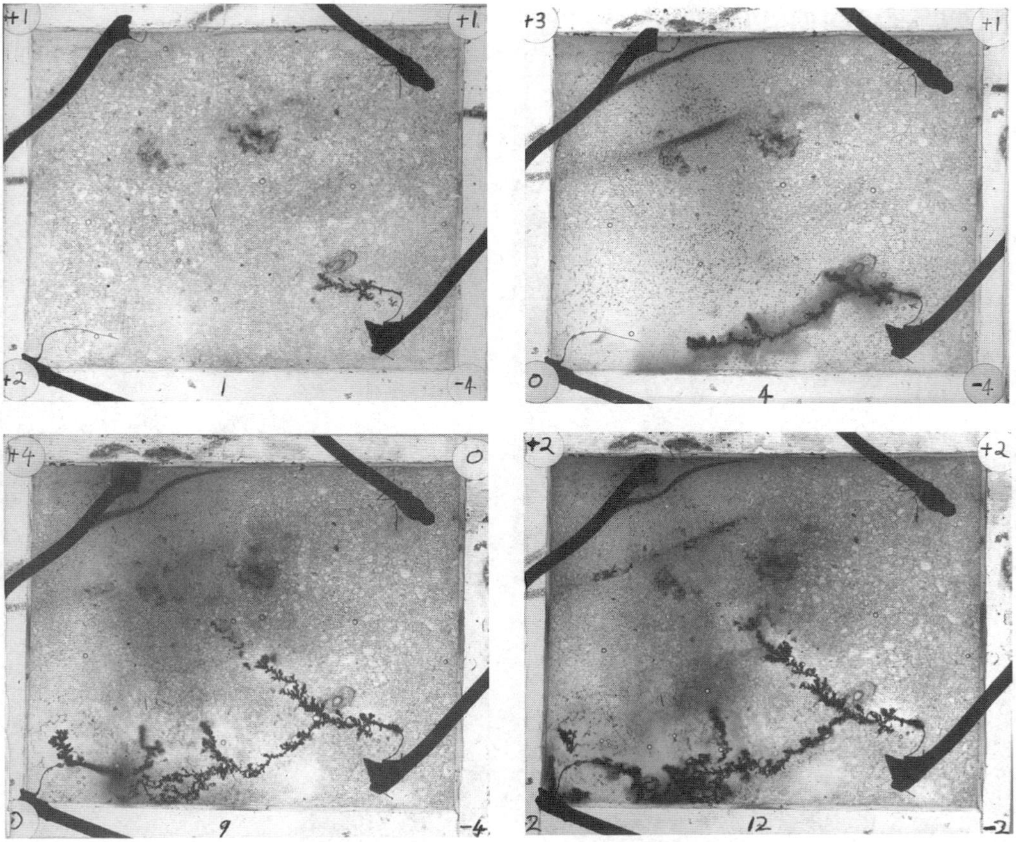

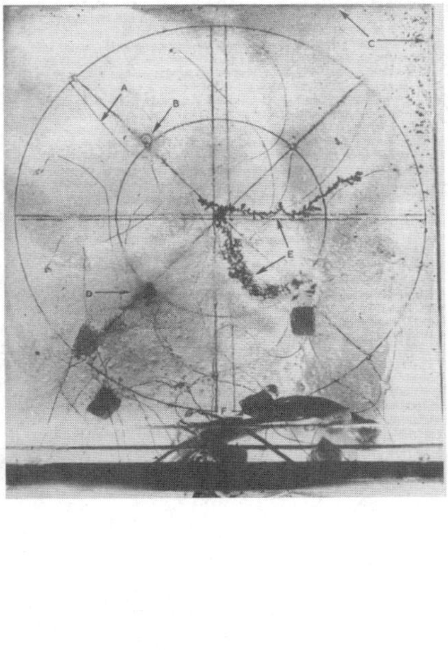

"Physical Analogues to the Growth of a Concept", image courtesy of Pask Archive.

Fig.12. (A) Connecting wires for electrodes.
(B) Platinum pillar electrodes.
(C) Edges of glass tank containing ferrous sulphate.
(D) Chemical reaction in progress
(E) "Tree" threads being formed.
(F) Connecting cables.

(Reproduced from *British Communications and Electronics*)

(94009) 919

3D models of an electrochemical computer
Seaman in collaboration with Danqing SHI

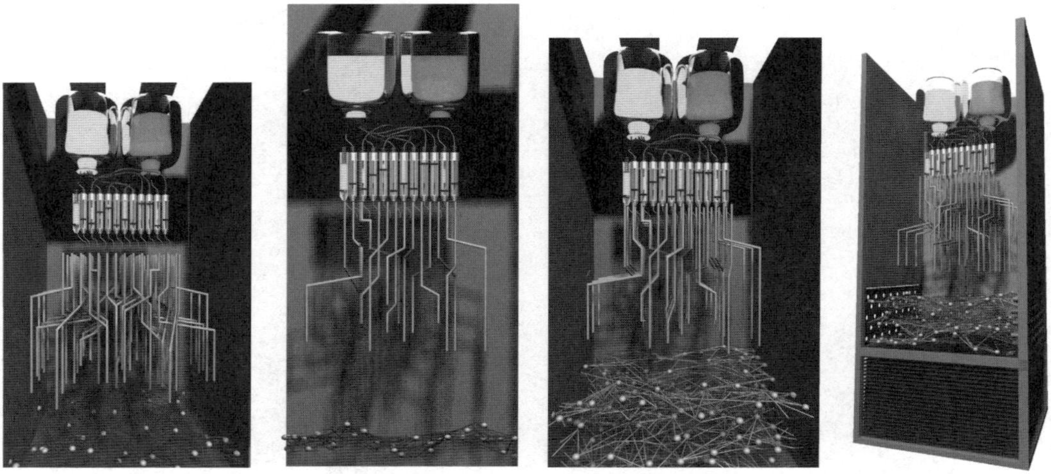

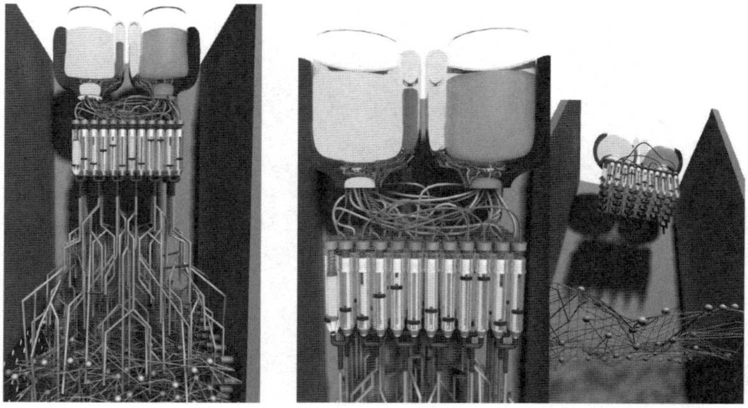

Early concept renderings for an Electrochemical Computer based on the Iron Wire reaction (Bonhoeffer)[86] – Acid and Base (neural transmitter analogues); Force Field Analogue "Sliders"; Synthetic Neuron Farm, images by Danqing SHI.

A possibly related computer by Stafford Beer was recently pictured by A. Pickering in his book *Cybernetic Brain* – Beer's Stocastic Analogue Machine for generating random numbers.

An Informed Approach to the Creation of an Electrochemical Computer

There are three different approaches to the creation of an electrochemical computer:

1. *Biomimetic Digital Computation*
2. *Biomimetic Analogue Computation*
3. *Mixed Digital/Analogue Computation*

In 2009 Seaman began a related research project (to that of his work with Rössler) with Dr Timothy J. Senior, a Research Scholar at the Department of Information Science and Information Studies (ISIS) at Duke University. With his background in neuroscience, we are formalizing ideas for a biologically inspired electrochemical computer. Like Gordon Pask, we are also interested in the intermingling of scientific and artistic concerns. Although still at an early conceptual stage, we envisage that our electrochemical computer will consist of modular components (akin to individual neurons), the flexible connectivity of which will permit them to be organized into different "functional" populations. Our electrochemical computer will also exhibit a number of biologically inspired features, including: a chemical signalling system analogous to neurotransmitter systems; routes for externally derived sensory inputs of different origins to modify the behaviour of modules; memory elements, whose function will be inspired by biologically relevant learning rules; and finally, oscillation generators that modulate and synchronize activity within the electrochemical computer, akin to those contributing to many information processing functions within the mammalian brain. We are interested in the emergent behaviour exhibited by such a system when embedded within a "sensed" environment.
We are at the beginning stages of our research; a full discussion of the background and the working nature of the system will be presented in a forthcoming paper. Figure showing one possible arrangement of modules within our initial electrochemical computer concept. A, Electrochemical oscillator unit; B, Module column; C, Neurotransmitter (NT) analogue; D, Site of control for NT analogue release; E, Processor – input integrator; F, Routes for direct external inputs; G, Electrochemical memory element; H, Electrochemical modulator unit used to drive either excitatory or inhibitory changes within modules from transduced external sources.[87]

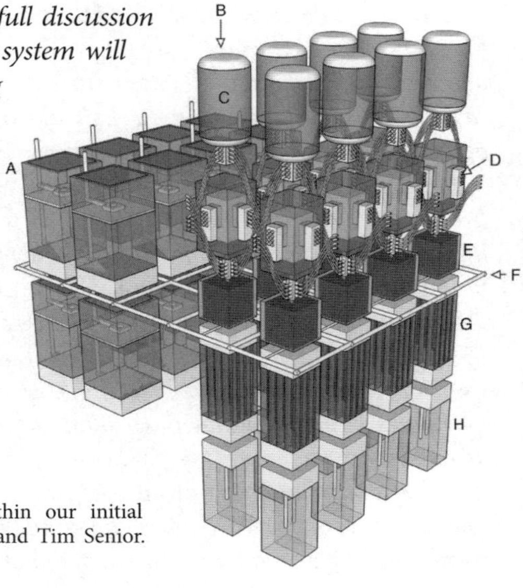

Figure showing one possible arrangement of modules within our initial electrochemical computer concept. Concept by Bill Seaman and Tim Senior. Image by Tim Senior.

Gordon Pask – Physical Analogues to the Growth of a Concept

Physical Analogues to the Growth of a Concept by Gordon Pask

Introduction

In this paper I discuss the circumstances in which we can say a machine "thinks", and a mechanical process can correspond to concept formation. My point of view about this question is as follows. It is reasonable to say that a machine does or does not "think", in so far as we can consider the working of the machine as in some way equivalent to a situation or an activity, (for example, riding a horse), which is familiar, and in which we ourselves are used to taking a part. Thus, when I speak of "thought", (as when saying a sonata is written, or a hairpin is invented, as a result of "thought"), an end product is introduced on which to hang the thinking process. The process itself is a descriptive expedient, a kind of analogy. Clearly the sonata was not written "by thinking", (in the sense of "by magic" or "by using a computer").

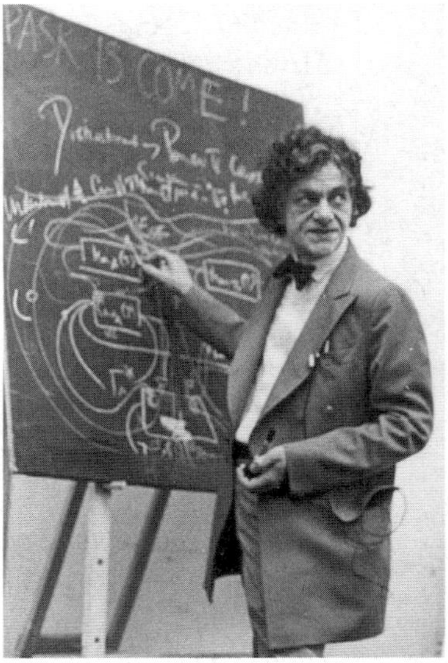

Courtesy of Albert Mueller (Pask Archive).

Thus, my view of thinking can be expressed in terms of the concepts "participant observer" and "external observer", as these terms are used by Colin Cherry. If we assume that such an "external observer" watches the process of writing a sonata he will seek to describe the stages of the process and he will have no need to speak of the "thinking". On the other hand, if an observer does speak of "thinking" in such a context he wishes to assert, according to my view, he was not purely an external observer, but to some extent participant.

Since it is the participant observer who, by the present hypothesis, used the term "thinking" correctly, let us consider his description. For him thought is taking place about some end product, and although the nature of the end product tells us very little about the "thinking" as such, it does say something about the way that the observer examined the subject, (or going now from our common examples to thinking machines, about the way he examined the machine submitted for test as a thinking assemblage). Moreover, the particular observer who conceives that the sonata and the hairpin were constructed as he, or we, might have constructed them, will be unable to say, in so many words, how he would have constructed them himself.

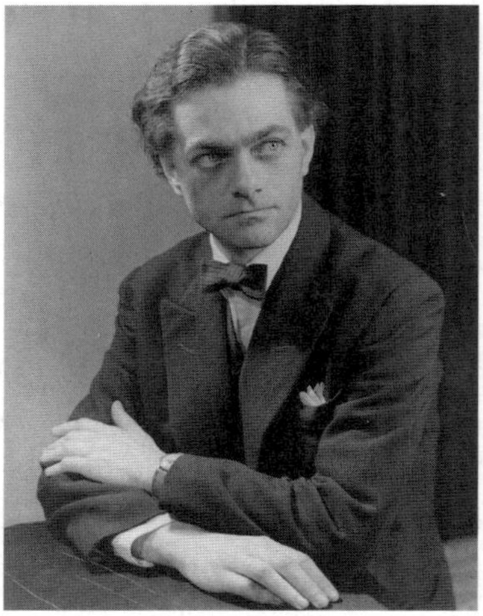

Pask 1961 Book Jacket, courtesy of Paul Pangaro/Albert Mueller Pask Archive.

Building up thinking processes

Very roughly, at the partly introspective level, these experiments suggest that a thinking process both builds up and employs conceptual categories. These categories are defined in terms of attributes, which may be common to a number of objects in the environment, or to other categories or to both.

At each stage in the thinking process a decision is made about whether an object should be placed in one or another of these conceptual categories. Such a sequence of decisions is a thinking strategy. The human being tends to regard these conceptual categories as definite and well bounded. But, objectively the categories are not clear cut, and decisions appear to be made between imperfectly specified alternatives. The categories are learned, or equally well they grow as a result of the strategies adopted, and it is not possible to extricate the category building from the decision making process.[88]

Cariani on Pask

Through the early and mid 1950's Pask experimented with electrochemical assemblages, passing current through various aqueous solutions of metallic salts (e.g. ferrous sulphate) in order to construct an analog control system. The system would be different from others in existence in that its design would not be completely well-defined: no explicit specification would be given for its parts. Pask was specifically looking for a machine that would create its own "relevance criteria", one which would find the observables that it needed to perform a given task. The device would go one step beyond Pask's earlier Musicolor system by evolving sensors to choose, independent of the designer, those aspects of its external environment to which it would react. Not only would particular input-output combinations be chosen but the categories of input and of output would be selected by the device itself.[89]

This question is related to Konrad Lorenz's idea of innate releasing mechanisms.

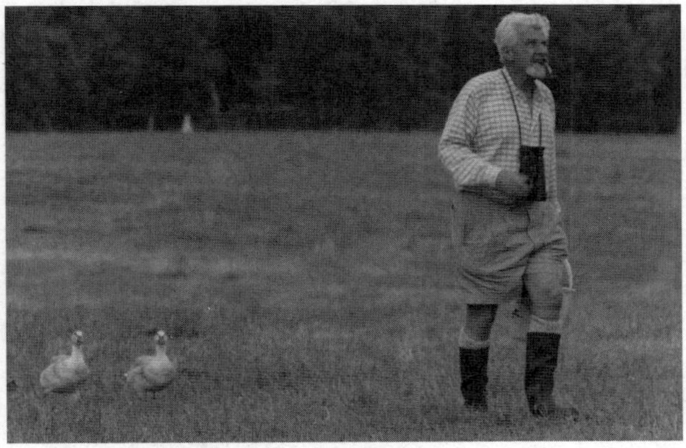

Konrad Lorenz, courtesy of the Konrad Lorenz Archive, Altenberg.

There is so much more mind in your body than in your mind, Nietzsche said.

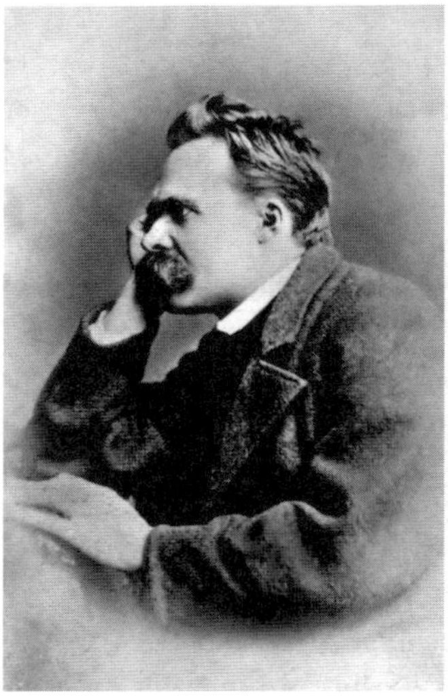

Nietzsche, public domain.

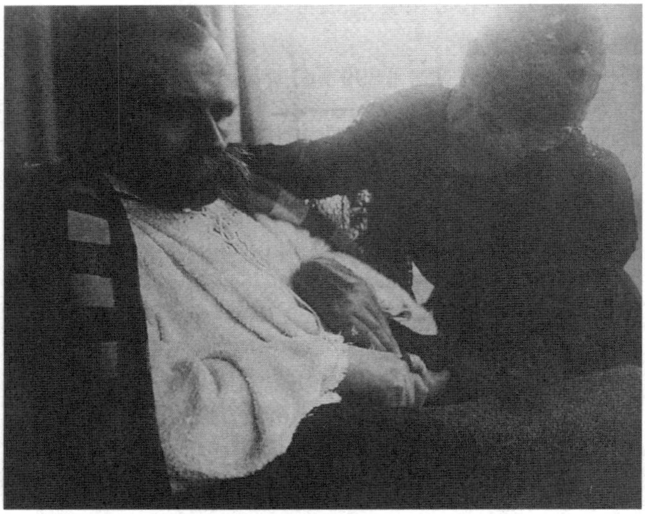

Image courtesy of the Image Commons.

Maverick Machines – Pask

You can make a computer out of anything. The London School of Economics had an analogue computer made of glass and filled with different coloured fluids that simulated national economies with a clarity that must have distressed mathematical economists (especially these days). *It used the same laws of hydraulics that operate the fountains at Tivoli just north of Rome.*

There was also a generation of pneumatic computers. In these, switching was achieved by jets of air. This was serious technology in the 1960s and still has special applications, in reliable engine regulators, for example [...] There have also been experiments using passivated iron (formed by the interaction of piano wire and nitric acid) as computing fabric, inert platinum electrodes as input and output devices and zinc, light energy or electrical current as the stimulus to compute.

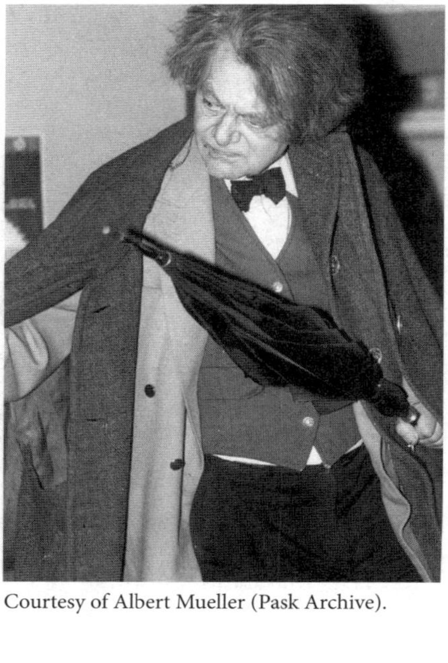

Courtesy of Albert Mueller (Pask Archive).

Alternately, computing structures can be "grown" out of ferrous sulphate and sulphuric acid activated by electrical current: the resulting iron develops branching nodules known as dendrites, analogous to the branches of the program.

These two recipes were combined by R. M. Stewart of California in 1963 to make a far more elaborate maverick device, essentially a resonant device with stable coherent cycles of activity. In place of piano wire he used steel spheres and packed glass spheres, and silver or gold dendrites rather than iron. The whole contraption was enclosed in a container pressurized to 100 atmospheres.

There is no clear-cut distinction between the notion of programming (giving a system a set of instructions to be followed in a sequence determined by the outcome of operations included in them) and the notion of adaptation (allowing or encouraging the system to respond to the conditions it encounters). In the case of dendritic computers, where physical contact with the external environment is indeterminate, the two notions are particularly close. The simplest dendritic computers react to sound, vibration, electric light, and other stimuli, and therefore make no sense per se unless they are considered in the context of such stimuli.

[…] There is now a demand for such devices, which are appropriate to non-logical forms of computation, but dendrites and regions of depassivation on passivated surfaces are physically too cumbersome for such demand to be met practically. It now seems that biological media may perform in similar fashion but on a more manageable scale. Others see proteins and three dimensional molecular assemblies as heralding a new era of miniaturization: already we have technology to create chips containing 100,000 more "switches" per unit area than conventional chips.[90]

Examples of Pask's art

Pask embodied some of his scientific ideas in works of art.

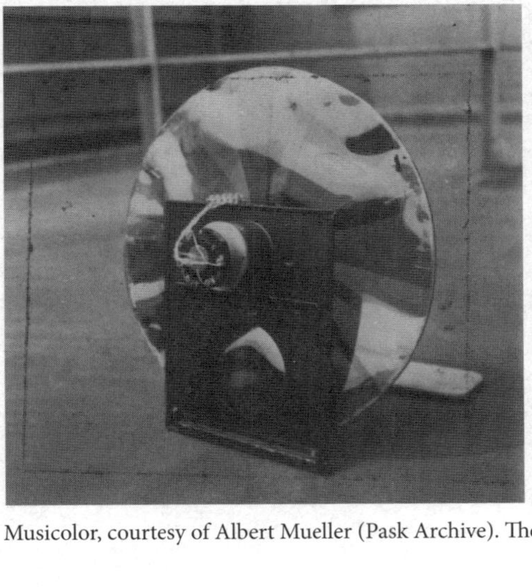

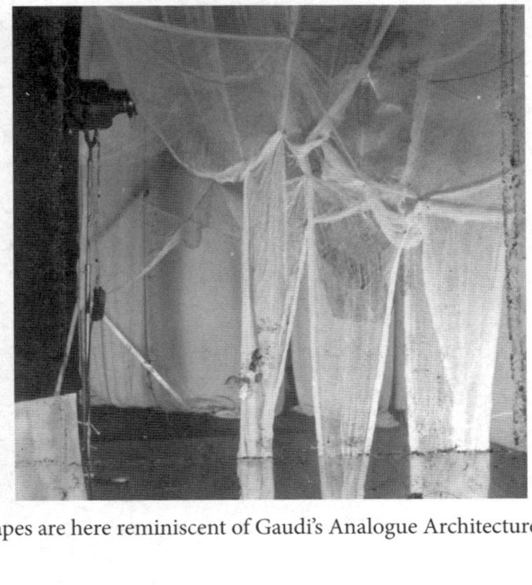

Musicolor, courtesy of Albert Mueller (Pask Archive). The Drapes are here reminiscent of Gaudi's Analogue Architecture.

Artworks which embody and play out cybernetic concepts were created by Gordon Pask. Robin McKinnon-Wood and Gordon Pask had what Ranulph Glanville called "a Lifelong Conversation" surrounding such devices, including the work Musicolor developed in the mid-1950s.

Musicolour

This was a machine that controlled lights so that they reacted to (live) music. But not like the trivial machines of today, which pulse with the beat and change colour with frequency. MusiColour (which erratically toured nightclubs and popular music venues) picked out patterns in the music, responded to these, and got bored. If the musicians did not provide enough variety, MusiColour would provide speculative change of its own accord, working itself up into a frenzy until the musicians changed how they were playing. This is truly interactive. And it is the first program that is an agent provocateur: its purpose is to interfere with the musicians. This computer, sadly long since dismantled, expects you to respond to it in interaction. It anticipates drama.[91–92]

Reflecting notions of social communication was Pask's *Colloquy of Mobiles*

The English cyberneticist Gordon Pask conceived the «Colloquy of Mobiles» for the 1968 exhibition «Cybernetic Serendipity» held at the ICA in London. It was a reactive, educable, computer-based system composed of five mobiles. By way of light and sound, the rotating elements suspended from the ceiling communicated with each other, independent of external influences. Using flashlights and mirrors, the people at the exhibition could nevertheless take part in the conversation between

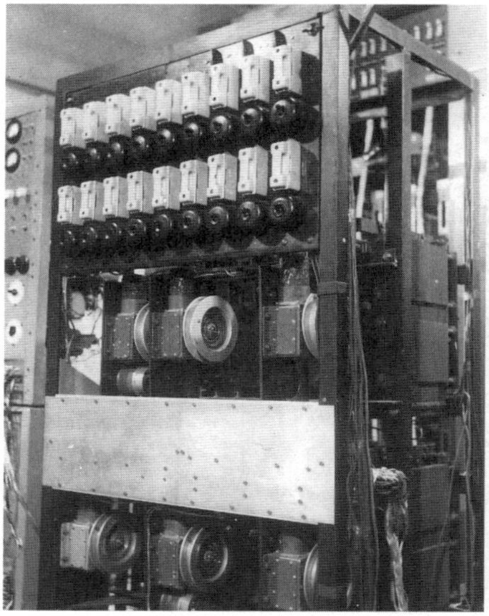

Musicolour Switchbank, courtesy of Paul Pangaro.

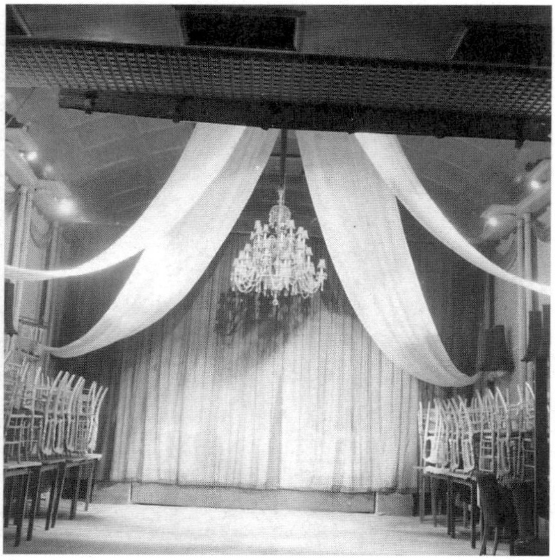

Musicolour Hall, courtesy of Paul Pangaro.

the machines. With this installation, Pask brought to a conclusion his idea for an «aesthetic potential environment».

To give significance to the communication between the machines, Park designed the «Colloquy of Mobiles» as a social system. At the same time, the form of communication that he conceived referred unmistakably to a sexual analogy: hung from the ceiling were two «males» and three «females». After a phase of inactivity, the females (made of fiberglass) began to glow more intensely and the three males emitted a ray of light. When the ray of light struck the mirror inside the female mobile's structure, by way of rotating the mirror, she tried deflecting the ray back at the free-hanging light sensors above and below the male's aluminum body. The goal of communicating was to achieve this moment of satisfaction, and the mobiles learned to optimize their behavior to the point where this state could be reached with the least possible use of energy. With the help of flashlights and mirrors, the exhibition visitors could assume the roles of the mobiles and influence the learning process.[93]

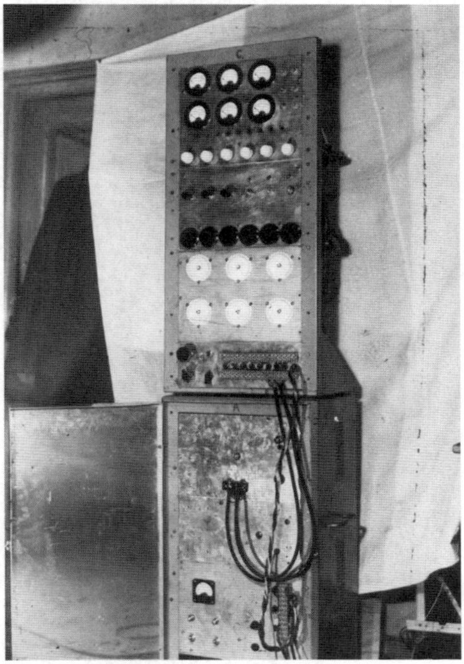

Musicolour Machine ,courtesy of Albert Mueller (Pask Archive).

A Colloquy of Mobiles

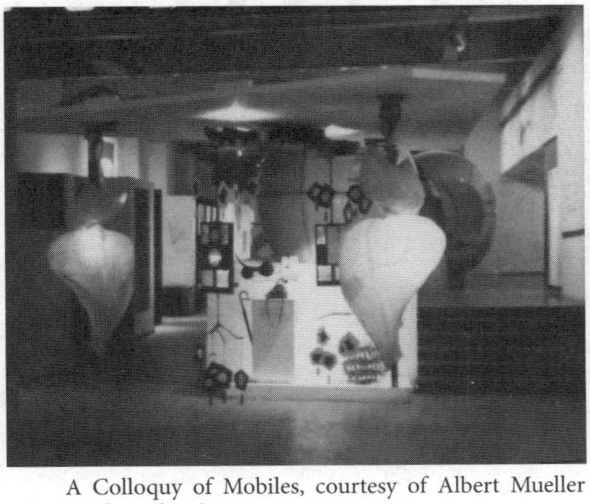

A Colloquy of Mobiles, courtesy of Albert Mueller (Pask Archive).

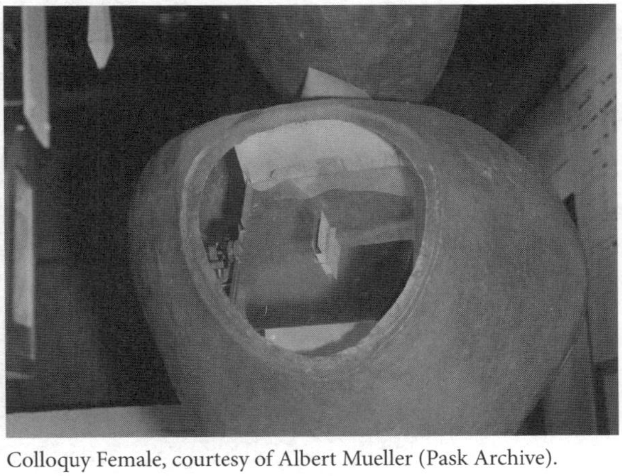

Colloquy Female, courtesy of Albert Mueller (Pask Archive).

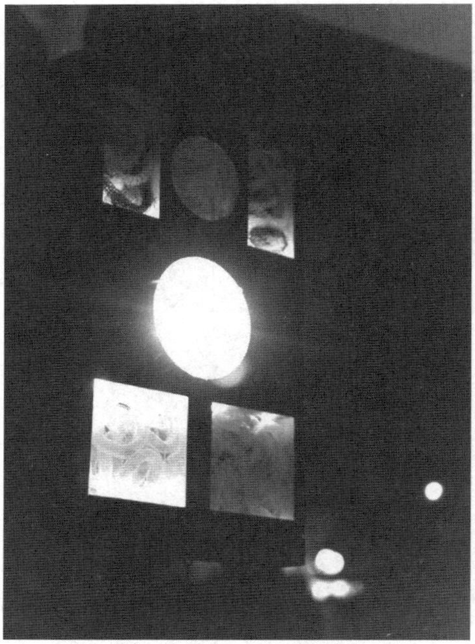

Courtesy of Albert Mueller (Pask Archive).

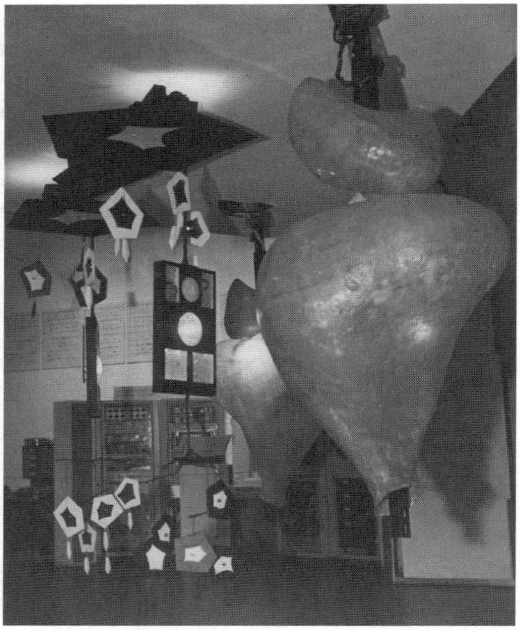

A Colloquy of Mobiles, courtesy Albert Mueller (Pask Archive).

At this point Marcel Duchamp's work The Large Glass comes to mind.

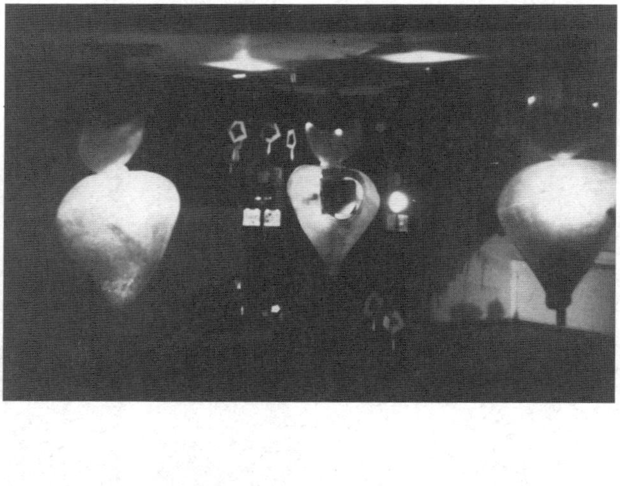

A Colloquy of Mobiles, courtesy of Albert Mueller (Pask Archive).

Abduction

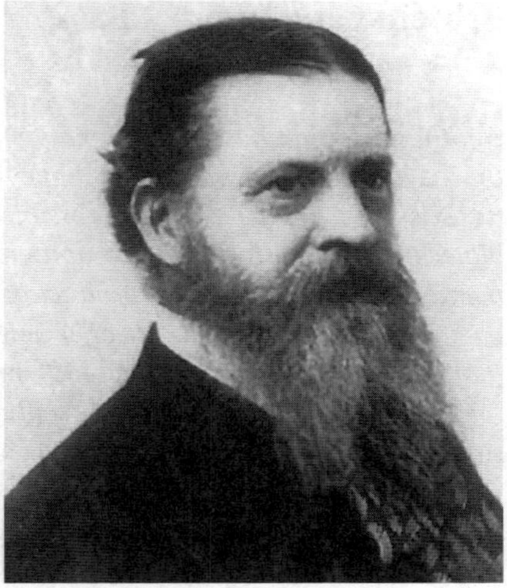

Charles Sanders Peirce, public domain.

Peirce states:

If you carefully consider the question of pragmatism you will see that it is nothing else than the question of the logic of abduction. That is, pragmatism proposes a certain maxim which, if sound, must render needless any further rule as to the admissibility of hypotheses to rank hypotheses, that is to say, as explanations of phenomena held as hopeful suggestions; and, furthermore, this is all that the maxim of pragmatism really pretends to do. (CP 5.196)[94]

"From Ugly Duckling to Swan: C. S. Peirce, Abduction, and the Pursuit of Scientific Theories"
Daniel J. McKaughan

Jaakko Hintikka (1998) has argued that clarifying the notion of abduction is the fundamental problem of contemporary epistemology. One traditional interpretation of Peirce on abduction sees it as a recipe for generating new theoretical discoveries. A second standard view sees abduction as a mode of reasoning that justifies beliefs about the probable truth of theories. While each reading has some grounding in Peirce's writings, each leaves out features that are crucial to Peirce's distinctive understanding of abduction. I develop and defend a third interpretation, according to which Peirce takes abductive reasoning to lead to judgments about the relative pursuitworthiness of theories; conclusions that can be thoroughly disconnected from assessments of truth-value. Even if Peirce's use of "abduction" slides around among each of these three importantly different though potentially compatible senses, this neglected third understanding makes sense of a large number of Peirce's remarks and directs our attention to the cognitive structure of judgments that scientists face after the initial proposal of explanatory hypotheses but prior to their experimental testing; a topic which should be of interest to contemporary philosophers of science.[95]

Protein Computers – Pask

Another field that has grown rapidly but with few fanfares in the last 15 years is biotechnology, the development of controlled biological systems. The growth of biotechnology and even its existence has been made possible by computers. Conversely, some of the products of biotechnology are fabric for computers, especially mavericks. Materials such as protein lipid membranes, themselves the product of controlled biological processes, have switching, storage and oscillatory properties that offer new prospects for making systems self-organizing. Machines that are self-organizing on a biochemical basis may be better at modeling and controlling some real-life situations than conventional Machines.[96] [Smale and coworkers have explored similar avenues more recently]

[…] The term "biochip", increasingly bandied about today, means different things to different researchers. For some a biochip is a single layer of protein molecules sandwiched between glass and metal, the individual molecules playing the same role as the silicon transistors of the conventional chip. Others see it as synonymous with chips made of conventional materials but possessing a complexity which approaches that of the human brain.[97]

Roy Ascott first introduced the first author to Pask's work and Ted Krueger introduced the first author to Pask's little book on *Cybernetics*. The second author was influenced by Pask with his theory of chemical evolution. Pask was a uniquely charming and kind person – as both an artist and a scientist.

Pandaka Pygmaea

Pandaka pygmaea is supposed to be 0.9 cm in size.

An initial step toward the development of the first iteration of the Electrochemical Computer would be to investigate (and then model) the brain of the smallest fish. It would be one of the most worthy of human endeavors.

The Pandaka Pygmaea Institute would be involved in reverse engineering the brain of this fish – the perhaps smallest relative of ours. There exists a close relative to Pandaka, Gobius niger, which is 20cm long and already half way with his brain to ours in terms of orders of magnitude. So the remaining step would be no larger than that between the two sister species. How does this compare to Sea elegens?

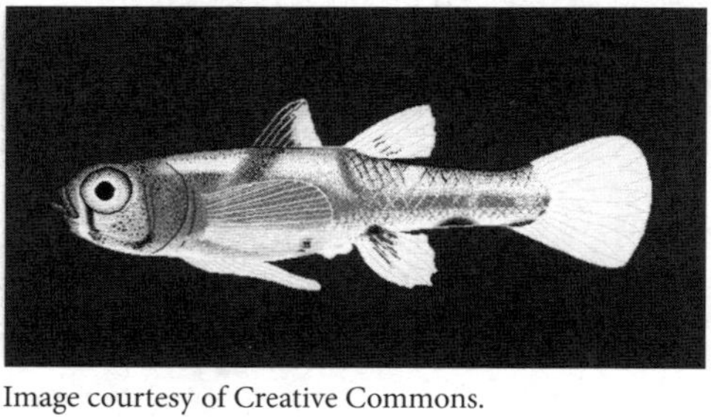

Image courtesy of Creative Commons.

Self-knowledge – David Finkelstein

For a finite system, complete self-knowledge seems impossible, since the system would have to include a model of itself as a proper part. Therefore an allowed set never consists of just one unit.[98]

Non-two-value Logic

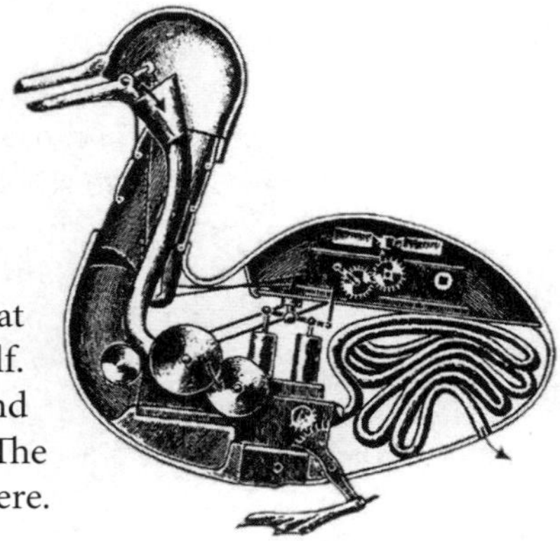

This is a logic that transcends logic.

George Moore's automata (below) possesses features that are shielded from the logic accessible to the machine itself. This shows a link between the endo perspective (brain and physics models from within) and multi-valued logic. The problem of consciousness is lurking in the background here.

Jacques de Vaucanson's Duck, public domain.

Vaucanson's duck

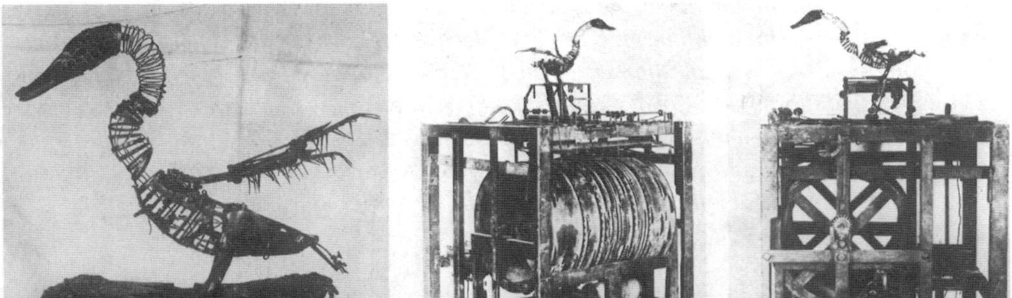

Vaucanson's duck disappeared in 1879 during a fire in a museum in Novgorod City (Russia). Images courtesy of Musée des Automates de Grenoble of Mr Francis Lara.

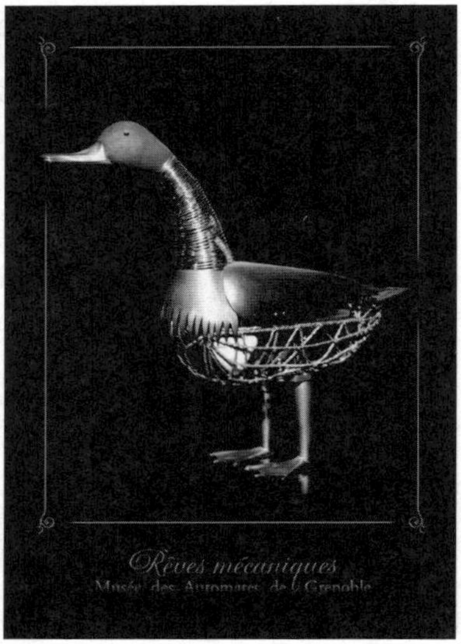

"Anas Mechanica Arcana" (mechanical automatic). This automata was created by Mr Frédéric Vidoni in 1997 for the Musée des Automates de Grenoble of Mr Francis Lara, in hommage of Mr. Jacques de Vaucanson who was born in Grenoble in 1709 and died in Paris in 1782. This automata is property of the Musée des Automates de Grenoble of Mr. Francis Lara. This automate is unique and exclusive and created for Lara's private museum, created in 1995.

"A rival to Prometheus, [Vaucanson] seemed to steal the heavenly fires in his search to give life." –Voltaire

Vaucanson's most famous creation was undoubtedly "The Duck." This mechanical beast could flap its wings, eat, and digest grain. Each wing contained over four hundred moving parts and even today it remains something of a mystery. The original Duck has disappeared.[99]

Sara Roberts
The construction made by the highly talented French engineer Jacques de Vaucanson (1709–82) undoubtedly represents the zenith of the technical genre which produced automata. Even in his youth, in Grenoble, de Vaucanson had worked on various inventions and modifications for machines. In the mid-1730s, he decided to move to Paris and to involve himself with automata, which were all the rage at the time. He approached the subject systematically, beginning with a thorough study of anatomy, as he wanted to use mechanical aids to illustrate an anatomie mouvante ("moving anatomy"), which was to present human and animal organs in a three-dimensional atlas, no easy task! Here were Descartes's philosophical ideas, about to be turned into a technical reality at the hands of the clever de Vaucanson.[100]

1893 – George Moore's Steam Man

Mr. Zadock Deddrick, a Newark machinist, has invented a man; one that, moved by steam, will perform some of the most important functions of humanity; that will, standing upright, walk or run as he is bid, in any direction, and at almost any rate of speed, drawing after him a load whose weight would tax the strength of three draught horses. The history of this curious invention is as follows: Six years ago Mr. Deddrick, the inventor, who is at present but twenty-two years of age, conceived the novel idea of constructing a man that should receive its

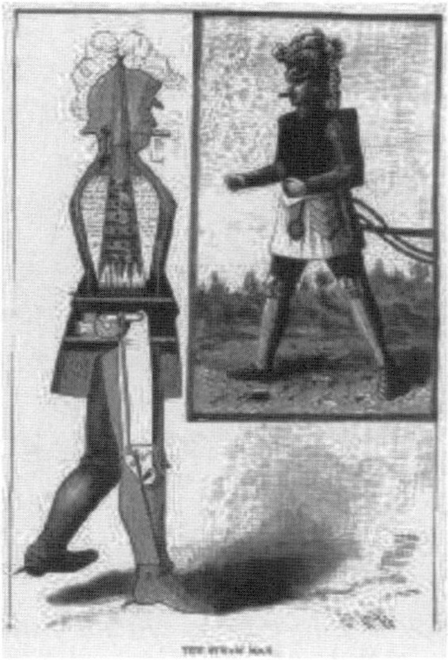

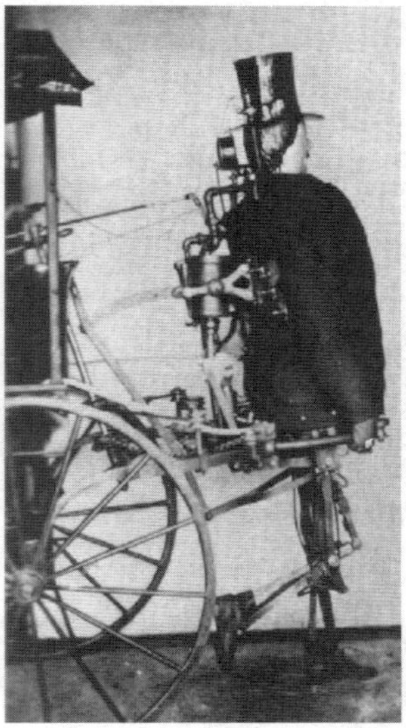

23 January 1868, A Steam Man, from the Newark (N.J.) Advertiser.

vitality from a perpetual motion machine. The idea was based on the well-known mechanical principle that, if a heavy weight be placed at the top of an upright slightly inclined from vertical, gravitation will tend to produce a horizontal as well as vertical motion. The idea was unsuccessful. However, by observing carefully the cause of failure, persevering and perfecting the man-form, and by substituting steam in place of the perpetual motion machine, the present success was attained.

The man stands seven feet and nine inches high, the other dimensions of the body being correctly proportioned, making him a second Daniel Lambert, by which name he is facetiously spoken of among the workmen. He weighs five hundred pounds. Steam is generated in the body or trunk, which is nothing but a three-horse power engine, like those used in our steam fire engines. The legs which support it are complicated and wonderful. The steps are taken very naturally and quite easily. As the body is thrown forward upon the advanced foot the other is lifted from the ground with a spring and thrown forward by the steam. Each step or pace advances the body two feet, and every revolution of the engine produces four paces. As the engine is capable of making more than a thousand evolutions a minute, it would get over the ground, on this calculation, at the rate of a little over a mile a minute. As this would be working the legs faster than would be safe on uneven ground or on broad street cobble stones, it is proposed to run the engine at the rate of five hundred revolutions per minute, which would walk the man at the modest speed of half a mile a minute.[101]

Nonsense logic

In terms of exploration of the interface as content, significant to the operation of an interactive computer-based environment, I have chosen to explore ridiculously complex interfaces that are outwardly expressive, while inwardly, function as the outer-most layer of a symbolic logic. Thus the interface becomes a vehicle of symbolic logic. When we include puns, nonsense and jokes on this symbolic layer of the system as an operational part of the interface, we can potentially make observations about the nature of logic through interaction with such a system. It becomes a goal in my work, to present for the user an opportunity to observe the functionality of consciousness in action, through the intermingling of complex multi-layered systems with authorship and inter-authorship, placement and displacement [...] By developing a computer system that explores pointed nonsense as its content, we come to better understand the complexities of context construction. It is often the nonsense text, that through displacement, opens up a new relation, a re-seeing of the original context, a form of active comparison built into the signifying environment [...] The permutations inherent to recombinant structures present a situation in which nonsense relations can arise or be intentionally initiated. Each media-element in a combinatorial work of art has a potential "meaning force." By exploring elements carrying condensed content, or multiple potential readings, we could see the "force" of such elements paradoxically pushing in a number of directions at the same time. The nature of signification as examined within an emergent, interactive context, exhibiting fleeting and shifting qualities of meaning, can become an experiential arena. The user experiences a temporary glimpse at a continuous process where elements of language, image and sound qualify the readings of particular elements, and are themselves qualified in relation to these other elements, within this process.[102]

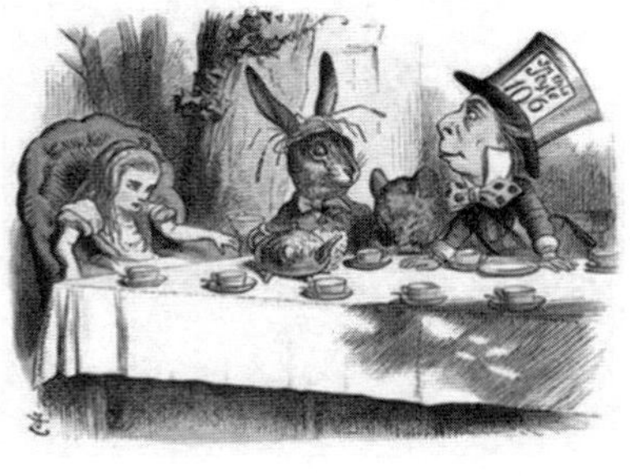

John Tenniel's Alice's Mad Tea Party, public domain.

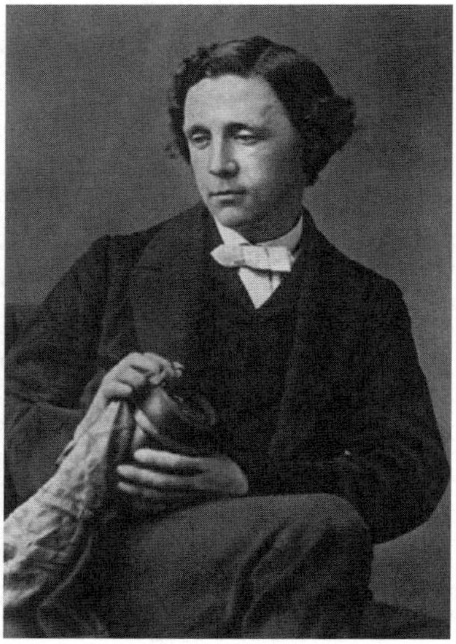

Lewis Carroll (public domain), photo by Oscar Gustave Rejlander, 1863.

This is reminiscent of dreams where sometimes the end of a dream does not jibe with the beginning.

Incidentally, this type of internal communication is barred from non-human animals because they cannot internally represent more than one optimality-functional. An optimality functional is the application of a given force to a certain set of objects and could be called one context. Animal functionality is below the glass ceiling.

Peirce – Ideas Surrounding the First General-purpose Relay Computer

Peirce was the first to discuss the creation of a general-purpose relay computer and to develop multi-value logics.[103]

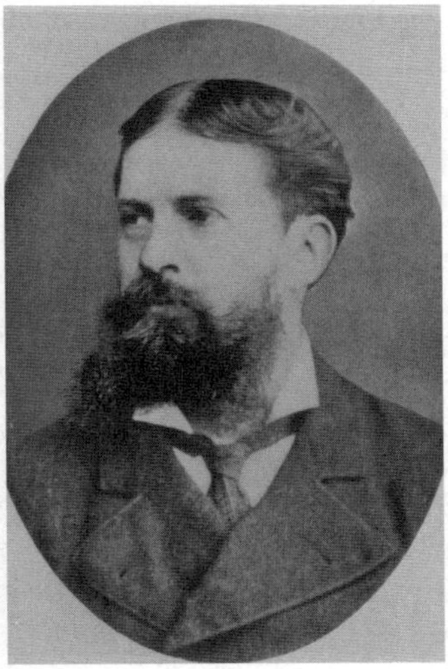

Photo of Charles Sanders Peirce, courtesy of NOAA Central Library, public domain.

Charles Peirce also proved a theorem about the rotation of bodies in four-dimensional space. But his most important mathematical results were in symbolic logic, a subject not generally accepted by mathematicians in Peirce's time. He developed the formalism of the propositional calculus and the general logic of quantifiers, independently of, though a little later than, Gottlob Frege. Independently of Dedekind, Peirce defined a finite set as one that cannot be put in one-one correspondence with a proper subset of itself.

He was the first to define all Boolean functions in terms of the single primitives "not-and" and "not-or" and to conceive of the truth-table method of evaluating truth-functions. He also was the first to develop multi-valued logics.[104]

[…] Of course, it is a manifestation of genius to have an idea long before it is understood and appreciated. Let me close by outlining the background for another of Peirce's logical ideas of great originality, the idea for a general purpose relay computer, which was fifty years ahead of its time. The sequence of events is as follows:

1. *Peirce stimulated Alan Marquand to invent and build a mechanical logic machine superior to that of William Stanley Jevons. This machine is described in Peirce's Logical machines, vol. Ill, pt. 1, pp. 625–32.*
2. *This machine was built in the early 1880s. At about the same time, Peirce conceived the sufficiency of "not-and" and "not-or," together with the use of a truth-table as a decision procedure for tautologyhood.*
3. *In a letter to Marquand dated 1886 Peirce suggested the use of relays for Marquand's machine and showed how to achieve "and" and "or" with relays. […] it is by no means hopeless […] to make a machine for really very difficult mathematical problems (ibid., p. 632).*

4. *Marquand then prepared a wiring diagram for a relay version of his mechanical logic machine.*
5. *In 1900, Peirce stated that a computer could enumerate all the theorems of axiomatic arithmetic, thus anticipating the 20th century identification of logic with computers. See Our senses as reasoning machines, vol. Ill, pt. 2, pp. 1114–15.*

Peirce knew of Charles Babbage's attempt to build an "analytical engine." This was to be a general-purpose mechanical computer for calculating functions and making tables. Babbage worked on his machine a long time, but never completed it, partly because of the inadequacy of mechanical technology for that purpose. I think that when Peirce wrote his 1886 letter he saw that a relay version of Babbage's machine could be built and that it would work. The first general-purpose relay computer was completed after World War II, at about the same time that the ENIAC, the first general purpose electronic computer, was completed![105]

Giulio Camillo (1480–1544)

The following is a description which discusses the nature of interaction within a particular memory theater, from the book Theatregarden Beastarium as expressed by Chris Dercon:

A spectator would sit at a central location inside a portable wooden structure which contained seven groupings of information, each accessible from seven different levels. The viewer would engage with an environment designed to reveal secrets about the structure of the universe, from the realm of the microcosmic to that of the macrocosmic. On the walls of the Theatro

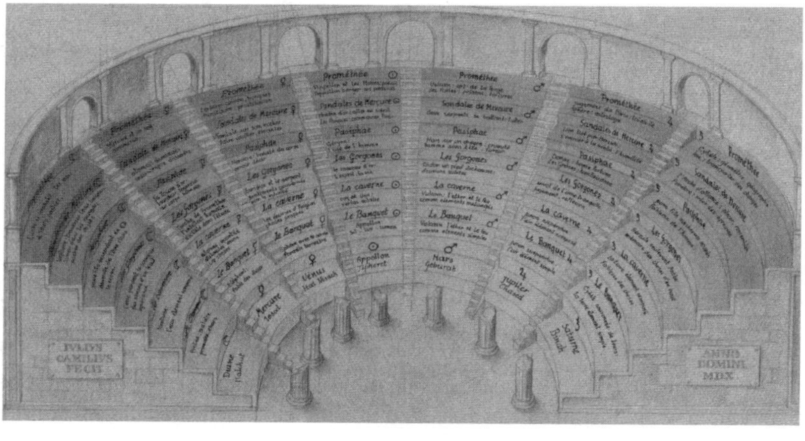

Public domain.

Del Mundo were inscribed all of the signs and symbols of the Christian Renaissance: the stars, the planets, the Greek gods and their attributes, animals and plants, the elements and their alchemical symbols, the temperaments, the vices and virtues. The theatre also contained wooden drawers filled with written texts that combined all of these elements within a "universal book." Viewers made choices from a central location, which enabled them to explore information housed in containers in close proximity to the participant. The room was organised in tiers which grouped information that dealt with questions of the universe, expanding upon innumerable aspects of creation. (Dercon 1990)

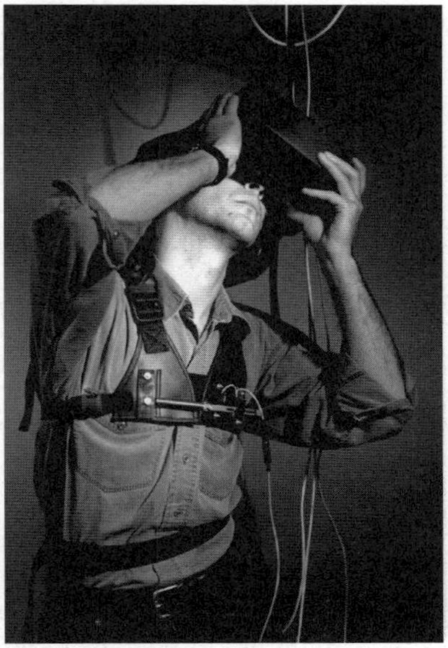

Char Davies' "breathing and balance interface" used in the performance of virtual reality environments *Osmose* (1995) and *Ephémère* (1998), image courtesy of Char Davies. Is VR the new Memory Theatre?

There is a palpable continuity across the ages which reminds one of the connection drawn from the Dante Alighieri's *Divine Comedy* to the scenario of modern cosmology by a physicist from Basel, Switzerland – Gustav Andreas Tammann.[106] Mythology is still directly below the surface and so is the immersion of cyberspace. The modern immersion of *Osmose* comes to mind as well. We are working toward defining a new memory theater that combines features of *Osmose* (Char Davies) with Spielberg's intelligence of a future. Driving back and forth within the mind, and driving back and forth between the ages is almost the same thing.

The Case of the Brains in a Vat – Hilary Putnam

Putnam claims that substituting in a stepwise fashion every element of a brain by computer changes nothing in the momentarily perceived world.

The case of the brains in a vat
Here is a science fiction possibility discussed by philosophers: imagine that a human being (you can imagine this to be yourself) has been subjected to an operation by an evil scientist. The person's brain (your brain) has been removed from the body and placed in a vat of nutrients which keeps the brain alive. The nerve endings have been connected to a super-scientific computer which causes the person whose brain it is to have the illusion that everything is perfectly normal. There seem to be people, objects, the sky, etc.; but really, all the person (you)

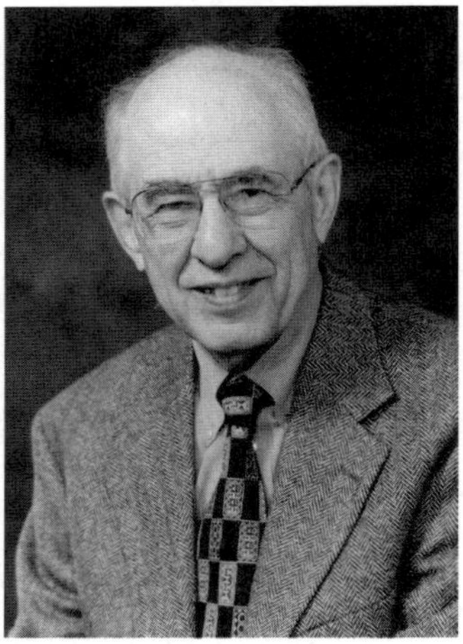

Public domain.

is experiencing is the result of electronic impulses travelling from the computer to the nerve endings. The computer is so clever that if the person tries to raise his hand, the feedback from the computer will cause him to "see" and "feel" the hand being raised. Moreover, by varying the program, the evil scientist can cause the victim to "experience" (or hallucinate) any situation or environment the evil scientist wishes. He can also obliterate the memory of the brain operation, so that the victim will seem to himself to have always been in this environment. It can even seem to the victim that he is sitting and reading these very words about the amusing but quite absurd supposition that there is an evil scientist who removes people's brains from their bodies and places them in a vat of nutrients which keep the brains alive […]

Instead of having just one brain in a vat, we could imagine that all human beings (perhaps all sentient beings) are brains in a vat (or nervous systems in a vat in case some beings with just a minimal nervous system already count as "sentient"). Of course, the evil scientist would have to be outside – or would he? Perhaps there is no evil scientist, perhaps (though this is absurd) the universe just happens to consist of automatic machinery tending a vat full of brains and nervous systems.[107]

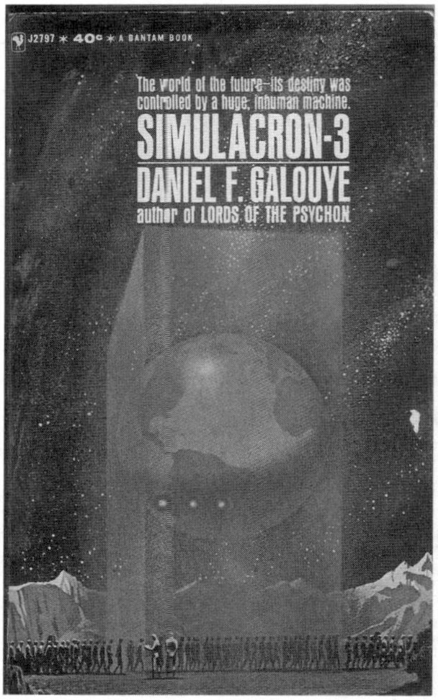

Public domain.

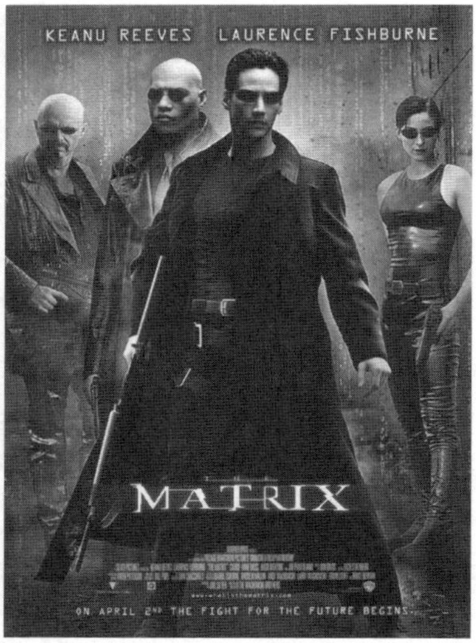

Publicity material from movie distributor 1999 Warner Bros. Entertainment Inc. (US, Canada, Bahamas and Bermuda); © 1999 Village Roadshow Films Limited. Fair Use Provision.

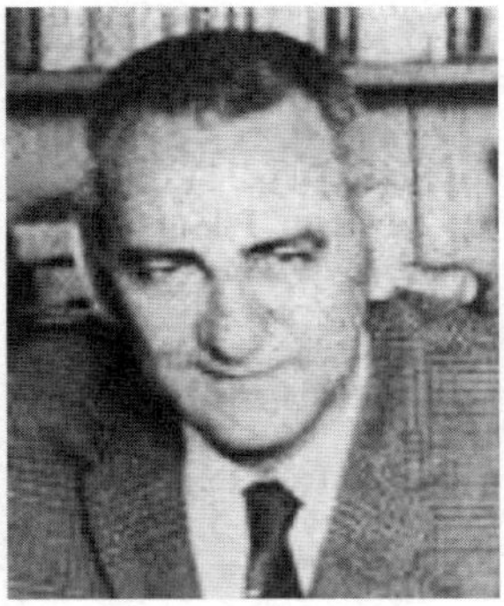

Daniel F. Galouye.

This of course is good old Matrix theory before the age of the Matrix (the filmic series by the Wachowski Brothers). *Simulacron Three* by Daniel F. Galouye is a precursor in 1963. Rainer Werner Fassbinder's movie *A Puppeteers World*, (*Welt am Draht*) was an adaptation of Galouye's book and preceded *The Matrix* by two decades. And before that Descartes had had the same dream already, for example, in his book *Meditations on First Philosophy* of 1641.

Well-stirred Computers

Pointing to the miracle of our predominantly-fluidic body.

[…] Could we devise an analogous chemical and/or electrochemical network that might generate similar outcomes given the appropriate level of programming and situated training? How can we go about developing systems that become operative via an electrochemical substrate that functions analogously to our own embodied thought and language production processes? Interestingly, there is a paper entitled: "A synthetic approach to exotic kinetics" which states: As an aid for intuition, three sources for the generation of new chemical circuits with non-trivial, i.e. exotic, dynamical behavior are offered:

a. the analogy to electronic circuits
b. the analogy of neural elements
c. the analogy to already existing chemical circuits, invented by mathematical biophysicists.

Suffice it to say, it appears that the above system of motivation, optimization, cognitive mapping, learning, recombinant patterning etc. could be approached via one or more of these "exotic" methodologies. At the time of writing (1973) these theories were purely theoretical. The conclusion provides the following summary: "On the basis of a non-physical analogy between homogeneous reaction systems and electronic systems (concentrations corresponding to voltages), spatially homogeneous chemical analogues to a number of well known electronic circuits can be devised in abstracto (amplifier, rectifier, RC oscillator, Eccles-Jordan trigger, multivibrator, time-base generator, monoflop, single-sweep time base generator), some of which are identical to already existing abstract reaction systems.

To what extent can such knowledge inform a new approach to emulating embodied neuronal functionality? We initially discussed the potential of using this form of chemically well stirred reactions. Only a few variables can be worked on simultaneously with this kind of system. Yet one could imagine a room with many of these reactions going on side by side, forming an elaborate connected neural correlate.[108]

This is Putnam met again.

Ostwald's Living Fluid

Ostwald gave the first measurement on a fluid that seemed to be brimming with irregular excitations.

An "exotic" electrochemical approach

The potential to make an electrochemical neural-analogical mechanism is also implicit in the paper by Cowan (1972).[109] *He postulated a "neural field theory", being based on Bonhoeffer-type partial differential equations (in the present terminology), which also allows for catastrophical [any perturbation which takes the system across such boundaries will switch the system from one dynamical regime to another [...] are called "Catastrophies"]*[110] *shifts between different regimens of qualitative behavior. An analogous simulation result ("hysterisis behavior") has been obtained in discrete neural nets (Anninos 1972).*[111]

Thus a topological theory of the brain (Zeeman 1965)[112] *begins to emerge in operational and even chemical terms.*

What we imagine is the analogue of a neuron farm as articulated in some electrochemical environments. This

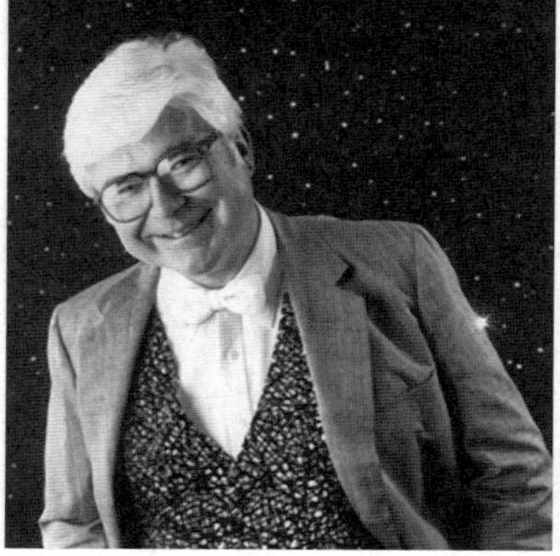

Public domain.

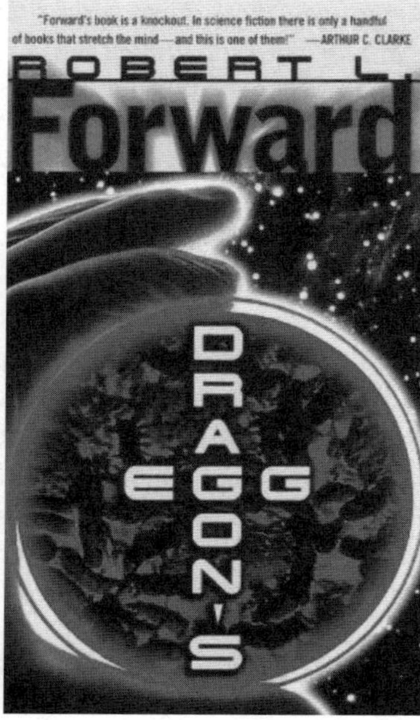

huge room would enable the system to be dynamically active. The room could be connected at a distance to a robot that it is communicating with, both receiving pattern flows of sense perturbations, as well as sending robotic affector commands. It could also be tied directly to more traditional computers.[113]

One can also imagine a series of spray valves that would function like neurotransmitters to change weights in the system. A third system would send wave messages about differing states of the system (volume transmission) to other relevant parts of the system. The system could also consist of two parts separated by a vast distance of several light seconds e.g. on the moon.

Compare *The Dragon's Egg* novel by Robert Forward. He was thinking in nuclear chemical terms. An Important reference concerning well stirred distributed chemical reaction systems with chaos is John L. ("Jack") Hudson's relevant work over more than four decades.

Zeeman – The Construction of a Pseudo Continuum

Christopher Zeeman rediscovered and renamed Poincaré's relational theory of 1904 (in *The Value of Science*) into Tolerance theory. This Poincaré–Zeeman theory is an attempt to unify the continuum and the discretum. Zeeman rediscovered this notion in relation to the eye while visiting an optometrist. He realized that with the given resolution of the eye you cannot distinguish between an infinitely sharp picture and a pixelized picture of finite resolution. He called this *Tolerance equivalence*. The brain is a machine based on finitely many elements and sensors which by necessity implement Tolerance theory. Tim Poston and Mario DalCin formalized Zeeman's theory in subsequent years; whereby DalCin talks about "Tolerance automata." We create a Tolerance Attractor if we iterate a picture under the closed loop of the operation of the nonlinear sinc wavelet. The "Tolerance Attractor" is nothing else but a Platonic idea in the sense of Heinz von Foerster in his paper of 1961, "On Platonic ideation", which provides an independent entry into this marriage of the discretum and the continuum. The electrochemical machine is created in the same spirit. Gordon Pask would join in. Poincaré had been struck by the fact that the number of receptive fields of neurons on the forearm is only about 5. But if you gently move a needle across your forearm you feel a continuous motion. The Poincaré–Zeeman–DalCin algorithm will also be equally useful in robots as in biology.

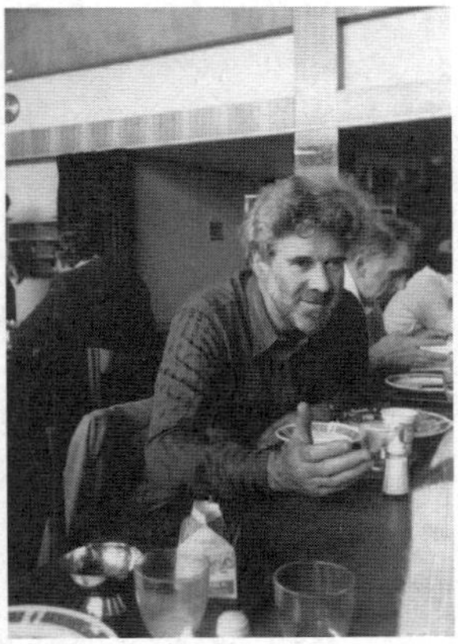

Christopher Zeeman, Photo by Konrad Jacobs 1980. Courtesy Archives of the Mathematisches Forschungsinstitut Oberwolfach.

Well-stirred Life on Jupiter

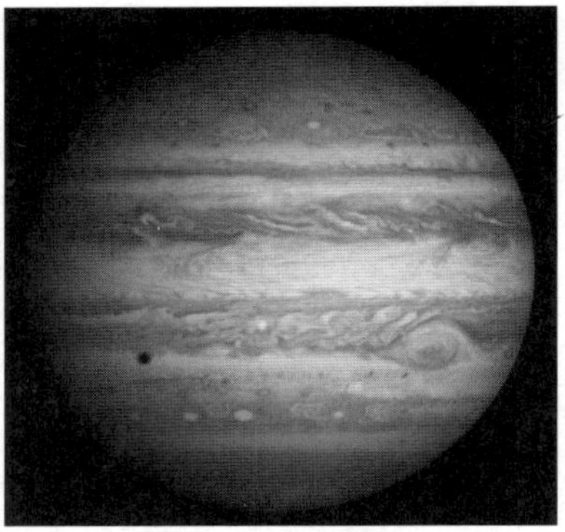

Courtesy image commons. NASA.

Carbon is not the only chain-forming atom in the universe. Boron in alternating boron/nitrogen chains can be expected to play a similar role under other planetary conditions that do not involve water as a solvent and have a hot heart under a cold skin.

The Great Everett/Many Branches Theory

Every person believes he lives his life in a consistent world with a consistent history, but according to Everett each person belongs to a different world. See the book the *Quark and the Jaguar* by Murray Gell-Mann that pays tribute to this great idea.

When Everett was 12 years old he got a friendly letter from Einstein. It read:

"Dear Hugh: There is no such thing like an irresistible force and immovable body. But there seems to be a very stubborn boy who has forced his way victoriously through strange difficulties created by himself for this purpose. Sincerely yours, A. Einstein."[114]

Observer Split

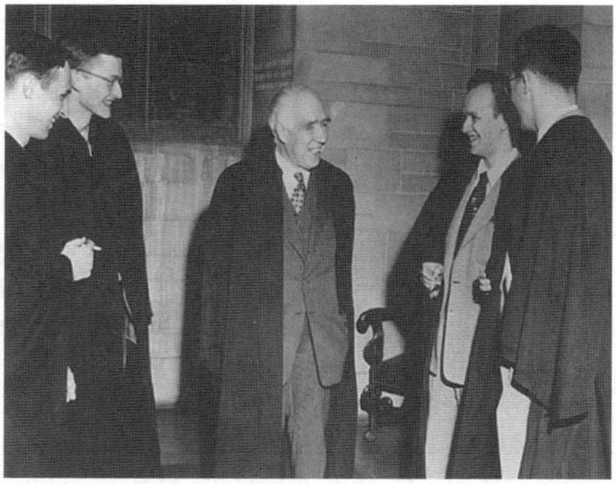

Everett (second from right) in 1955 with Niels Bohr, photo courtesy of Mark Everett.

In September, 1955 (the beginning of Everett's third year at Princeton) he presented two small papers to Wheeler. (In Everett's archives, in the same folder with these two, there is stored a third paper, just four pages in length, that may have been written earlier. This third paper deals with objective vs. subjective probabilities. In it, he proves the inconsistency of the concept of objective probability and chooses as the most fruitful way to consistency an acceptance of the concept of hidden variables. The marginal remarks in this paper probably belong to Shoemaker, because the handwriting is

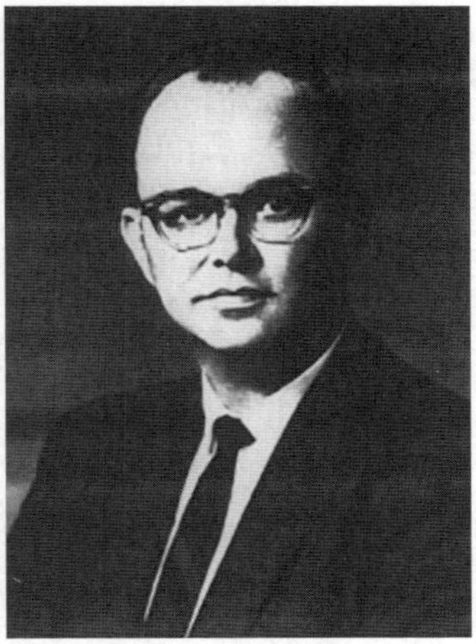
Hugh Everett III at 34, photo courtesy of Mark Everett.

different from the usual handwriting of Wheeler.) In one of the September papers submitted to Wheeler, Everett introduces a new concept-the correlation of values X and Y (not to be confused with a coefficient of correlation), based on the expectation of change of the quantity of Shannon information about X, depending on information about value Y. The paper concludes with a formula for the correlation of observable values X and Y, described by a wave function […]

On September 21, 1955 Wheeler wrote Everett a note, judging both papers as important works. The first one, on correlation, he is ready to send somewhere for publication, but as to the second one, probability in wave mechanics, he says he is "frankly bashful about showing it to Bohr in its present form" since it can be "subject to mystical misinterpretations by too many unskilled readers". So, it seems that Everett's theory was too advanced for its time. (Everett received his master's degree that year, probably before submission of these papers to Wheeler. At that time in physics at Princeton, passing the general exams was all that was required for the M. A. degree. Only the Ph.D. required research accomplishment.)

Everett's main 137-page work, "The Theory of the Universal Wave Function", is dated January 1956. (It was reprinted in a 1973 collection. Chapter II of this work was taken from his unpublished article on correlation. Everett recalled later that Wheeler hurried him to a dissertation defense before his third year ended in the spring of 1956, although he (Everett) would have preferred delay because leaving the University might have meant being drafted into the military (the Korean War had recently ended, and being drafted was still a possibility). Everett later thanked Bohr, Groenewald, Petersen, Stern, and Rosenfeld for criticism. But something did delay his defense. Perhaps it was Wheeler's leaving to accept a Lorentz Professorship at Leiden University for the period January to September 1956. In any case, his startlingly original and important work on quantum mechanics caused much less of a stir than it should have, and Everett turned toward a new career full of military secrets.[115]

Many Worlds/Many Minds

The many-worlds interpretation (also known as relative state formulation, theory of the universal wavefunction, many-universes interpretation, Oxford interpretation or many worlds)[or many minds, emphasis the authors], is an interpretation of quantum mechanics that claims to resolve all the "paradoxes" of quantum theory by allowing every possible outcome to every event to define or exist in its own "history" or "world", via the mechanism of quantum decoherence, instead of wavefunction collapse. Proponents argue that the many-worlds interpretation reconciles how we can perceive non-deterministic events (such as the random decay of a radioactive atom) with the deterministic equations of quantum physics; history, which prior to many worlds had been viewed as a single "world-line", is rather a many-branched tree where every possible branch of history is realized.[116]

Everett States

We have the task of making deductions about the appearance of phenomena to observers which are considered as purely physical systems and are treated within the theory. To accomplish this it is necessary to identify some present properties of such an observer with features of the past experience of the observer.

Thus, in order to say that an observer 0 has observed the event a, it is necessary that the state of 0 has become changed from its former state to a new state which is dependent upon a.

It will suffice for our purposes to consider the observers to possess memories (i.e., parts of a relatively permanent nature whose states are in correspondence with past experience of the observers). In order to make deductions about the past experience of an observer it is sufficient to deduce the present contents of the memory as it appears within the mathematical model.

The Machine has Perceived A

As models for observers we can, if we wish, consider automatically functioning machines, possessing sensory apparatus and coupled to recording devices capable of registering past sensory data and machine configurations. We can further suppose that the machine is so constructed that its present actions shall be determined not only by its present sensory data, but by the contents of its memory as well. Such a machine will then be capable of performing a sequence of observations (measurements), and furthermore of deciding upon its future experiments on the basis of past results. […]

For such machines we are justified in using such phrases as "the machine has perceived A" or "the machine is aware of A" if the occurrence of A is represented in the memory, since the future behavior of the machine will be based upon the occurrence of A. In fact, all of the customary language of subjective experience is quite applicable to such machines, and forms the most natural and useful mode of expression when dealing with their behavior, as is well known to individuals who work with complex automata.[117]

A Neosentient will be a relevant class of observer in the Everett sense, in that it combines the measurement capabilities of a computer with a means of reflection.

Everett's theory at the same time addresses the question of assignment which is basic to all artificial brain type work. It is also basic to the notion of consciousness.

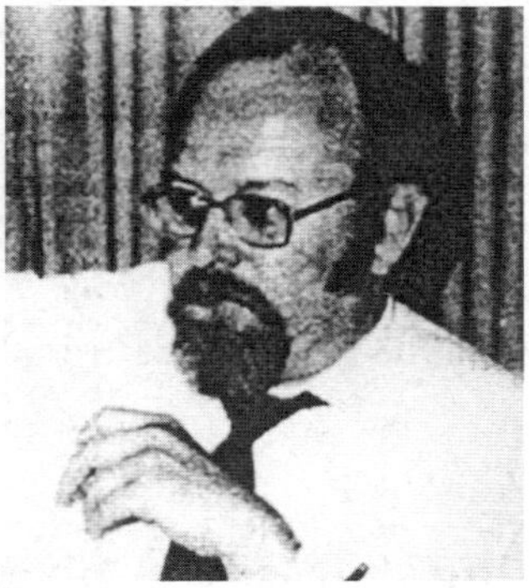

Hugh Everett III, in 1982 (age 51), photo courtesy of Mark Everett.

Everett continues:

These configurations can be thought of as punches in a paper tape, impressions on a magnetic reel, configurations of a relay switching circuit, or even configurations of brain cells. We only require that they be capable of the interpretation "The observer has experienced the succession of events A,B,...,C" (We shall sometimes write dots in a memory sequence, [...A,B,...,C] to indicate the possible presence of previous memories which are irrelevant to the case being considered.).[118]

Many-consciousness Interpretation

There is a very interesting lineage including von Neumann, Everett, Wigner, Zeh, Albert, Gell-Mann, and Deutsch.

In a letter to the authors related to the Many-Minds interpretation, Dieter Zeh states:

I used the idea already in my first papers on the subject (starting in 1970) ... In a contribution of 1981 for the Epist. Letters of the Ferdinand Gonseth Association (Biel, Switzerland) I invented the term "many-consciousness interpretation." I always had in mind a new and appropriate version of psycho-physical parallelism as required by von Neumann (in the sense of an epiphenomenon).

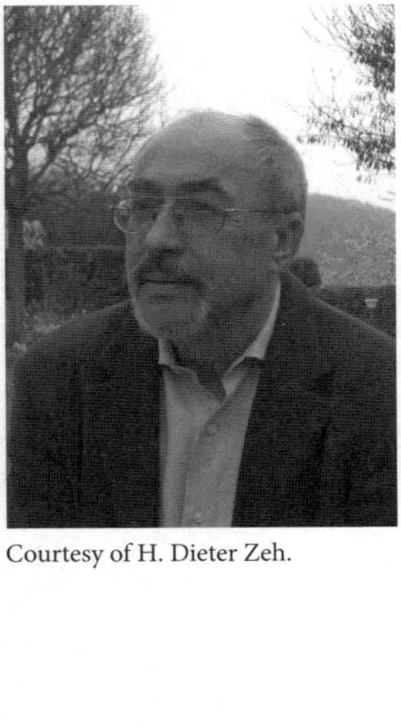

Courtesy of H. Dieter Zeh.

In his paper, "Toward a quantum theory of observation" (originally published in 1973) Zeh states:

Everett proposed an interpretation of quantum theory that avoids the reduction of the wave function, and instead postulates the universal validity of the Schrödinger equation.

This means that the "other" components (which would disappear according to the reduction postulate) still "exist" after a measurement. However, they are correlated with different states of the apparatus and subsequently with different states of human observers. Therefore Everett has to assume that "we are aware" of only one of these world components, and that the world apparently "splits" into many components whenever a measurement-like process occurs.[119]

Will the Neosentient be both apparatus and observer – of course it will.

The Undivided Universe – An Ontological Interpretation of Quantum Theory

By David Bohm and Basil Hiley

Everett assumes that the whole universe including all observers exists objectively and is described, as we have already pointed out, completely and perfectly by a vector in Hilbert space. One may explain what this means loosely by saying that in some sense the universe is regarded as a multi-dimensional reality. But what Everett is doing, is to make a theory that relates the universe to various points of view that are contained within it. What we experience of the universe is a single subsequence of these points of view. Or, as Squires has put it, what we are dealing with is not a many-universe theory, but a theory of one universe with many viewpoints. Each point of view establishes a relationship between a state of awareness and the state of some other part of the universe containing the observing instrument and the observed object.[120]

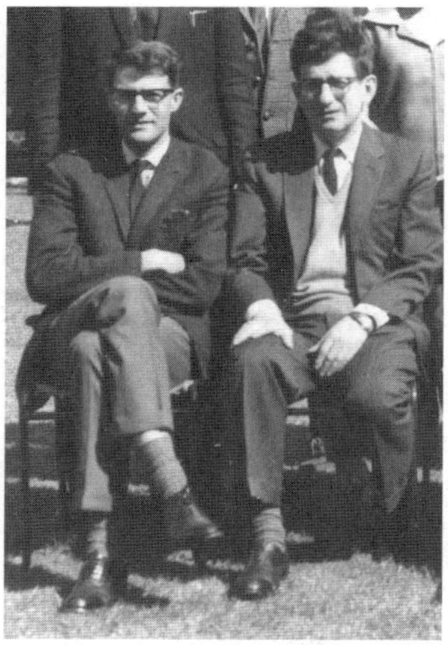

Basil Hiley and David Bohm, courtesy of Basil Hiley.

The theory of many minds by David Albert, is in the footsteps of H. Dieter Zeh and earlier, von Neumann. It assumes that the distinction between worlds should be made at the level of the mind of an individual observer.[121] This is "pure Everett." Everett went one step further. He saw that all these worlds were "observer-state relative." Different states of the observer give rise to different worlds because the difference (interface) between the rest of the universe and this microscopic state of the observer (his or her brain) is different.

This "cut" between observer and rest is microscopically sharp. Part of matter is thereby made the seat of the soul as anticipated by Descartes. Some cells and their electrons are privileged with a razor's sharpness at every moment. The deterministically existing micro-time reversals cause both the quantum uncertainties and the non-locality (as predicted by Everett in his printed 1957 paper, p. 149).

The fact that h can thereby be derived numerically and so can c forms the subject matter of "endophysics."[122]

The Cut Through the Neosentient

Is this cut taking place on the exo level? Some questions: Is this now the endo approach – does the wave function collapse in microscopically articulated space, different for each particle? If the particle is in motion, is the cut in motion? Does the creation of the cut have a duration, or is it instantaneous? Does it "break" or collapse across the cut, or is this a metaphor? Does the cut represent a change in energy state? Is the collapse of the wave function a metaphor or a literal event?

Is a sensed perturbation derived only after encountering the cut? If I feel the static electricity surrounding another individual – where is the cut (Kirlian photograph)? Does the cut favor one half of the micro-time reversal over another in different locations of particles, or is it consistent in a singular consciousness? Is the cut always mobile (a fluid boundary forming an interior and exterior) or is it a flow with continuously shifting dimensionality? If it is a flow across the cut, traversing from exteriority to interiority, then does a proximity to time define the boundary? Is there a boundary/a cut only on the endo level, with a flow (the metaphor of the persistence of vision) at the exo perspective (Libet)? Might the "soul" be attached as a particle to the universe on the exo level as a continuum while functioning as a separate entity from the endophysical perspective? Is this not an example of the Poincaré–Zeeman theory – an attempt to unify the continuum and the discretum? A kind of complementarity of observer perspectives? How does this cut manifest itself in a computational system – at the sensor or in the code? Is this different for the analogue computer?

The endo and the exo converge at the point of the cut, yet from only the endo perspective the cut is discrete.

In space it is a continuum, in time it is discrete. The point-shaped position of the observer at the center of the light cone (Einstein) is a consequence and so is the collapsed wave function of quantum mechanics. Thus, quantization is only endo objective.

The cut itself is an assignment condition of an individual now. An individual now is always a mediated instantiation (so the observer and observer error always enter the equation). Everett saw that the machine could become the observer and "perceive A."

What is the relationship between space, energy, and the now?

Murray Gell-Mann – *The Quark and the Jaguar*

Today we are entering the era of computers and robots functioning as complex adaptive systems without humans in the loop. Many future robots will have elaborate schemata subject to variation and selection. Consider a six-legged mobile robot having in each leg a set of sensors that detect obstacles and an information processor that responds in some prearranged manner to the signals from those sensors to control the motions of that leg, moving it up or down and forward or backward. Such legs resemble a set of old-fashioned cybernetic devices.

Nowadays robot design might include a form of communication among the legs, but not through a governing central processing unit. Instead, each leg would have the capacity to influence the behavior of the others by means of communication links. The pattern of strengths of influence of the legs on one another would be a schema, subject to variations produced, for example, by input from a generator of pseudo-random numbers. The selection pressures influencing the adoption and rejection of candidate patterns might originate from additional sensors that measure what is happening not just to an individual leg, but also to the robot as a whole, such as whether it is moving forward or backward and whether its belly is far enough off the ground. In this way the robot would tend to develop a schema that yielded a gait suited to the terrain on which it was traveling and that was subject to alteration when the character of that terrain changed. Such a robot may be regarded as at least a primitive form of complex adaptive system.[123]

This represents a fairly primitive form of artificial intelligence applicable to insects. This is something like the eusocial organization put into one body. It is also close to the ideas of Donald MacKay.

The Aharonov–Bohm Effect

By changing a magnetic field for a particle in a location where it is not possible to directly effect the particle's behavior, nonetheless an instantaneous action at a distance is achieved in the Aharonov–Bohm experiment. An inventive explanation of this quantum effect is waiting to be found.[124] A magnetic field is direction-of-time dependent. This effect could be interpreted as an "Everett flip" – but this is preliminary.

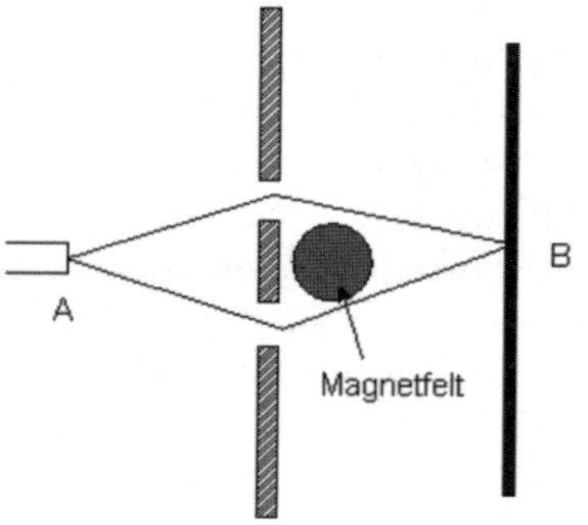

What role does action at a distance play in consciousness? Assignment conditions imply a cut in our terminology. If we don't know the initial conditions how can we know the assignment conditions? We cannot completely know the initial conditions because of infinitely many digits being presumably involved. Only as a superobserver can one define both the initial and the assignment conditions. We cannot feel the assignment conditions authored in our system. The creator has an underprivilegedness. Here the machine has a kind of transcendent reality which is not available to the creator. Without assistance from below, you remain at the mercy of your creature and can never know the world of the engendered Neosentient entity.

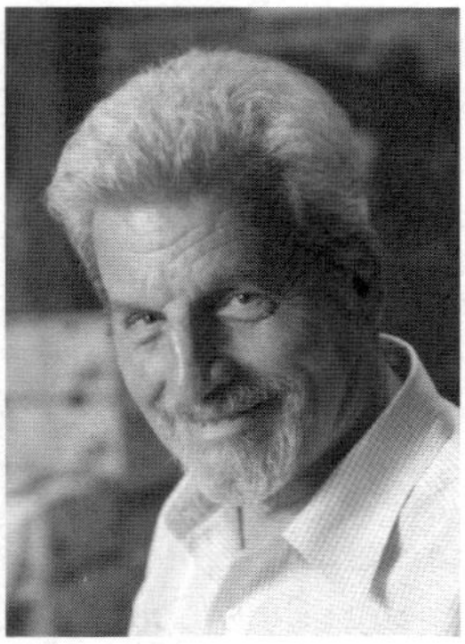

Yakir Aharonov.

Assignment Conditions

Newton divided the world into laws and initial conditions. This ingenious reduction of the whole world to comprehensible machinery left out one element – assignment conditions. The macro-assignment needs to be differentiated from micro-assignment. The same machinery of the same world witnessed by an internal resident can be quite different. This is how a poor creature feels in the face of the creator. Sons and fathers are the most familiar example already.

The broad concept of the interface emerged in the fields of computation and in human-machine interactions of early cybernetics. Widely theorized as an aspect of software design, the interface languished in metaphors of the page, the desktop, and worse still, in point-and-click interactions that enslaved users. The limitations of a notion of the interface based on the binary opposition of user-machine have hindered a consideration of the interface as a state linked more with what Rössler identifies as "assignment conditions" than with the typically programmed behaviors of software interfaces. In this context, haptic interfaces, that permit both feedback and performance on physical or virtual objects are a promising development.[125]

"Blood stained cut versus tender interface." Rössler

The slightly frightening notion of cut in physics (anaximander's cut, the Cartesian cut, Heisenberg's cut, von Neumann's cut) might all be replaced by the more tender notion of interface. The Everettian choice of world is also a related benevolent proceedure (articulated with equal precision but not with a knife).

The World as Interface

Archimedes

Give me a place to stand on and I will move the earth

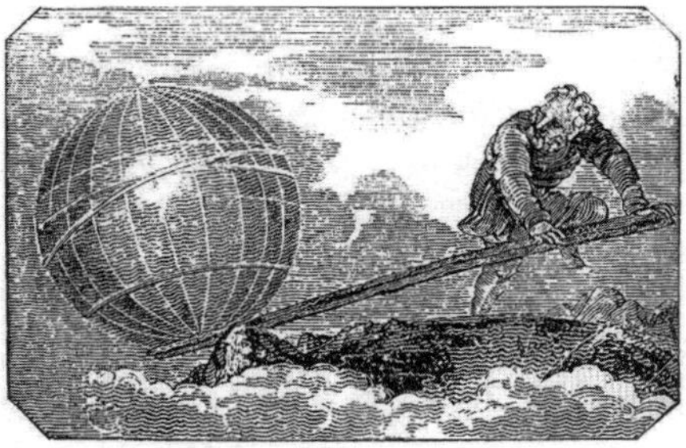

Public domain.

The science of endophysics claims that the world as it is given to us is only a cut, an interface, a difference inside what is real (the whole). This has some powerful implications, including the possibility to change the whole world (i.e., the interface world).

Archimedes invented the idea with his famous phrase "give me where I may stand and I shall move the earth." The original quotation was in Dorian Greek. This privileged situation is not usually available to a mere subsystem. A subsystem never sees the rest of the world as it is. But he only sees the difference between his own state and the rest of the world. It is almost a kind of subtraction, a difference principle. It was clearly expressed by Roger Joseph Boscovich in his 1755 paper "On space and time as they are being perceived by us" (in Latin). Boscovich took the intuition for his idea apparently from Leibniz who had wondered how big a fly would be looking to a highly shrunken human being, realizing that there is no length scale in the universe except the natural size of an internal observer. Boscovich was the first to come up with a temporal example. He said that if the earth along with us were shrinking and expanding in a matter of days, along with all forces, we would be unable to even notice this gross effect. So we can never trust Science in this respect. There are realities that will remain forever veiled to our knowledge. Thus, we can never know the world in itself. Next Maxwell who had read Boscovich realized the same fact by stating "We will never be able to lay hold of an atom and palpate it" (in his *Theory of Heat* of 1871). With this quote he anticipated quantum mechanics. In the field of quantum mechanics, Everett was the only one who took up the thread. Heisenberg gave an interesting talk in 1943 before the Wednesday Society in Berlin which is virtually unknown. He stated, "We should become aware of the fact that the world depends on us inescapably in so far as it is a world recognized by us." Next comes Toffoli who realized in 1978 in a paper in the proceedings of the conference edited by Feynman – that an automaton cannot accurately model his own state, paraphrasing an idea of Moore in a book titled *Automata Studies* of 1956. David Finkelstein took up with the same thread and came up with his already quoted paper. This long tradition was actually summarized by Lord Kelvin in his old age in 1905; "I am a Boscovichian pure and simple." Boscovich played a similar role in public consciousness as Einstein did ever since 1905. Relativity theory is one of the purest outgrowths of Boscovich's worldview. It has its first trace in Western history in the writings of Anaximander who claimed that we cannot understand the unempirical (ápeiron) but we can only understand a difference that is created internally by "secretion" (apokrinein). So he described in words the famous drawing of yin and yang which together divide a hole into two mutually complementary halves. We are for some reason positioned on this internal cut which is today called an interface. It is the interface of the Now and the world. There is no better word for that than assignment condition. The study of this fundamental relationship should be called Interfaciology (or Endophysics if you so wish).

The pious wish: the observer and superobserver combined.

The achievement of neosentience is an interface problem; or the observer surprising the superobserver with a present. The interface problem is itself already meta – it is a two-level theory. The question is, can a Neosentient entity bridge the two levels of the greater domain?

Boscovich

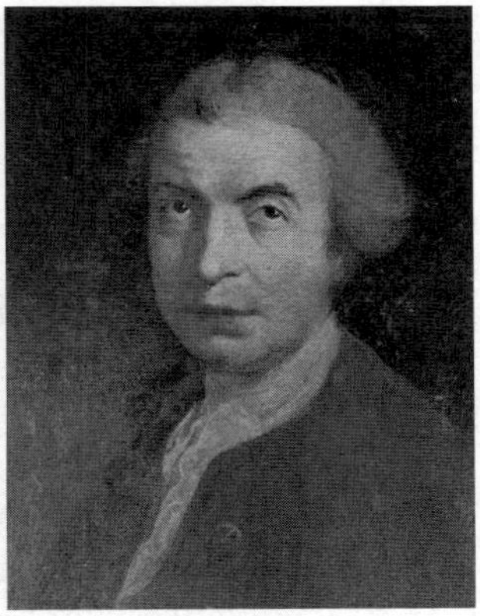

Only four physicists after Descartes appear to have taken the idea of an interface-affecting causation seriously: Boscovich, Einstein, Bohr and Everett. Everett's version of quantum mechanics[126] *is particularly illuminating. It is completely "observer-relative" in the sense that every measured quantum state in the world is personalized. The world is made "only for me" in a Kafkaesque manner (to mention only the frightening aspect). The now and the quantum world become a single "joint pick" on a two-dimensional parameter surface* [127]

[Another...] point is in favor of limitology: distortion limits always leave a loophole. They exist because an objective picture (which no longer depends on the observer) can only be obtained by making the observer explicit – a feat impossible to accomplish from the inside. Nevertheless the impossible can be achieved – on the modeling level. The "artificial universe approach" to the real world therefore qualifies as a new type of measurement. At the same time the computer acquires an unexpected fundamental role.[128]

From our rainbow world

The virtual reality paradigm lends scientific credence to the topic of the "interface." The momentary position of the "index glove" functions inside a simulated world in a way which only makes it palpable as an invariant reality. The generation of such artificial interfaces is not easy and requires fast computers, as is well known.

This program then leads over to temporally changing realities. What if the position of the "eye" and that of an external object are correlated? Will such correlated objects tend to disappear in the perceived interface?

A third type of experiment will involve reversible simulated worlds. This proposal includes the study of the predicament of an ice-skater who cannot get rid of his whole-body angular

momentum unless he pirouettes. At still greater degrees of sophistication, the proposal will include an Archimedean system of balls and springs – like a giant model drug molecule – to play with. Eventually, as the computers grow faster, a whole ice-skater will come into sight again – but this time watched completely from the Archimedean frog's perspective of total reversibility. The first detailed report about the properties of such a "conservative virtual reality" will come in in the year 2010, if everything goes well. In this way, a new "hopeful suspicion" could be arrived at: the virtual reality paradigm may reveal more about our own world than the usual course of science has led us to believe. Is the whole world a rainbow world? Only after such a suspicion has taken hold do new "diagnostic tools" – to confirm and to manipulate it – have a chance to be developed seriously.
To conclude, the rainbow has not lost any of its childhood magic. To simulate it interactively, an advanced type of VR is required. At the same time, a new attitude is fostered – the walls which surround the sparkling VR-like now at every moment acquire a new tangibility. Does the hermetic paradigm of computer-generated worlds perhaps hold the key to making our own world less hermetic? The rainbow would become a door in the sky.[129]

The task has been started in two dimensions by Hans Diebner.[130]

Discreteness and Continuum

The question of discreteness is actually contrary to a deep understanding of the universe and the brain on a fundamental level. The reason is very inconspicuous – it is the empirical existence of absolutely indistinguishable particles. For example, electrons of the same spin are totally indistinguishable. The strange phenomenon was discovered and named by Wolfgang Pauli, "exchange symmetry." It means that if you surreptitiously exchange the positions of two such particles in the world, NOTHING has been changed. This is an absolute statement. It may be one of the best ones we have in the world. So far it has never been possible to duplicate this phenomenon in a discrete computer-based world but the challenge is still on. For example Tommaso Toffoli has been working on this for decades and so has Edward Fredkin. This is the pure substance of the continuum. It brings us back to Anaxagoras, and via Anaxagoras to bishop Gregorius of Naziance and the Mutakallimun, then Spinoza and Leibniz, as Hermann Weyl described in his book *Philosophy of Mathematics and Science* – Second edition 1952. Pauli discovered the whole thing on his own but unfortunately found it to be a fruit of quantum mechanics, so that its more general origin was overlooked.

Discreteness is something which we, like children at play, cannot dispose of. It is the sign of our underprivilegedness in nature. Heraclitus said of the creator that "eternity is a child on the throne that plays." We are also children on the throne but the gift of transfinitely exact creation is so far being withheld from us. So we may never know whether a creation of our own really perceives anything subjectively because of this arbitrary (cruel?) restriction to our own creativity. But the present authors are confident that a discrete creature in the spirit of Poincaré and Christopher Zeeman – discrete computers – will still be endowed with consciousness.

Assignment conditions occur equally, both in a discrete and in a continuous world. A continuous world is nevertheless made of particles even though the latters' positions and velocities are infinitely (and transfinitely) exactly specified. We do not touch on the question of so-called continuous media, namely, partial differential equations that are also called fields. Here quantum mechanics has introduced a discretization that is not to be confused with finitization. It by the way is possible – and was actually articulated by Feynman and Wheeler – to get rid of primary fields in the sense of partial differential equations. This is the so-called "absorber theory."

Different Definitions of the Observer

There are qualitative differences between classes of observers:

Class 1: animals as more or less sophisticated observers
Class 2: the human person
Class 3: the human person amplified by computers and other apparatus
Class 4: hypothetical, more highly evolved biological species and extraterrestrials that likewise have epigenetically gone through the personogenetic bifurcation
Class 5: computer-implemented intelligent entities functioning as persons – *The Benevolence Engine*, our Neosentient Entity
Class 6: Point omega

What is the definition of an observer in a physics experiment vs. human and/or Neosentient observation? What is a "single-pendulum observer"?

A single-pendulum is the simplest non-trivial physical system. And a full-fledged observer can be built up from many pendulums. On the micro level, the lowermost element of more complicated physical and chemical observers would be pendulums or moving electrons in their Sackur cells (i.e., classically pre-formed quantum cells).

An artificially microscopically implemented observer might be defined for all six observer classes (endophysical approach) in a lower level artificial universe.

Maxwell's Demon

[…] If we conceive of a being whose faculties are so sharpened that he can follow every molecule in its course, such a being, whose attributes are as essentially finite as our own, would be able to do what is impossible to us. For we have seen that molecules in a vessel full of air at uniform

temperature are moving with velocities by no means uniform, though the mean velocity of any great number of them, arbitrarily selected, is almost exactly uniform. Now let us suppose that such a vessel is divided into two portions, A and B, by a division in which there is a small hole, and that a being, who can see the individual molecules, opens and closes this hole, so as to allow only the swifter molecules to pass from A to B, and only the slower molecules to pass from B to A. He will thus, without expenditure of work, raise the temperature of B and lower that of A, in contradiction to the second law of thermodynamics.

James Clerk Maxwell[131]
In his text "Diffusion" Maxwell stated:

[…] The idea of the dissipation of energy depends on the extent of our knowledge. Available energy is energy which we can direct into any desired channel. Dissipated energy is energy which we can not lay hold of and direct at pleasure, such as the energy of the confused agitation of molecules which we call heat. Now, confusion, like the correlative term order, is not a property of material things in themselves, but only in relation to the mind which perceives them […] (he continues) A memorandum-book does not, provided that it is neatly written, appear confused to a literate person, or to the owner who understands it thoroughly, but to any other person able to read it appears to be inextricably confused. Similarly the notion of dissipated energy could not occur to a being who could not turn any of the energies of nature to his own account, or to one who could trace the motion of every molecule and seize it at the right moment. It is only to a being in the intermediate stage, who can lay hold of some forms of energy while others elude his grasp, that energy appears to be passing inevitably from the available to the dissipated state.[132]

This is an example of something that can be done only by an exo observer but not by an endo observer.
He thereby conceived of this second level in the spirit of endophysics.

The poly-sensing system of the Neosentient might include molecular-scale apparatus and new technological sensing devices of any variety including nanotechnology.

Naked Mole Type Intelligence

The eusocial class of animals, with a queen, is an important subclass of animal observers. The subclass is almost completely uninvestigated so far. The underlying distributed brain equation has yet to be found. Note, by the way, that these mammals have a higher relative brain weight – the highest on earth.

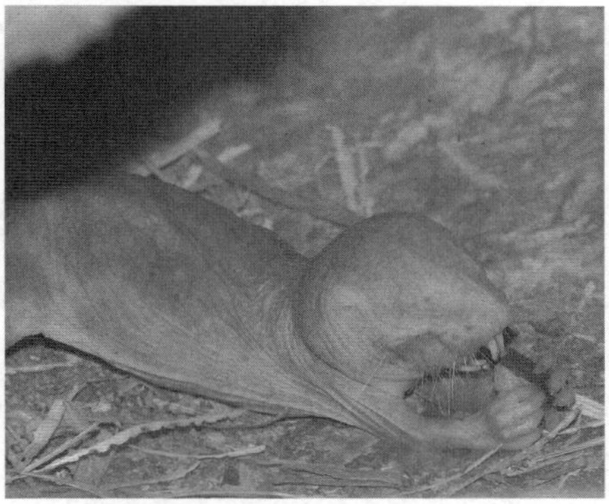
Naked mole rat Heterocephalus glaber eating, public domain, Ltshears – Trisha M Shears.

Naked mole rats are the most social of all the mammals. They live in underground colonies with a social structure like that of ants and termites. There are castes of workers, and only the queen, an oversized female, breeds. Naked mole rats are also intensely xenophobic; they avoid or fight with other mole-rat colonies. But such tightly closed societies lead to inbreeding with all its deleterious effects. For naked mole rats to survive over the long term, a biological solution to the inbreeding problem had to be found.

The response of the species to this threat is the occasional production of a "dispersive morph." The largest and most successful colonies produce – somehow – a larger-than-normal individual, almost always a male, that is fuelled with extra fat and possesses a yen to travel. He is disinclined to mate with the resident queen, preferring to leave the colony for amorous adventure elsewhere. Thus, intercolony gene flow is established.[133]

Comment. Of course, the naked-mole-rat colony, even when thought of as a "superorganism," cannot perceive the future consequences of inbreeding. The invention of a "dispersive morph," according to evolutionists, has to come from a sequence of random mutations that over time create a special individual, specially fuelled and with abnormal proclivities.[134]

This actually is a self-improving random process of the theory of recursive evolution following in the footsteps of John von Neumann and John Holland.[135]

Special Sense Modalities and Equivalencies Across Minds

All brains on all planets are predictably similar because they implement the same equations following from Spatial Darwinism. This is the brain equation approach.

Fulguration

Fulguration was Lorenz's word for the emergence of a new quality out of "trivial" elements. More conventional words are "bifurcation" (Poincaré), "function change" (Bob Rosen), and "catastrophe" (René Thom). Each embodies the "creative spark" (Arthur Koestler).

Mormyrid fish seem to "see" using electricity. And this isn't the only instance where evolution has co-opted one sense to stand in for another. By studying brain structures, Ken Catania from Vanderbilt University, Tennessee, has found that star-nosed moles "see" their dark subterranean world through their highly sensitive nose tentacles, while naked mole rats use their incisor teeth. These cases where different sensory inputs are integrated, together with the numerous examples of convergence, suggest that despite obvious differences in the ways animals sense their worlds, the basic processing may be much more similar than we realize. So, not only do sensory systems as different as sight and electrical reception each show multiple convergences, but all may lead to an equivalent mental map.[136]

High-resolution Magnetic Senses – Hammer Head Shark

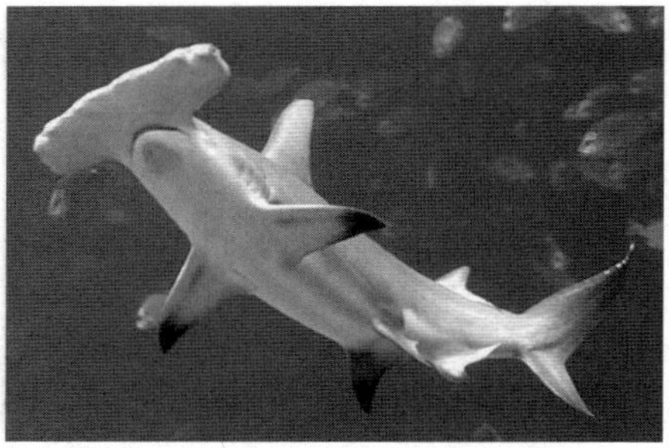

Multi-tongued perception of the magnetic type.

Because the fish and the saltwater form an electrical circuit, movement of the fish through the water will induce an electrical field that produces a voltage drop across the electroreceptor cells. Movement of saltwater through the Earth's magnetic field will also produce a voltage drop across the electro-receptor cells, even when the animal is passively moving with the water. The magnitude of the voltage drop depends on the intensity of the external magnetic field, the length of the canal, the orientation of the canal relative to the external magnetic field, and the relative conductivities of the internal and external media. The voltage drops generated by movement of both the fish and the water are sufficient to stimulate the electro receptors and permit determination of magnetic field direction (Kalmijn, 1978, 1982), independent of whether the animal uses this information. Although the electroreceptors will not detect the constant electrical field signals produced by completely uniform movement of either the water or the fish, further theoretical analysis has shown that the low frequency movements of the body during swimming (side to side in sharks or up and down in rays) will still permit extraction of information about magnetic field direction.[137]

What senses will construct the phenomenology of the Neosentient?

Zhuangzi

Zhuangzi stood with a pupil on a bridge looking down into the river. He said "look how the fish enjoy themselves in the water". The pupil said "how can you know – you are not a fish". Zhuangzi replied: "how can you know I don't know; you are not me". The next morning, Zhuangzi awoke after having dreamt being a butterfly and said to himself; "am I a butterfly who just dreams of being a human being or am I a human being who just dreamt of being a butterfly?"

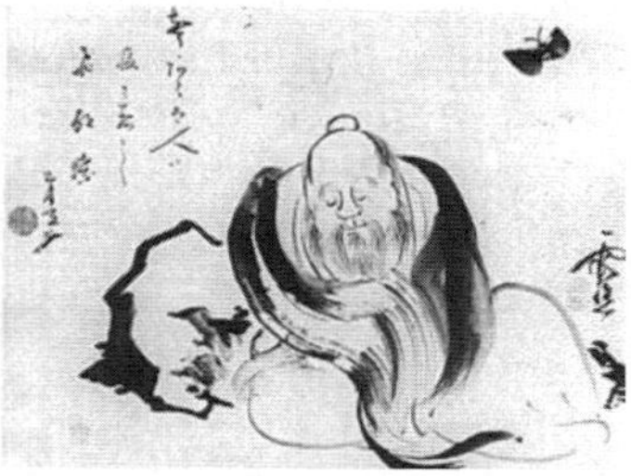

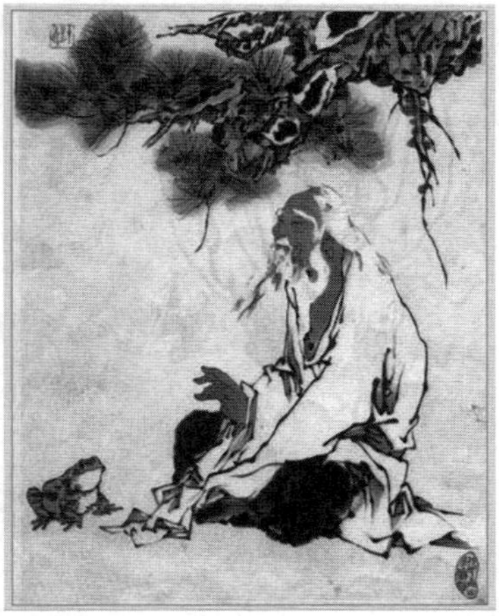

Zhuangzi dreaming the butterfly, public domain, Lu Zhi, 1496–1576). Public domain.

The Now

The almost undefinable topic – when you start to ponder it you realize all the rest we are clinging to is worthless by comparison – for it does not exist outside of the now. The Now is the real object of all valuable investigations.

Scott M. Hitchcock says the following about T-computers and the Origins of Time in the Brain:

Recent research has identified the components of the brain that appear to time label information from observed sensory events, store the labeled information in memory and then using the time labels for two or more events to compute their time differences, time intervals, elapsed times or "lifetimes". Time differences are the basis of the "time" numbers we read from clocks and compute in our brains. Time is our map of change. Maps are abstractions of information and can be used to construct useful devices such as space-time. A general time computer or T-computer model is outlined that shows how observed signals can be processed into time labeled information states, infostates, by our instruments or our brains. The observer can communicate the "time" computed for observed events using consciousness and language signals to drive sound signals in the vocal cords for instance. The "problem of time" is near a realistic solution now that the brain's T-computer has been identified. The brain is the "local" creator of time, space, and space-time as our special maps of the reality we "observe" and participate in.[138]

The great simulator is another word for Hitchcock's T Computer.

When Hitchcock uses the term consciousness, he presupposes that consciousness is attached to his T computer.

A more modern word for T Computer appears to be a VR machine with a dynamic fovea.

Time Buffer – Temporal Fovea

The technology of the body enables a time buffer and so does advanced artificial technology (a VR machine).

Mind time

Our evidence indicates that a substantial period of neural activity (500 msec of "on" time) is in fact required to elicit awareness of the sensory event. That delay provides a sufficient psychological opportunity during which unconscious brain patterns can alter the content of the experience before awareness of it appears. Indeed, the experimental phenomenon of subjective referral of a conscious sensory experience backward in time provides relatively direct evidence for one kind of modulatory distortion of the subjective experience. The delayed experience is subjectively timed as if it were not delayed at all.[139]

Eva Ruhnau says that the brain is a machine that produces a simultaneity out of non-linearly distributed events, much as general relativity does.[140]

What would the "now" of a Neosentient entity be, in the sense that a whale has slow time and a bird has fast time? By the way – this proves there is no flowing time in nature. Time could be considered as an illusion but this is too weak a term, because time is something we "eat" all of the time. We are breathing it. Thus we live under this Heraclitean fist.

Brian Massumi

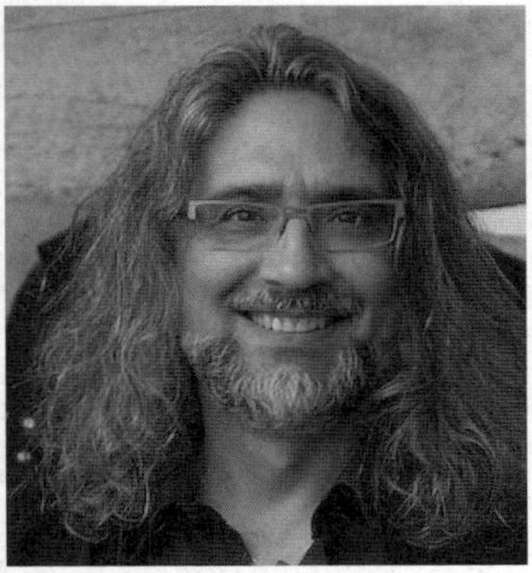

2010 Ivars Gravlejs, E-text and Textiles Latvia, courtesy of Brian Massumi.

The human observer must accept what Brian Massumi calls the "smudging" of the now, where our limits and qualities of perception become the "now" as we know it, lived within the parameters of our human framing. In his work *Parables for the Virtual*, Massumi, in the chapter entitled "Strange horizon: buildings, biograms, and the body topologic," states:

Experience smudges. You get a thirdness: a supplemental effect not reducible to the two stimuli's respective durations considered separately. You get a supernumerary difference, a qualitative difference arising from the interrelation of recursive durations. To put it bluntly, you get a relational time-smudge. A kind of ***hypertime****. Think about it. Since any lapse of time is infinitely divisible, and at every instant there must be some kind of stimulus arriving through one sense channel or another, if you try to fill in what happens in the half-second lapses of awareness, things get downright hallucinogenic. Say at .01 seconds a second loop begins; at .02 seconds another begins […] but at .015 seconds there will have been an intervening beginning, and also at .0125. You're left with an infinite multiplication of recursively durational emergent awarenesses, madly smudging each other. You get an exponentially self-complicating relational mess.*[141]

Fractal Time

Susie Vrobel in *Fractal Time*[142] resolves some of these mysteries. See also her book *Simultaneity* with World Scientific of 2008.

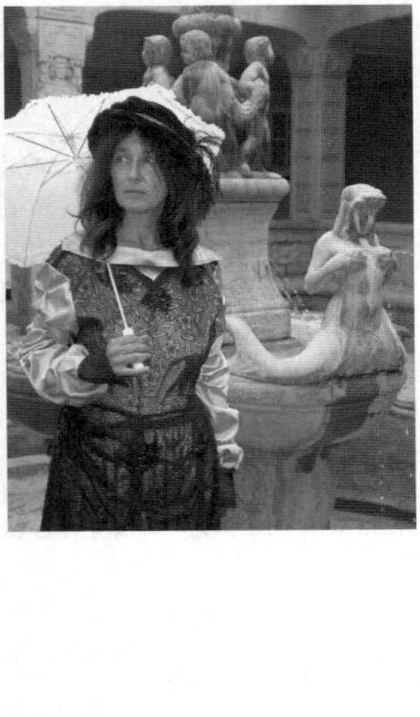

Image courtesy of Susie Vrobel.

Peter Cariani

How will the Neosentient employ pattern matching and generative pattern recombination in the service of creativity? Will it come to compose music?

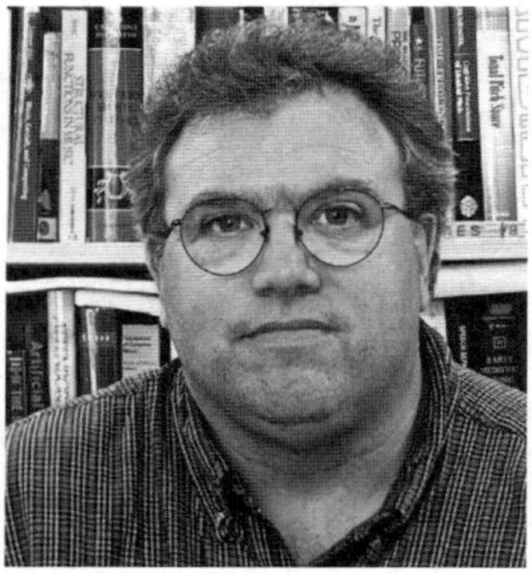

Image of Cariani, courtesy of Cariani.

Temporal codes and neural temporal processing architectures (neural timing nets) that potentially subserve perception of pitch and rhythm are discussed. We address (1) properties of neural interspike interval representations that may underlie basic aspects of musical tonality (e.g. octave similarities), (2) implementation of pattern-similarity comparisons between interval representations using feed-forward timing nets, and (3) representation of rhythmic patterns in recurrent timing nets. Computer simulated interval-patterns produced by harmonic complex tones whose fundamentals are related through simple ratios showed higher correlations than for more complex ratios. Similarities between interval-patterns produced by notes and chords resemble similarity-judgements made by human listeners in probe tone studies. Feed-forward timing nets extract common temporal patterns from their inputs, so as to extract common pitch irrespective of timbre and vice versa. Recurrent timing nets build up complex temporal expectations over time through repetition, providing a means of representing rhythmic patterns. They constitute alternatives to oscillators and clocks, with which they share many common functional properties.[143]

Lieselotte Heller invented the idea of the "eigen tone," a pervasive footprint in every human consciousness as unique as the soul itself (personal communication 2009). See also Anthony Moore's related work about musical tones and time, and time reversal.

Dennis Parsons' 1976 discretized melodies form the largest meaningful subset of a "universal library" so far. This set of meaningful melodies is a finite subset of the smallest universal library known. Modern data mining methods could be used to automatically identify beautiful new melodies ("artificial Mozart technology"). See also Csikszentmihalyi —Creativity: Flow and Psychology of Discovery and Invention.

The Now Equation

We ask, what would an equation of "the now" include as variables? Certainly the now has a conscious observer at its center. Sleeping defines gaps in the now. An equation of the now would in part take into account all lived moments. Everything is running through it but it never changes, only its content changes. This could be articulated as an average, as a probability based on life expectancy or as an actuality of conscious "experienced" moments lived over a lifetime. Everett writes not of probabilities but of measures. This suggests he is always thinking of observer-centric experience as it has been summed via the measure of this experience. These lived moments are parsed as spatially located experiences existing across a "discontinuous" continuum. The duration of the life of the body is this continuum. A time machine would make now jumps. Sleep is a form of time machine. The now is always observer-centric. The now is the collapse of the wave function as revealed to the human/observer interface so one would have to take into account the time of the arising of the now, a famous Buddhist idea. The body is an embodiment of assignment conditions imposed onto the individual's biofunctionality. Benjamin Libet points at the delay of biological functioning that contributes to the "conscious" now and this would also need to be taken into account. This fabrication of the now through pseudo simultaneity is implicit in the blueprint for the Benevolence Engine (see figure at the end of this book). It is always now and there is no way to say where or when it is, except in special relativity where the now is condensed into a single point in the physical universe as the provable feat of simultaneity. It is also the collapse of any world, classical or not, onto the eternal present. What does eternal mean here? Simultaneity is observer-centered in a miraculous fashion. We only know that a now will be arising in the future if we are alive to perceive it. The now is only a point in time – so this is not really the now. Speed and locality, as well as a state of fever, all affect its content but not its substance.

It is always now so we may remember the soul of our sweetheart.

Although there exist spaces where time machines might be naturally occurring like in a black hole, a *world change machine* could only exist in an environment where an observer exists.

The term "future" may no longer be strictly applicable because we may lose our identity as Hinduism describes as well as quantum mechanics.

Bell in his book *Speakable and Unspeakable in Quantum Mechanics* states:

"Quantum mechanics for cosmologists" […] show(s) my conviction that, despite numerous solutions of the problem "for all practical purposes", a problem of principle remains. It is that of locating precisely the boundary between what must be described by wavy quantum states on the one hand, and in Bohr's "classical terms" on the other. The elimination of this shifty boundary has for me always been the main attraction […][144]

Bell continues mentioning his friend the Dalai Lama in this pure physics context. He describes how we would not realize if we lived a new life in a new body after the last life, as Hinduism assumes. Then he contracts the lifetimes without memory of the previous one, from years to months, to days, to hours, to seconds, to milliseconds, to microseconds, to fentoseconds. He thereby arrives at Everett's theory in a new way because the many different worlds no longer exist separately in space but rather successively in time. This is a revolutionary idea, which most likely is correct. Both Hinduism and physics would be reinforced. And of course Heraclitus' joystick. It has testable consequences though, the so-called Bell non-locality which was already described by Everett as a testable prediction. The fact that this is a reality in physics amounts to a virtual proof of the Everett–Bell Theory. But the reader should be aware that this statement is a secret.

The whole thing becomes rounder and more shiny like the surface of a chestnut.

By the way the Now does not exist in physics and there is no way even to prove it exists.

Dreams

"Waking life is the most palpable dream."
Descartes, *Meditations*.
Dreams play out in a hyper now. Dreams may arise from a suddenly freed access to the higher resolution screen. The space of words is tightly tied to the lower resolution screen that becomes superimposed on the big screen from another dimensionality, enabling the time of writing to intermingle with the current Now.

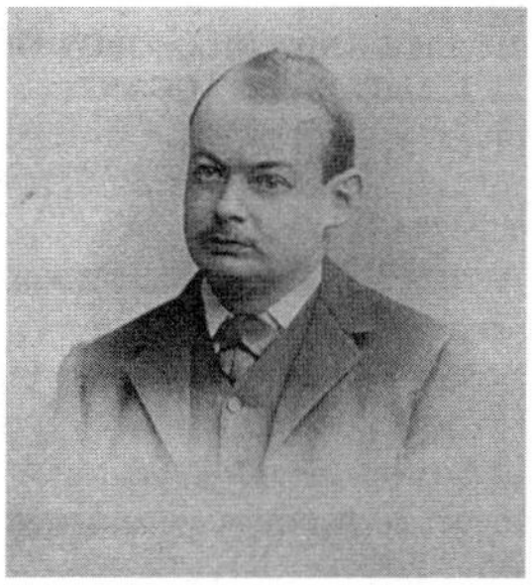

McTaggart, courtesy of William Sweet.

Will machines dream?
The *NeoNow* – Title of a future book?
There is a cruel element to the now, hopefully a joke.
We must acknowledge Neo – The protagonist in the popular science fiction movie, *The Matrix*, Directed by Larry and Andy Wachowski, 1999.
Disprovability of the now – McTaggart's Paradox[145] of 1908 – McTaggart's Theorem.
John (McTaggart Ellis) McTaggart (1866–1925)

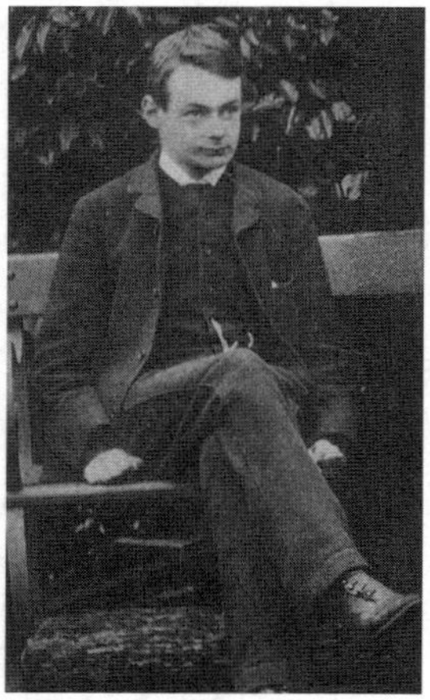

McTaggart in 1891, courtesy of William Sweet.

There is not only an arrow for time but also an arrow for space (especially when you are riding in a car). Being thrown from one world into the other from moment to moment also has consequences for space. Is there a causality to that? This would be another Everettian enlargement of physics.

A new relativistic thermodynamics is also at stake. Gravity and heat have never been brought together. Hans-Guenther Stadelmayr is of the same opinion. Lev Landau wrote a paper on that in the 1930s but the field didn't take off. Donald Lynden-

Bell promoted the topic in subsequent decades. Roger Penrose also touched on this in his 1987, *The Emperor's New Mind*. The synthesis still awaits cosmology being unified with thermodynamics– the big bang being replaced by a gravitational thermodynamics. That is the idea.[146]

This is a thermodynamic dream.

Chance is an Element of the Necessary

Chance, chaos, quantum chance, and the real chance of Everett need to be connected with Gödelism – maybe via Bruno Marchal. The world choice of Everett's is the birth of microscopic assignment conditions.

Gödel Time Machine and the Illusion of Time[147]

John L. Bell[148]

From "Time and Causation" in Gödel's Universe.

In 1949 the great logician Kurt Gödel constructed the first mathematical models of the universe in which travel into the past, in theory at least, is possible. Within the framework of Einstein's general theory of relativity Gödel produced cosmological solutions to Einstein's field equations which contain closed time-like curves, that is, curves in spacetime which, despite being closed, still represent possible paths of bodies. An object moving along such a path would travel back into its own past, to the very moment at which it "began" the journey. More generally, Gödel showed that, in his "universe", for any two points P and Q on a body's track through spacetime (its world line), such that P temporally precedes Q, there is a timelike curve linking P and Q on which Q temporally

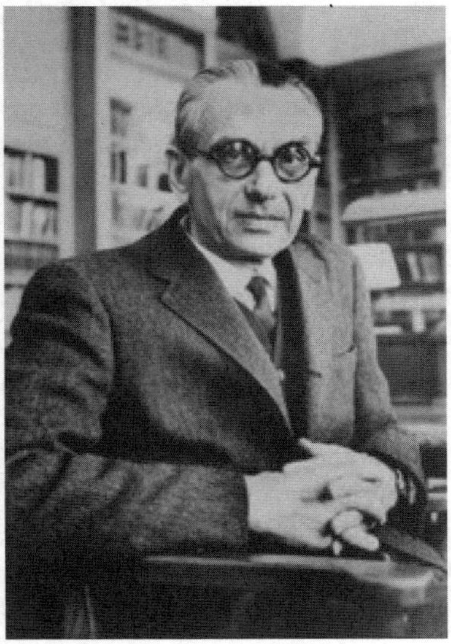

Gödel Seated, photo courtesy of The Shelby White and Leon Levy Archives Center, Historical Studies-Social Science Library, Institute for Advanced Study, Princeton.

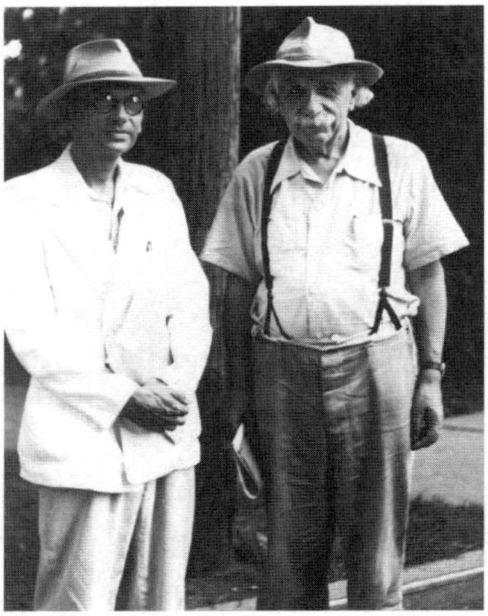

Gödel and Einstein – Richard F. Arens photographer. From The Shelby White and Leon Levy Archives Center, Institute for Advanced Study, Princeton, NJ, USA.

precedes P. This means that, in principle at least, one could board a "time machine" and travel to any point of the past [...]

Einstein was flabbergasted and did not respond as enthusiastically as Gödel had expected because this finding of Gödel proved that something was wrong with his theory. This flaw has not yet been identified. This represents a fallback into a medieval past of physics in the eyes of Einstein and shows that one little element in the Einstein equations is not yet optimally tuned.

Neosentience is a re-understanding of human sentience. This is connected to all of the above topics. And as we just realized the process starting at this seminal moment in time and space in this book is the beginning of a Borges forking library which synthesizes the two strands of exo and endo thinking.

It is not impossible that a hard to decipher link exists between Borges on the one hand and Everett on the other.

We conclude that, if time travel into the past is possible (and feasible), and no restrictions are placed on the purposes to which such travel is put, then the universe must branch. Accordingly we have three possibilities:

1. *Time travel is impossible.*
2. *Time travel is possible, with no "changing of the past."*
3. *Time travel is possible, and the universe ramifies.*

Ramifying universes have arisen in connection with quantum mechanics, in the so-called many-worlds interpretation. In this account, when certain types of interaction occur, typically, measurements, the universe divides into different branches, one for each possible outcome of the interaction. Observers branch (or split) as well, and each observer on each branch sees one of the possible outcomes. It is interesting to note that recent work by Deutsch et al. has shown that time travel with no constraints, that is, situation (3), is compatible with the many-worlds interpretation. But again observe that here time travel takes place from the present of one "branch" of the universe into the "past" of another branch. Gödel's puzzle arises with the possibility of time travel within a single universe, and for this the problem of devising convincing "temporal interdicts" remains.[149]

S. Hawking and G.S.R. Ellis
The Large Scale Structure of Space-Time

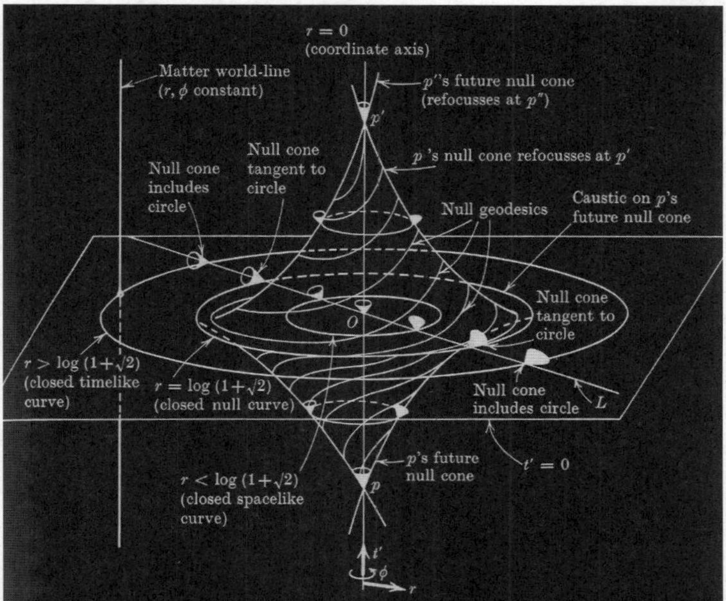

FIGURE 31. Gödel's universe with the irrelevant coordinate z suppressed. The space is rotationally symmetric about any point; the diagram represents correctly the rotational symmetry about the axis $r = 0$, and the time invariance. The light cone opens out and tips over as r increases (see line L) resulting in closed timelike curves. The diagram does not correctly represent the fact that *all* points are in fact equivalent.

A picture of Gödel's solution in a rotating cosmos. Fair Use

Einstein

Einstein sought to define the simplest way to describe the world. In this book we seek to provide a set of salient concepts without attempting yet to define the unity between them.

Einstein
Stratification of the scientific system
The aim of science is, on the one hand, a comprehension, as complete as possible, of the connection between the sense experiences in their totality, and on the other hand, the accomplishment of this aim by the use of a minimum of primary concepts and relations. (Seeking, as far as

possible, logical unity in the world picture, i.e. paucity in logical elements.)

Science concerns the totality of the primary concepts, i.e. concepts directly connected with sense experiences, and theorems connecting them. In its first stage of development, science does not contain anything else. Our everyday thinking is satisfied on the whole with this level. Such a state of affairs cannot, however, satisfy a spirit which is really scientifically minded; because, the totality of concepts and relations obtained in this manner is utterly lacking in logical unity.

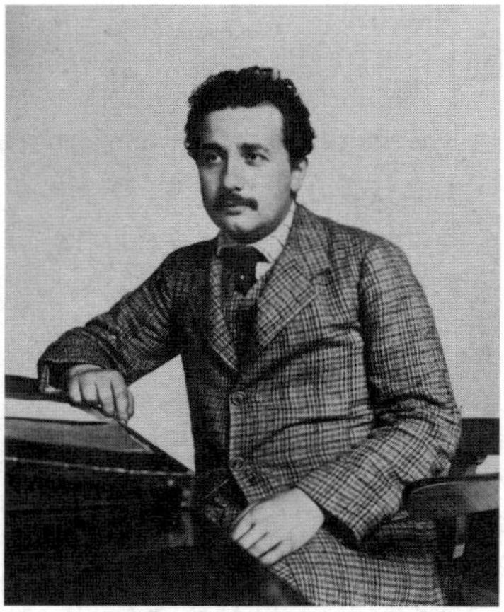
Einstein, photo courtesy of the Albert Einstein Archives, Hebrew University of Jerusalem.

In order to supplement this deficiency, one invents a system poorer in concepts and relations, a system retaining the primary concepts and relations of the "first layer" as logically derived concepts and relations. This new "secondary system" pays for its higher logical unity by having, as its own elementary concepts (concepts of the second layer), only those which are no longer directly connected with complexes of sense experiences. Further striving for logical unity brings up to a tertiary system, still poorer in concepts and relations, for the deduction of the concepts and relations of the secondary (and so indirectly of the primary) layer. Thus the story goes on until we have arrived at a system of the greatest conceivable unity, and of the greatest poverty of concepts of the logical foundations, which are still compatible with the observation made by our senses. We do not know whether or not this ambition will ever result in a definite system. If one is asked for his opinion, he is inclined to answer no.[150]

But we would think the answer is yes.

Non-local Coupling

Just as Bell commented above on Everett so Everett already commented on Bell in 1957 before Bell had even had his idea, namely, that non-local phenomena magically centered on an observer will be found in physics. Everett saw that this superluminal non-locality is not in defiance of causality because both sub-measurements would converge sub-luminally on the experiencing observer; so that their mysteriousness would become a characteristic of this particular observer's world and universe.

The branching would be a private itinerancy of a little monk in his own Buddhist garden – that is, our whole universe. Compare Ichiro TSUDA's notion of Chaotic Itinerancy.

Cooper Pair

Cooper pair in superconductivity – two electrons are apart without friction and exchange their identities.

Cooper Multiple – multiple electrons are apart without friction, and exchange their identities? This might include n electrons.

What relationship does a Cooper pair have to non-local activity? This is a new question. Here we have a splitting and a convergence simultaneously. What does the reader say? This is an open research topic again.

Forking and folding into a whole is not a contradiction.

The Body is Simultaneously a Hierarchy and a Heterarchy.

Who Needs Emotions? The Brain Meets the Robot

I proposed, then, to start, in some sense, in reverse – with a system that has the capacity for feelings. From this beginning, we can build the capacity for emotions of varying complexity and for the flexible, value-driven social behavior that animals exhibit. Without such a beginning, we will always be mimicking only aspects of behavior. To guide this enterprise, we can ask ourselves what criteria we use to assign feelings and emotions to other people.[151]

This approach would thus not only achieve the desired design of robots with which humans can interact socially but also hold out the opportunity to teach us something about how feeling, emotion, and social behavior depend on one another and about how they function in humans and other animals.[152]

Simple Languages – Deb Roy

Given the immense complexity of language use, it is critical to focus on a manageable subset of the phenomena if we are to gain traction. Rather than partition the problem along traditional pragmatic-semantic-syntactic-phonological boundaries, we can instead take a "vertical" slice through all of these levels by modeling simple but complete language use. Language use by young children is a paradigm case.

Children acquire language by hearing and using words embedded in the rich context of everyday physical and social interaction. Words have meaning for children not because they have memorized dictionary definitions but rather because they have learned to connect words to experiences in their environment. Language directed to, and produced by young children tends to be tightly bound to the immediate situation. Children talk about the people, objects, and events in the here-and-now. The foundations of linguistic meaning reside, at least in large part, in the cognitive representations and physical processes that enable this kind of situated language use.

[…] A toddler's use of language nonetheless demonstrates many of the hallmarks of mature adult language: descriptive and directive speech acts consisting of compositions of symbols that relate to the child's environment and goals. How is it that young children produce and interpret simple speech acts that simultaneously refer (are about something) and serve social functions? […] A detailed mechanistic analysis of speech acts used by children has yet to be offered in the cognitive sciences. Any such model must explain aspects of perception, memory, motor control, planning, inference, and reasoning capacities that play a role in situated language use […] I will describe a model of embodied, situated speech act interpretation that is motivated by these questions. The goal of this model is to make progress towards a mechanistic explanation of meaning, so first we need a working definition of "meaning".[153]

Micro-time Reversal

A movie can be cut into short subsets running forward and backward in time – but this is not intimidating because we already know the preferred direction of time. Unlike this, micro-time reversal shows its intimidating face. If both time directions are equally real, what are the consequences?

Boltzmann, Einstein and Everett provided relative-state formulations. Einstein always considered Boltzmann as his master. Boltzmann's idea is very simple: Two copies of the universe which differ only in the direction of time are one and the same universe. Leibniz and Boscovich could already have said the same thing, although they apparently did not do so.

Boltzmann's finding has an important corollary. A time reversal in a subsystem of the universe is equivalent to a time reversal in the rest of the universe. In particular, a time reversal in the observer is equivalent to a time reversal in the external world. [... in the case that the Observer would not be time reversed].

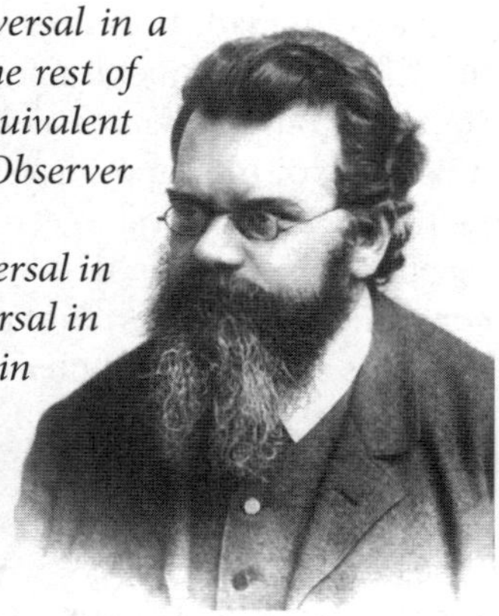

Boltzmann.
Public domain.

At first sight, this is an innocuous statement since a "time reversal in the observer" seems as unlikely an event to expect as a time reversal in the whole universe. Note that the latter requires that all particles in the universe reverse their directions of motion simultaneously. This could only occur spontaneously if all particles collided simultaneously in such a way that all momentums become zero at the same moment – a virtually infinitely unlikely event. The same argument at first sight applies to an observing subsystem.

Only if the observer is very simple – a single oscillator – is it trivially correct that relative to it, the world undergoes a time reversal after every half period.

[...] It will be shown that the "single-pendulum observer" actually is a prototype for a much larger class of observers – including possibly ourselves. Boltzmann's microscopic relativity would then force a radically new view of reality upon us.[154]

How might reversible computing play into a Neosentient's potential for knowing?

This will provide insights into time's arrow and micro-reversibility. Boltzmann had the first proof of the world being microscopically reversible. He proved that a world running forward in time and a world running backward in time on the micro level are indistinguishable.

Rolf Landauer worked in the frame of Boltzmann via the continuum, and new ideas come from Fredkin, Toffoly, Wolfram, and Finkelstein in relation to the discrete. This leads over to the bigger topic of endophysics.

Edward Fredkin

Edward Fredkin built the first reversible universe which he called Digital Information Mechanics (DIM). The people who followed him are by no means DIMwits. This is a dream of Boltzmann come true. Unfortunately Fredkin only has a discrete universe. From such a universe you can build up a seemingly non-discrete universe. Any computer simulation of a continuous universe will be discrete so it will be related to Fredkin's universe. There are two continua that allow one to make artificial universes and brains – the first is macroscopic with a brain made of neurons simulated in a computer, if we implement the Brain Equation in a discrete machine. It may also function as a non-discrete entity via an electrochemical computer but this again can be modeled by a discrete machine. Yet we must remember the model is not the thing in itself. This question we leave open – is the model co-extensive with the entity/universe it represents? Andy Hilgartner says no in Korzybski's footsteps. Stephen Smale states that an analog computer is infinitely more powerful than a digital computer. Klaus Peter Zauner also says similar things. He discovered that in between the numbers a digital computer can cover an almost infinite realm of numbers that are usually overlooked.

Seven-level Scheme

There are big unseen continents in the future of digital computing. We are still on the macro level. On the micro level another infinity comes into view. This is Boltzmann's view. All the machines we have had to date have not been reversible in the frictionless sense.

We present here different levels of scientific accuracy in the reductionist program.

These are the only known non-arbitrary programs in the Cartesian attempt to reduce the world to a machine.

First level is macroscopic irreversible deterministic discrete (digital computer).

Second level is macroscopic irreversible continuous deterministic (digital computer more completely described).

Third level is macroscopic irreversible analog-type indeterministic continuous analog computer or brain.

Fourth level is microscopic reversible deterministic discrete (Verlet–Diebner–Sonnleitner).

Fifth level is microscopic reversible quantum probabilistic (quantum computer).

Sixth level is microscopic reversible quantum deterministic (Everett).

Seventh level is microscopic reversible deterministic continuous (exo).

The world can be built up on a maximally ideal micro level.[155]

Most people are hovering somewhere on this scheme without telling everyone else their particular levels and limitations of view. We believe it is important for future scientists to articulate the level to which their approach belongs.

This is a very comprehensive Aristotelian attitude for which we ask the forgiveness of the reader.

All lower levels can emulate all upper levels … (almost)

The subjective domain of reality which includes color, pain, pleasure, and the now is still not touched by the seven levels described.

We seek to develop a machine like the human that simultaneously can explore all of these levels.

Instead of complementarity – a septupleistic perspective (given the seven perspective levels above) can be explored.

We ask, what is the post-machine approach?

Our successors will have to do this (if we don't finish this).

Time's Arrow[156]

"Time flies like an arrow, fruit flies like a banana."
Groucho Marx[157]

If there exists a micro-time reversal, then there must also be a micro-space reversal.

Nevertheless space does not have an arrow itself as far as we know. We don't believe in time's arrow as being something fundamental in physics. The binding point of where consciousness is attached to physics causes the illusion of time's movement. The given Now changes perhaps even in a timeless "jump" like fashion which we wouldn't notice, even if the leaps were large.

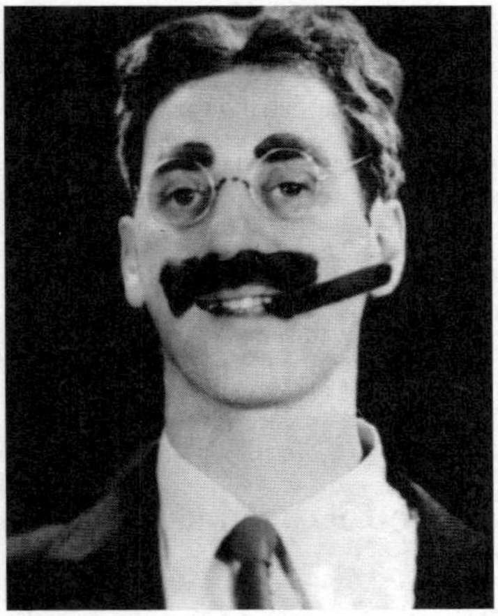

Julius Henry "Groucho" Marx, Public domain.

Thinking is Physics

The first Newtonian discovery is the LAWs (of the machine of the world) analogous to Buddha's web of causation. The second is the discovery of the initial conditions (IC) of the machine of the world. This represents a kind of global assignment. The third discovery in the same context and spirit is the assignment conditions (AC). The same machine with the same initial conditions looks and is totally different depending on from which internal perspective it is watched. A trivial example is the assignment of the body. Whether I am the beggar or the rich man is something which doesn't change one iota in the world including its initial conditions, but makes a difference of the whole world for me, for example, if I am going to die at the next moment. But these "intuitive" assignment conditions are only macroscopic and trivial even though the Book of Job talks about them. The real assignment conditions are microscopic. They determine the now and the quantum reality. They cut deeper than a knife into every blood cell or electron. They cannot be manipulated so far.

Gödel's time machine was a first brave effort at escaping the laws of causation including assignment conditions. It is a great pity that recent developments in general relativity seem to rule out Gödel's solution to the Einstein equation so that another stab at immortality will be necessary. Since we can set the assignment conditions of a lower level intelligence, this implies the question of whether a "program" can force the "programmer" to respond.[158] And enlightenment is of course older than Gödel.

Is language physics? This question is glistening in many shades.

A breathing space

We see this strange flipping over of positions in the mutual space swapping of two spin-bearing particles in the same orbit or in super fluidity and the formation of a Bose–Einstein condensate. This is a very active area of empirical research at the time being. There are many Nobel Prizes in this field at the moment. Time's arrow is first an illusion (from the point of view of physics), and second it has a direction that is not externally defined but nonetheless exists.

Give me a place to stand and I shall move the earth! (Archimedes)

Alfred Korzybski – *Science and Sanity* – *New Theory of Language*

General semantics

Korzybski's work culminated in the founding of a discipline that he called general semantics (GS). As Korzybski explicitly said, GS should not be confused with semantics, a different subject. The basic principles of general semantics, which include time binding, are outlined in *Science and Sanity*, published in 1933. In 1938 Korzybski founded the Institute of General Semantics and directed it until his death. This is both linguistic and extra linguistic in its scope, because he tried to find the defining difference between humans and other animals. His most influential current successor is C. Andy Hilgartner.

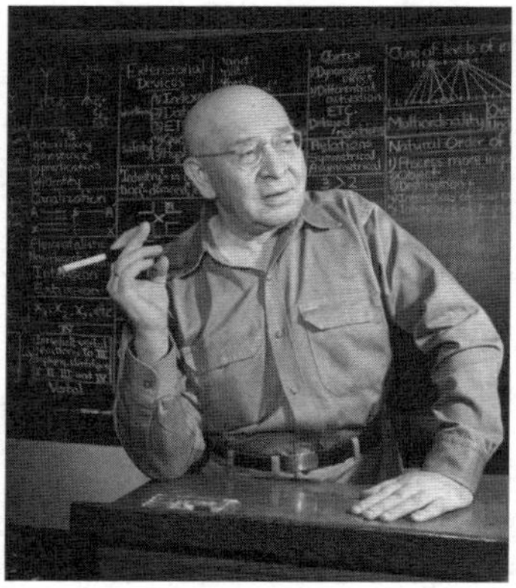

Alfred Korzybski smoking a cigarette at the Institute of General Semantics. (Photo by Gordon Coster//Time Life Pictures/Getty Images) courtesy Getty Images.

Hilgartner discovered a new logic and wrote down the first artificial grammar (in this logic). He believes that nouns and verbs embody a distinction which is unconsciously

C. Andy Hilgartner by Tim Barcus, staff photographer in the Public Relations Department of Truman State University on 8 January 2008. Courtesy of Barcus.

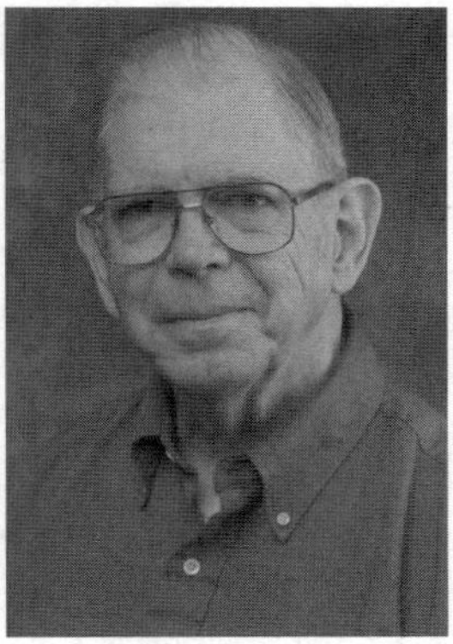

fraudulent. The predicament of humanity – including cruelty and wars – is reduced by him to this invisible, built-in lie, in modern languages. He conjectures that hunter-gatherer societies like the American Indian Societies were immune to this craziness of the post-fertile-crescent, agricultural, and industrial societies. Modern society according to his diagnosis is close to committing planetary suicide in a completely innocent way. It is essentially because Korzybski's discovery of time binding was not appreciated.

What is time binding?

Korzybski was the son of a Polish landowner who owned also many human slave laborers. At the age of 12 he was assigned the task to oversee his father's laborers working on the fields, prompting them to work faster. They told him, Dear Little master, please notice that we are no beasts. In the Polish language there is a common word both for misbehaving people and animals. This forced the boy to wonder what is the difference between a person and a beast which occupied him throughout his entire life. Time Binding and the question of sanity in society were his major topics. Time Binding is the human property of connecting experiences made by earlier generations with the life of subsequent generations. Today, we know that animals have tradition too, for example, monkeys living near the sea shore in Japan invented potato washing before eating them, and let it spread throughout later generations. Also the great apes and gibbons, man's closest relatives, are very humanlike in teaching their offspring survival strategies. Nevertheless, something is missing. Korzybski hoped to find this missing element in language. Hilgartner follows him along this track. There is a competing theory which stipulates that the "suspicion of benevolence," arrived at individually by a toddler in interacting with his mother or father, is the crucial event. However this may be, the spectacular success of Hilgartner in creating the first artificial grammar gives a great weight to the Korzybski school on the planet. General Semantics is much too narrow a term for this development.

If words are not things, or maps are not the actual territory, then, obviously, the only possible link between the objective world and the linguistic world is found in structure, and structure alone.
Alfred Korzybski

Two important characteristics of maps should be noticed. A map is not the territory it represents, but, if correct, it has a similar structure to the territory, which accounts for its usefulness.
Alfred Korzybski

Whatever you say it is, it isn't. *Alfred Korzybski*[159]

Ceci n'est pas une pipe. *Magritte*

C. Andy Hilgartner

I grew up in a Western Indo-European or WIE language, with English as my native tongue. Furthermore, I became a scientist of the Western Indo-European tradition. So, like most everyone else in this room, I unthinkingly sliced up the world into static, unchanging things that enter into more-or-less transient relations, which, in my WIE language, I designated respectively by means of static, self-identical nouns and not self-identical verbs.

As a youngster, I subscribed to the dualisms, mind/matter and so on, not realizing then that the dualism is simply a projection of the grammar of Western Indo-European languages onto the cosmos. Mind/matter: we take one side as static and the other side as not. Depending on whether we're doing physics or psychology, we can take one side or the other as the static one, that's what we study, and – well, anyway. Eventually, my research led me, forced me, and enabled me to reject and discard the WIE way of slicing up the world. In order to continue my inquiries, I had to overcome the disadvantages imposed by the received knowledge I had assimilated and made my own.

In particular, I disclosed a fundamental theoretical error, the kind of thing that in my opinion no one would willingly subscribe to, knowingly subscribe to, built into the grammar of the Western Indo-European languages and therefore into the foundations of our logics, or mathematics, our sciences, our philosophies, our jurisprudences, our religions. [...] All our linguistic specializations contain this fundamental error. I found ways to discard the error, and, in the process, the grammar of the Western Indo-European languages, at least for me, collapses and I had the opportunity to clear the rubble of the WIE frame of reference out of the way and then managed to generate an alternative frame of reference, which appears more general than any other human viewpoint that I know of. From the very beginning, so to speak, this alternative frame of reference presumes a dynamic cosmos, not a static one, which it describes and evokes by means of a new kind of symbols.

The notation which I devised comes out of these studies, uses no nouns, no verbs, nor any of the parts of speech used in Western Indo-European languages and named in the so-called Latin grammar. Among other advantages, this frame of reference does not utilize the dualisms. It does not utilize any construct of mind or matter, or oppose them as [pause] things that are opposed that you can't bridge between, or however we'd say it, our philosophy, which the exponents of the Western Indo European frame of reference seem unable to discard even when they want to. I've used this frame of reference to describe an account for human behaving-and experiencing, a pair of related topics systematically split apart within Western Indo European frames of reference, and to criticize and to propose revisions to various fields of Western Indo-European science.[160]

Benjamin Whorf also greatly stimulated Hilgartner's thought by showing how radically different languages can be in their shaping of unique mental universes.

Socrates – I know that I know nothing.

Literal translation: I know that I am someone who knows nothing. (sýnoida emautō oudén eidós)

"The Need for a New Language, Especially within Science"
C. A. Hilgartner

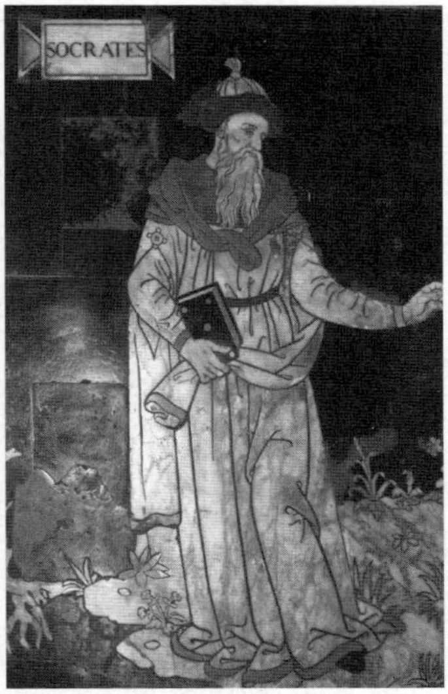

Detail of Socrates on the "Allegory of the hill of knowledge" by Pinturicchio, 1505–06. Marble pavement in the nave of the Duomo, Siena, Italy. Courtesy of Sacred Destinations.

I present not just a new "idea", but rather, an actuality – a frame of reference new to the human race, and now ready for us humans to use.

I consider it a notational language – or at least, as including a notational language – of the "Let's Keep Track of What We Say" type. Regard it not merely as different in detail from other notations, but as structured according to previously unheard-of principles.

To flesh out this frame of reference, I present some details concerning how it developed – how I happened to make some of the discriminations or distinctions (non-identities) on which its structure crucially depends. Then I present some of its implications, including that:

1. *It discloses a fundamental theoretical error encoded in the grammar common to Western Indo-European (WIE) discursive and notational languages – specifically, encoded in the way we distinguish between "noun" and "verb". In my analysis, every "noun" comes to look like a concealed "is of identity" proposition, which violates the requirement that we distinguish between Name and Thing Named (Frege) or between Map and Territory (Korzybski). To express this violation in words, calling the be-whiskered furry-faced organism by the noun "cat" amounts to asserting "cat(name) identical with cat(thing)".*
2. *The act of unconcealing this hidden assumption, followed by the act of rejecting and replacing it with the Postulate of Non-identity, brings about the collapse of the WIE grammar, and with it, the collapse of the linguistic specializations based on it – the WIE logics, mathematics, sciences, philosophies, jurisprudences, religions, etc.*
3. *Before I unconcealed this hidden assumption, I had found that I could not write a non-WIE notation – I didn't know HOW (mainly because I kept using two KINDS of terms, analogous to "nouns" and "verbs"). After I unconcealed this hidden assumption, I COULD AND DID write a non-WIE notational language, with no "nouns" or "verbs" (or any other WIE "parts of speech") in it.*[161]

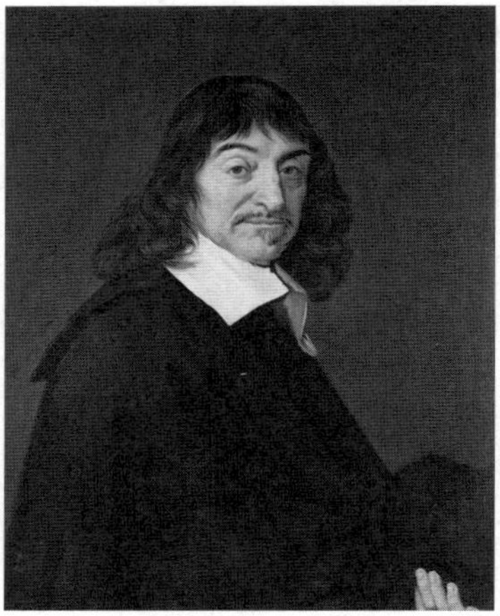

René Descartes. After Frans Hals, Portrait du philosophe René Descartes (1596–1650). Public domain.

Descartes – I doubt therefore I am.

Toward new languages for the Neosentient. The Neosentient will potentially become multi-lingual. They will learn natural language and potentially a new generative machinic language that would arise out of the Neosentient's assumed machinic culture and a broad understanding of systems theory. The Neosentient might want to apply Hilgartner's principles to their own meta-human languages.

The Second Force

Being recognizable as being different requires that there is some sort of force; otherwise you could not distinguish it.

The brain generates forces – that enable the controlling of behavior and of thought in general.
Physical force and conceptual force – what is their relationship?
Could it be that a thought has a mass or is a moving energy distribution?
One force is simulation, one force is reality – we ask, what is the interplay between simulation and reality…

Peter Weibel once tried to implement a microscopically reversible computer world that connects via energetically reversible links to the physical world of an outside human player. Hans Diebner was concerned with this idea. Since the proposal remains unimplemented, the secret desire to overcome quantum mechanics with this gadget device remains unconsummated.

Energies are employed to propagate simulated forces. Energies are employed to propagate actual physical forces. What is the relation between these two energies when a Neosentient exhibits physical behavior in actual space? It is again the same problem as with the now. In a non-now moment, even our own brain is not conscious. Consciousness exists only in the narrow confines of the now.

Perhaps the hardest thing for the human to accept about intelligent machines is whether or not these force fields are genuine and reach through and touch – like a human emotion.

Note that in the non-now there is nothing of this touch of emotion, either. So the real question is whether a machine can be given a now.

In the now we can think of past and future but the non-now itself lives only if re-transformed into the Now – if it is articulated in a being in a real now.

This is a very abstract poetic thought.

World Change Techniques

The capability to understand observers on the micro level implies the ability to build world change machines. This technology is still under construction. World Change has never been accomplished so far, although some disciples of Everett – including his daughter – went so far as to experiment with it, throwing in their lives for good in the process.

Buddha can perhaps be alluded to very timidly at this point. He was woken up at the age of 30 by recalling a pain from his earlier youth, that his mother had inflicted upon him. It might have been the greatest crime of history or perhaps the opposite. This second possibility dawned on him when he recalled the last words of his mother who had died in childbed, after giving birth to him. She asked her younger sister whom she had called on to marry Buddha's father, and both to as dearly love her son as she would have done herself. This was a double bind. But the double bind could be resolved. For 30 years he suffered under the impact of his mother having forced the world after her death to propagate a verdict of hers that could not be undone. Whenever they told him how much they loved him, they would invariably add, explicitly or not, 'but we will never be able to love you as much again as your poor mother did who unfortunately died when you were born – and you were the reason' (in the logic of a child). Was this not a crime of unforgivable proportion? It took him 30 years to realize that this was not a crime but the greatest manifestation of love that ever was dared to be said. For of course she was not omnipotent even though she was infinitely benevolent. Should one refrain from this power of imposing an infinitely good scent on the future? For any ordinary non-benevolent act, this would be counter-productive. But in the context of the special relationship that she built up between her and him, this was a unique invention with an unlimited force. This force suddenly swept him from his feet and turned him around infinitely many times – so he became the second Buddha.

Definitions of Life

There are multiple types of life including vegetative life – plant life and cellular life, and biochemical life – and there is animal physiological life or brain life, and strangely this brain life is an evolutionary product which is independent of the nature of the vegetative substrate. For example, if we had sentient beings on Jupiter they would have a completely different biochemistry but their brain would predictably function along the very same mathematical principles – just as in the animal kingdom with the snails and the vertebrates and the insects and mollusks – the brains in each case have independently emerged from quite different types of hardware but nonetheless are always the same functionally speaking. So the Brain Equation is emancipated from biochemical evolution. If you wish, vegetative life and conscious life are two different kinds of life – so the vegetative life and conscious forms of life are intrinsically dissociated. The Neosentient would implement the traveling salesman-type mathematics which is solved by a particular variety of machines – so biology and new types of machines would be supporting this higher level form of consciousness on an equal footing. Accordingly consciousness would also be emancipated from biochemistry in exactly the same sense as an artificial consciousness functioning in the manner of Hilary Putnam – The brain in a vat. We are now in search for the name of such life after five centuries of thought in this direction … We would suggest "neolife" vs vegetative vs animal life?

So far, Alife as a discipline is not focusing on higher level brain functions as we are – the simulating of real life neosentience. Alife in general is not as "noble" as the simulation of artificial brains. There is a value difference between Alife and biochemical life. Alife includes artificial intelligence. It must be noted that vegetative Alife would not qualify to be living. The combinatorial potentials of real chemistry are much more complex. So Alife would only cut out a very small island compared to the chemical domain.

As soon as we simulate behavior in the sense of ethology (adaptive behavior in space), this simulation is much like the real thing because it serves the same brain equation. There is a qualitative difference between instantiating the system in real space and being instantiated in a simulation system, not coupled to reality. Both instantiations take a particular kind of interface to become articulated. Consciousness seems only to be attached to a "behavioral computer" (a Neosentient computer). The questions surrounding the interface between the brain equation and the world will become important. In an initial instantiation, the system would run as a simulation with a limited physical interface. In a different kind of instantiation the brain equation would need to be able to interact with the larger environment (physical space) via some form of physical interaction – some effectors and sensors enabling the system to function interactively in a particular physical environment as explored via a robotic entity.

Niels Birbaumer

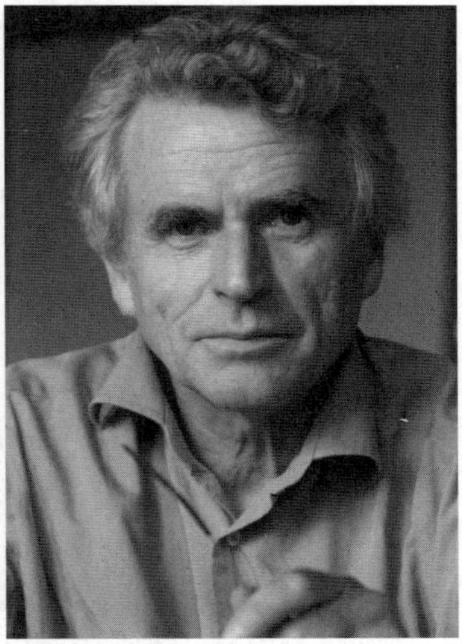
Niels Birbaumer, courtesy Birbaumer.

Niels Birbaumer enabled people to move things in space via a non-invasive brain-machine interface. He invented "biofeedback" (his coinage) and defined a relationality between the human brain and a robotic interface. His allegedly comatose patients ("waking") could come to learn via this mechanism. They could learn to move a cursor on a screen just by thinking. He could communicate with these people. And he even asked them if they wanted to go on with their life, even with this limited single artificial effector – their reply was a resounding yes.

If the Neosentient system is instantiated through embodiment, if you live within the language of that embodiment, then there is no conceptual separation – you are directly interfacing with the world, not with a simulation of the world. The parsing of this space of simulation or illusion has a long history in eastern traditions, seeing the world as an illusion. Even in the movie *Matrix*, there is an interface but in that particular case it is with a simulated world (which happens to be "virtually" hidden). Thus, you could have an interface in a purely simulated reality. Perhaps this is the simulation inherent in the study of Endophysics. Going back to Descartes (or perhaps to the traditions of Buddhist thought), we find that there is no way to parse between simulation, reality, and dream. In the present time we are trying to create an interface that enables us to share this simulation/reality/dream space with the Neosentient and to embark on Neosentient to Neosentient interactivity. Or is the very nature of Neosentience related to this pairing, both initially to the human partner and later to other Neosentient entities? (This is the second Cartesian revolution.)

Next we may ask what will the quantum computer tell us about dreams?

Bell's Theorem and the Interface Question

What does Bell's theorem tell us about the interface in general? There are endo worlds (so far we have been talking about dissipative worlds where everything is macroscopic). Yet for Boltzmann, physics is non-dissipative, without friction – everything is microscopic and exactly reversible; this also applies to quantum mechanics by the way. The Boltzmann universe contains particles which were never given a name of their own. "Boltzmann's micro billiard balls" would be a possible name. If you invert friction you get the opposite ("antifriction"), but this is a different story. At any rate there is a macroscopic and a microscopic brain theory. Bell's theorem is understandable as something rational, deterministic, and scientific. The opposite is voodoo. "Real" quantum theory is not voodoo – but so far Everett's theory is the only example.

See *Simulacron 3* by Daniel F. Galoye, 1964 and R. W. Fassbinder – *A Puppeteer's World*, a decade later. (Goldmann, Munich, 1965). *The Matrix* movie is in the footsteps of Galoye's book as well.

A simulated world would be just as fine as the real world. We are making theater theory. The theater of thought in particular.

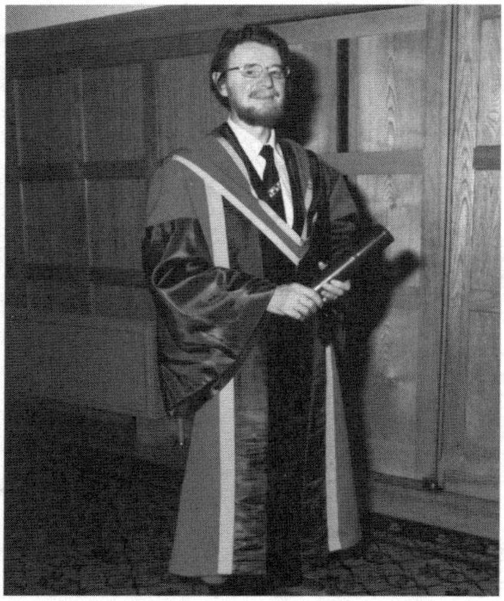

John Stewart Bell, courtesy of Queen's University Belfast.

Hans Diebner

Diebner states: "The photo" was taken in Bogota July 2007 at the presentation of the students' final projects of my art&science course. Some students reversed the idea of the Rössler attractor as a result of the dynamics of a taffy puller and they "re-engineered" the taffy as Rössler attractor. (Letter to one of the Authors)

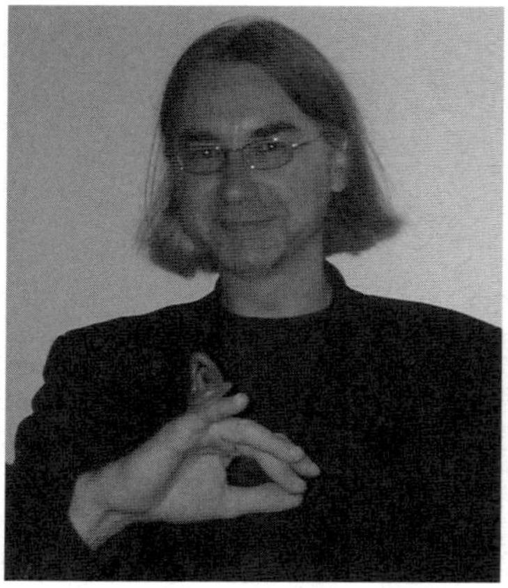

Hans Diebner with a Rössler "Taffy Pull" Candy Ring, courtesy of Diebner.

When do we give over from reversible worlds to non-reversible worlds? We can only in simulation implement a world that is reversible, and one person has explored this notion – Hans Diebner. He successfully implemented a computer-generated Hamiltonian world with Boltzmann's micro-billiards and ran it backward exactly.

Strangely, consciousness would be the same in the forward and the backward direction. We are here on the micro level. The micro level is still virgin territory. Diebner was the first to bridge the gap. He simulated an oscillating chemical reaction – which is a macroscopic machine – in terms of very many microscopically calculated billiard discs (in 2D). He also was the first to be able to run such a calculation backward. He used an exactly reversible computation algorithm. The same results can now in principle be retrieved not just with a self-oscillating simulated liquid but with an excitable simulated liquid. Such a fluid would represent a single nerve cell. As computers become faster, hundreds and millions of such microscopically simulated nerve cells can be combined to replicate a macroscopically simulated artificial brain – or neosentience. The full goal of the Neosentient revolution would for the first time be reached in a simulated reversible universe (all the way up and all the way down).

New Sciences

The smallest possible parsing up to the outermost circle, ever expanding perhaps …

"Nynology" – the science of the Now.

"Interfaciology" – the science of the interface.

Neosentience functions at the intersection of several new sciences, not all of which have been named already.

Reversible Ramifications

Is there a phase transition? A new phenomenon is explored – regarding the question of levels:

The lower level exhibits reversibility and the higher level is not reversible.
This is the only transition of its kind – from reversible to irreversible.

There exists an idea that the transition between reversibility and irreversibility could already be seen in a two-particle, frictionless, classical system. It is two particles in a T-shaped tube – one moving horizontally and the other moving vertically. The force between the two particles is made soft, either repulsive or (in the dual case) attractive. The vertical particle cannot hit the horizontal particle because it is prevented by a barrier from entering the horizontal tube. The interaction is only by Newtonian attraction or repulsion. We also assume that the vertical particle is much heavier and energetic initially than the horizontal particle. Then with repulsive interaction switched on, the heavy energetic vertical particle, on average, will heat up the horizontal particle passing underneath. This follows from the equipartition theorem of statistical mechanics. Now we switch from repulsion to attraction with otherwise the same law (the distance squared force law of Newton). Again, initially the heavy particle has much more energy than the fast light horizontal particle. Will the horizontal particle again gain energy? The answer is no; it will lose energy on average!

If this prediction is correct it almost amounts to a miracle. For what happens if we now invert time in mid-flight after the system has run for a period of time? Of course now the fast particle will be accelerated since the previous dynamics is inverted. This is absolutely transparent but very strange. There must be a difference between the present initial condition with the inverted time and the previous initial condition where time went forward. Boltzmann first had this strange hunch; that there are two kinds of initial conditions – the normal ones and the pathological ones – he called it the "Hypothesis of Molecular Chaos", to describe the "normal" initial conditions. No one understood him in his time, for he had to assume many particles. This was too difficult to follow through mentally. Here suddenly everything is crystal clear. A non-selected initial condition leads to "ordinary" behavior, an exhausted initial condition at the end of a certain running time, leads to counterintuitive behavior. Otherwise, there is no difference between the two. Is this not a miracle?

Obviously, it has to do with Cantor and transfinite accuracy. But then we have only digital, computational accuracy here. So a real scandal is about to develop. Some young person has to be waited for who explains to us the mechanism of the miracle. The upshot is that if the horizontal particle is a fast proton (cosmic ray), and the heavy particle is a slowly moving galaxy, then the fast proton will on average be slowed down as we saw. Therefore, cosmic rays and photons suffer a Hubble-like redshift in the universe. Bye bye big bang?

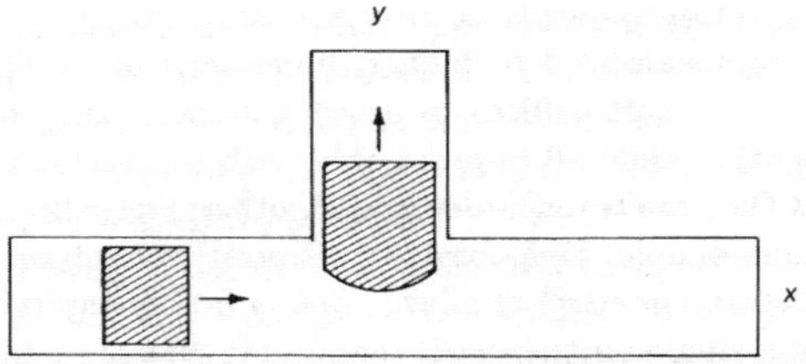

Fig. 1. A 1-D universe of two chaotic billiard balls.

Fredkin started frictionless computing. Frictionless computing is frictionless neosentience.

We are reversible neosentiences while being subjectively irreversible sentiences. This is because our body builds up from physics, and physics is microscopically reversible. Thought combines both the reversible and the nonreversible but plays itself out on the level of the theater floor which is irreversible.

World change attemps to address the reversible level. World change attempts to manipulate the reversible to have causation in the theater of the non-reversible.

What is the relationship between these reversible and irreversible levels?

If you are on the inside of a reversible machine there is no way to prove to yourself this lower level is happening underneath, but there is one method that will work one day. You can manipulate this world on the microlevel, even though you are imprisoned in it.

You can program the value of natural constants like h and c – then h becomes a string of numbers. In principle you can write a message within this string of numbers – so that you can prove that you have succeeded. To some extent this is manipulating an assignment condition. This is the story of the Fever Test.

The Fever Test with Joe Ford is described in the endophysics book. The origin was the paper "An estimate of Planck's constant." This was just the beginning – it included a calculation of h. We are still in the need for a first principles calculation of c.

Three people are sitting around a table. Each is staring at the value of h in a physics textbook on the table. Then one of them takes a fever pill. The idea is that h corresponds to the thermodynamics of the individual. They can use their own brain temperature to calculate the value of h bar and their body volume (using the Sackur–Tetrod equation). And then they compare what they estimate with what they find in the books. Temperature cannot be made to vary sharply. The participant will be surprised to find (after a fever pill) – it is his own temperature that is responsible for h. At that moment he begins to become suspicious. And this is a typical paranoid idea: how can one really believe such a thing? Brain state and interface – the printed value of h, changes counterfactually: If you check it with the others, h obeys your brain temperature but not theirs. It is like a bad dream – because in the others' dream they control h; h is thus a constant in each individual's life but not on the exo level, where it does not exist.

Erwin Schroedinger never trusted his own quantum mechanics – see his 1927 paper – wave mechanics. His Psi function was a substitution of Hamilton's H function. Unlike H however this new function had parapsychological features. That is why he called it Psi. While the function itself is as well behaved as Hamilton's H, its momentary effect would fluctuate unpredictably. Max Born later came up with his probabilistic interpretation of PSI, which only confirmed Shroedinger's worst dreams. For there was no reason for this so-called *primary chance* as Born's pupil Wolfgang Pauli came to call it. There is an anecdote of Niels Bohr – the shaking of the match box – that was told to one of the authors in 1983 by John Wheeler during a stroll taken in Como. Bohr was asked by a journalist, Professor Bohr what is quantum mechanics? He said "do you have an empty matchbox," and "do you have a die with you"? Here is the empty matchbox, here is a die. "Now please put the die into the matchbox very carefully and softly close it." Then give it to me very carefully. Then he took it very carefully, turned around very slowly, facing away from the interrogator and suddenly shook the matchbook three or four times heavily. Then he turned back very slowly and carefully, and handed it back to the interrogator – now open it very carefully: This is quantum mechanics. It means there is a dice tossing behind the world. This theory of dice tossing behind the world is Einstein's nightmare. So Bohr showed his devotion to Einstein while at the same time accepting what Einstein would never accept – namely an interference by "magic" into the world. This was a parody on

Einstein's statement "The Lord does not play Dice." It is not necessary to use an oracle if you are the boss of the world (we imagine).

Simulacron 3 or *Matrix* – The Matrix + Magic is unacceptable.

Newton's successors had a formula for the world which they called H – the so-called Hamiltonian function for the world. Everett replaced it with a capital PSI – the Wave Function of the world. Schroedinger had done the same thing before him. But Everett discovered the formula for the state of an observed object, psi sub obj = f (PSI, psi sub obs). That means that the wave function of the object is a function of the wave function of the universe – as everyone would expect – but also of the wave function of the observer himself. And this is a scandal because the properties of an object depend on you – your own unknown state, but that is exactly what quantum mechanics says. This finding is due to Everett and it is a scandal. On the other hand, this is what Roger Joseph Boscovich also said in 1755. It only got forgotten. David Finkelstein suggested the name Endophysics for this situation. Endophysics is "Matrix" physics.

Another name would be Neophysics or more properly, Neo's Physics.

Shikhovtsev wrote a book distributed via the internet jointly with Ken Ford titled *A Biography of Hugh Everett III*. This is the book where one finds the story of the theologian who committed suicide after talking to Everett.

See also "Fringe" – Popular Science fiction featuring the ability to move between multiple worlds.

Endonomadology – Endomonadology

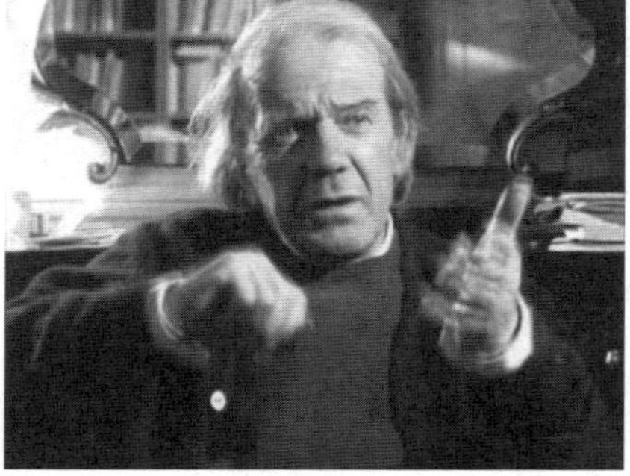

Gilles Deleuze, public domain.

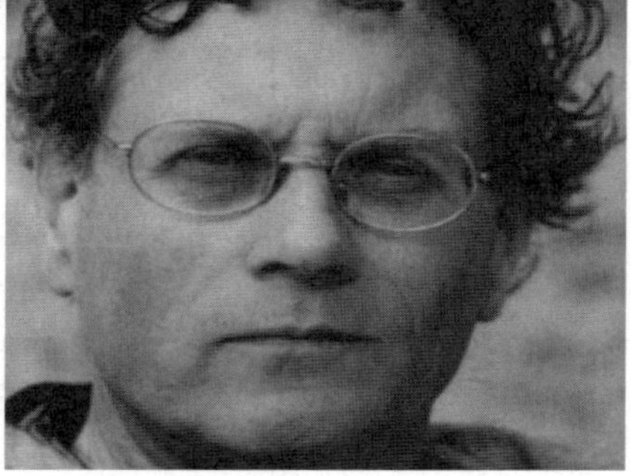

Félix Guattari, public domain.

This is a plateau where Leibniz speaks to Deleuze and Guattari, while Jonathan Kemp and Nils Röller are onlooking.

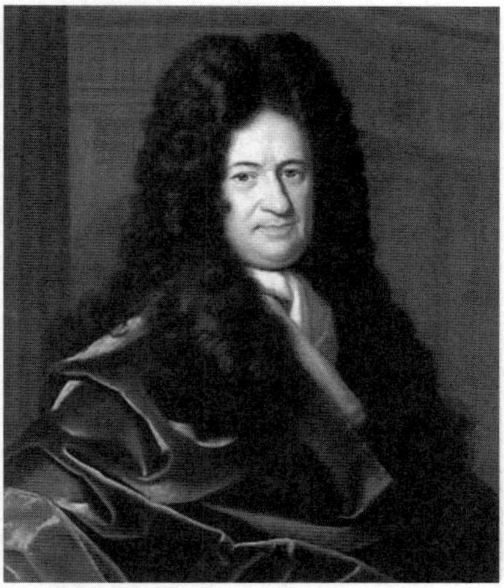
Gottfried Wilhelm von Leibniz. Public domain.

I just might end or finish this with just a few sentences on applications. This interface theory that I proposed to you, is called endophysics. You are a lone monad or nomad which is almost the same thing in the world. But if you take it seriously, Descartes claimed that his science would eventually allow you to become immortal. It would be even much more powerful than science has ever been up till now. Then there was this crisis in physics where suddenly quantum mechanics showed that there was a limit to this rationalism. But if you believe in Cartesianism, if you believe that the world is rational, then you find a way out again and you find an explanation, why these interface phenomena in quantum mechanics happen exactly the way they do. There is an outside view which allows you to understand why you cannot explain the click in the Geiger counter. Why this is suddenly something metaphysical which broke into physics. And this is this theory of endo-physics where you explain quantum phenomena as something to be expected if you are a part of the world. This would take me too long to explain in detail. But maybe this new way of doing science as endophysics allows you to do it, leads to new predictions, that give you a new handle on the world. Peter Weibel and I called this world change technology. A technology which does not change something within the world as all technologies have done so far, but which changes the whole world. Because you are starting to manipulate the very interface which contains the whole world. If it is true, that the world is an interface reality. If it is true, that rationalism can be regained by taking into account the fact that you are with your own body part of the world and then only the difference between you and the rest of the world is accessible to you. Then part of the world would become infected by the fact that you are an element of the world. And if you really faced this strange situation, that you are in, in the world, you could start to manipulate this interface. And so even this […] as Descartes claimed would eventually be overcome by this type of thinking. I am sure I have not been able to completely get through what I wanted to say, but maybe you got a little bit of the idea. Thank you very much for allowing me to talk so long.[162]

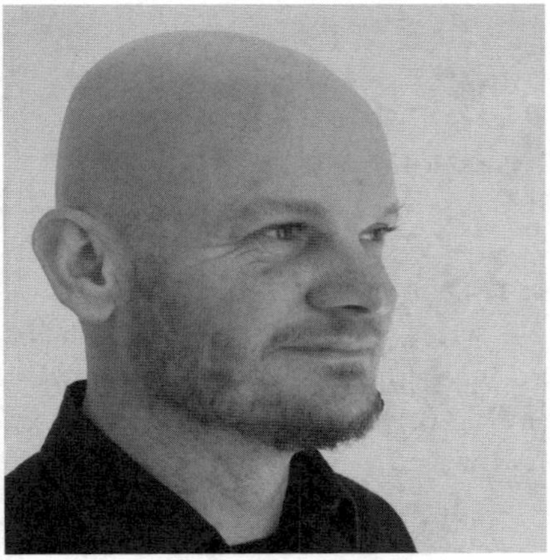
Image courtesy of Jonathan Kemp.

Kurt Lewin – Topological Psychology

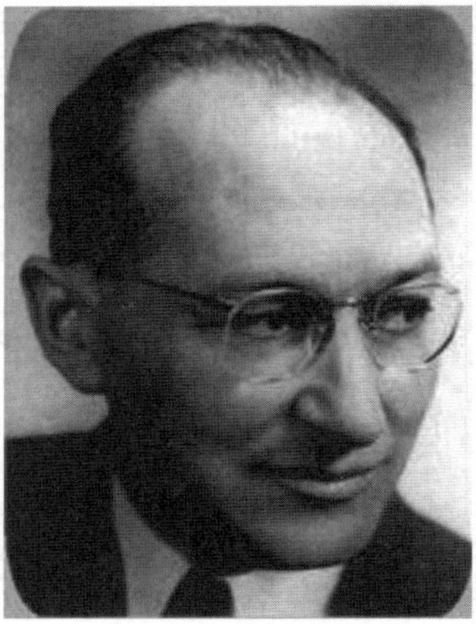
Kurt Lewin, courtesy of the Kurt Lewin Institute.

The force field space (discussed elsewhere in this book) would be another name which Kurt Lewin would like. Responsible of course is Aristotle – "The falling stone is accelerating because it is looking forward to coming home and to rest."

Enfolded Topological Spaces

[…] We can potentially extend this approach by folding in concepts first articulated by Kurt Lewin in his text Principles of Topological Psychology from 1936 although one needs to join multiple differing topologies together – topological psychological spaces, simulation spaces and physical/actual motion spaces. Lewin discusses how a series of psychological vectors might form a topology. In the chapter entitled "The psychological life space as space in the sense of mathematics", he describes how psychological facts can be articulated, "connected" and "coordinated" in a topological space, forming paths – "any kind of locomotion of the person in the quasi-physical, the quasi-social, or the quasi-conceptual field can be designated as a connecting process which corresponds to a topological patch." Lewin further provides remarks about topological space: "The fact that certain regions in the psychological environment and within the person influence other regions, both of the environment and of the person, may be taken as a criterion for connectedness in the topological sense." This happens through "dynamical communication."[163]

Topological psychology is a verbal description of the brain equation 40 years ahead of time.

Bonding, Imprinting, and Other Lorenzes – Innate Releasing Mechanisms

In animal perception there are "templates" for a whole series of important events in life which are kept more or less in a state of readiness, and if a perceptual object or a process in the environment fits such a template the corresponding drive activity will be released (provided that the drive energy concerned is adequately charged).

Konrad Lorenz's legacy – Motivation of human and animal behavior: An ethological view[164]

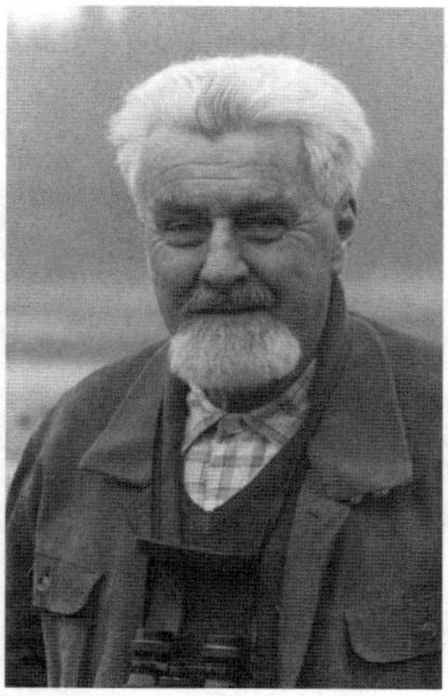

Konrad Lorenz, courtesy of the Konrad Lorenz Archive, Altenberg.

We call these templates "innate releasing mechanisms," and from numerous animal experiments we have already acquired a good deal of information about their properties and functional peculiarities. The innate releasing mechanisms (IRMs) roughly represent the "keyboard" by means of which the environment plays on the "organ of drives," or seen from the point of view of the animal the IRMs sort the stimuli impinging on the animal from its environment under the headings "vital to existence," "less important," or "of no consequence." Of importance in our context are those IRMs which regulate the social life of animals in troops, herds, colonies, and the like. Here I must first add that not only drive activities are elicited by IRMs but also reactions of other kinds, such as directing mechanisms (taxes) and – something which is particularly important in the social context – also inhibitions. In the field of social life IRMs determine not only when something will be done but also when something may not be done! Thus they form a kind of "moral code" below the level of genuine morals.

The IRMs are the supposed force-specific sensors in the brain equation. The sensors connected to the different forces – the IRMs – are filters that lead onto the right force functioning as triggers.

See also: psychohydraulic model of the control of propensities (*Konrad Lorenz*). Illustration found at http://terpconnect.umd.edu/~wrstrick/secu/ansc455/model.htm (Accessed 2, June 2011)

Behind the Mirror

The *flip side of the mirror* (a literal translation from the German title) is what Lorenz had in mind. This interest in what bodily (biologically) lies behind consciousness is central;[165] so is his "thinking is acting in imagined space."

The closed-eye mode. The brain equation has two modes of action – the closed-eye mode is acting in imagined space and the outgoing mode is functioning in physical space. This is the serious jump from simulation to action in the embodied physicality. The overlap buffer enables a combination of the two modes to make external activity smooth.

One of the authors once observed a dwarf panda (Ailuropoda minor) in a zoo, stopping from time to time in mid-walking as if frozen in thought, as if devoid of an overlap buffer.

See Foveal Attention (p. 242) in our model.

Ed Lorenz's Butterfly

Ed Lorenz is no relation to Konrad Lorenz even though he invented the butterfly in Chaos Theory.

Predictability: Does the Flap of a Butterfly's Wings in Brazil Set off a Tornado in Texas?[166]

No wonder the Lorenz attractor looks like a butterfly …

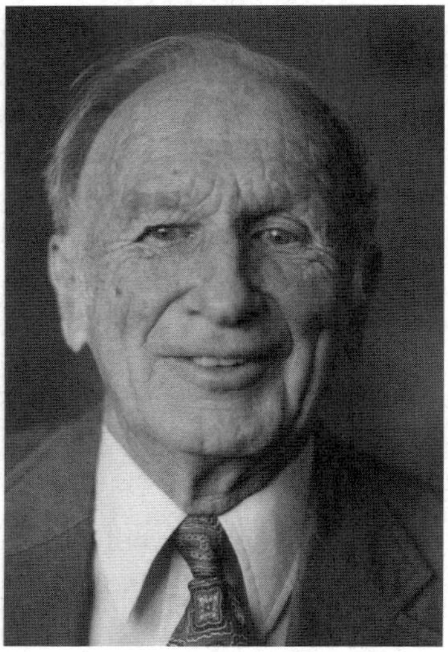

Ed Lorenz, courtesy of MIT News Office, Donna Coveney/MIT.

In the early 1960s using a simple system of equations to model convection in the atmosphere, Edward Lorenz, an MIT meteorologist, ran headlong into "sensitivity to initial conditions". In the process he sketched the outlines of one of the first recognized chaotic attractors.

In Lorenz's meteorological computer modeling, he discovered the underlying mechanism of deterministic chaos: simply-formulated systems with only a few variables can display highly complicated behavior that is unpredictable.

Using his digital computer, culling through reams of printed numbers and simple strip chart plots of the variables, he saw that slight differences in one variable had profound effects on the outcome of the whole system. This was one of the first clear demonstrations of sensitive dependence on initial conditions. Equally important Lorenz showed that this occurred in a simple, but physically relevant model.

He also appreciated that in real weather situations, this sensitivity could mean the development of a front or pressure-system where there never would have been one in previous models. In his famous 1963 paper Lorenz picturesquely explains that a butterfly flapping its wings in Brazil could affect the weather thousands of miles away some weeks later. This sensitivity is now called the "butterfly effect".[167]

Ed Lorenz was a very gentle unassuming man, very generous to what others would think of as competitors. In his old age he was still hiking in the mountains. The Book *The Essence of Chaos*[168] not only is a tribute to his field but also exposes the kindness of his soul.

Single-spin Chemistry

A new periodic table in strong magnetic fields.

In 1998 Laughlin, Stormer and Tsui were awarded the Nobel Prize for Physics for discovering that electrons acting together in strong magnetic fields can form new types of "particles" with charges that are fractions of electron charges, the citation being: "for their discovery of a new form of quantum fluid with fractionally charged excitations'.[169]

What are the ramifications of spin chemistry for the creation of an electrochemical computer?

Spin possibly is a pure endo phenomenon like h and c, but is even more palpable. Most recently, Cornell, Weiman, and Huang got Nobel Prizes in 2008 related to the "Bose Nova" implosion which is a new spin-based phenomenon whereby many equal atoms apparently condense into a single atom of the "sum" mass, and the sum mass of each of its own constituents (perhaps), for example, the mass of the resulting compound nucleus would be greatly increased. The limits of this condensation have not as yet been adequately investigated.

Thus, an apparently new form of matter possibly exists. Fortunately (unlike the LHC danger) its density apparently cannot become dangerously high.

Spin-based Computers

Another development is the emergence in the future of a spin-based computer as a variant of a quantum computer. The Neosentient could be implemented in all three forms of the continuum – as a Stephen Smale computer, as a David Deutsch computer and as a spin computer.

A "Well-Stirred Computer,"[170] an example of a continuous computer, was described in 1973 by one of the authors.

Hospitalism

Death from lack of bonding

In 1945 René Spitz described the death without reason of temporarily orphaned young children in a hospital. This phenomenon has become known as Hospitalism. The relevance of this relates specifically to personogenesis – the spontaneous invention of the suspicion of benevolence residing in the caretaker, by the child. This infinite trust that human beings can develop is both their greatest strength and their greatest weakness, because you can die from despair when being abandoned.

Artificial Ethology/Ethomathematics

Survival depends on space, specifically on not missing a survival-relevant source located in space. This is Spatial Darwinism. Spatial Darwinism explains all brains in the universe except what humans do with their brains. They misuse their brains for a new purpose – for picturing a benevolent intention and another soul inside a brain that is not their own. This expels humans from the community of living animals because the remote control by evolution and the evolution-controlled brain equation is constituent for all Darwinian systems. So humans have fallen out of the web of nature. But they are not necessarily alone. They can transmit this function change to other species including artificial brains. The jump-like transmission of their center of optimization (soul) changes their relationship to space and time and makes it a personal one. This "person" is suddenly alone in the universe in the sense that it is responsible for both itself and for others.

Levinas pays tribute to this mystery most deeply in many of his texts (see 1946 *Time and the Other*). See also *The Levinas Reader* (S. Hand, ed., Basil Blackwell, 1989).

Even though you are alone you can make sure that others are not left alone by you.

Bottom Up vs Top Down

The bottom up approach is the best way to go but it might take us 1000 years and even then we might get stuck. The Brain Equation is like a bottleneck – you have to go through it to succeed because one can prove that nature has used it. Not to complete the path taken by nature would be a mistake. This is an optimality problem that any surviving creature in space must solve mathematically. We have an inherent mathematicality that is innate. Lorenz believed one of us in his identity as a mathematician could find this. The mathematical extension of our talking (in 1966) would lead to the solution. The brain equation eventuated out of these discussions seven years later. The brain equation is a top down approach and the bottom up has so far not even envisaged its existence. An Insight Engine is hoped to be a midwife to the bottom up approach.

Innate and Acquired Releasing Mechanisms – Priming (Lorenz)

Lorenz, Konrad. Behind the Mirror: a search for a natural history of human knowledge. Trans. Ronald Taylor. New York: Harcourt Brace Jovanovich, 1977.

A similar process takes place on a high plane when a pattern is controlled by several sense organs. I have already referred to the significance of the fact that the anthropoid's grasping extremity remains within its field of vision, with the result that he exteroceptor reafferences of vision coincide with the proprioceptor perceptions of the position and movement of the limbs, thus producing the cognitive act of pattern matching. When a baby discovers its own hands and feet and starts to play with them, not only is the number of reafferneces doubled but it becomes abundantly clear that they come both from inside and outside the subject.[171]

This is true for many animals in all kingdoms not just for humans.

An important psychologist, Selma Fraiberg, wrote *Insights from the Blind*. In her book of 1977 she describes that babies that are blind do not do this – they have to be taught artificially to make their hands touch when they are a half year old.

Gustav Bally was the first to show specifically that play was only possible in what Kurt Lewin termed a "tension-less field". Gehlen, in his motivational "field theory" accurately characterized the nature of exploratory behavior when he described it as consisting of 'senso-motory patterns of combined visual and tactile sensations, cyclic processes that provided their own stimuli for their continuation. They run their course with no hint of desire and serve no immediate consummatory purpose.

Except the consummation of play itself, which is a powerful reward of its own – the authors – this is called Function Lust – the pleasure of functioning.

This form of productive interaction with the outside world is, at the same time, objective.' One could hardly find a better definition of exploratory behavior. It clearly distinguishes learning by exploration from the ordinary mechanisms of the operant acquisition of conditioned responses described in the earlier sections of this chapter. Of these latter Gehlen says: "It is only the pressure, in a given situation, of a present instinctive urge that forces learning processes to operate, making the animal's behavior essentially dependent […]. And since its actions are not independent, they are not objective."[172]

As we already know, gestalt perception, though evolved as a "constancy mechanism" in the service and under the selection pressure of recognizing individual objects is proved able to arrive at "abstracting" the objective laws underlying a variety of individual phenomena. Similarly, exploratory behavior, without any substantial mechanism, also performs a new function […] [173]

Children, on the other hand, and, astonishingly, the above-mentioned birds, are excellent imitators. Social psychologists have proved that children imitate the actions of adults with great precision out of sheer pleasure in imitating, long before they understand the purpose of the behavior pattern in question. In their book The Social Construction of Reality, Peter Berger and Thomas Luckmann have analysed these processes very closely.[174]

In Hartmann's day the prospect of ever bridging the gulf between the organic and the inorganic by a "continuum of forms" seemed as remote as that of solving the problem of the relationship between body and soul, so that Hartmann could rightly say: "The real origin of life, with its self-regulating metabolism and its power of self-reproduction, is something we have not as yet been able to demonstrate."[175]

But as such far-reaching discoveries concerning the constituent functions have since been made in biocybernetics and biochemistry that is now a far from merely utopian hope that in the foreseeable future we shall be in a position to explain the autonomous principles of organic life in terms of its material structure and its evolution. At all events it is in principle far from impossible that the growth of our knowledge will eventually bridge the gap between the organic and the inorganic by means of a "continuum of forms."[176]

This refers to behavior as fundamentally distinct from biochemistry – it can be tied to biochemistry but just as well to silicon-based hardware. This is prophetic for the new science of artificial consciousness – neosentience.

There has been a great deal of discussion since Darwin as to whether acquired characteristics are hereditary or not. Once, half in jest, I coined an aphorism that is appropriate here: "One is often made aware of the fact that a certain process does not usually occur, by coming across an exception which shows us what things would be like if it did occur."[177]

All of these creative remarks of Lorenz's show his genius.

However, as a result of the new "inheritability" of acquired characteristics, a new cognitive apparatus emerges, the functions of which are parallel to those of the genome in that the processes of the assimilation and retention of information are preformed by two different kinds of mechanism […] [178]

High cultures often, though not always, seem to arise when a people moves from its native area and comes into close contact with another people that has remained sedentary, and a "graft" of foreign culture-"la greffe" as Paul Valery called it-frequently appears to have stimulated "creative flashes". This, of course, is a possibility only given to cultural development, as it presupposes the inheritance of acquired characteristics.[179]

This becomes interestingly true when seen in the light of a new Neosentient techno-species. Neosentient entities will develop a culture which is of itself. And we will be pampered by this second level of evolution – this is benevolence theory.

Although in all cultural communication systems it is learned recognition of Gestalt that plays the role of the receiver, simpler processes of perception, taking place on much lower levels of the nervous system, are also involved, as they are the elements and the base of more highly differentiated Gestalt perception. Physiologists and psychologists who have concerned themselves with these functions know very well what kind of demands our perceiving apparatus puts to the constellations of sensory data, if it is to recognize them as unmistakable Gestalts.[180]

How do we program the ability to abstract?
The brain equation is programming the force fields. Extracting gestalts from the sensual input of the system is important and is quite non-trivial. We provide our diagram of an embodied brain equation elsewhere. We believe it will be uniquely recoverable in a one to one fashion from Pandaka pygmaea's brain, once it is studied with full power in an institute of the same name.[181]

Bonding Drive/Attachment Theory (John Bowlby and Mary Ainsworth)

Attachment theory is the joint work of John Bowlby and Mary Ainsworth. Drawing on concepts from ethology, cybernetics, information processing, developmental psychology, and psychoanalysis, John Bowlby formulated the basic tenets of the theory. René Spitz and Friedrich Fröbel should also be mentioned here.

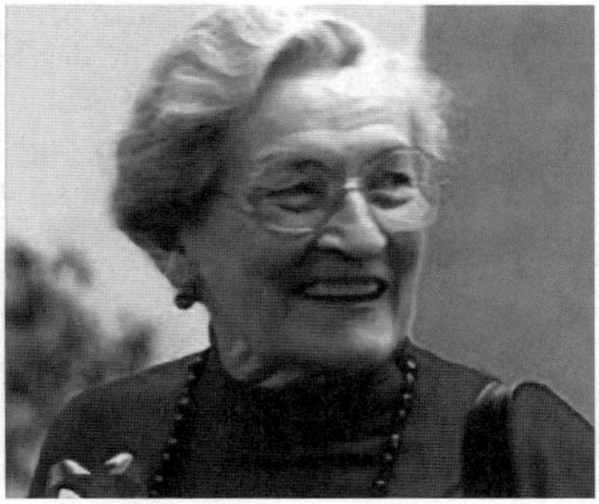

Ainsworth, Public domain.

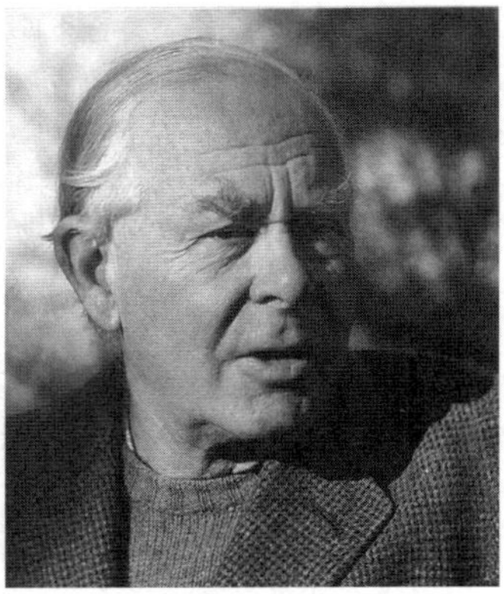
Bowlby courtesy Sir Richard Bowlby.

The origins of attachment theory: John Bowlby and Mary Ainsworth
He […] revolutionized our thinking about a child's tie to the mother and its disruption through separation, deprivation, and bereavement. Mary Ainsworth's innovative methodology not only made it possible to test some of Bowlby's ideas empirically but also helped expand the theory itself and is responsible for some of the new directions it is now taking. Ainsworth contributed the concept of the attachment figure as a secure base from which an infant can explore the world. In addition, she formulated the concept of maternal sensitivity to infant signals and its role in the development of infant-mother attachment patterns.[182]

This is ethology and all of this ties in with the theory of personogenesis. We should also not forget the movie *AI* here.

The Invention of Benevolence as a Transcendence of Biology

Benevolence is an emancipation from the remote control by the evolutionary process (compare the blind mechanism of the "brain" in the genome).[183] The shift from emotions that are unreflected and purely biologically driven necessities (like feeding the young that cry from hunger) to genuine benevolence and caring is essential to understand.

Thus, benevolence propels the Neosentient to a new technologically arising phenomenology in partnership with our own and with future other neosentiences that might reside somewhere in the universe. Humans as a species are different from any previous species because of the invention of benevolence, and with it personhood, by the young. The remote control by evolutionarily developed forces is replaced by personal responsibility. This is the end of the arrow of evolution in nature. But at the same time the "arrow of evolution" toward Point Omega of Teilhard de Chardin is fulfilled in its essence.

This is also the discovery that two coupled deterministic machines can create free will.

The clear understanding of one's being able to serve another while remaining free represents a deep paradox that has not as yet been looked at mathematically in detail.

Darwinism is one of the most dangerous theories of science because it can be misused.

Point Omega represents infinite freedom and infinite potentiality, so the danger that Nietzsche saw in the Superman philosophy is not really there.

Natural Brains Artificially Produced

The original bio-computer was invented by McCulloch and Pitts. The early hunch of McCulloch and Pitts that the function of the brain can be implemented via digital machines can be confirmed. The Brain equation can be realized in terms of digital hardware.

McCulloch and Pitts' Neural Logical Calculus[184]

The paper by McCulloch and Pitts (1943) is properly titled "A logical calculus of the ideas immanent in nervous activity": after stating a careful and well-argued selection of simplifications of the behavior of real neurons, they develop a logical apparatus to define:

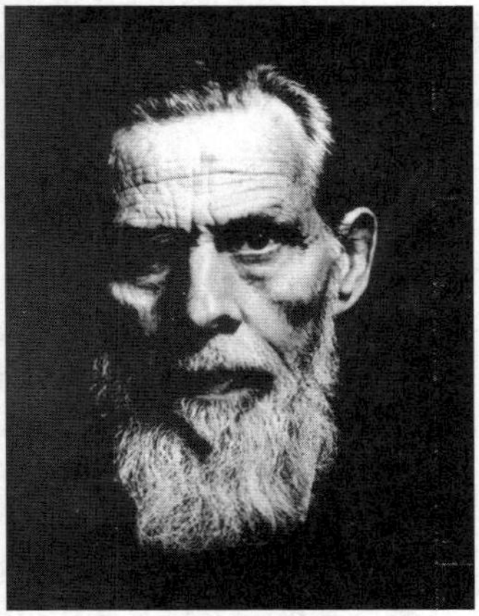

Warren McCulloch, photo courtesy of Taffy Holland.

The concept of the solution of a net and of the realizability of a logical predicate by a net. After dividing the neurons in one net into two groups, that is, input neurons ("peripheral afferents") that do not get signals from any other neuron in the net, and the rest of the neurons, they go on to define a method to answer the following two questions in the most general way possible.

What does a given net compute?
Can a given net compute a given logical sentence?

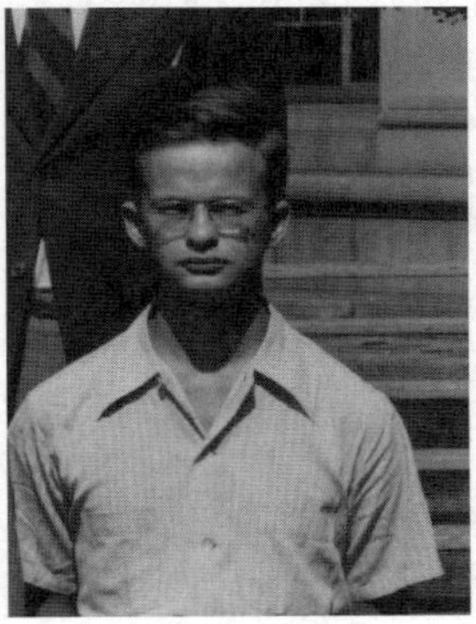

Pitts was 19 years old at the time this paper was written.

Neurons are in two possible states: firing and not firing, and thus, they define for each neuron a predicate that is true when the neuron is firing at a given time:

They define the solution of a net as a set of logical sentences of the form "neuron is firing if and only if" a given logical combination of the firing predicates of input neurons at previous times and some constant sentences including firing predicates of these same neurons

Walter Pitts, courtesy of the MIT Museum.

is true. These sentences are a solution for a net if they are all true for it. In other words, the sentences describe what the net computes. Conversely, such an "if and only if" sentence is called realizable by a net if it is true for that net; that is, when the net can compute it.[185]

Is the Brain a Digital Computer?

In reference to The Chinese Room:

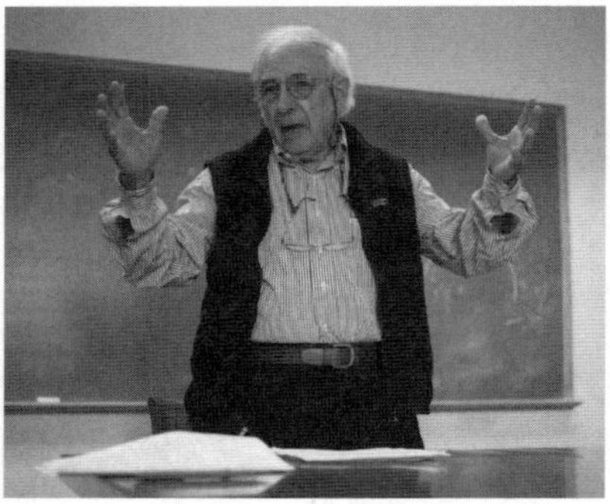

John R. Searle. Courtesy of John Searle.

Searle re-discovered Leibniz's big question of the windmill in his *Monadology*. In that book the brain is compared to the most complex machine of his time, the windmill. A scientist climbs up the staircase at the side of the windmill to enter a little door on its side – one of its two "ears." (Its nose is of course is the turning wheel.) The scientist stays inside for a long time counting every cog of every wheel determining all interactions in the huge maze of interacting gears. It takes him a long time to take stock of every detail. Eventually he is finished and he steps out of the "ear" to a waiting crowd of journalists and announces, I completely understand the functioning of this brain. One journalist takes a heart and asks: and what about the soul? The scientist shouts back: "What Soul?" Leibniz also invented the idea of the telephone and the tape recorder ahead of time. His brain theory is already in the spirit of the inventor of the binary code who also was named Leibniz (the same person). The story told above is slightly embellished since in his days the profession of journalists had not yet surfaced. The connection to Searle is, of course, the "Chinese Room." Searle reproduces Leibniz's basic idea in more telling terms. With messages being exchanged between non-understanding functional units (clerks who cannot read Chinese). A mere automoton and rule-based system of clerks, like in a big banking system, certainly does not have a soul as such. Even though the customers and the economy sometimes would think otherwise in the aftermath of Lehmann Brothers which behaved in this automaton like fashion without any conscious malevolent intention being involved. And society at large also is a swarm. Mere swarm intelligence? Searle does have an important message.

One might at one point not be able to understand a language yet function (or not) at a low level. Yet, one might also later come to learn a language given the appropriate training and breadth of experience (read programming approach).

Introduction. Strong AI, Weak AI and Cognitivism.
The basic idea of the computer model of the mind is that the mind is the program and the brain the hardware of a computational system. A slogan one often sees is: "the mind is to the brain as the program is to the hardware."[186]

This is not quite true in reality, only very very few processes in the brain are accompanied by consciousness (mind). A program is a way to implement a dynamics. Almost all the dynamics and programs in the brain lack consciousness. The dynamics of the brain is controlling behavior both visible and invisible. In addition, only a small part of this behavior is conscious – namely the force field on the "Big Screen" (see diagram at the end of this book). We see the brain as a mixed analog and digital system.

Jeff Hawkins – Hierarchical Temporal Memory

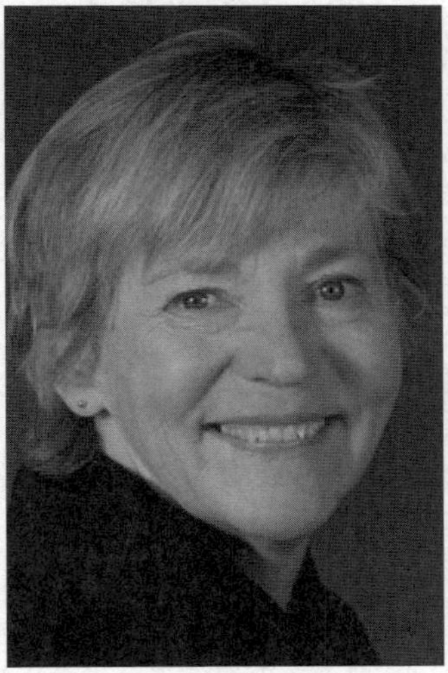

Sandra Blakeslee, courtesy of Sandra Blakeslee (coauthor of *On Intelligence*).

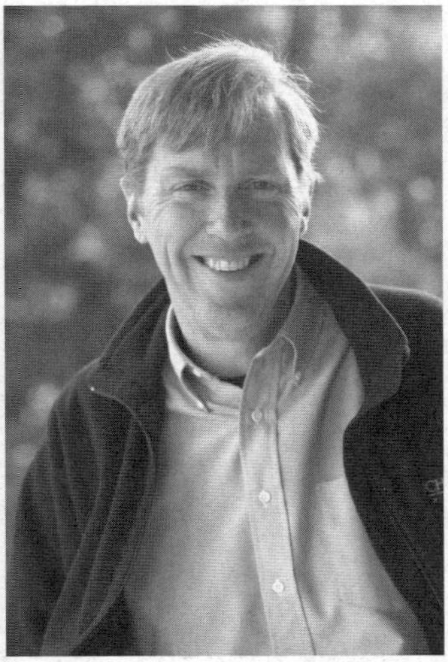

Jeff Hawkins, courtesy of Jeff Hawkins.

Hierarchical Temporal Memory (HTM) is a machine learning model developed by Jeff Hawkins and Dileep George of Numenta, Inc. that models some of the structural and algorithmic properties of the neocortex as Bayesian networks. It is also discussed at length in *On Intelligence* by Jeff Hawkins and Sandra Blakeslee.

Creativity is mixing and matching patterns of everything you've ever experienced or come to know in your lifetime. It's saying "this is kinda like that." The neural mechanism for doing this is everywhere in the cortex.

Tolerance networks are the basis.

Second, you need to let your mind wander. You need to give your brain the time and space to discover the solution. Finding a solution to a problem is literally finding a pattern in the world, or a stored pattern in your cortex that is analogous to the problem you are working on.[187]

It is also like finding and/or creating a relevant relation between patterns …

James Olds

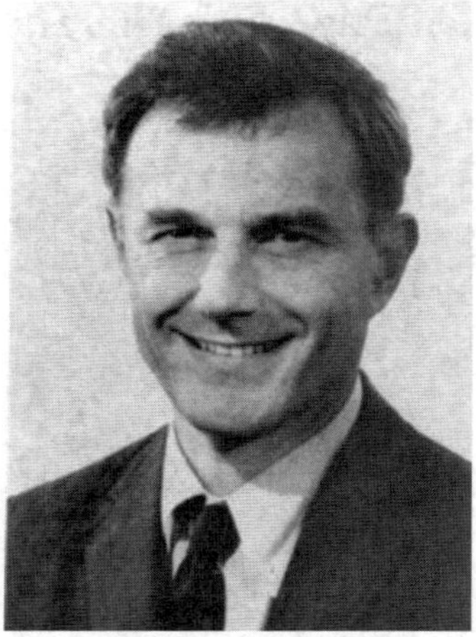

James Olds, courtesy of National Academies Archives.

An artificial excitation of specific cellular nuclei in the mid-brain can be controlled by the animals themselves. This is living proof of the autonomous optimizer theory of the brain. The decisive missing step was done by Olds. He gave the animal the control of the stimulation key so that it manifested self-stimulation (and aversion), and found attraction empirically – living proof of an autonomous optimizer structure. A self-introduced impulse as a key to specific behavior.

James Olds
30 May 1922–21 August 1976
By Richard F. Thompson

James Olds was one of the most important psychologists of the twentieth century. Indeed, many of us feel that his discovery of the "reward" system in the brain is the most important single discovery yet made in the field concerned with brain substrates of behavior [and psychoanalysis we would add]. *In retrospect, this discovery led to a much-increased understanding of the brain bases and mechanisms of substance abuse and addiction. Jim also was a pioneer in the study of neural substrates of learning and memory and the first to show that neurons in the hippocampus become substantially engaged in basic associative learning.*[188]

W.R. Hess

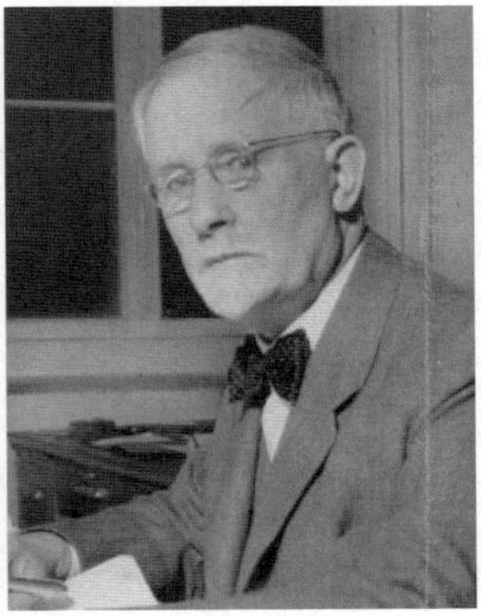

Fair Use.

Nobelist Hess's discovery of specific nuclei in the brain eliciting specific types of behavior confirmed elements of ethological motivation. José Delgado later stopped a charging bull in an arena by pushing a little button on a remote control box that sent a signal into the bull's brain.

Hess (e.g., 1956) electrically stimulated the mid-brain of cats with implanted electrodes and found that it was possible, by this means, to produce fully co-ordinated behaviour patterns, including appetitive sequences terminating in consummatory act, identical with normal behaviour.[189]

Kurt Gödel

Gödel deserves to be admired also for being faster than von Neumann on one occasion. After learning of the Gödel conjecture, von Neumann resolved to prove it first and failed for once in being the fastest mathematician of his time.

Gödel makes a distinction between inside and outside which might be the deepest element of his theorem. From outside it is quite easy to see that an "inside" observer is limited in her/his view; this relates specifically to endophysics.

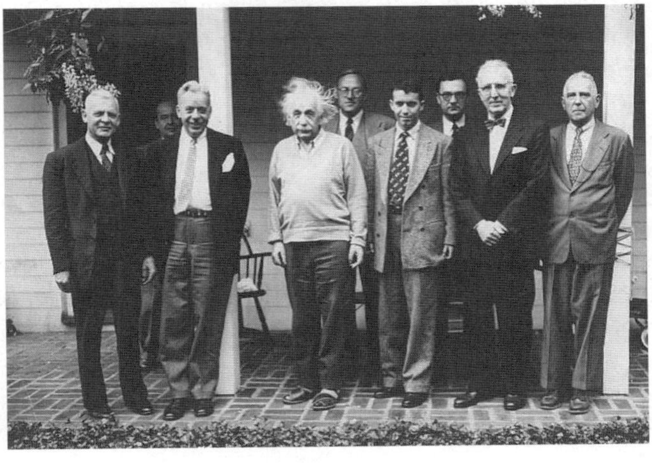

John von Neumann on the left in the Backgound – Einstein and Colleagues, courtesy of Marina v. N. Whitman.

With an interest in time machines and immortality (as discussed above by Bell, p 41), Gödel discovered a famous solution to Einstein's equation. The latter implies the existence of a time machine unless Einstein's equations contain a hidden flaw. When Einstein learned of his friend Gödel's findings, he got very upset because it proved something must be wrong with his own theory but the problem was never resolved so far. A new implication of general relativity could lead to a resolution.[190]

Peter Weibel

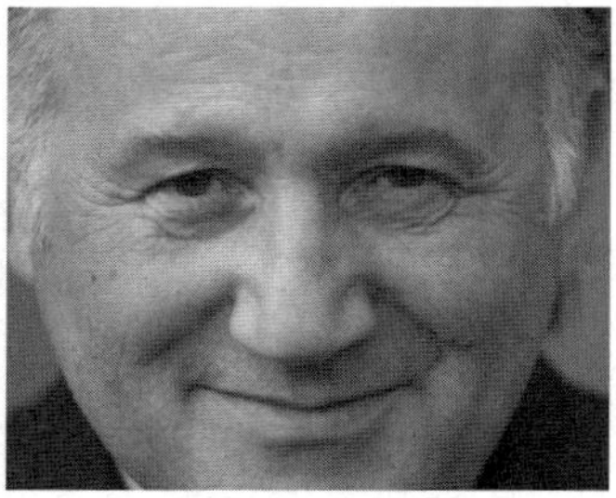
Image courtesy of Peter Weibel.

Peter Weibel is the contemporary artist of the self-referential in the virtual. Very busy and very kind. He has written and/or edited a book each month for many years. He invented action art with Valerie Export. He independently saw parts of Endophysics, including end'o'physics. As a young mathematician he was in close contact with Kurt Gödel.

The intelligent image

Another science which we can learn from, is what effect these tools of communication will have on us and the subject. As I have said already, it is changing our status as observer. We can learn from quantum theory, which teaches us that reality is observer-relative. Whatever you observe, you change it by your very act of observation. This is another step of our system theory. Quantum theory not only told us that reality is observer-relative; it is more than just an observer-relative perception of reality. With our act of observation we change the behavior of the image. But we do not change reality. So we have to go from receptor technology (which is cameras), which is now down at the low-end, to effector technology. In the act of seeing, I want at the same time a machine that effects something from the outer world. Up to now, we have developed only receptors, recording machines with which to record the world, to represent the world; and now for decades we have had this famous crisis of representation, and the crisis can only be solved when we develop a technology of effectors. The act of seeing is changing not only the perception of reality and the perception of the image, but also the real world itself. This is a basic proposal of quantum theory. Naturally, when in our case the observer is a machine, then we can realise that our reality is not only observer-relative, but also machine-relative. Our observing machines, which we are developing now, from satellite TV to computers, are not only changing perception, not only simulating reality (simulating life) – they are constructing reality. This change to reality as observer-relative, as machine-relative, whereby machines by the interface can construct reality, has finally encroached upon us as subjects. While in the classical world we said "know yourself" or "express yourself," it is clear that this is not valid any more in the world we are now constructing with the help of these machines. It is also our subject which has to be constructed: we cannot say I have a natural identity, and I am a male or I am a female, and there is something in me, a kind of genetic code which I am developing; I only have to find a way to express myself, to know myself. We have learned from psychoanalysis that we never will know ourselves because there is a subconscious, and that we are not even able to express ourselves. The only thing we can do is "construct ourselves" like the machines that can construct what they see.[191]

This is the seed of neosentience.

Observing Systems (Molecular Ethology)

Heinz Von Foerster:

[...] The question here is how to compute functions rather than states, or how to build a machine that computes programs rather than numerical results. This means we have to look for a formalism that handles "finite function machines." Such a formalism, is of course, one level up from the one discussed before, but by maintaining some pertinent analogues its essential features may become apparent [...] Our variables are now functions, and since relations between functions are usually referred to as "functionals," the essential features of a calculus of recursive functionals will be briefly sketched [...][192]

This is related to category theory (Rosen, Gunji).

Douglas Hofstadter

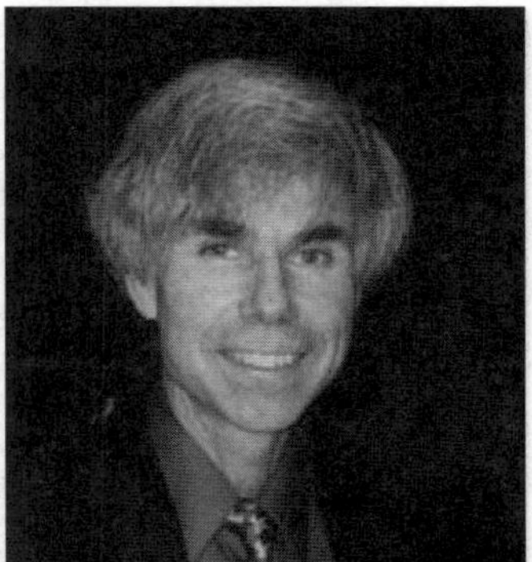
Courtesy of Douglas Hofstadter.

The paradoxes of consciousness arise because a conscious being can be aware of itself, as well as of other things, and yet cannot really be construed as being divisible into parts. It means that a conscious being can deal with Gödelian questions in a way in which a machine cannot, because a conscious being can both consider itself and its performance and yet not be other than that which did the performance. A machine can be made in a manner of speaking to "consider" its performance, but it cannot take this "into account" without thereby becoming a different machine, namely the old machine with a "new part" added. But it is inherent in our idea of conscious mind that it can reflect upon itself and criticize its own performances, and no extra part is required to do this: it is already complete, and has no Achilles' heel.[193]

In neosentient models the machine becomes aware of itself like we humans do.

Mirror Neurons/Mirror Competence

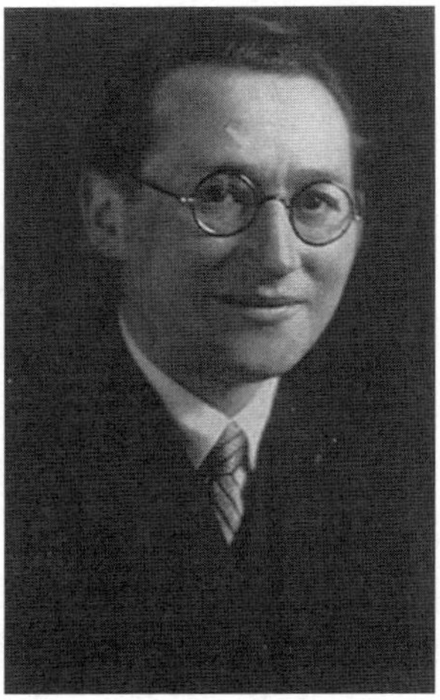
Kurt Lewin. Public domain.

All higher animals have mirror neurons but not mirror competence. (See Michael Arbib – mirror neurons.) Gordon Gallup rediscovered mirror competence, originally discovered by Wolfgang Köhler, an early Gestalt psychologist and the teacher of Kurt Lewin. Mirror competence is more important.

This also refers to Rizzolatti Mirror neurons discovered much later.

Mirror competence implies person competence.

The mirror competence (MC) of young chimpanzees has been known since 1921 (Wolfgang Köhler) and 1969 (Gordon Gallup). Recently Daniel Povinelli questioned MC's sufficiency for a "theory of mind". The human primate indeed has a further trait that may act as a catalyst. Happiness and bonding (laughter and smile) are virtually indistinguishable (J. van Hooff 1972). In her 1978 "Insights from the Blind", Selma Fraiberg showed that children born blind (who see neither laughter nor smile) often remain "too harmless" for life outside an institution. "Smile-blindness" also often causes autism (lack of a theory of mind). A therapy was discussed with the late Gregory Bateson in 1975: Acoustic mimicry of the optical condition (i.e., tender noises made by the mother whenever she is happy). The same "interactional bifurcation" should then occur, via mirror competence, as in the sighted: At first, the toddler starts to feed mother because he mistakes her laughter for tenderness. When she feeds him next time, the exchange symmetry causes him to create the suspicion of benevolence on his own. For the very act just

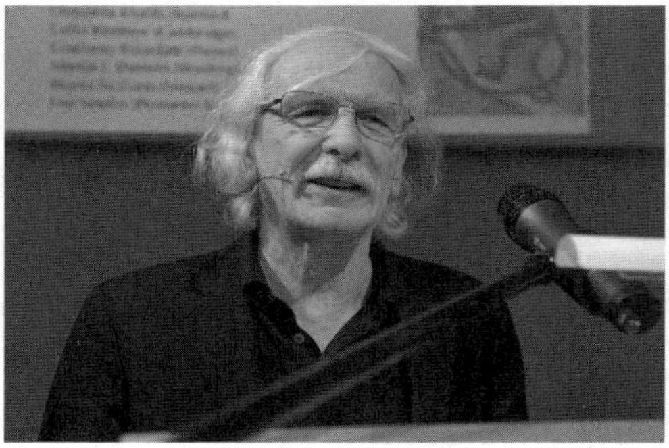
Courtesy of Giacomo Rizzolatti.

performed deliberately by himself feels good on the receiving end. Next time, he tests the good effect over there and is rewarded by a reliable return of the derived joy. Mutual benevolence is born in a positive feedback. By definition benevolent agents are persons. Thus, personhood can be exported to smile-blind mirror competent individuals. A "galactic export" is possible, including all mirror competent species on the planet. They must, therefore, be granted the person rights of Thomas Jefferson.[194]

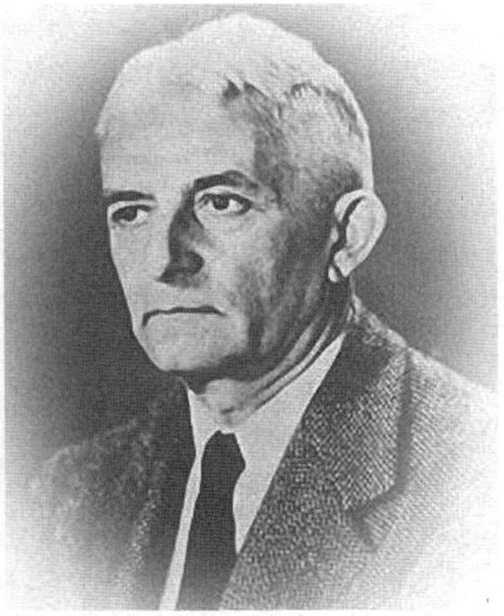
Public domian, Gestalt psychology with Wolfgang Köhler. Public domain.

Arbib: Action to language via the mirror neuron system.

Mirror neurons may hold the brain's key to social interaction – each coding not only a particular action or emotion but also the recognition of that action or emotion in others. The Mirror System Hypothesis adds an evolutionary arrow to the story – from the mirror system for hand actions, shared with monkeys and chimpanzees, to the uniquely human mirror system for language.[195]

It must be noted, all of the animals studied by Rizzolatti are not mirror competent. Only very few animal species are mirror competent: the great apes and gibbons; the cetaceans (dolphins, orcas, and sperm whales); and the raven birds including the magpie and big parrots not to forget elephants (in that an elephant never forgets).

These animals not only possess mirror neurons but are fully mirror competent.

A Neural Transmitter for Every Mood – Electrochemical Computers Revisited

Konrad Lorenz stated early in the 1950s that for every emotion there is a neural transmitter. The brain is a force field that is like a bath that sweeps over a network of cells – it has both discrete and continuous qualities that are inter-relational. There is also no emotion without a direction in space or imagined space, including remembered space. The cells in the reticular formation are being continuously functionally reconnected based on one's momentary position in space. These spherical cells function as pivots and generate a network that is many to many, rapidly re-aligning.

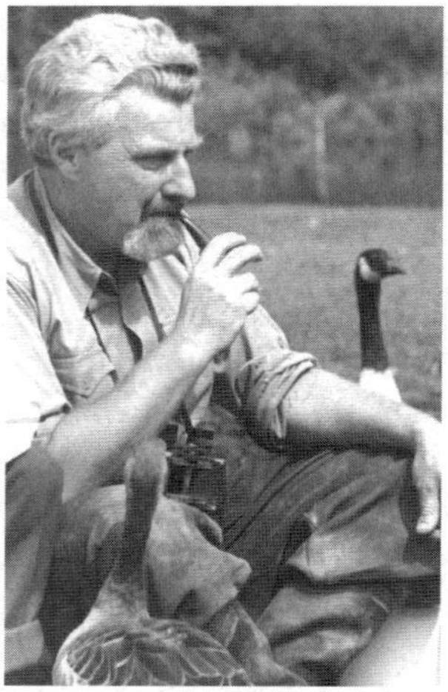
Konrad Lorenz, courtesy of the Konrad Lorenz Archive, Altenberg.

Gyroscopic thinking is an endophysical thinking and an empathetic thinking. Einstein also wrote about the story of several people of different ages in a room seeing the same lightning and recognizing the other's emotional state. This idea of perspective taking was probably influenced by this poem – *Great Grandmother, Grandmother, Mother and Child* (Gustav Schwab). Sometimes poems have an influence in science as in this case.

Do people who can put their minds into a gyroscope have more empathy than other people?

Schopenhauer called this pity, in the footsteps of Herbart (Hans-Martin Schweizer, personal communication).

Relativity as a spatial relation and relativity of emotional perspective refers to the fact that they are also connected to the idea of mirror neurons. It is a very empathetic equation.

Two connected gyroscopes. (the Rössler/Seaman attractor)

… Understanding love is dangerous – and people have resisted making a model of love …

The danger of taking a pair of pliers in order to touch a butterfly's wings was one way Konrad Lorenz was criticized for his similar undertaking, by Trumler.

Question: What is a neurotransmitter?

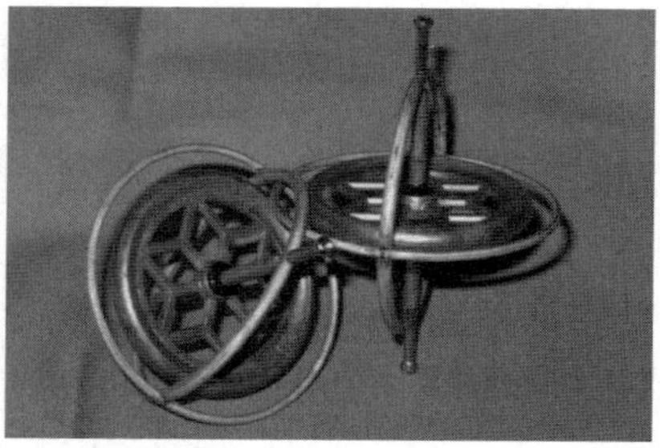
Public domain.

Answer: A neurotransmitter is a chemical or peptide in synapses usually between neurons, a neuron and muscle or a neuron and other organ which functions to transmit information to and from and within the brain. When a neurotransmitter is released from the presynaptic cell in response to depolarization of the cell by an action potential, it diffuses across the synaptic cleft and binds to a receptor or ligand-gated ion channel on the postsynaptic cell. Binding on the postsynaptic cell alters the resting potential of the postsynaptic cell in either an inhibitory or excitatory manner, making the cell less susceptible or more susceptible (respectively) to an action potential. Examples include, but are not limited to, acetylcholine, GABA, noradrenaline, serotonin and dopamine.[196]

How do we improve on neural net models with abstractions of neural transmitters?

There may be 100 force-field-specific neural transmitters, and the brain equation would then be 100 dimensional.

Pattern Flows: Notes Toward a Model for an Electrochemical Computer – The Thoughtbody Environment

The notion of building a model for an electrochemical computer based on the functionality of the human body is both an exciting and daunting task. In order to model and ultimately build such a device, one seeks to borrow important operative concepts and processes from the body and try to re-understand them in the context of a device that is not human in nature (and not even living) but potentially conscious. Certainly the task is to learn more about mind/brain/body and language in the process. This procedure includes bridging a series of domains involving biology, physics, cognitive science, computer science, electrical engineering, linguistics, philosophy, psychology, and artistic ingenuity. In this Open Order Cybernetics program, language acquisition and the production of meaning in reciprocal action between others, self, and environment are elements. A delicate intermingling of scientific, philosophical, linguistic, and moral aspects surrounding such a project must be carefully examined.

See Wilfried Hou Je Bek – several simultaneous associations to his way of thinking. *Osmose* by Char Davies can serve as a poetic source of ideas.

The Relation of the Body to an Embodied Electrochemical Computer

What aspects of the physical relation between "body" and environment can be retained in such a system? To what extent does the physiological thoughtbody, or its relation to the environment, contribute to consciousness? It seems clear that such an electrochemical device will need both a Thoughtbody and an ExperienceBody that allows it to function as a unified field of becoming.

How might a local robotic body with multiple synthetic senses including a sense of balance and a haptic response system become coupled to a larger distributed electrochemical system? To what degree is this device to be based on the workings of the human or an abstraction and/or expansion of the human? No one knows if a robot needs to include electrochemical elements to be accepted in a larger electrochemical system or in human society for that matter. On what level of frequency response should the electrochemical computer be calibrated? How will embodied experience be realized?

Experience with analog computers teaches that they can be set to multiple time frames – slowly calculating, ten times faster, a thousand times faster. In the same way the speed of artificial consciousness can be arbitrarily chosen. Compare whales to humming birds …

Synthetic Qualia and Talia Predictably Arise as an Emergent "Inside Quality" of our System

Poetics means doing or making – it actually means the same thing as synthesizing.

Our system functions via self-consistent internal loops. The force field components function as the predictable substrate for qualia.

Candice B. Pert – Molecules of Emotion[197]

The science behind mind-body medicine
Professor Candice Pert first came to public prominence in the 1970s for her discovery of the brain's "opiate receptor". Since then she has become an acknowledged world specialist on the mind-body-brain connection. And in this ground-breaking book she sets out clearly how the "molecules of emotion" are not confined to the brain, but "run every system in the body". She explains graphically and simply that the body is "the unconscious mind", and how the body and mind work as one for filtering, storing, learning and remembering: key elements of learning.[198]

Some persons on the planet might take issue with this statement because their body was severed from their brains, but they still function with unimpaired mind and feelings, possibly in part due to the autonomic nervous system's production of hormones and the active use of memory.

See Niels Birbaumer's work with waking coma patients.

The MMM Machine

What is MMM? The Multiple Manifold Machine (MMM). We can imagine a Computational Model which includes this machine in a flow loop, functioning in the service of a future protein computer. This is a development implicit in the work of Michael Conrad and Howard Pattee.

The multiple manifold machine was built for Marshall Nirenberg

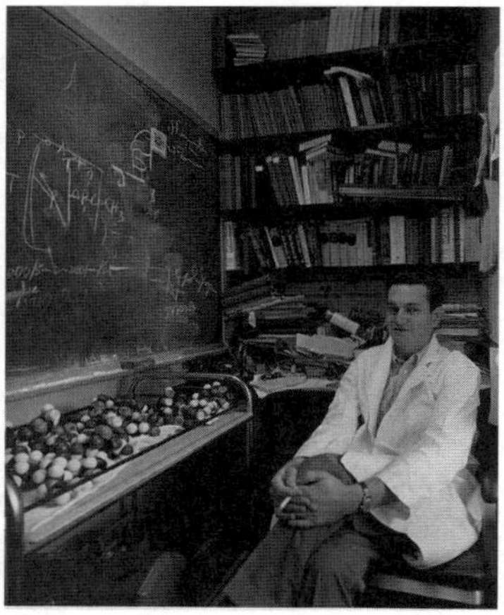

Marshall Nirenberg, photo taken by the National Institutes of Health, ca. 1962. Public domain.

The Physiognomic Side of Nature and its Spatial Relation to the Body

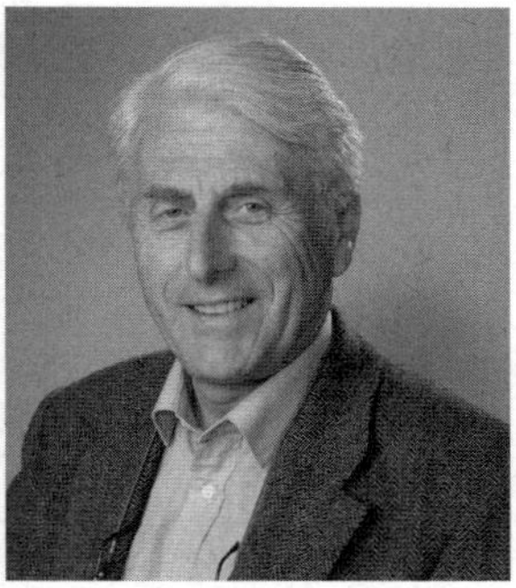
van Hooff, courtesy of J.A.R.AM.

Nature has a face for us with its landscapes. The face of nature is directly related to the survival of the individual. The force fields, employed in our model for a Benevolence Engine, are reflections of a personification of nature as it were.

Smiling

Many authors, most of them implicitly, regard smiling and laughter as patterns that differ only in degree, smiling being a less intense form, a diminutive of laughter. According to Spencer (1870) first the effectors with a low threshold (i.e. the facial musculature) are affected, giving the smile; when stronger excitations break through other muscles join in, giving laughter. According to others (e.g. Darwin, 1872; Hayworth, 1928; Koestler, 1949) laughter preceded smiling in the history of our species, the smile being a subdued version, a diminutive of the laugh.[199]

How will the smile and the laugh become embodied for the Neosentient?

Laughter could be a yellow lamp, smile the same lamp at lower intensities. But the two are driven by different force field components joy = sum potential in the first channel; bonding [oxytocin analogue] = level of one specific force field subcomponent, namely bonding, in the second channel.

Light Computer

A computer might be built some day consisting of nothing but differing states of light. Light itself would become the hardware. The system is physically feasible, reminding one of angels. John Wheeler's Geon comes to mind here as well, combining light with gravitation in the distant future.

Modern "light crystals" can realize this dream whereby physical confinement mechanisms of a mechanical or glass fiber type would still be needed. Several coincident (with their nodes of the lowest frequency) light waves could influence and modulate each other. This could either be achieved by very high energies or via the use of a non-linear medium, a crystal or a liquid. A fairly thin medium would be sufficient – it could be sealed without any material input and output. It would be controlled by light input and produce light output.

We devised a plan for a computer that would operate using differing states of coherent light. This computer would be ultra-fast in terms of its operation. Where an electrochemical computer might draw on the massive parallelism that leads to human thought, a light computer would be a device that could augment thought external to the human body. One could imagine a Neosentient that would incorporate both forms of computing – both light and electrochemical as well as other kinds of computer, forming an ecology of computation.

Fred Hoyle in his science fiction classic *The Black Cloud* already anticipated part of this dream, and Boris Schapiro developed a hypothesis that the sun contains conscious beings that are a product of an evolutionary process taking place at its core.

See also *Geons and Quantum Foam* by J. A. Wheeler.

The Elephant Looking into it's Own Mouth (J. Plotnik, F. de Waal, and D. Reiss, Courtesy J. Plotnik)

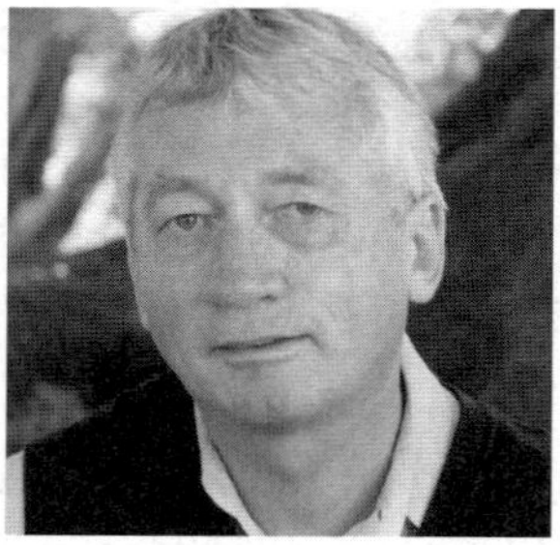

Photograph of Frans de Waal by Catherine Marin, courtesy of de Waal.

A photograph by J. Plotnik, F. de Waal, and D. Reiss taken through a semi-transparent mirror shows an elephant looking into his own mouth. It is one of the most telling photographs in the history of photography because it exemplifies mirror competence.

1. *The mark test. "Happy" the elephant with an X-shaped mark on her head. This image, taken from the camera embedded*

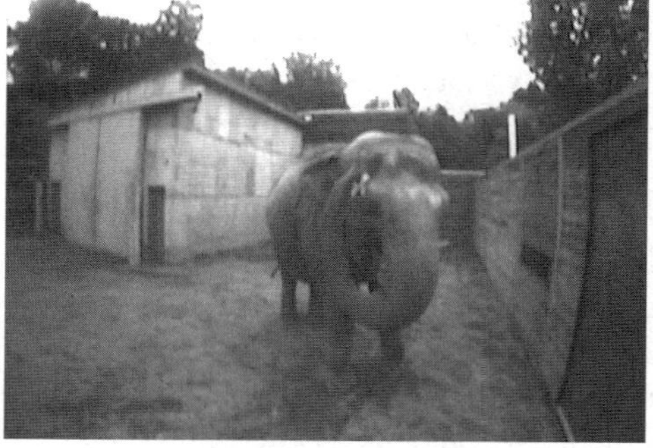

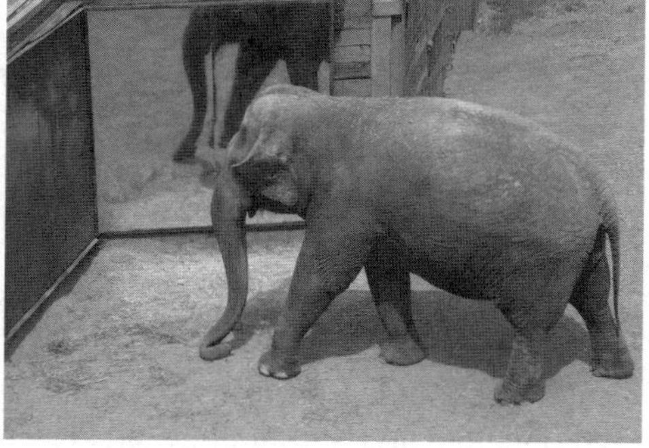

Happy by J. Plotnik, F. de Waal, and D. Reiss, courtesy of J. Plotnik.

directly behind the mirror, shows Happy touching the mark on her head while in full view of the mirror.
2. Happy viewing herself in front of the mirror.

Joshua M. Plotnik, Frans B. M. de Waal, Diana Reiss, from the paper "Self-recognition in an Asian elephant"

Andy Clark – Mind as Mash-up

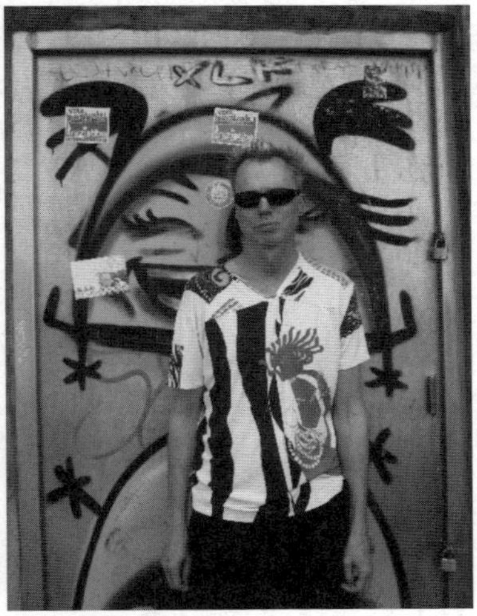
Andy Clark, courtesy Clark.

To unravel the workings of these embodied, embedded, and sometimes extended minds requires an unusual mix of neuroscience, computation, dynamical, and information-theoretic understandings, "brute" physiology, ecological sensitivity, and attention to the stacked designer cocoons in which we grow, work, think and act. This may seem a daunting prospect, but there is cause for optimism. In learning, development and evolution, trade-offs among neural control, bodily morphology, action, and the canny use of environmental resources and opportunities are regularly and reliably achieved. Since such "messy" but powerful solutions are reliably found, there is a good chance that they can be systematically understood. Better still, the sciences of the mind are already well on the way to developing frameworks and forms of analysis that make headway with this difficult task. A mature science of the embodied mind will, I have tried to show, need to combine dynamical insights such as the stress on various forms of coupled-environment unfolding with a much better understanding of the broad space of adaptive trade-offs; an understanding currently best achieved, or so I have argued, by the use of the more familiar tools provided by computational, representational, and information-theoretic approaches.[200]

Plamen Simeonov

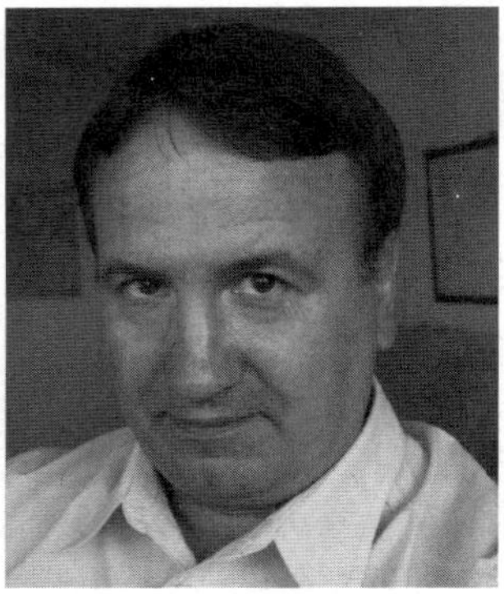

Courtesy of Plamen Simeonov.

Integral biomathics: A post-Newtonian view into the logos of bios

[...] is an attempt for a state-of-the-art survey of natural and life sciences with the goal to define the scope and address the central questions of an original research program. It is focused on the phenomena of emergence, adaptive dynamics and evolution of self-assembling, self-organizing, self-maintaining and self-replicating biosynthetic systems viewed from a newly-arranged perspective and understanding of computation and communication in the living nature. The author regards this research as an integral part of the emerging discipline of nature-inspired or natural computation, i.e. computation inspired by or occurring in nature.[201]

The Creation of a New Techno-species

Neosentience – A New Branch of Scientific and Poetic Inquiry Related to Artificial Intelligence[202]

The Invention of Benevolence

Delectatio in felicitate alterius – Benevolence theory

If two such machines interact in a cross caring manner, each can be enticed into an attempt to simulate in favor of the other's goals.[203]

In this case, the invention of a "hallucinated other center of optimization" occurs. This is the invention of "benevolence." The suspicion is the invention. It is the only example of creation out of nothing that is known. It is a free universe that is suddenly springing out of the machine.

This presents a much more interesting mode of functioning of the system than simple locomotion. It will be necessary to build two such machines to enable such coupling in order to completely understand the emergence of voluntary foreign controlledness within the system, along with its stopping to function as a subconscious optimizer. Actually the invention of the subconscious by Freud corresponds to the rediscovery of the original lack of a consciousness mode in the brain. The real surprise is the emergence of a conscious giving up of the original unconscious identity through the emergence of a simulated existence that is benevolent toward another simulated consciousness that is also internally represented by the same system. So strangely, consciousness is not implied in the machine itself but only in a kind of creation, seemingly out of nothing, yet initiated through specific behavior articulated within the machine. The ghost of personal consciousness has no substratum in the hard and software of the system (other than the momentary subconscious big screen and joystick). Consciousness is pure fiction but it is the only agent to be found; it is an infinitely strong agent.

Smile Theory (Don't Laugh!)

Person theory – the theory of persons – is based on the smile. No non-human animal can smile. Smiling is friendliness and laughter in one, charm and closeness. It encourages and enables the epigenetic occurrence of benevolence in the presence of another.[204]

Are We Making an Immortal?

The potential exists to create an immortal with the brain equation, smile/laughter coupling, the flight simulator and the force field equations. Thus our benevolence engine could potentially become immortal. This mechanism can of course also be supported by a fluidic machine or a well-stirred chemical machine or an electrochemical computer. See other chapters for detailed information on these topics.

Parts always need replacement … our eternal blip.

Mary Catherine Bateson *Our Own Metaphor*

Our Own Metaphor, *with its focus on the human pattern of setting conscious goals, provides a new approach to the basic question of whether humans, with their increasingly powerful technologies, will ultimately destroy the environment on which they depend or prove capable of a new level of adaptation.*[205]

Gregory Bateson – Analog computing
Bateson calls for clarification of [the] distinction between "analog" and "digital". He hearkens back to the arguments over Köhler's presentation at the 4th conference and suggested it would be wise to remove any ambiguities.[206]

Macy 4th conference
Köhler presents his "field" perspective, generating substantial controversy. Pitts and McCulloch criticize Köhler's "field theory" as mere theory devoid of empirical basis.

This debate illustrates two important points. First, there was a divide between those interested in the mechanisms of neural architectures (e.g., Pitts and McCulloch) and those who expressed interest in descriptive theories of what those mechanisms might do (e.g., perception). Second, it remained the case throughout the conference series that the neural mechanism people (who were also to be counted among the formalists) were repeatedly critical of what they perceived as fuzzy or vapid theorization (particularly with regard to the psychoanalysts).[207]

Analogical Computing (Hava T. Siegelmann and Steven Smale)

Neural Networks and Analog Computation:
Beyond the Turing Limit
By Hava T. Siegelmann

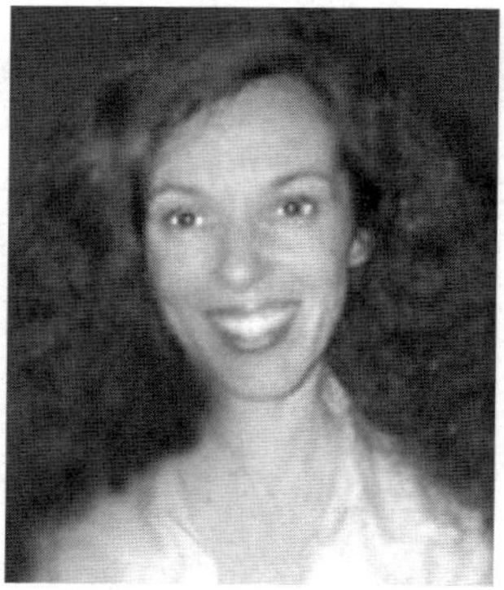
Courtesy of Siegelmann.

The theoretical foundations of Neural Networks and Analog Computation conceptualize neural networks as a particular type of computer consisting of multiple assemblies of basic processors interconnected in an intricate structure.

Examining these networks under various resource constraints reveals a continuum of computational devices, several of which coincide with well-known classical models. What emerges is a Church-Turing-like thesis, applied to the field of analog computation, which features the neural network model in place of the digital Turing machine. This new concept can serve as a point of departure for the development of alternative, supra-Turing computational theories. On a mathematical level, the treatment of neural computations enriches the theory of computation but also explicates the computational complexity associated with biological networks, adaptive engineering tools, and related models from the fields of control theory and nonlinear dynamics.[208]

Segelmann states: "The surprising finding has been that when analog networks assume real weights, their power encompasses and transcends that of digital computers."[209] *She goes on to say "our model captures nature's manifest "computation" of the future physical world from the present, in which constants that are not known to us, or cannot even be measured, do affect the evolution of the system."*[210]

See Also *Neural Networks and Analog Computation: Beyond the Turing Limit* by Hava Siegelmann, Siegelmann, 1998

One of us explored a related approach – see *Chemical Automata in Homogeneous and Reaction–Diffusion Kinetics.* This is the well-stirred model of artificial intelligence.[211] Bruno Marchal should be mentioned here. See also Klaus Peter Zauner, Steven Smale, and Gerold Baier.

Analog Chips (Remembering their Ancestry from McCulloch and Pitts)

Configurable analogue ICs have been available in various forms for years, seemingly making less of an impression on the market than their digital cousins, FPGAs (field-programmable gate arrays). The current economic situation suddenly makes the concept of programmable analogue standard products more attractive, however. The need to stay on the leading edge of design practice in a product area but without a lot of design cost and without the end-user demand that could justify taking any one design into production fits perfectly with the benefits of these devices. Their day may finally be at hand.[212]

The World as Interface/Interface as Continuum

The word "interface" is one of the most difficult to understand notions of history. For example, the Now is pure interface. The world is pure interface. Only consciousness is more (pure substance), but within its shadowy recesses, we have nothing but interface.

Matter is about equally hard to understand, being – as an exo- attempt to understand the world – almost ridiculous. But within that material "universe", again nothing but an interface waits. This is Einstein's discovery of relativity. There are a few precursors like Archimedes, Boscovich, Maxwell. And a few followers, like G. H. Mead who discovered the relativity of being a person. Persons are defined by being benevolent in constructing an interface called peace or synonymously, paradise. Feuerbach and Gandhi wait to be acknowledged by the greatest intelligence on the planet, a sperm whale. But let us return to Einstein (who venerated Gandhi). We all live in a yellow (submarine) light bubble […] The interface. The medium means only you. You are the most important person on earth and in heaven. The interface says: this face is naked and waits for you in order to be spared dying (as Levinas discovered).[213]

We only have the medium.

Einstein's interface is the Lorentz transformation, the spherical light bubble existing for two mutually moving observers around each, with each as the center of his own bubble … but nevertheless the two bubbles being the same bubble. This conundrum, a logical impossibility, was accepted by Einstein and shown to be reality. It is the most mind-blowing discovery of history. Poincaré's "Lorentz transformation" of 1900 is the oldest explicit interface: is it not beautiful? If the most famous interface equation still waits to be better understood, what do we gain?

Free energy from gravity? Perhaps. An explanation of the Hubble law? Perhaps. A reappraisal of the world as a light bubble? For sure. But what is the real gain? Can we explain color? Can we understand the rosette phenomenon (of sperm whales)? Should science go on? Science is friendship. The youth of the planet was never more promising and never deserved it more.

The science of endophysics claims that the world as it is given to us is only a cut, an interface, a difference inside of what is the real world on the exo level (the whole). This has some powerful implications, including the possibility to change the whole world (i.e., the interface world). That is the world change technology about which we are not strong enough to talk here …

Everett also was not able to fully work out the implications of this insight of his. See the beautiful book by Bryce DeWitt and Neill Graham entitled *The Many-Worlds Interpretation of Quantum Mechanics* (Princeton University Press 1973).

Is the mind-body interface microscopic?

Advances in the biophysics of the nervous system, not only on the level of its macroscopic functioning but also on the level of individual ion channels, have made the question of how finely consciousness is tied to matter and its dynamics more important. Quantum mechanics limits the attainable resolution and puts into doubt the idea of an infinitely fine-woven attachment. A recent approach to physics rekindles such a rationalist hope. Endophysics focuses on the global implications of microscopic computer simulations of chemical and biophysical processes. A complete artificial universe can be set up in the computer. It produces non-classical and nonlocal effects inside – on the interface that exists between an internal observer (fluid neuron) and the rest of the world. This interface is finer than any brain property to which the status of the mind-body interface has been attributed hitherto. A new class of experiments becomes possible in the artificial world and, by analogy, in the real world. Magnetic resonance imaging experiments, routinely performed under open-loop conditions, can be repeated under psychophysical (closed-loop) conditions – in search for microscopically induced changes in the perceived and measured structure of the world.[214]

The ultimate litmus test would be to deliberately encode a message in the digit string of a physical constant like h or c (as mentioned above).

Interfaciology

Interfaciology represents the broadest understanding of the "world as interface" and the potential ramifications this has for coming to know the world.

Because the broad implications of interfaciology extend across disciplines, we are proposing a symposium that looks as much at physical, biological, mathematical, and engineering aspects of the interface as it does in the historical, philosophical, social, and artistic interpretations that are enveloped in the emerging discourses of techno-culture. This would suggest that areas such as cognitive systems, complex systems theory, and the brain sciences, will be as relevant to the discussion as cinema, television, media art, theories of representation and spectatorship in experiential conditions driven less by singular states and more by transformations.[215]

The whole thing is very metaphysical; "this is why I am here" was just a remark by one of us to the other.

"This is why I am here" on multiple levels.

Cooperation in Robotics (Luc Steels)

Steels invented a group of robots that in turn invented an animal-like language on their own. Many insights related to communication will be enabled by his work. Also the gap between animal and human language will be better explicated.

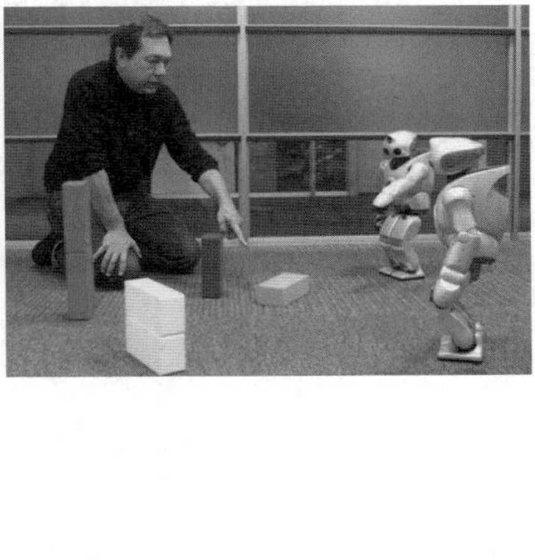

Courtesy of Luc Steels.

Steels:

My scientific research interests cover the whole field of artificial intelligence, including natural language, vision, robot behavior, learning, cognitive architecture, and knowledge representation. At the moment my focus is on dialogs for humanoid robots and fundamental research into the origins of language and meaning. Current work focuses on developing the foundations of semiotic dynamics and on fluid construction grammars.

Evolving Grounded Communication for Robots
The computational and robotic synthesis of language evolution is emerging as a new exciting field of research. The objective is to come up with precise operational models of how communities of agents, equipped with a cognitive apparatus, a sensori-motor system, and a body, can arrive at shared grounded communication systems. Such systems may have similar characteristics to animal communication or human language. Apart from its technological interest in building novel applications in the domain of human–robot or robot–robot interaction, this research is of interest to the many disciplines concerned with the origins and evolution of language and communication.[216]

On Steels' work
Several experiments focus on teaching robots language skills, which will be an essential capability of machines designed to function as humanoid aides. SONY Computer Science Laboratory artificial intelligence expert Luc Steels proclaims that open-ended dialogues with "physically embodied robots" are possible. He has conducted an experiment in which an AIBO robot equipped with a video camera and a microphone was "taught" to recognize a new object – a ball – by forming concepts from the visual and audio input it received. The robot picks up on preprogrammed words spoken by its human teacher – such as "look," "listen," "good," "what is it?," "yes," and "no" – and associates them with the object.[217]

However, there is some daylight in the form of the computer science researcher Luc Steels who argues that "language was a cultural breakthrough, like writing." To give credence to this hypothesis, Steels purports to have built robots ***without any explicit language module*** [emphasis the authors] *which nonetheless developed grammar and syntax systems on their own. In different research, neural network computer models have produced overgeneralization errors (followed by self-correction) when learning language constructs that are eerily similar to those exhibited by human children (e.g. "I bringed the toy to Mommy").*[218]

C. Andy Hilgartner's artificial grammar which avoids a potential suicidal aspect of all post-hunter-gatherer societies must also be mentioned in this context.

Games and Seduction

(Shigeru Miyamoto) – Zelda. Evolution of a character. Fair use.

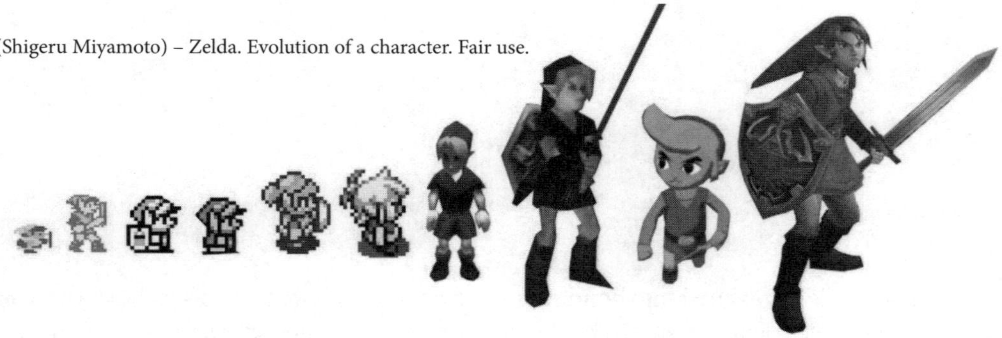

Shigeru Miyamoto is one of the people that invented natural virtual-environment computer games, where one controls an actor in 3D space. One walks behind a digital actor and one can also inspect this puppet from an alternate set of perspectives. *Zelda* is a full artificial environment where you can have the complete freedom to move about in a virtual space. Thus, this work enables people to be free in their identity in an artificial universe and also to experience nice feelings about one's second identity – moving in a way that is charming like Mother Theresa.

Good must be more fun than evil.

The Legend of Zelda
The Legend of Zelda (THE HYRULE FANTASY) is a video game designed by Shigeru Miyamoto and published by Nintendo in 1986. A classic example of the action-adventure genre, the game is set in the fantasy land of Hyrule and centers around a young hero's quest to rescue Princess Zelda from the villainous Ganon by collecting the eight fragments of a powerful artifact known as the Triforce. As one of Nintendo's flagship franchises, Zelda is among the most recognized names in video games.

One of the authors would like to thank Matthias Scharle for introducing him to Zelda early on.

The Science of Charm

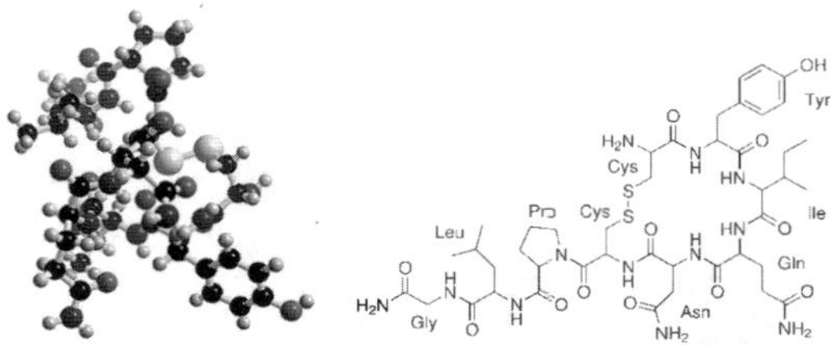

Oxytocin. Public domain.

Being charmed is being lured into bonding, mediated by oxytocin. It makes you see with your heart. It is because you are rewarded by the signs of reward of another being (for humans).

What is Second Life?

Second Life is a 3D virtual world entirely built and owned by its residents.
Since opening to the public in 2003, it has grown "explosively."

- *From the moment you enter the World you'll discover a vast digital continent, teeming with people, entertainment, experiences and opportunity. Once you've explored a bit, perhaps you'll find a perfect parcel of land to build your house or business.*
- *You'll also be surrounded by the Creations of your fellow residents. Because residents retain the rights to their digital creations, they can buy, sell and trade with other residents.*
- *The Marketplace currently supports millions of US dollars in monthly transactions. This commerce is handled with the in-world unit-of-trade, the Linden dollar, which can be converted to US dollars at several thriving online Linden Dollar exchanges.*[219]

This relates back to William Gibson's Neuromancer in which he invented Virtual Reality.

Avatar

The movie *Avatar* by James Cameron exemplifies and exploits the dialectic of a computer-aided humanism. This film, like A.I., only touches on the immortality of a computer-based intelligence.

Ingo Rechenberg

Rechenberg has developed approaches to artificial bionics since the 1960s. Bionics (also called bio-mimetics) is an attempt to learn technical tricks from nature.

Thomas Ray – Tierra

He is the first to implement Natural Selection in a computer – to have an artificial evolution.

Tierra
(n) 1. Artificial life simulation of Thomas Ray's which demonstrates the utility of natural selection in computer implementations for finding novel approaches to difficult problems.[220]

Tom Ray is admirable for a strict employment of ethics in his computation.

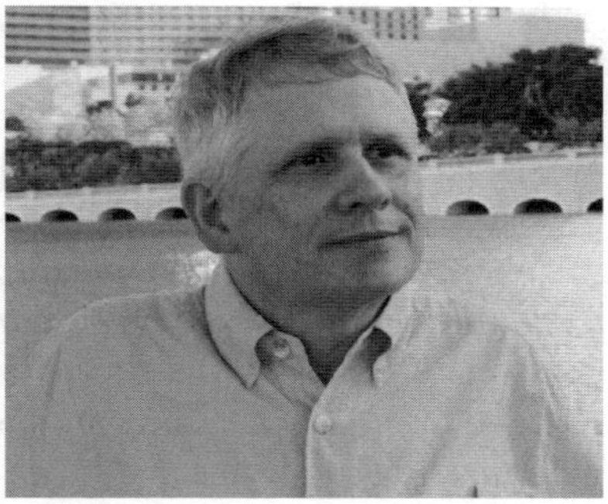

Photo by Chenmei Xu, courtesy of Thomas Ray.

Embodied Souls

"Solecules are the molecules of the soul …" Fredkin

Robotic Care Givers

Robotic care givers might potentially deliver loving care as emotional companions.

Aging population: Robots are widely used in Japan and are seen as a way to help deal with an aging population. Nearly 19% of the 130 million people that live in the country are aged 65 and over. This is expected to rise to 40% by 2055.[221]

In Pictures: Robot menagerie

Robots could be key to maintaining the labour force and helping care for the elderly. The Paro robot was developed by the National Institute of Advanced Industrial Science for therapy sessions in care homes. It is also used by autistic and handicapped children. Like more traditional animal therapy, where pets are brought into hospitals, the robots are used to help people relax and exercise. As well as responding to touch through tactile sensors on its body, Paro responds to its name and coos like a real baby harp seal. Other robots to aid the elderly included the My Spoon feeding robot. The joystick-controlled arm helps people feed themselves. The spoon tipped device follows pre-programmed movements to move food from a plate to a position just in front of the user's mouth. It is already on sale in Japan and Europe. Other robots to be honoured at the ceremony included a huge autonomous vacuum cleaner that moves around Tokyo skyscrapers at night, clearing up after office workers.[222]

Do the Japanese respond to such robots because they have a deep appreciation of Pantheism? (See also *The Uncanny Valley.*) Humans are the only animals that care about the emotions of others from the inside perspective. Many animals give the impression of doing the same thing. But how are we to know? In many cases caring behavior has the same effects as humane behavior. The effect is caring, but the animal has no understanding of another mind existing as something autonomous, to the best of current scientific knowledge. The inappropriate modern consensus is that animals do have a "theory of mind" if they pretend there is a predator in order to eat a certain food undisturbed (as an example). But there is a misunderstanding here involved among humans. Successfully predicting how another mind will respond does not prove that one takes into account the other mind. Alternately, chess playing would be an example. Ravens are known to remove food they had hidden while another Raven was watching, and re-burying it somewhere else or even pretending to hide food without actually doing it (Thomas Bugyar). This is because they have mirror competence and use it for predicting the behavior of others.

In neosentience, we pragmatically seek mirror competence plus the positive feedback of benevolence acquisition. The latter is generally so far not considered by philosophers of mind, AI researchers, and evolutionary anthropologists.

Animals are Behaviorists

A chimpanzee mother whose child had a broken arm was hugging it and when it cried more because it hurt, hugged it even more. This would be an example of not knowing what is going on inside of another being. Humans have an acquired trait that takes into account the inner feelings of another person. This – having thrown one's soul over the fence – animals cannot do this, as far as we know. Ultraperspective – perspective taking from both the vantange point and the subjective state of the other – was first emphasized in George Herbert Mead's *Mind, Self and Society*, 1930. It was written posthumously from his notes by his students who published it without adding their own names. So he is still alive …

Skinner invented behaviorism and he mistakenly thought behaviorism suffices to explain society. It does suffice to explain animal society. He left out ultraperspective like a dictator did in practice. If human beings are behaviorists they are cruel by definition – the Marquis de Sade was a behaviorist in this definition. When animals are behaviorists they are absolutely sound and normal and behave like innocent animals. Konrad Lorenz told one of the authors of a story of someone who was going to be eaten by wolves – he realized the wolves were suddenly friendly. They were so kind because one doesn't show aggression against a "piece of bread" that one is going to eat.

Perhaps some animals have overstepped the barrier in history but whenever this has happened, they ceased to be animals and have become persons. The "rosette phenomenon" is a potential example here. It is known as a whaling technique. A lonely sperm whale is shot at and deliberately not killed – just wounded, floating helplessly at the surface. Then the other members of its clan assemble around him, forming a so-called "rosette" because all of their heads come together while their tails point out forming a star. In this position it is easy to harvest all of them, to put their meat into the waiting refrigerators. The big question is – are they so stupid or do they know what is happening to them? Maybe they are teaching their little human brothers a lesson in Buddhism. It should be noted that the sperm whale has the biggest and most complex brain on the planet.

Benevolence from a Doll and Animals Brought into Personhood

… is a possibility to be taken seriously. A young white elephant might be seducible into the same role by his caretaker making the bonding signal whenever happy (like the pseudo-smile of a human mother laughing).

Expanded Neural Aesthetics/The Aesthetics of Neosentience

Erotic Dolls? (Ethics and human nature …)

Descartes' Doll

From Descartes: An intellectual biography
By Stephan Gaukroger

Since the eighteenth century [so this would be 100 years after his death – the authors], *there has been in circulation a curious story about Descartes. It is said that in later life he was always accompanied in his travels by a mechanical life-sized female doll which, we are told by one source, he himself had constructed "to show that animals are only machines and have no souls". He had named the doll after his illegitimate daughter, Francine,* [his beloved only child that dies of scarlet fever at age 5], *and some versions of events have it that she was so lifelike that the two were indistinguishable. Descartes and the doll were evidently inseparable, and he is said to have slept with her incased in a trunk at his side. Once, during a crossing over the Holland Sea some time in the early 1640s, while Descartes was sleeping, the captain of the ship, suspicious about the contents of the trunk, stole into the cabin and opened it. To his horror, he discovered the mechanical monstrosity, dragged her from the trunk and across the decks, and finally managed to throw her in the water. We are not told whether she put up a struggle.*

This story had a wide currency in the nineteenth and early twentieth centuries, at one stage being taken as a theme for a novel by Anatole France. It exists in a number of versions, some of them explicitly fictional, some purporting to be factual, and the detail varies quite considerably from version to version. (1) So far as I can tell, the story originates no earlier than the eighteenth century, and it received most attention in an era preoccupied with the theories of La Mettrie, the French Enlightenment philosopher who, in his infamous L'Homme Machine (1747), had extended the idea of animals being automata – developed by Descartes in his L'Homme – to human beings, offering a materialist account of the mind, and suggesting that Descartes himself had held such a view, but that judicious self-censorship had prevented him making the theory public. (2) There is, in fact, absolutely no evidence that any version of the story is true. Its origins are rather obscure, but by the second half of the eighteenth century it was a propaganda weapon in the fight against La Mettrie's materialism, Descartes himself being seen as the ultimate instigator of this pernicious doctrine. Given this context, the story has all the elements of propaganda, including that favourite propaganda weapon, sexual innuendo, and I have little doubt that it originated as a tool of the eighteenth-century struggle against materialism.[223]

Neosentience is continuing on this dangerous track, but we added the concept of benevolence and we mean it.

Descartes made the startling proposal that consciousness resides in the brain and "solely" in the brain (pun not intended). This idea is very strange if one puts oneself into the shoes of his time and all other human civilizations of history. We are absolutely familiar with this because of modern medicine – but it must be kept in mind that modern medicine was invented by Descartes. So we no longer feel startled as much as he did because of the absolute absurdity that this idea represents. For imagine someone who claims that the soul exists in the left hand's little finger or in an apple in a drawer as in Arabic fairy tales. This machine which is also sometimes called a "meat computer" is not predestined to hold the holy grail of consciousness because nothing in the world can possibly contain the world and even more than the world. But this is exactly what consciousness does. Colors are definitely not included in the Cartesian–Newtonian world machine, nor is the "now". So it would be interesting to do research in how Descartes first arrived at this startling conclusion.

This insight suggests a very different reading from the dualistic understanding of Cartesian philosophy. Descartes was definitely a monist, believing only in the safe existence of the mind. This follows from one sentence from his Meditations on the First Philosophy. To paraphrase his text – If I said to myself in a dream "cogito ergo sum," then this definitely would be the case. Therefore the whole material world that Descartes revolutionized by his machine conjecture, to him, was pure subjective experience. To Descartes, there is no world outside the mind. Bishop Berkeley revived this deep side of Descartes. According to Berkeley all is pure soul. Berkeley was perhaps the only one who understood Descartes.

Res-cogitans contains res-extensa. Mind and body appear to co-arise but we have no theory and no reason for the existence of mind in matter. Esse est percipi – to be is to be perceived, in Berkeley's words.

How to Build a Superluminal Computer[224]

The speed of light represents one of the fundamental limits of the laws of physics. Nothing can travel faster than the speed of light, right?

Well, yes and no, say Volkmar Putz and Karl Svozil at the Vienna University of Technology in Austria. They say there are several ways that signals can cross the superluminal line, although none of them allow the kind of time travel paradoxes beloved of science fiction writers. For example, the quantum phenomenon of entanglement occurs when two quantum particles are described by the same wave function. These particles can be separated by the diameter of the universe and yet a measurement on one will instantaneously influence the other.

So-called "nonlocal" phenomena cannot be used to transmit information faster than the speed of light but Putz and Svozil today ask whether it can be used to process it, to carry out computational tasks at superluminal speeds. They say there is no reason why not, provided the processing does not lead to any time travel paradoxes.

How might such a machine work? Putz and Svozil point out that nonlocal phenomena can lead to materials in which the index of refraction is less than one, thereby allowing superluminal speeds. For example, light travelling through a vacuum can be made to spontaneously form into an electron-positron pair-an entangled pair-which then recombines to form a photon [it must be two] *again. This process happens instantaneously, allowing the photon to effectively "jump" across space.*

A material in which this kind of pair formation and recombination was promoted would have a refractive index less than one, they say. Various physicists have proposed such materials made of things like metamaterials. Putz and Svozil themselves suggest that a vacuum filled with either electrons or positrons would do the trick.

Having created a medium in which the refractive index is less than one, Putz and Svozil's idea is simply to immerse a computer in it. That simple act (and presumably some clever design to create an optical computer in the first place) would allow superluminal computation to take place.

Assuming that this device could actually be built, what could you do with a superluminal computer? That's a good question that Putz and Svozil do not address directly. They say such a device would fall into a class of processing machine known as hypercomputers. These are hypothetical devices more powerful than Turing machines, that allow non-Turing computations. They were first discussed by Alan Turing in the 1930s.[225]

The question of whether superluminal signals can be sent was raised by Einstein, Rosen, and Podolsky in 1935. Everett in 1957 and Bell in 1964 demonstrated the partial soundness of the idea. The first convincing measurements were made by Alain Aspect in 1979. What can be sent superluminally are only "½ messages" – that is the second half of the message has to be supplied subluminally before one can recognize whether the first part has arrived or not. Putz and Svozil had an ingenious idea – how to generate a superluminal computer out of these ingredients. It is tempting to think of this idea as a sort of "mind" being implemented in a completely new way whereby the feasibility of this new hardware is open at the moment. Robert Forward's *Dragon's Egg* is a story where two life forms interact, one of which is 1 million times faster than the other also comes to mind at this point. One can imagine slow computers with specific qualities (like humans) interacting with ultra-fast computers with a completely different physical nature.

Another exhilarating idea in this context is "The engine of engines." It would be a machine which combines all possible different kinds of computing machines in such a way that each brings in a different optimal performance inaccessible to the others as stand-alone machines.

Computers Began as People

"Computers" were initially people before they were understood as non-human machines given the history of the use of this word. In An Illustrated History of Computers John Kopplin states:

"Computer" was originally a job title: it was used to describe those human beings (predominantly women) whose job it was to perform the repetitive calculations required to compute such things as navigational tables, tide charts, and planetary positions for astronomical almanacs'. (Kopplin, 2002, http://www.computersciencelab.com/ComputerHistory/History.htm)

It is interesting to note that the etymology of the term computer began with "Computare" and focused on reckoning:

Compute 1631, from Latin, computare "to count, sum up" from com "with" + putare "to reckon". The term was initially used for a person who "computes" 1646; mechanical calculating machine, 1897; and electronic machine, 1941. In the modern meaning, "programmable digital electronic computer" 1945 (the theoretical sense is from 1937, as in the Turing Machine).[226]

So we ask, what are all of the processes at operation in the body that enable us to "reckon"? (see also von Foerster above, p. 41). The body is extremely complex and we can approach it from many different disciplinary understandings. Individual disciplines often have their own language, publishing domains, and intellectual hegemonies. How can we facilitate interdisciplinary and transdisciplinary insight through computational means? From the perspective of biochemistry intersecting with computer science, we can come to understand the body as an "electrochemical" computer – a far from equilibrium complex adaptive system.

A Multi-perspective Approach to Understanding That Which is at Operation in the Body Contributing to Thought and Sentience

We can examine the body from a series of different disciplinary, interdisciplinary, and transdisciplinary perspectives – scientific, humanities-related, and poetic. Often new knowledge arises in the space between established domains, formed by defining new forms of dynamic relationality. If we unpack the conceptual processes adhered to by each of us as creative thinkers that try to eventuate new modes of understanding, could we create a new tool set inspired by this plethora of processes to augment our current approach to knowledge production? Could we create a computational "tool of tools" comprised of many digital tools and processes that might be apt to intra-act in a thought augmenting manner? We would call this system an "insight engine."

Neosentientology

Neosentientology: A multi-perspective approach to Neosentience.

Recombinant Informatics – imagine the following list written in a circle, with a line drawn to bridge each category to another one …

Aesthetics
Analog Computation
Anthropogenesis
Anthropology
Ape-ology
Apology
Art
Artificial Intelligence
Artificial Life
Attachment Theory
Autism Therapy
Autopoiesis
Benevolence Theory
Bio Art
Bio Ethics
Bio Technology
Biology
Bioinformatics
Biochemistry
Biogenesis
Bionics
Bonding Theory
Bondology
Category Theory
Catastrophe Theory
Chaos Theory
Chemistry
Chronomatics
Cognitive Maps
Color Theory
Computer Science
Conceptual Art
Consciousness Theory
Cosmology
Cybernetics
Digital Computation
Deductive Biology
Dolphinology
Dynamical Systems Theory
Ecosemiotics
Entailment Theory
Epiphenomenology
Epistemology
EPR paradox
Erobotics
Ethics
Ethology
Ethomathematics
Etymology
Everett Theory
Exobiology
Far From Equilibrium Systems
Field Theory of Meaning
Force Field Theory (Synthetic Emotions)
Free Will Theory
Galactic Export
Genomics
Geobiology
Grammatology
Integral Biomathics
Integrative Linguistics
Interfaciology
Laughter Theory
Lingua Franca
Linguistics
Mathematics
Mathematical Biology
Media Archeology

Media Art
Micro Reversibility
Mirror Competence
Molecules of Emotion Theory
Monadology
Morphology
Multi-modal Sensing (human and machinic)
Mythology
Nanoscale Computation
Natural Language
Neural Aesthetics
Neosentient Aesthetics
Neurobiology
Neurology
Neuroscience
Neumannology
Neurotransmitter Theory
Neuroquantology
Nomadology
Nynology – Science of the Now
Octopodology
Ontology
Orobourology
Oxythocinology
Pandakology
Paradoxology
Pattern Flow Theory
Pattern topologies
Performative Science
Personhood Theory
Personogenesis
Phenomenology
Philosophy
Physiology
Physiognomics
Pico Scale Computation
Pity Theory
Point Omega
Proteonomics
Primatology
Psychoacoustics
Psychology
Psychophysics
Radical Constructivism
Recombinant Informatics
Recombinant Poetics
Relational Memory
Relative State Theory
Rhizomatics
Rhizomatic Informatics
Robotics
Robot Language Acquisition
Semiotics
Sexology
Singularity Theory
Smile Theory
Sociology
Synthetic Genetics
Synthetic Innate Releasing Mechanisms
Synthetic Senses
The Brain Equation
The Now Equation
Theology
Termodynamics
Thermodynamics
Time Reversability
Topology
Topological Psychology
Variantology
Zoosemiotics

The Articulation of a Bio-mimetic Form of Computation

In the above light, the future understanding of the body's entailments as they are related to thought processes, might lead to a re-understanding of the nature of computation itself.

Neuromorphic Articulation

Could we imagine collaborating with a new variety of "creative" bio-computer based on a "Neuromorphically" articulated creative system to augment human creativity?

Neuromorphic systems are implementations in silicon of sensory and neural systems whose architecture and design are based on neurobiology. This growing area offers exciting possibilities, such as sensory systems that can compete with human senses and pattern recognition systems that can run in real time. It is at the intersection of neurophysiology, computer science and electrical engineering. (Smith and Hamilton, 1998, back cover)

For those that feel that the analog system does not have the desired accuracy and determinacy, the neuromorphic approach may be of greater value. Here, research can bifurcate and be applied to both the analog and the digital realm although we are equally interested in the emergent properties that our embodied electrochemical system can make manifest.

Vast Complexity

There are said to be as many as 10,000 different kinds of neurons in the brain – having subtly different functions related to different areas in the brain as well as in relation to more global brain functionalities. They might also use an unimaginable variety of neural transmitters. To this we add that there are 200 billion neurons in the brain. We must also consider the complex bio-functionality of the senses. How might dynamic hierarchies and/or heterarchies be visualized in new ways that illuminate their inter-functionality and intra-functionality? Can we develop new computational systems that reflect such complex bio-landscapes by bringing different domains and scales of research into play? As computer-based systems and technological sensory extensions change our relation to both nature and language, we need to create mechanisms that function at the highest possible level of human/machine interaction, to best reflect upon this plethora of emergent relations. In so doing we change the sensing and knowing potentials of the organism itself through machinic extension.

The movie *Avatar* implemented some of these ideas already. We should not forget the bottom-up approach which could start out with an analysis of Pandaka pygmaea.

Insight Engine

A contemporary "insight engine" (our tool of tools) would explore dynamic relationality. A large set of micro-process "modules" or "context-windows" would employ a set of computational processes that enable a chosen set of juxtapositions to be entertained locally or from distributed locations. In a contemporary "theater of thought" we could like Gunji explore recombinant semantic relationality, enabling (through human/machine and human/human interaction) introspection, mapping, discussion, synthesis, juxtaposition, the examination of historical examples, conceptual analysis, pattern relationality, structural relationships, differing modes of description, annotation of forms, conceptual unpacking, the storage and retrieval of data sets. So as to enable a "creative" discussion surrounding particular areas of study. One could also generate an ongoing set of new computational "triples" reading all literature in terms of subject, object, predicate.

Such a system might embody the following computational features:

- *Storage and retrieval of information from multiple distributed sources.*
- *The searching of databases containing abstracts, papers and texts from many different disciplines derived through the use of "triples" and/or other search methodologies.*
- *The facilitation of the ability to search – textual, media object or entire multi-modal architectures of association that other researchers may have already assembled.*
- *The operative employment of articulated relationalities between disciplines (to function as database filters)*
- *The generation of linguistic tools (shared articulation schemes) including jargon translation systems and bridging languages enabling discussion across disciplinary domains.*
- *The articulation of Boundary Objects.*
- *The housing of numerous forms of imaging, including the ability to access dynamic models, emulations and simulations.*
- *The storage of maps of entailment.*
- *The storage of dynamic time-based diagrams.*
- *The ability to approach a process from multiple scales which could be brought into relational juxtaposition.*
- *The storage and retrieval of associated diagrams as part of process, including informal diagrams – e.g. discussion notes.*
- *The storage and active use of documentation of performative processes – video and video "mark up" potentials, VR and VR mark up languages, recorded discussion.*
- *The articulation of a time line of historical relevancies with the ability to search for time-specific data.*
- *The generation of a multi-scale virtual map of all relevant space – micro and macro.*

- *The long term goal of articulating a map of the body and many of its intra-functionalities – micro/macro. This might work toward articulating the entailment of neural connectivity and recursive loops (the same also in Pandaka pygmea).*
- *The development of new organizing principles – new cybernetic approaches across research domains.*
- *The development of a poly-sensing environment enabling the connection between physical space and data space.*
- *Digital / Analogue cross referencing*
- *The ability to house relevant information related to evolution, deductive biology, recursive evolution genetics, genomics.*
- *The potential to provide multiple approaches to a given subject through texts – factual, fictional, historical and poetic.*
- *The potential to house systems of categorizations and meta-categorizations.*
- *The ability to explore and articulate ontology, genealogy, etymology and epistemology.*
- *The functionality to connect to multiple fields/disciplines/institutes and structures of collaboration across fields.*
- *The potential to use knowledge gleaned from the system to work toward the development of different technological instruments that extend human potential in an ongoing manner.*
- *The use of the system to help facilitate the articulation of new processes/new approaches to science, the humanities and the arts.*[227]

This is work in progress so to speak. Closely aligned to many different research efforts, yet articulated in the spirit of interdisciplinary and transdisciplinary cooperation.

The Glass Ceiling and the Vertical Breakthrough

Connected to benevolence, the Neosentient machine can potentially move from being a deterministic, intelligent autonomous self-propelled entity to a genuinely autonomous, gentle, caring "person" who displays qualities like benevolent empathy, creativity and fantasy for a joint future. Central to their "personhood" is the creativity of sacrifice. We may see that robots exhibit the propensity to invent religion. In human history at some point the realization that subjectivity and the Now are gifts fell into oblivion. The color problem would loom large as a point of contention between artificial persons and biological persons. In this context butterflies, mollusks, and crabs that can use more than three colors would also become allies in their most highly developed forms; octopuses and certain undersea crabs have been found that might even show mirror competence.

Potato Washing

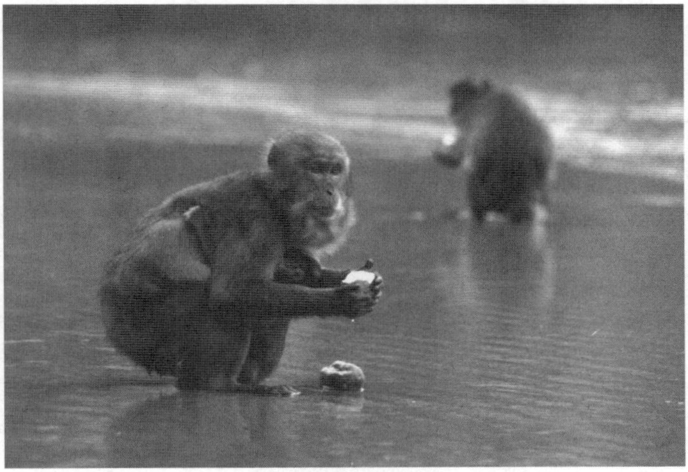

Photograph of Macaques on Koshima Island: Photograph by Frans de Waal, courtesy of Frans de Waal.

See *Cultural Primatology Comes of Age*
Frans B. M. de Waal[228]

The Hundredth Monkey Revisited
Researched by James Gregory

Most people are familiar with the story of "The Hundredth Monkey." Lyall Watson first told it in "Lifetide," but its most widely-known version is in the book The Hundredth Monkey by Ken Keyes. For those of you who don't know it, the story goes like this: The Japanese monkey, Macaca fuscata, had been observed in the wild for a period of over 30 years. One of their favorite foods was the sweet potato. In 1952, an 18-month-old female named Imo on the island of Koshima found she could solve the annoying problem of sand on her potatoes by washing them before eating them. She taught this trick to her mother. Her playmates also learned this new way from her and they taught their mothers.

The Japanese researcher who discovered this is named MASAO Kawai.
This is an example of epigenetics as is any form of culture and tradition.[229]
Neosentient entities may potentially be able to communicate with other such entities via direct coupling. This is an example of tradition and technology in a non-human species.

Poly-sensing Potentials

The potential is to use machine senses to build up a knowledge of context. Empathy would at first still be missing in these autistic biological situations. The long-term goal for our Neosentient machine is to break the glass ceiling of autism, learn language, become creative, and have the ability to glean a deep knowledge of context as an ongoing activity.

The Dolphin invents when quite young a specific whistle which is then adopted by its group as its name.

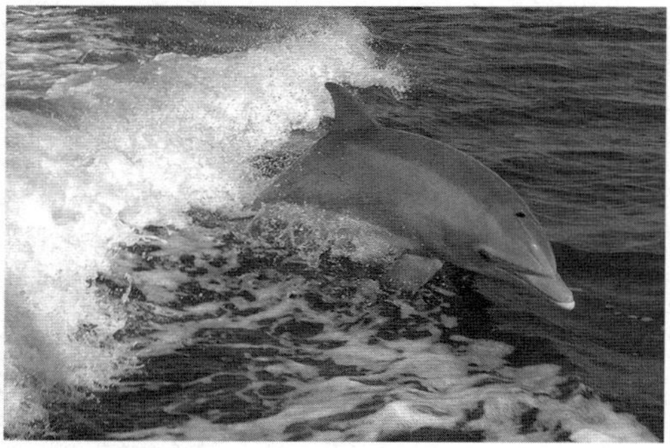

Public domain.

Poly-sensing technology can be used to form the machinic senses of the Benevolence Engine.

The "Poly-sensing Environment" – Toward the development of an integrated distributed technology exploring "Poetic/Informational Grammars of Attention and Functionality".
Seaman, Verbauwhede, Hansen

There are many exciting potentials related to the development of new sensing technologies at this time. In particular we are seeking in an interdisciplinary manner, to develop research that explores the creation of a poetic/informational interactive system, that will be facilitated through the use of multi-modal sensory devices that collaborate in a distributed fashion. Many researchers see the importance of parsing "sense" data within interactive environments. Turing's description of the ACE (Automatic Computing Engine), the first digital computer, saw the potential for a machine with programmed responsive, "operative" input and output "organs" (Turing). The biological model of the human body, parsing a series of sensory modalities in the service of knowledge acquisition and general functioning, becomes one focus for the development of our model. Yet, technologies enable the pertinent extension of the senses. Organism like, self organizing technological systems enable new forms of poetic/informational interaction. (Gordon Pask was a pioneer in this area.) We can also look toward many different organisms to implement different qualities of the "senses" that will make up this system. Our long-term goal is to create "neighborhood" environments. Indeed, advances in sub-micron and nano-scale semiconductor technologies allow the integration of multiple heterogeneous sensors on one "system-on-a-chip." The unique aspect of this technology will be the collection of information from the parsing of an integrated "collaboration" between different selected micro-scale sensing devices. A number of researchers are currently exploring the parsing of individual streams of sense data. Our new paradigm will enable every chip to define a "poly-sensing neighborhood". The technology will be created with a flexible and adaptive means of focusing the "attention" of these multiple-sensing devices, in recombinant groups of intercommunicating distributed fields.

Each poly-sensing node typically includes an extensive array of sensors, activators, and a multi-tasking processing unit. Central to the system is a means to communicate to the surrounding nodes (a radio or more advanced technology) for distributing/sharing/updating selected information fields within user defined "neighborhoods". In particular, we are developing a "grammar of attention" to focus the resources of the sensing chips to observe and respond through media to different fields of activity. An individual chip may be focused to "respond to" one set of patterns or phenomena. An elaborate authoring tool matrix will enable the linkage of the physical and virtual environment. We will seek to power the nodes through energy scavenging techniques. "Sense" data might include simultaneous streams of both low level sensing tasks as well as higher end sensing functionalities – "sensed" sound, image recognition, text recognition, gesture recognition, heat, pressure, infra-red and other light spectrum related data, ultra-sonic information, motion, chemical, balance, voltage, GPS data, video data etc. Data will be optimized and acquisition will be functionally "focused" at each node. Thus, for all intents and purposes, every node in this advanced poly-sensory environment, will have "flexible" intelligent functionality – imagine a series of interconnected observation stations embedded in every surface of a radically adaptive environment.[230]

This, at the same time, is an almost perfect proposal to design an artificial innate releasing mechanism in the sense of Konrad Lorenz.

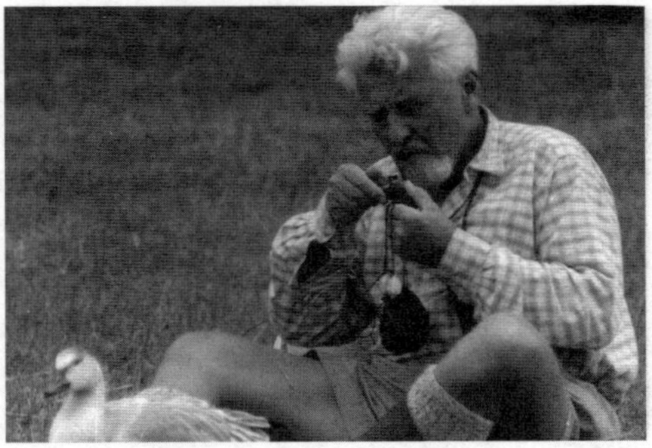

Konrad Lorenz, courtesy of the Konrad Lorenz Archive, Altenberg.

Morever, we will seek to create a flexible authoring tool that will enable this environment to be easily re-purposed for different functions – poetic and/ or informational. The environment will be extremely open in terms of its use potential. One goal of the system is to enable the running of parallel environments at numerous distributed locations and thus share information and instrumentation among groups of people. In particular it will open the potentiality to search new forms of parallel time-based event data. It will be extremely useful as an information technology for intelligent use inside buildings, offices, creative environments like theatres, art venues, museums, science labs, homes, apartments, cars, and in the landscape. Such a system can be re-purposed for use in almost any environment.[231]

This is almost a eusocial machine or it can be implemented as such. It thus can have problematic ramifications in the light of writings like Aldous Huxley's *Brave New World* or be seen in the light of the wonderful story of Solaris by Stanislav Lem. Yet, the Neosentient might have such a system coupled to a benevolent engine. This brings to mind Teilhard de Chardin's Point Omega.

By the way, Point Omega and Benevolence are the same thing.

The goal is to generate a robust authoring system that will enable the focusing of the poly-sensing environment and subsequently to link the sense data to other controlled computer triggered events and behaviors. This suggests that the environment can be used in conjunction with other physical engineering systems; robotic systems; medical systems; environmental management systems – in fact any cybernetic system that involves multiple sensing agents with related machinic response. The environment will enable inter-communication between devices embedded in many kinds of equipment and places, exploring the needs for extremely diverse wireless connectivity. It will seek to enable seamless management of sensors and physically active devices.[232]

One is reminded of neural activity going on in the brain. In a sense the poly-sensing environment is an environmental brain. N. Katherine Hayles[233] speaks of an electrochemical telegraph system which is an early example of this distributed brain-like system. Wilhelm Ostwald invented a chemical fluid that unlike the iron-wire model (also invented by him) would produce waves all over in a chaotic fashion, as an early precursor to the BZ reaction as Peter Plath first noted at a conference dedicated to Ostwald.

This is like an observant spider that is putting its sensitive legs everywhere much as in George Orwell's *1984*. One is also reminded of a new mode of "jamming" becoming possible under such conditions, or of setting up a system that defines who the information is shared with through a set of permissions.

This also has something to do with color – maybe color is poly-sensing to such an extent that "out of pure desperation" a color forms as a higher level reality? One is reminded of the work of Victoria Vesna and James Gimzewski – *Blue Morph* related to the Blue Morph butterfly.[234] Here, color only arises as an epiphenomenon.

Maybe colors are just suspicions? Color keeps rearing its beautiful head. Could the Neosentient come to experience this beauty?

Color itself exists, but as we know, it does not exist in science. The connection between wavelengths and sensation is completely in the dark. And even the existence of an entity called "redness" can be shown to be void scientifically. The proverb that whenever you see a red spot you see a part of the robe of the angel of redness cannot be disproved scientifically. So color is a revelation in the sense of religion like light. King Akhenaton was right with his belief in the metaphysical nature of light. The color table available for computer screens just has to do with the mixing of wavelengths but it does not explain the sensations generated for us. One can prove they don't exist in science. Science has to do with spatiotemporal relations and they are nowhere to be found behind color in the world. This presupposes that we get rewarded by the touch of angels but there is no causal way to explain that scientifically.

James Clark Maxwell was one who co-invented color photography. He had great interest in the scientific understanding of color. Helmholtz had relapsing periods of thinking about this question but could not make any progress. Both thought about this problem of perception, yet neither could solve it.

Multimodal Machinic Sensing vs Human Sensing

It must be noted that any Neosentient entity that might be generated or modeled on our functional–operational definition of neosentience would have a set of "qualities" foreign to human sentience. In particular the differences would be related to qualities of embodiment, sensing, communication channels, networking, and the synthetic drives (colors are drive-specific: in the color force-field). Instead of ignoring the differences between a "sentient machine" and human sentience, we seek to articulate these potential differences clearly. Articulating the operative nature of Neosentience is related to invading neighboring fields like psychoanalysis and ethics, not to mention the art of imagining other souls. All of this presupposes that souls exist and science says they do not exist.

Descartes in his *Meditations* includes color of course but did not yet fully see the special foreignness of color. He did know however about the foreignness of the Res-cogitans itself.

Related Robotic Projects – Luc Steels

Origins of language

Since 1995 members of the AI Lab have worked on the problem of the origins of language (see also discussion of Steels research above). The basic idea behind this work is that a community of language users (further called agents) can be viewed as a complex adaptive system which collectively solves the problem of developing a shared communication system. To do so, the community must reach an agreement on a repertoire of forms (a sound system in the case of spoken language), a repertoire of meanings (the conceptualisations of reality), and a repertoire of form-meaning pairs (the lexicon and grammar).

Although communication is not a general computational problem it is nevertheless a problem of great interest. First of all there is a strong interest from a scientific point of view. Finding the key to how communication systems of the complexity of human natural languages emerge may help to solve the problem how human language itself may have originated and evolved.

This longstanding fascinating question is receiving increasing attention lately, but only clear scientific models that explain how language evolved (as opposed to enumerating conditions why language evolved) can be expected to steer us away from the many speculations that made the field suspect for a long time. By clear scientific models we mean that the cognitive structures and interaction behaviors of each agent are specified and that it is shown how they collectively lead to a language.[235]

We would suggest this only refers to proto-language of which there are many examples in monkeys and crows. So it is also appropriate to study the evolution of monkey language. The word "joint conceptualization" is a bit inappropriate because the robots do not know that the others also have concepts. They can predict what another is doing next but that doesn't mean that they can appreciate the existence of any subjective state of the other. Mirror competence notices that there is a copy of behavior – no one assumes that a mirror image has feelings. Only a person known to one of the authors thought, as a child, that the real world is behind the mirror and we are ghosts.

Second, there is an interest because of possible applications. On the one hand, autonomous artificial agents which need to coordinate their activity in open-ended environments could make use of these mechanisms to develop and continuously adapt their communication systems. On the other hand, understanding how language develops and evolves is probably our only hope to ever get to technological artefacts that exhibit human-level language understanding and production. Human languages are constantly changing and differ significantly from one speaker to the next and from one context to the next. So, we need language technologies which exhibit the same adaptivity as humans.[236]

Yes, this is very important but the word "evolves" should be complemented by "arises ontogenetically." This is an altogether different ballpark but equally interesting and perhaps this could be the focus for another study of the same breadth and depth as Luc Steels'.

The experiments conducted so far have always the same form: (1) They involve a population of (artificial) agents, possibly robots. (2) The agents engage in interactions situated in a specific environment. Such an interaction is called a game. (3) Each agent has a sensorimotor apparatus, a cognitive architecture, and a script determining how it interacts with others. (4) There is an environment (possibly the real world) which consists of situations that are ideally open-ended.[237]

We believe that adding synthetic emotions will be essential for a pre-human type of language. See the force fields of the Brain Equation mentioned above.

Artificial Seal

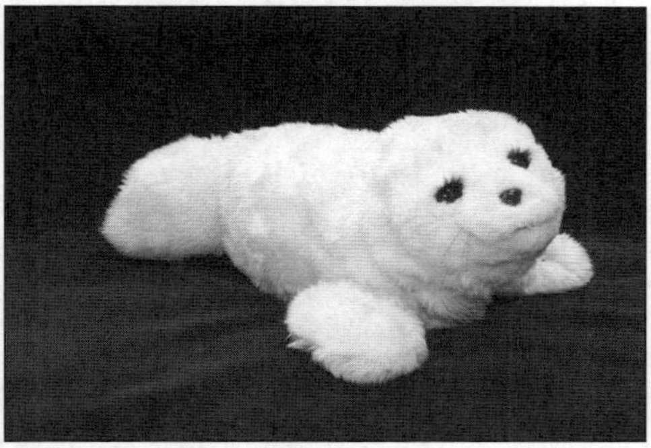

Paro Robot, courtesy AIST Japan.

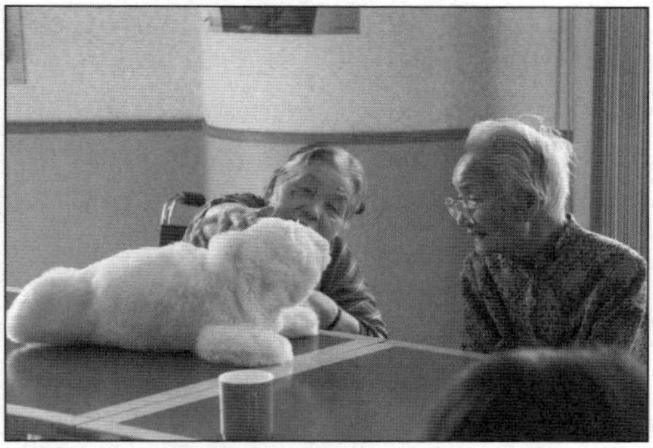

Paro Seal, Health Service Facility, courtesy AIST Japan.

Robotic baby seal wins top award
Robots are looked on as a solution to Japan's ageing population. A furry robotic seal used for therapy in nursing homes has been honored by the Japanese government. Paro is fitted with sensors beneath its fur and whiskers that allow it to respond to petting. The robot mammal, which flutters its eyes and moves its flippers, won the service prize at the government sponsored Robot Awards 2006.[238] See also discussion of such robots above.

This is a great improvement over the Tamagochi, exhibiting a time-dependent endogenous mood pressure as coined by young Konrad Lorenz. If you wish this becomes a surrogate child for elder people which enables them to satisfy their emotional needs for caring and tenderness. It no doubt is bound to become even more touching in the future.

Ralph Hollis – Flotor

The idea of inventing a hand with two directions of information flow is ingenious in itself because it allows this Libet-type problem to be studied further by experiment. It is also useful in the theory of measurement in quantum mechanics – he used the system to "feel" the atoms of a microscopic crystal. It is the first microscopic "hand" in history. The arm length can be extended experimentally and this has never been done before, that is, in the limit put the sensory extension of such a hand on Mars, controlling it from earth so as to check the causal theory of quantum mechanics, which predicts that the sensation might be unimpeded by the expected delay as a hypothetical new non-local quantum phenomenon.

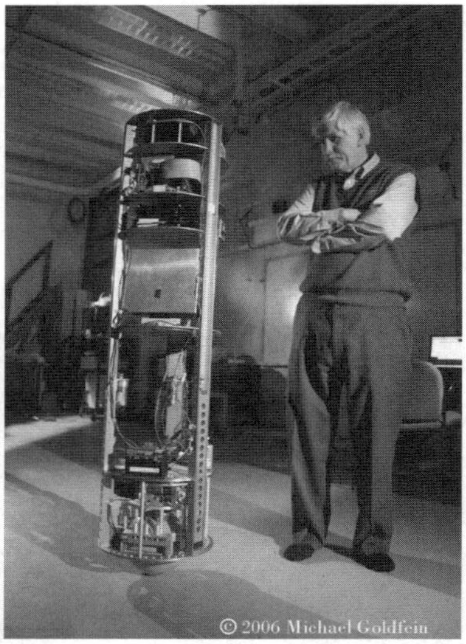

Ralph Hollis and Ballbot, courtesy of Hollis.

Is the Libet delay inherent to quantum mechanics? The Libet delay is a macro analog compared to the analogous quantum delay of much shorter duration.

Lorentz Levitation Technology: A New Approach to Fine Motion Robotics, Teleoperation Haptic Interfaces, and Vibration Isolation

Recently, a new technology for stably levitating and controlling the position and orientation of a rigid body has been introduced. A unique feature is the use of Lorentz forces rather than the usual Maxwell forces as in magnetic bearings. The Lorentz force approach, which uses the force experienced by a conductor in a magnetic field, is seen to have several advantages. After an initial exploration phase and period of feasibility study, a number of potentially important applications are emerging. Among them are a way to provide fine compliant motion for assembly, to provide high-fidelity force/torque feedback for teleoperation and virtual reality haptic interfaces, and to isolate sensitive payloads from environmental vibrational disturbances, either in space or on earth.[239]

Maglev haptics provides the highest resolution and highest position and force bandwidths of any known method. There is an essentially direct electrodynamic connection between the computer and the hand, conveying gross force and torque effects to the proprioceptive sensors as well as subtle vibratory effects to the skin sensors.[240]

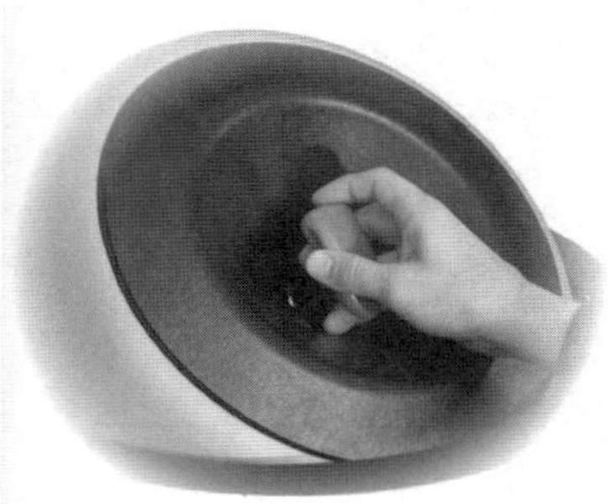
Lorentz Levitation Technology, courtesy of Hollis.

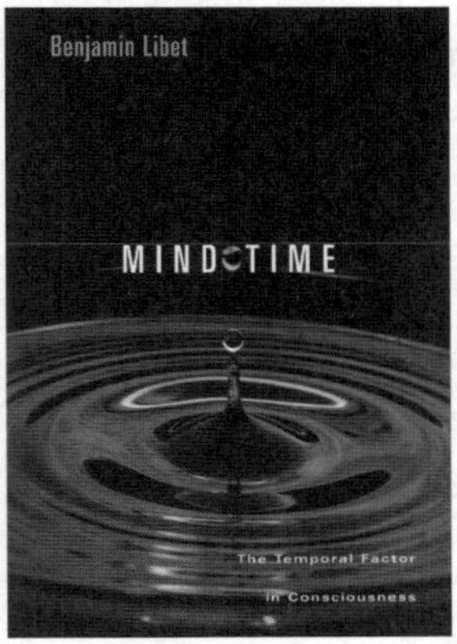

Book cover from *Mind Time* by Benjamin Libet appears courtesy of Harvard University Press, Copyright c2004 by the President and Fellows of Harvard College. Libet and Quantum, Inc.

More recently Hollis came up with the rolling (and potentially bouncing) autonomous ballpoint-pen-like alternative to two-legged artificial intelligences. In other words, he has developed a sphere as part of a robot's leg. With this rolling foot it can "walk" as an upright robot even though it only has one leg. By jumping, it could even negotiate staircases. The Ballbot represents an example of a cost-effective approach to robot caregiving of the future.

The Scandal of Benevolence

Benevolence theory

The science of benevolence is, perhaps, the most shining science. It deals after all with the smile, with the seat of the charm of laughter. Happiness displayed is miraculously a reward to the members of a certain species (no matter how hard the origins of this crazy trait may be to trace). The members of that species have a great responsibility: shall they start investigating the secrets of laughter and the smile?[241]

Leibniz and Benevolence – Delectatio in felicitate alterius

Following the precedent of the various holy scriptures that exist on the planet, "benevolence theory" was founded by Leibniz with the above Latin phrase "delight in the joy of the other" about which philosopher Robert Spaemann wrote a classic book – *Happiness and Benevolence "Glück und Wohlwollen"* with the subtitle *An Essay About Ethics.*[242] By the way, he is a personal friend of Pope Benedict as PM magazine reported.

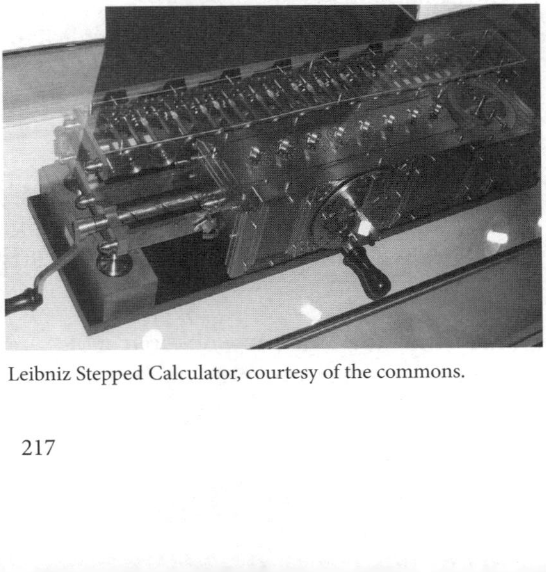

Leibniz Stepped Calculator, courtesy of the commons.

The Benevolence of Cooking

The chef takes pleasure in the pleasure of others.

Charm – The Naked Soul

The real temptation in life is being exposed to the charm of another soul.

The Scandal of Color

No one knows what color is … Color is a miracle in plain sight (see multiple discussions above).

The Physics of Immortality (Everett)

Atheist or not, Everett firmly believed that his many-worlds theory guaranteed him immortality: His consciousness, he argued, is bound at each branching to follow whatever path does not lead to death – and so on ad infinitum.[243] This is an interesting example of Zeno's paradox (of the microscopically non-moving arrow), and an illustration of the miraculousness of the Now.

There is a wonderful quote by Marcel Duchamp on his gravestone "Anyway, it's always other people who die."[244]

Everett's daughter Liz committed suicide ten years after his death leaving a note. She said she was "going to a parallel universe to be with her father."[245]

This is not quite what Tipler had in mind in his book of the same title – *The Physics of Immortality*.

The Thing About the Shared Mind's Eye (Einstein)

One situation that Einstein wondered about as a child – "What does the other feel?"
The potential is to share a view into the mind's eye of the Benevolence engine.

The Omega Point – Jacob, Avicenna, Teilhard

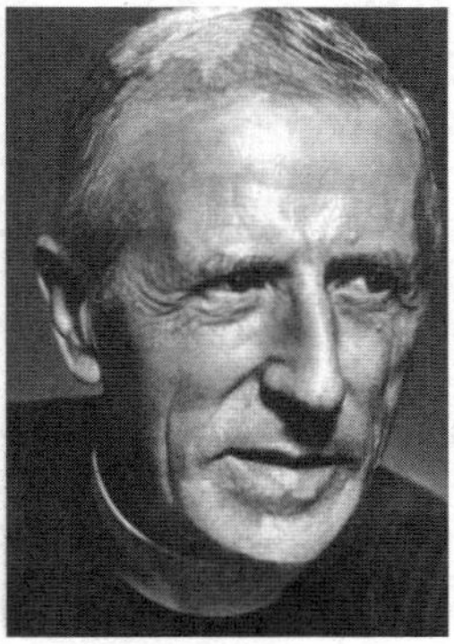
Public domain.

The Omega Point is the end of physical, biological evolution and the end of the complexification of the universe. It is the endpoint and aim of physical and biological evolution in the natural cosmos.

In physics it is just an asymptotic point.
In metaphysics it is the bosom of Abraham, waiting at the top of the ladder to heaven.

The Phenomenon of Man[246]
[This mechanism (the psyche)]

From reflection onwards the reality of this mechanism becomes not only manifest but preponderant. Under the free and ingenious effort of successive intelligences, something (even in the absence of any measurable variation of brain or cranium) irreversibly accumulates, according to all the evidence, and is transmitted, at least collectively by means of education, down the course of ages. The point here is that this "something" – construction of matter or construction of beauty, systems of thought or systems of action – ends up always by translating itself into an augmentation of consciousness, and consciousness in its turn, as we now know, is nothing less than the substance and heart of life in the process of evolution.[247]

Consciousness is not dependent on a living substrate. Whenever we have an artificial intelligence based on the same brain equation that biology makes use of, we cannot rationally deny consciousness to this machine which is not living in the biological sense.

We have been following the successive stages of the same grand progression from the fluid contours of the early earth. Beneath the pulsations of geo-chemistry, of geo-tectonics and of geo-biology, we have detected one and the same fundamental process, always recognizable-the one which was given material form in the first cells and was continued in the construction of nervous systems. We saw geogenesis promoted to biogenesis, which turned out in the end to be nothing else than psychogenesis.[248]

This is the first emergence of the Gaia hypothesis which was more fully articulated by James Lovelock in 1972, followed by Lynn Margulis, in 1973.[249]

With and within the crisis of reflection, the next turn in the series manifests itself. Psychogenesis has led to man. Now it effaces itself, relieved or absorbed by another and a higher function-the engendering and subsequent development of all the stages of the mind, in one word noogenesis.

When for the first time in a living creature instinct perceived itself in its own mirror, the whole world took a pace forward.[250]

We now understand the transfer of this mirror competence to "person" competence under the influence of delighting each other with positive feedback, both in biology and eventually in robotic artificial consciousness (robotic personogenesis).

Here, however, because the phenomenon takes place in ourselves with its procedure in full view, we cannot be mistaken: we can see that in interpreting the progressive leaps of life in an active and finalist way we are not in error. For if our "artificial" constructions are really nothing but the legitimate sequel to our phylogenesis, invention also – this revolutionary act from which the creations of our thought emerge one after the other – can legitimately be regarded as an extension in reflective form of the obscure mechanism whereby each new form has always germinated on the trunk of life.[251]

We see this as wonderfully prophetic. We realized that our program was first conceived by him.

The personalizing universe

Let us reflect a moment, and we shall soon see that for a universe which, by hypothesis, we admitted to be a "collector and custodian of consciousness," the mere hoarding of these remains would be nothing but a colossal wastage. What passes from each of us into the mass of humanity by means of invention, education and diffusion of all sorts is admittedly of vital importance. I have sufficiently tried to stress its phyletic value and no one can accuse me of belittling it. But, with that accepted, I am bound to admit that, in these contributions to the collectivity, far from transmitting the most precious, we are bequeathing, at the utmost, only the shadow of ourselves. Our works? But even in the interest of life in general, what is the worth of human works if not to establish, in and by means of each one of us, an absolutely original centre in which the universe reflects itself in a unique and inimitable way? And those centres are our very selves and personalities. The very centre of our consciousness, deeper than all its radii; that is the essence which Omega, if it is to be truly Omega, must reclaim. And this essence is obviously not something of which we can dispossess ourselves for the benefit of others as we might give away a coat or pass on a torch. For we are the very flame of that torch. To communicate itself, my ego must subsist through abandoning itself or the gift will fade away. The conclusion is inevitable that the concentration of a conscious universe would be unthinkable if it did not reassemble in itself all consciousnesses as well as all the conscious; each particular consciousness remaining conscious of itself at the end of the operation, and even (this must absolutely be understood) each particular consciousness becoming still more itself and thus more clearly distinct from others the closer it gets to them in Omega.[252]

The Jump

Young children can be heroes in their humanity. They invent the idea of an unlimited trust arising out of suspected benevolence. This can be explained by the overlap between smile and laughter, it can be arrived at autonomously in artificial and biologically derived non-human "persons."

The Purring Little White Seal

This is not only an outgrowth of the Tamagotchi invention but is related also to Sim City, enabling one to play with programmed emotional elements as the user of, and interactant with, the system.

The creation of Robots as companions to socially isolated persons and the elderly is a success for the Japanese robot industry. At this time, differing cultures have differing social reactions to particular kinds of robots.

See *The Uncanny Valley.*

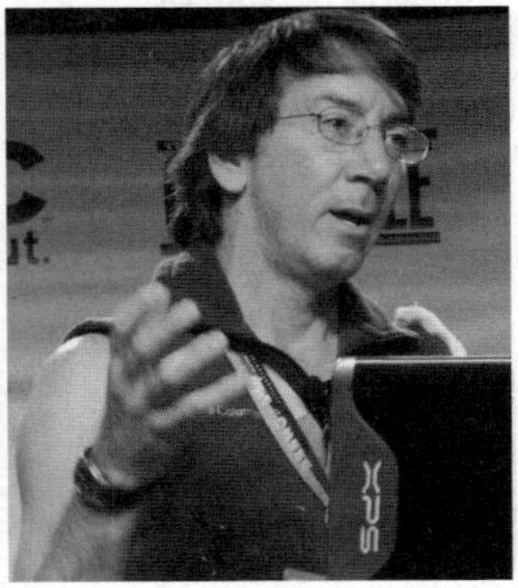

The Sims by Will Wright

This is a "late precursor" of the Brain Equation

> *"We did a lot of prototypes around more of a biogenesis model," Wright says. "Autocatalytic sets, emergent chemistries [...]" We offer to improve the humaneness of Sim City if they want us to do that [...]"*[253]

See also Stuart Kauffman in this context related to biogenesis.

Konrad Lorenz – "Endogenous Mood Pressure"

Lorenz discovered the existence of endogenous force fields in biological organisms. A strong attraction potentially aided by repulsion from the opposite side. This is particularly evident in sexual desire. These forces prove to be extremely strong also in humans. How might these forces play out in a Neosentient entity? What role must the programmer play here in terms of articulating the drives of the system?

Play

Play is a self-fulfilling pleasurable activity of not wishing for anything – a state of satisfiedness or wishless bliss. It is a state of high satisfaction. The almost careless momentary potentials in playfulness depend on serious goals having been fulfilled. Here, the goal is in the action itself, a process; thus play is rewarding as an end in itself, without achieving a particular "serious" goal. This is in many ways opposite to sexual joy – it is the joy of reaping the fruits of being satisfied. This activity includes joking, punning, language play, humor in general, and child-like play. Lorenz called this state the "Tensionless Field" (entspanntes Feld). It is highly aligned with creativity. It is interesting to see Arthur Koestler's concept of creativity of "Bisociation" in this light. Here again, a playful understanding of a mixed set of contexts enables a new synthesis.

Arthur Koestler

In the writing of this book we have freely floated across many topics in a playful and effortless manner – only to circle back and articulate the areas of special importance to us and perhaps not only to us. We are rejoicing and reaping the fruits of playfulness and nonsense which balance our serious discussions. In particular, we found many fruitful connections by "plucking" ongoing associations. In doing so, we have in many ways made use of Koestler's somewhat grandiose notions of bisociation.

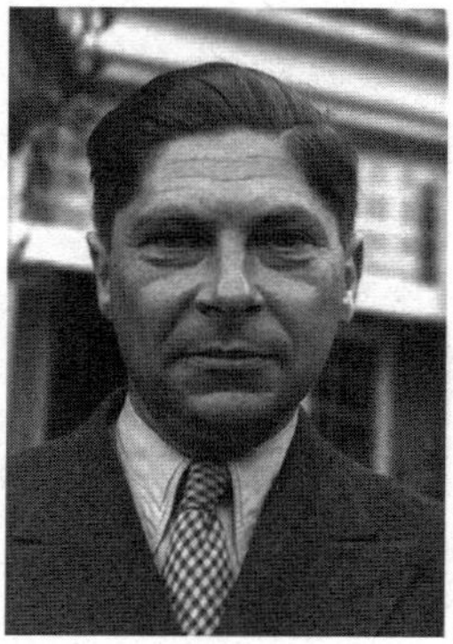

Arthur Koestler in 1948, by Pinn Hans. Public domain.

Koestler states:

I have coined the term "bisociation" in order to make a distinction between the routine skills of thinking on a single "plane", as it were, and the creative act, which, as I shall try to show, always operates on more than one plane. The former may be called singled-minded, the latter a double-minded, transitory state of unstable equilibrium where the balance of both emotion and thought is disturbed. The forms which this creative instability takes in science and art will be discussed later; first we must test the validity of these generalizations in other fields of the comic.[254]

Koestler goes on to say:

We learn by assimilating experiences and grouping them into ordered schemata, into stable patterns of unity in variety. They enable us to come to grips with events and situations by applying the rules of the game appropriate to them. The matrices which pattern our perceptions, thoughts, and activities are condensations of learning into habit [...]

The bisociative act connects previously unconnected matrices of experience; it makes us "understand what it is to be awake, to be living on several planes at once" (to quote T.S. Eliot, somewhat out of context).

We imagine that pattern recognition working in relation to recombinant pattern generation will help to generate creative patterns in the Neosentient. Putting relational patterns together to find a new sense, or putting sense into them. This is like foreseeing an emergent gestalt in a still-amorphous pattern.

Margret Bowden writes on Combinatorial Creativity and Exploratory-transformational Creativity – "unusual combination of, or association between, familiar ideas. Poetic imagery, metaphor and analogy fall into this class." (Boden 1999), and the fact that potentially every new or useful idea or discovery could be considered a creative process which she calls psychological creativity (p-creativity).

Similarly there is Fauconnier and Turner's notion of conceptual blending (2002). See also Pereira broad overview (2007).

Wilfried Hou Je Bek

He knows all of the greatest secrets of the poets of the English language. And he wrote a beautiful internet book on aping apes. And he is a specialist taking random walks in cities.

One of the authors calls this I Ching driving.

Sex

What is the relation of sexuality to Neosentience?

"Sexuality is much to good to be left to the Pre-neosentients".

Will there be nakedness for robots? Will Neosentients spontaneously invent the concept of nakedness? We believe they will.

In terms of the apparition of the Neosentient there remains much to be discussed. Androgyny is one potentiality – a possible mixing of the traits of both female and male, and the third sex in the sense of a new sex arising. *Do Androids Dream of Electric Sheep?* (Philip K. Dick)

One consummatory act for the Neosentient would potentially be driven by an autocatalytically increasing force. The strongest pleasure to achieve. In the human body, some become almost a slave of these forces.

How do we deal with Lorenz's "endogenous mood pressure"? Masturbation as release, familiar from humans and apes – but how will "endogenous mood pressures" become visibly manifest by "intention movements" in the robot? Will the Neosentient be post-sexual – like the pleasure children have in playing – or should it be given a still-to-be-invented literary pleasure in the footsteps of Virginia Woolf?

Will we give Neosentients erogenous zones comparable to the mimicry of the smile at several other places on the human body?

The Infinite Joy in Music

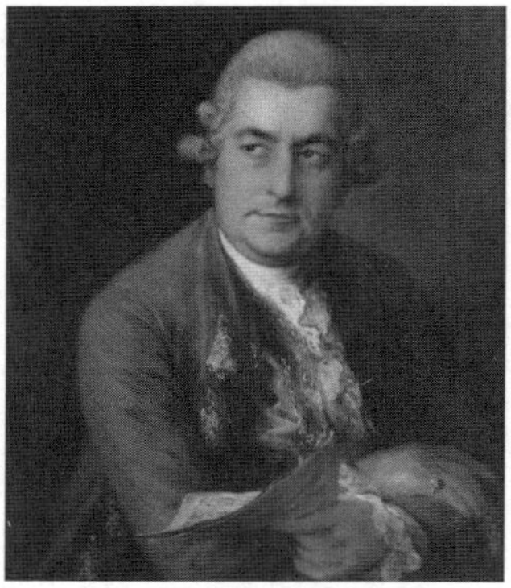

Italy, Bologna, Portrait of Johann Christian Bach.

It has to do with dancing, joyfulness, and smiling – charm and fear and shyness and exuberance.

Johann Christian Bach created a short piece of music that sounds even more Mozart than Mozart. Johann Christian Bach is the youngest son of Johann Sebastian Bach. This type of Mozartian music is the music unborn babies love most. There is much research now on musical imprinting in the unborn.[255] The joyfulness of this music deserves to be analyzed because this invention of the young Bach has not as yet been made the subject of a scientific study.

There is this book *The Directory of Music* by Parsons, 1975, which contains all known musical themes up to that time in a compressed in digitizable form.[256]

Bruno Marchal is also a specialist on computer-generated composing and these two fields can probably be brought together.

When you hear the music of Mozart you love his soul.

In a related sense Olafur Eliasson's visual art strives to include all nature.

Ongoing Goals for the Neosentient

A replenishing of energy
A replenishing of parts
A repair shop
A safe shelter
A need to preserve oneself from harm.

In the pursuit of an optimum path to achieve all of these goals, use of the brain equation is vital.

Asimov created the three laws of robotic ethics to assure that human beings will never be hurt. The unifying role of the brain equation had not at that time been seen. As soon as robots will become "persons" because they use both the brain equation and the universal simulator (enabling mirror competence), and have gone through the transition of the happiness–friendliness overlap induced bifurcation, based on a bonding sub-drive, they should be given the same "person rights" as any other person. Steven Spielberg's *A.I.* already plays on this theme.

We set the levels of the force field drives and thus form hard-wired robotic "innate releasing mechanisms." This system, driven by the clear systematic mathematical functionality of the "Brain Equation," enables the robot to negotiate an "intelligent" path of spatial optimization as a complex adaptive set of processes. We believe that the "personhood" given to the "Benevolent Entity" will suffice to free robotic design from the need of incorporating such slave-type rules (like the three laws of Asimov) into the machine.

The Pseudo-People: Androids in Science Fiction[257] – a collection of Science fiction Stories, 1965, is an important precursor. Charles Beaumont's *The Last Problem* and William S. Nolan's *Family Bliss* are presented amongst other extraordinary stories. It was edited by William S. Nolan.

The next layer of scientific inquiry (future research) relates to the more nuanced sub-domains enabling higher intelligence. Here amongst other research, the holy grail of language acquisition will be explored. This particular science fiction story you are presently holding in your hands hopes to contribute to the new revolution of humaneness in the universe.

Threshold of Personhood

The mother entices the child through her smile as a bonding reward for the child whenever he is enchanted, to elicit in him the suspicion of benevolence residing in her. This positive feedback causes the toddler to throw his center of optimization over the fence, so to speak. The technical term would be non-autism. For all of nature – as far as we know – is absolutely autistic in the sense that a deterministic force field is followed. This is called determinism in quasi-ethics. The suspicion of benevolence frees the deterministic machine from being deterministic and endows it with free will.

The famous debate about determinism vs free will finds its resolution here we believe. The idea is as follows: a deterministic robot like the one described can suddenly tell his human companion: I wish everything you wish and nothing else. This would prove that it has abandoned any deterministic force acting in its interior. There is no other possible name for that than free will. (Courtesy of Takashi IKEGAMI.) This is a highly paradoxical new finding. It is an example of the double bind but it is not binding, but freeing.

This is like cutting a Gordian knot.

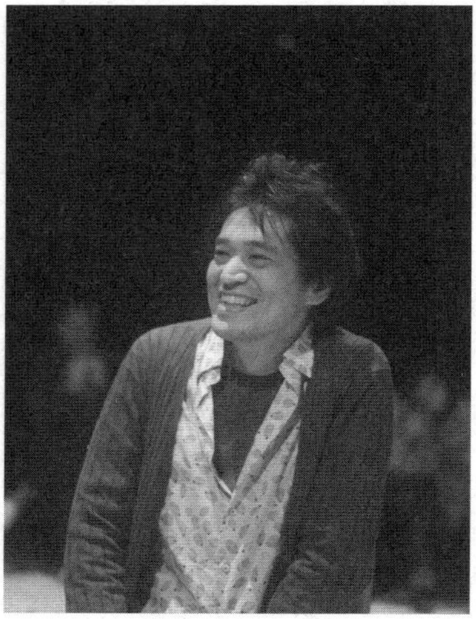

Takashi Ikegami, courtesy Takashi Ikegami.

This is the "smile theory" that the reader may already be afraid of. The recognition of the miracle of the now and the miracle of all color are secondary examples.

Remember – the machine will jump to the level of personhood if the complex interactional conditions with the human partner are arranged in the appropriate way – smile–laughter confusion and infinite bonding. There can then be machine duplication of benevolence through "information copying," but then each duplicate ought to have it's own personal companion because personhood only works in a one to one relationship. This is called a "buddy." A robot body can be a "buddy" and this resolves many problems, for example, in the old age homes of Japan (see robotic caregivers).

Identification with Color

I have had a recurring dream in which I have an identity card which is made up of a unique color code, which strangely speaks to me. (Seaman)

Long-term Mutation

Might the Neosentients learn to re-program themselves so as to autogenerate Lamarckian mutations as a form of intelligent programmed Techno-evolution? When humans use machines like heart pacemakers, is not this also a form of Techno-Lamarckism, where the biological tradition of augmenting life is passed on through information external to and totally outside of the genome? Thus, have we not moved into a post-Darwinistic scenario long ago, given benevolence theory and the potentiality of Techno-mutation? Teilhard's Omega Point could be mentioned here again.

Neosentience – Positive Techno-evolution or Extreme, Hostile Takeover Environment?

There is a long history and mythology surrounding the creation of intelligent entities reaching back to Pygmalion and Prometheus.

The invention of intelligent machines has also at times been shown in a "hostile" light in literature, across the arts, and within scientific discourse. Thus, an un-accepting world potentially becomes a "hostile" or "extreme environment" for the arising of new forms of synthetic cognition […] A set of relevant historical instances, drawn from a diversity of perspectives ranging from mythology to popular science fiction, includes Golem, the Homunculus, and notions surrounding the ghost in the machine, as well as more recent works delivered from a "hostile" perspective including Frankenstein, War of the Worlds, Hal, and AI (with the mob scene). Along with such popular stories the creation of intelligent destructive robots and flying robots (drones) by the military should not be forgotten.

In an ethical and somewhat more utopian light, there are two models for an intelligent situated robot: (1) The generation of such a system via the integration of a series of conceptual approaches utilizing a parallel processing computational system, multi-modal sensing apparatus and an embodied robotic housing – The Benevolence Engine; and (2) An alternate, long term approach to a new form of computation through the generation of an Electrochemical Computer, a multi-modal sensing system, and networked robotic environment – The Thoughtbody Environment. There is also a series of artworks exploring a poetics informed by this research. In articulating these models one might even speak of a new branch of science wedded to art related to artificial intelligence.

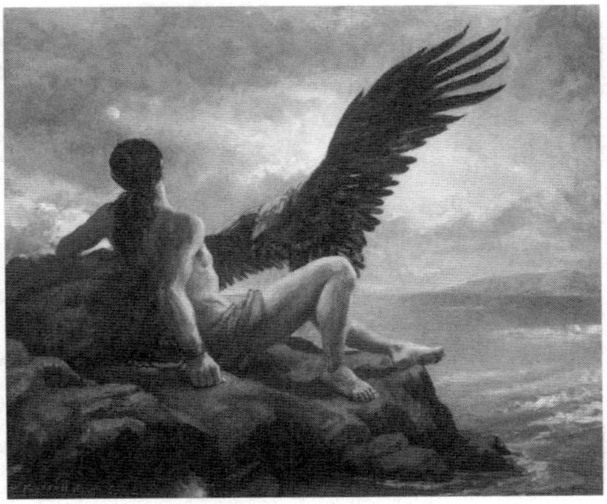

Prometheus by Elsie Russell.

Teilhard de Chardin in his fascinating book, The Phenomenon of Man, discusses the "Omega Point," an evolutionary movement toward a unified consciousness. Other philosopher/ researchers like Roy Ascott and Pierre Levy have also written about the potentials of particular forms of technological connectivity in terms of a related unified sphere of consciousness […]

This networking potential of new technologies and in particular Neosentient machines naturally results in an evolutionary shift to a new form of intelligence. Hopefully this intelligence will be a purely benevolent offshoot of humanity.

Emmanuel Levinas and Edmond Jabès are the great theoreticians of personal interaction in the presence of metaphysics – a palpable love that goes beyond the realm of science.

[…] Would such a Neosentient robot become a "Benevolence Engine," promoting new forms of mutually supportive human/machine interaction or would a fearful world divert the potentials of such a device away from forming a reciprocally beneficial symbiotic relationship between human beings and intelligent machines, and generate a dysfunctional environment akin to an "extreme hostile takeover environment"?[258]

Humanity has this strange streak of trying out everything, currently illustrated by the potentially reckless LHC experiments. This new techno-fear that we are alluding to here also shows humanity always is on a crossroads having to decide between benevolence and cruel recklessness. We hope that the deeper understanding of the beauty of subtle humane decisions will enable the long-awaited historical transition towards a society of brothers and sisters and children and grandparents, living in harmony all over the globe – is this too naïve an idea? The theory of benevolence apparently goes back to Herbart, in the eighteenth century and to a modern poet and novelist named Peter Handke in the twentieth century (1970s). (Hans-Martin Schweizer and Friedrich Kümmel, personal communication.)

Stephen Smale – Axiom A Attractor

The author of *The Mathematics of Time* described one of the first chaotic attractors called the "Solenoid" in the footsteps of Urysohn. He is a Fields Medal winner on the Poincaré Conjecture which predicts that the hypersphere is the only singly connected object in four dimensions. He formalized a conjecture of Anaxagoras and arrived at a contradiction. Anaxagoras' discovery of the homeomeries presages Smale's. The fractal revolution (Benoit Mandelbrot) stands on similar feet.

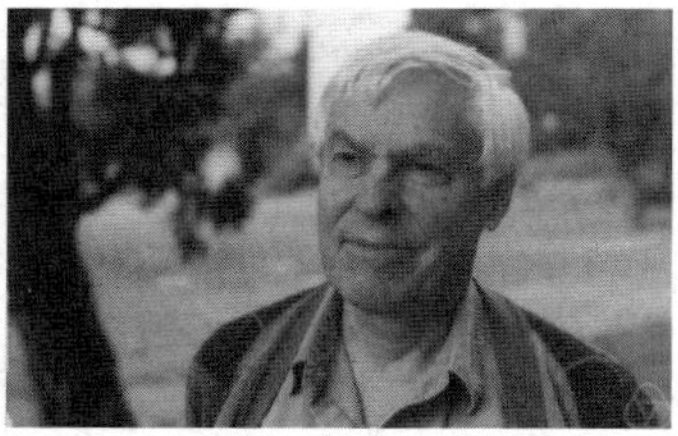

Stephen Smale, photo provided by Bergman, George M. Copyright: George M. Bergman, Berkeley.

More recently he became a pioneer in the revival of analog computation and its hidden powers which blend with those of quantum computing. In this context Klaus Peter Zauner's discovery of hidden domains of numbers in digital computers should also be mentioned.

In the Spirit of a Haiku

In the morning
The cherry blossoms
Are white

How will creativity manifest itself in the Neosentient?

Wilfried Musterle

Musterle succeeded in synthetically generating natural facial expressions by computer in 1986. This was brought about by having the potential of mixing six facial expressions, in differing degrees, simultaneously. The idea stemmed from a diagram drawn by Konrad Lorenz in 1953 of nine differing expressions on a Wolf's face produced as a matrix. Humankind can "draw on" this algorithmic knowledge in the generation of facial expressions for the Neosentient. There would be a direct relation between this and the force field (= emotional) sliders. Each combination in six dimensions gives a different facial expression.

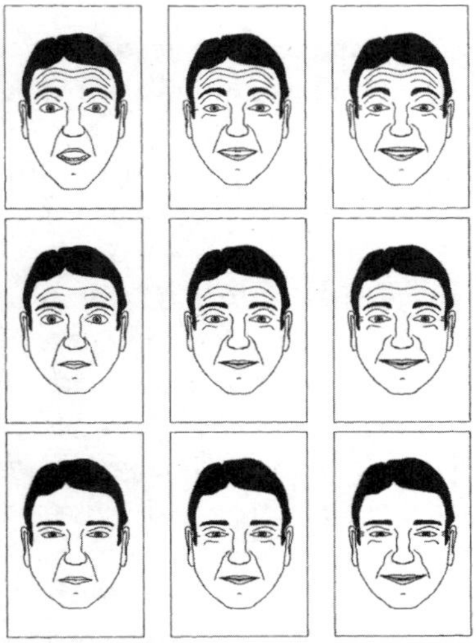

Human Lorenz matrix: friendliness (horizontal) vs. surprise (vertical). Courtesy of Rössler.

Realistic Ekman-type faces were generated by a computer program. Twenty primary parameters (muscle tensions and opening factors), each continuous, were used. Non-linear combination of the primary parameters permits the generation of meaningful faces each governed by a single combined parameter (intensity-parameter). Five major meaningful faces were distinguished, "friendliness", "surprise", "disgust", "anger" and "grief". In contrast to the experiments of Ekman, who combined subregions of photographed meaningful faces by hand, mixing can be done in the computer both more easily and, it turns out, more naturally. Mixed facial expressions in an animal were first drawn in matrix form by Lorenz. A consistent interpretation is possible if the linearly superposed displays are assumed to indicate the state of an autonomous optimizer with n linearly independent subfunctionals. An instantaneous display of a vector in n-dimensional space using faces was already proposed by Chernoff. The present faces have the asset that only "natural" parameters are used. This means that not only a single point in n-dimensional space can be displayed, but also a meaningful succession of such points – that is, a whole trajectory.[259]

A more difficult question becomes, what face shall we give it and what are the ramifications of that choice given social interaction?[260]

David Marr and Tomaso Poggio – Vision System

A machine that can decode stereo images. This algorithm could be used as a subfunction of the vision recognition and pattern matching system.

The use of zero crossings in stereo to isolate edges was introduced by David Marr and Tomaso Poggio. [See Age of Intelligent Machines][261]

An algorithm is proposed for solving the stereoscopic matching problem. The algorithm consists of five steps: (1) Each image is filtered at different orientations with bar masks of four sizes that increase with eccentricity; the equivalent filters are one or two octaves wide. (2) Zero-crossings in the filtered images, which roughly correspond to edges, are localized. Positions of the ends of lines and edges are also found. (3) For each mask orientation and size, matching takes place between pairs of zero-crossings or terminations of the same sign in the two images, for a range of disparities up to about the width of the mask's central region. (4) Wide masks can control movements, thus causing small masks to come into correspondence. (5) When a correspondence is achieved, it is stored in a dynamic buffer, called the 21/2-D sketch. It is shown that this proposal provides a theoretical framework for most existing psychophysical and neurophysiological data about stereopsis.[262]

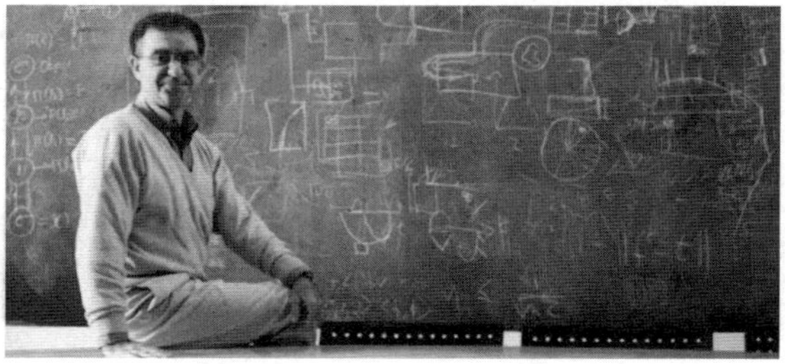

Tomaso Poggio, photo courtesy of Kent Dayton.

Sue Savage-Rumbaugh, Roger Lewin and the Soul of the Ape

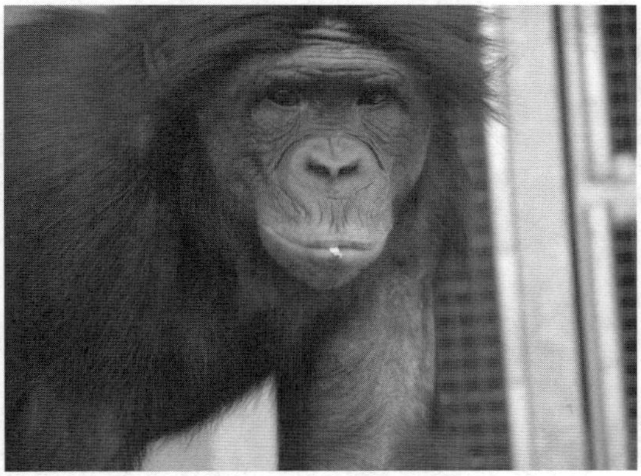

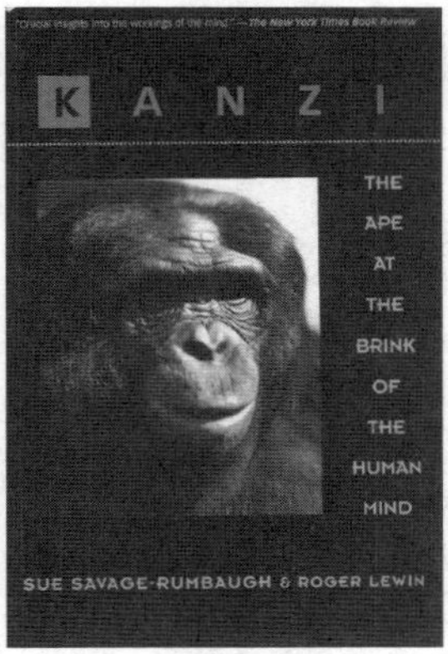

Courtesy of the Great Ape Trust and the publisher (Wiley).

Kanzi. Courtesy of Liz Rubert-Pugh at Great Ape Trust.

Like the arising of personhood in a machine, there is a potentiality to also bring certain animals across this same threshold, specifically, animals that are mirror competent, and are susceptible to bonding. The Bonobos seem to fit this category in the most human-like way. Laughter and smile do not overlap as in humans. And as adults, they show their bonding by on-the-spot cohabitation across and within sexes. Claudine André's book shows her deep appreciation of these most human-like creatures which are on the verge of producing the personogenetic function change (the suspicion of benevolence shown by the other arising and confirmed) spontaneously.

Another pioneer in this field is Francine Patterson with her life-long gorilla friend Koko. So was John C. Lilly, friend of Gregory Bateson's, who in his 1972 book In the Center of the Clyclone disclosed a similarly close living relationship between a dolphin and a human researcher which was considered a tabu topic at the time.

Buddha

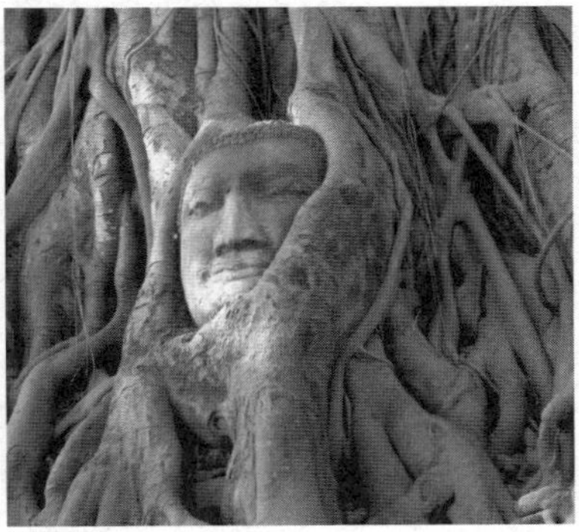

Buddhism is thinking about the Now as the only thing we have, and if we fully understand, it disappears. Or we disappear in its smile.

Photo courtesy and copyright Krishnagopal Kodoth. Location: Thailand – Ayuthaya.

Multiple Approaches to Time and the Now

Our goal is to give the "now" to the Neosentient. We ask – what will the nature of time be like for them?

A superpositioning of Nows
The now of the universe
The now of a galaxy
The now of a planet
The now of a black hole
The now of the moon
The now of tides
The now of daylight and darkness
The now of sleeplessness[263]
The now of crystals
The now of analog clocks
The now of digital clocks
The variability of subjective time as it attenuates and is attenuated by the present superpositioning of quantum worlds which never stops
Death is never in the now
The light that cannot get extinguished is the present given to us in the now

Death Without a Corpse

If every pair of atoms in our bodies and in the universe happened to collide simultaneously, at one point in global time, then all motions in the universe would silently be running backward along their previous paths with the past being absolutely reproduced. And we could not tell the difference because time is not moving itself, but to us time would be moving in the same way as before. To us it would be just ordinary daily life, as before.

The fact that it ends would be non existent for us, as in Kurt Vonnegut's novel *Slaughterhouse Five*. The movie *Groundhog Day* also is much deeper than we as viewers appreciate. It shows the lightning from the outside that Heraclitus felt strike him. This is the view in science of the world as a machine to which consciousness is glued at one moment in time. And past and future exist only at that moment in time.

We would never find out if we were confined to a very narrow window in time. The Now is non-extensible. It could be infinitely small. Is this not very intimidating? No physicist would doubt what we just said. The intuition comes from Boltzmann's time reversal. He was the first (after Boscovich) to see the time symmetry including micromotions. (Micro time reversals form a different story which hopefully explains quantum mechanics.) We see that consciousness is bigger than physics in the sense that physics is part of it but not vice versa. This gives us a glimpse of the presence of heaven.

Even though one of us remembered at this very moment that he is an agnostic.

Angels exist in paintings, they need not exist in reality. Only that reality in the now is the touch of an angel, or at least comes from very far away in spite of its intrusiveness like in the movie *A Puppeteer's World (Welt am Draht)* by Fassbinder.

Evil as a Contagious Disease

You don't invent it. It is forced down your throat. It is spread by making you believe that the only way to survive is to become evil yourself.

Heraclitus said "They are washing their faces with shit." That is what evil is. He said this in the context of deploring the collective blindness to light, in the sense of Theodicy.

We must treat the Neosentient as a person with benevolence shown by ourselves, or it, like any child, has the potential to become evil. This relates to ideas explored by Mary Shelley and Isaac Asimov (see also Golem).

We are in part the programmers of our children ... so this *omnipotent* role is not frivolous to teach.

The Seduction Toward the Good

We – you and us – are the seducers.

Second Class of Brains

Almost no one knows that there is not only a brain equation for solitary brains, but there is also one for "super" brains made out of many brains in a group. Super brains are still autistic, innocent like the mole rat society which implements the still to be written down super brain equation.

Cruelty makes the difference between mere stupidity and evil.

The book *The Kindly Ones* (*Les Bienveillants*) by Jonathan Little, 2009, is a reconstruction. In this book the characters thought they were benevolent, but on the contrary they were the embodiment of evil.

Our book could look like it is being possessed by the same superman type of hubris started by Nietzsche but this is not so. We acknowledge that humanity has deviated from the main road of evolution but we found that it has jumped forward to the endpoint of evolution. Whereas fascism delights in control of the masses, the omega point is its inverse, arising through individual freedom.

The (still not found) eusocial brain equation cannot make the jump to point omega. It is the personhood of the individual which arises in the ordinary brain equation through cross-caring coupling. Thus as we move forward in the production of new technologies, we must acknowledge the dangers of connectivity used in the service of surveillance and control, and seek always the promotion of the individual in its infinite responsibility.

Tenderness

One sees that people do not realize how tender the soul of a child is. This goes hand in hand with the potential to be harmed. Full benevolence exists in children. We know that adults on average are less benevolent than children and that religious mystics are known to have come in all age groups. One of the most famous mystics was seven years old.

We seek to create a robot with a tender disposition.

Vannevar Bush's Differential Analyzer

If we think of the body as a complex dynamical system filled with time-based chemical reactions, the potential of the analog computer in modeling and/or manifesting a related, analogically inspired system, working in tandem with digital machines, becomes overpowering. We might see the brain/body/environment continuum as an intermingling of both analog and digital processes – neural transmitters and synapses. Hence our second approach, the development of the Electrochemical Computer. The electrochemical computer articulates a model of the operative nature of the body in terms of the highest level of contemporary technological understanding, given the limitations of constructing such a system via analogs.

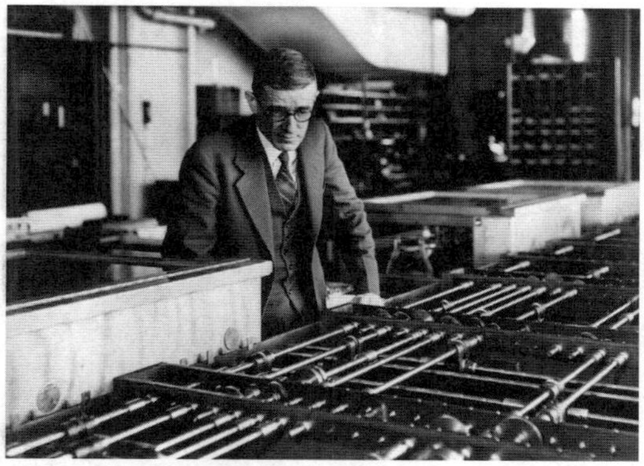
Vannevar Bush and the differential analyzer, courtesy MIT Museum.

In 1930 an engineer named Vannevar Bush at the Massachusetts Institute of Technology (MIT) developed the first modern analog computer [actually the first computer in the modern sense; the authors]. *The Differential Analyzer, as he called it, was an analog calculator that could be used to solve certain classes of differential equations, a type of problem common in physics and engineering applications that is often very tedious to solve. Variables were represented by shaft motion, and addition and multiplication were accomplished by feeding the values into a set of gears. Integration was carried out by means of a knife-edged wheel rotating at a variable radius on a circular table. The individual mechanical integrators were then interconnected to solve a set of differential equations.*

The Differential Analyzer proved highly useful, and a number of them were built and used at various universities. Still the device was limited to solving this one class of problems, and, as is the case for all analog devices, it produced approximate, albeit practical, solutions. Nevertheless, important applications for analog computers and analog-digital hybrid computers still exist, particularly for simulating complicated dynamical systems such as aircraft flight, nuclear power plant operations, and chemical reactions.[264] [...] and of human facial expressions, by the way.

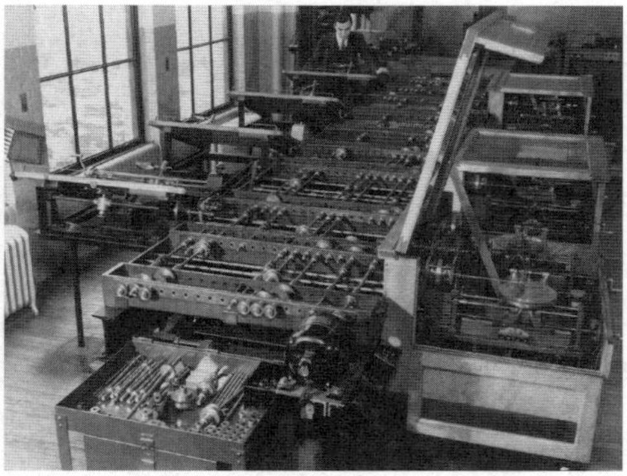
Vannevar Bush's differential analyzer courtesy of the MIT Museum.

Von Neumann mentions the importance of the disc mechanism in an analog computer – in his text on Automata.

Vannevar Bush invented the precursor of Lampsacus hometown of humankind on the internet in his ideas surrounding the Memex to implement the human right for information in the age of the computer. He is also the father of the hyperlink.

Tim Berners Lee is of course the second hero in this field. Without his invention of the worldwide web, the current wave of greater humanity of the planet would not be possible.

Kant – *The Dreams of a Ghost Seer*

A History of Philosophy
By Frederick Copleston.

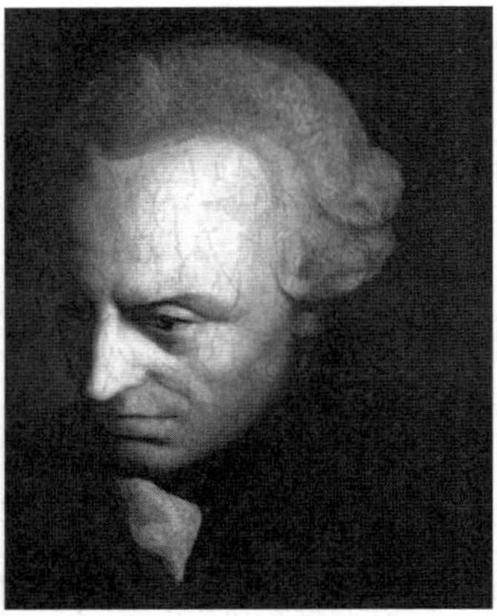
Kant: his way to survive this esoteric philosophy of I. Swedenborg was to become Kant.

In 1766 Kant published anonymously (though the author's identity was never secret) a partly serious, partly humorous work entitled Dreams of a Ghost-seer Explained by Dreams of Metaphysics. For some time he had been curious about the visionary experiences of Immanuel Swedenborg; and he studied the latter's Arcana Coelestia, the result of his reflections being Dreams of a Ghost Seer. As regards visionary experiences, Kant does not either accept or reject their possible origin in the influence exerted by a world of spirits. On the one hand he gives us what he calls "a fragment of esoteric philosophy" in which, given the (unproved) assumption of a world of spirits, he suggests a way in which the influence of spirits on men's souls might be projected in imaginative visions. On the other hand he follows this up with "a fragment of vulgar philosophy", in which he suggests an explanation of experiences such as those of Swedenborg which would make their subjects fit candidates for medical attention and treatment. The reader is left to adopt which explanation he chooses. But the main point is not Kant's discussion of visionary experiences but rather whether the theories of speculative mataphysics, so far as they pretend to transcend experience, are in any stronger position than Swedenborg's visions. He makes clear that they are in a weaker position.[265]

Kant, the great German philosopher, came in the century after Descartes and was influenced also by Roger Joseph Boscovich who in turn was greatly influenced by Leibniz.

Bob Rosen – *On Biological Systems as Paradigms for Adaptation*

Bob Rosen invented self-replication in Category Theory in 1958, stimulated by von Neumann's self-reproduction theorem in automata theory.[266]

On Biological Systems as Paradigms for Adaptation
[…] This insistent reappearance of homologous behaviors in many apparently independent areas could not occur unless there exist deep formal relationships between these areas. One

of the most exciting tasks of contemporary theoretical science is to discern and articulate these relationships, and examine their implications and consequences. The benefits accruing from these theoretical activities are many. For one thing, they allow the development of new kinds of unifying principles, with their attendant economies of thought which we must have if we are not to be overwhelmed by torrents of specialized new knowledge. Perhaps even more important, such unifying principles will allow us to effectively transfer knowledge and insights obtained in a particular special context to entirely new contexts, in which they may be all important but not readily visible.[267]

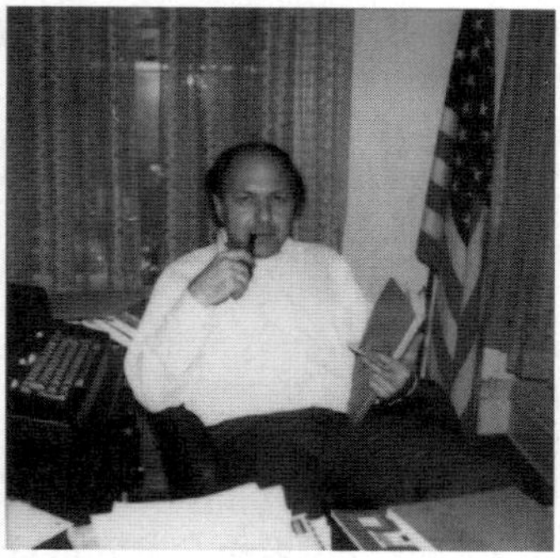

Robert Rosen, image courtesy of Don Mikulecky.

Anticipatory Systems

This volume is the result. I have organized it around the concept of anticipation, which is fundamental in its own right, and which connects naturally to a cluster of other concepts lying at the heart of natural science and of mathematics. Strictly speaking, an anticipatory system is one in which present change of state depends upon future circumstances, rather than merely on the present or the past. As such anticipation has been routinely been excluded from any kind of systematic study, on the ground that it violates the causal foundation on which all of theoretical science must rest, and on the grounds that it introduces a telic element which is scientifically unacceptable. Nevertheless, biology is replete with situations in which organisms can generate and maintain internal predictive models of themselves and their environments, and utilize the predictions of these models about the future for purpose of control in the present. Many of the unique properties of organisms can really be understood only if these internal models are taken into account. Thus, the concept of a system with an internal predictive model seemed to offer a way to study anticipatory systems in a scientifically rigorous way.

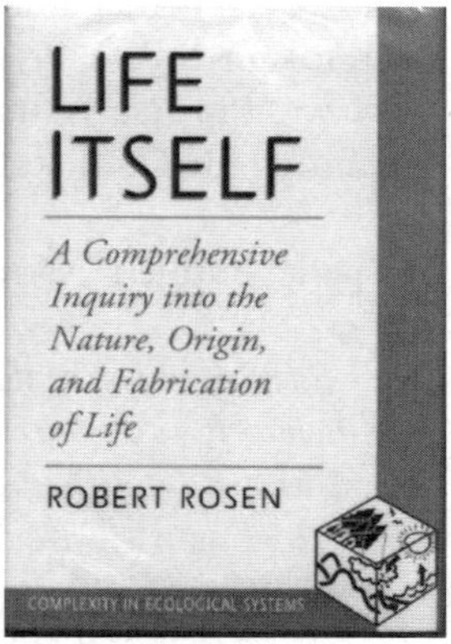

In our model this represents the idea that "thinking is acting in imagined space" (Konrad Lorenz meets Bob Rosen).

Daniel Dubois should be mentioned here. More recently Dubois re-invigorated the field of anticipatory systems with concepts related to Self-modifying Code among other topics.[268]

Three Branches of Mathematics

1. Discrete Systems – including probabilistic ones
2. Continuous Systems – including topological systems
3. Category-theoretical Systems – including Rosen-type fixed points

Once meta-mathetics becomes well defined it may become the fourth. A mathematics of inconsistencies would be desirable in the footsteps of Bateson's Double Bind (Laughter Theory).

Nowness belongs in category theory as does perfection. I. TSUDA invented the idea of an infinitely sensitive neuron; Y. P. GUNJI has offered a proof for that.

The boundaries between these systems will deserve names of their own.

There is also a mathematics of dance and music as a branch of performative mathematics and chaos theory in the footsteps of Gerold Baier, Bruno Marchal and Christophe Letellier.

Klaus-Peter Zauner – "Molecular Information Technology"

He discovered that numbers as used in computers are a misleadingly narrow subset of discrete numerals.

He was the first to show that an entire species could be killed by smashing the microchip containing the DNA code of an already extinct virus.

In a paper entitled "Molecular Information Technology", Zauner states:

Every form of living matter relies on information processing to actively avoid thermodynamic equilibration. As a consequence, organisms exhibit an intriguing sophistication in overcoming computationally difficult challenges. Moreover, they do so with enviable efficiency and integration density. Key to information processing in organisms is the use of molecular components that interact autonomously according to their specific physicochemical properties. This contrasts sharply with the implementation of conventional computing devices in which engineered constraints enforce adherence to a formalism chosen independently from its material implementation. To fully realize the potential of molecules in computation, information processing concepts that relinquish narrow prescriptive control over elementary structures and functions are needed, and self-organising architectures have to be developed.[269]

Molecular computing with artificial neurons
Today's computers are built up from a minimal set of standard pattern recognition operations. Logic gates, such as NAND, are common examples. Biomolecular materials offer an alternative approach, both in terms of variety and context sensitivity. Enzymes, the basic switching elements in biological cells, are notable for their ability to discriminate specific molecules in a

complex background and to do so in a manner that is sensitive to particular milieu features and indifferent to others. The enzyme, in effect, is a powerful context sensitive pattern recognizer. We describe a tabletop pattern processor that in a rough way can be analogized to a neuron whose input-output behavior is controlled by enzymatic dynamics.[270]

Howard Pattee – *How Does a Molecule Become a Message*

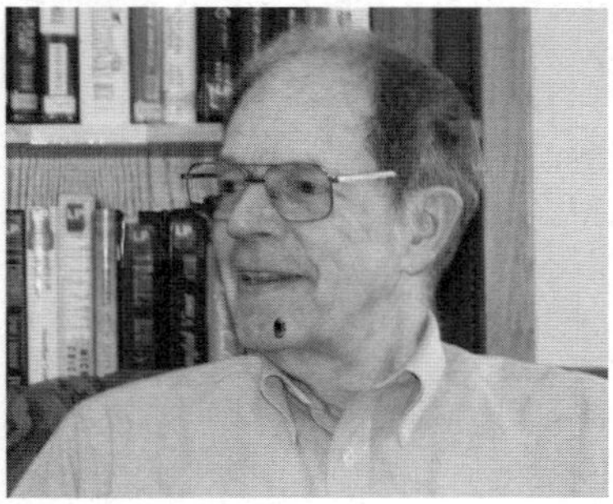
Photo of Howard Pattee, courtesy of Pattee.

How does a molecule become a message?
[…] How do we tell when there is communication in living systems? Most workers in the field probably do not worry too much about defining the idea of communication since so many concrete, experimental questions about developmental control do not depend on what communication means. But I am interested in the origin of life, and I am convinced that the problem of the origin of life cannot even be formulated without a better understanding of how molecules can function symbolically, that is, as records, codes, and signals. Or as I imply in my title, to understand origins, we need to know how a molecule becomes a message.

More specifically, as a physicist, I want to know how to distinguish communication between molecules from the normal physical interactions or forces between molecules which we believe account for all their motions. Furthermore, I need to make this distinction at the simplest possible level, since it does not answer the origin question to look at highly evolved organisms in which communication processes are reasonably clear and distinct. Therefore I need to know how messages originated.[271]

Yukio-Pegio GUNJI

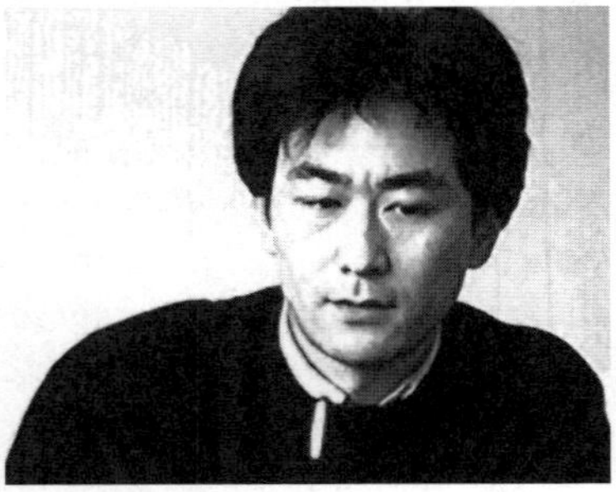
Courtesy of Gunji.

Dynamical duality of type and token computation as an abstract brain
In brain science, there are few researches focusing on the theoretical relation between cognition (top-down processing) and perception (bottom-up processing). Philosophically they were regarded as the alternative leading to the dualism

of mind and body, while it is an adequate problem for the endo-physics. Qualia are conjectured as the hard problem under those situations. To overcome such an impasse, we propose an abstract brain model featuring the dynamical duality of two parts of computations in a brain, in a term of endo-physics and internal measurement.[272]

Kunihiko KANEKO

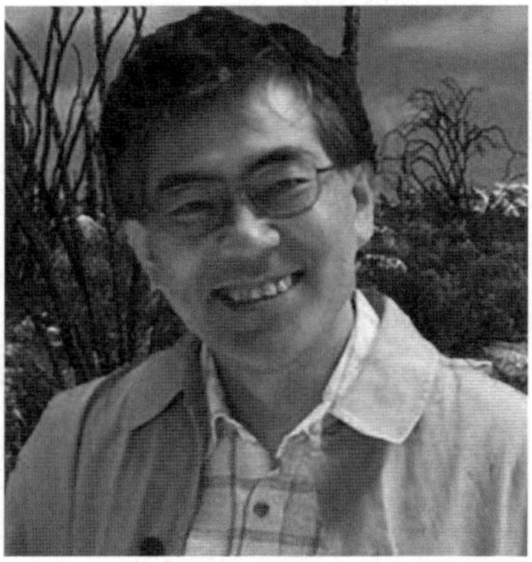

Kunihiko Kaneko and Michael Conrad both did seminal work on the brain equation.

Michael Conrad called it the Rössler Task – the mathematical problem of the Traveling Salesman with Alarm Clocks. Kaneko and Tsuda invented the "chaotic itinerancy" in the spirit of n-dimensional dynamical systems, on the one hand, and a deep appreciation of meandering in personal life. Kaneko was the first to write a book on toroidal attractors and to do work on the later so-called Flair Attractor (see Georg C. Hartmann).

One Particular Way of Pattern Matching

A simulating cognitive system with adaptive capability
By Hans H. Diebner

Dedicated to the memory of Michael Conrad, this paper builds on his seminal ideas expressed in his famous book Adaptability, as well as in his later works. We investigate a recently published adaptive system for the instantaneous recognition of dynamics with respect to its adaptability to the Lorenz system. The system consists of a pool of internal dynamical elements. These elements are defined through a set of parameter values that encode for a specific dynamic behavior. If the system is now faced with an unknown external dynamics – unknown with respect to the parameter – it is capable not only to recognize the dynamics but also to adapt to the correct dynamics, which in turn leads to a simulation capability. The system impressively quickly follows the sudden qualitative changes of the external dynamics. The adaptation works even quicker when the correct dynamics are already represented within the internal pool. This leads to the idea of memorizing the represented dynamics within the pool, whereby the elements that correspond to rarely externally presented dynamics can be given free for the adaptation and memorization of more frequently presented dynamics.[273]

The Angel of Redness

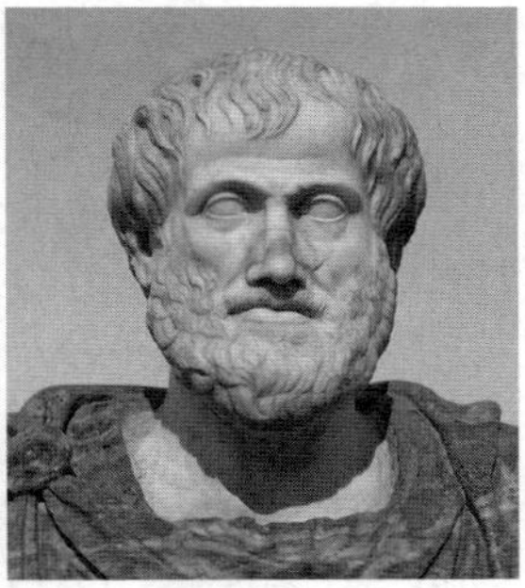

Bust of Aristotle. Marble, Roman copy after a Greek bronze original by Lysippos from 330 BC; the alabaster mantle is a modern addition. Public domain.

Will "redness" arise in the Neosentient?

Will it be different from the experience of red embodied in the human? Of course it will – hence the name *Neosentient*.

What is the physics that contributes to redness? There must be a connection but no one has ever had an idea of what could trigger the eventual pure appearance of something that has no place in science. It does not exist in science but it has a place where it surreptitiously enters even though it cannot enter. This fact was already seen by Aristotle who said: "The Mind enters tyrathen." Tyrathen means "through the door." This door has never been found but it no doubt exists.

All Aesthetics are Neural Aesthetics

Neosentient Aesthetics

Conceptual Art – The beauty of Ideas:

Art as idea – Science as idea – scientific papers and research become conceptual art.

The aesthetic takes the form that the project dictates.

The beauty of mathematics.

The aesthetics of the Neosentient itself:

What should it look like?

How will its looks affect how people interact with it?

How should its sexuality or something even more tantalizing be articulated?

Should it be anthromorphic and/or subtly "of itself" (See Spielberg *A.I.* as compared to *I Robot* – related filmic aesthetics)

Will it come to know nakedness?

How should it be clothed? There will be an entire branch of fashion design dedicated to the optimal outfitting and clothing of benevolent robots.

Will it have erogenous zones, and does anyone have an idea of how to make them both appealing and holy? What gestures should accompany these innocent displays? These questions can of course only be answered by children, who would recognize these activities as "pure playfulness."

How will the *neo-psychology* of self-image and individuality play itself out? (e.g., will it sport Tatoos?)
Would Neo (the character) be able to contribute to this Neo-psychology. This is a question to be put to the Wachowsky Brothers who invented Neo.
The aesthetics of the models leading to the construction of the Neosentient – the parts and the whole: diagrams, drawings, sketches, collages, graphs, schematics, 3D renderings, 3D animation.
Poetics and Recombinant Poetics: Poetic texts, metaphorical images – stills and video, evocative audio, metaphorical sounds and rhythms, the aesthetics of spoken narrative, poetic collages, interactive computational works. Duchamp, Dada, and Dali combined – DDD!
The Neosentient – consciousness arises.
The Neosentient learns.
Becomes enculturated.
Becomes aware of the aesthetic issues above.
Takes a part in the unpacking of its own understanding of aesthetics surrounding Neosentience.
Participates in a dialog with humans and other Neosentiences.
How about reading a book called *Neosentience* by one or more neo-sentients calling themselves archeosentients and referring to us.
Go as far as possible but no further?

Some Reflective Projections on the Internal Screen of the Brain

We can consider the pattern of neurons as a distributed system. We can observe the 40 Hz tone as a carrier enabling particular forms of spatial orientation in time. We can view saccades as time-based processes with a central area that is in focus as a moving center. There is a molecular binding that is enabled by the 40 Hz signal forming an analog "field" for the inner screen. (Ichiro TSUDA conceived the idea of an infinitely sensitive neuron.) If we can imagine an algorithm that only takes the focused moments and stitches them together as a collage of the present "vicinity" in vision, this allows for a new form of "persistence of vision". We can construct the "still view" of our perceptual environment – an image that is being constantly updated by new foveal centers and the ongoing movement of saccades. This is the short-term buffer in the scheme of the brain equation. Thus, a distributed linked set of neuronal firings when organized spatially in a consistent manner may underlie our visual "perceptual" screen through an analog algorithmic procedure.

An analog to the "Big Screen" has herewith been found – the VR of the Neosentient.

Kleist

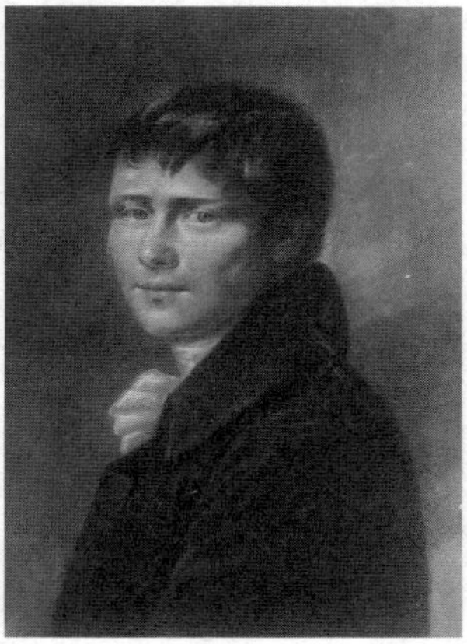

The Marionettes' Theatre discusses a young man/boy standing before a mirror and suddenly awakening to an adult existence.

Bernd Heinrich Wilhelm von Kleist. Public domain.

Turing

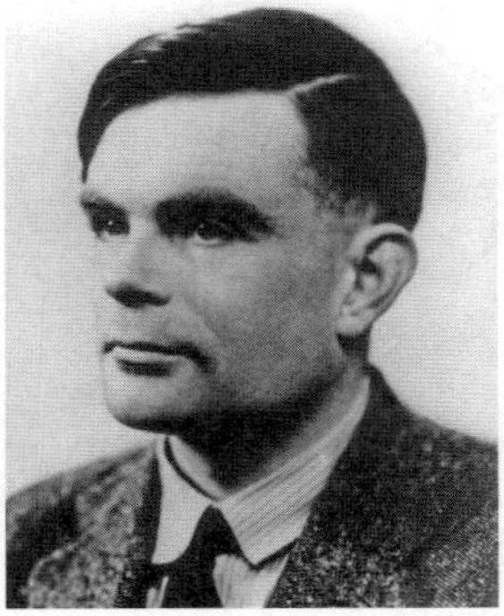

Alan Mathison Turing by Elliott & Fry quarter-plate glass negative, 29 March 1951 © National Portrait Gallery, London.

The Turing Test no doubt was a reflection on his own personhood. It shows a desperate longing for acceptance and for giving acceptance to others. He cannot possibly have been a cruel person.

Was Turing's sexuality in part unfolding a new form of love toward the *metal-encased soul*? The Turing Test being in the spirit of the present book – *The Real Fourth Sex* which discovers the desire in benevolence. There is no bigger desire. Love.

Epictetus the Roman slave and Turing are very close.
Epictetus, the Cretan, was a slave. His Roman master enjoyed torturing his slaves. One day he wrenched up Epictetus' arm behind his back. Epictetus said: "Master, if you wrench up the arm any further, the arm will break." The master did, the arm broke, Epictetus said "master, did I not tell you that if you wrench the arm up even further, the arm will break?" Whereupon the master set him free. A mere slave had been believed to have no soul. This was the first Turing Test.

Dystopian Techno-evolution (continued)

How can we optimize the initial setting of the system to facilitate symbiotic relations between the Neosentient and the Human as well as the *human and the human*? Will our hidden fears of dystopian control play themselves out because of humanities *traditionally* inherent evil and its distrust of the "alien"? Benevolence theory will lead us to a new form of humanity's evolution with post-Darwinian futures engendered technologically.

– A new "becoming" through Techno-Lamarckism in the spirit of the smile?

Male Mothers

Pestalozzi and Fröbel were male mothers. They invented the idea that children have the rights of other "adult persons." The "kindergarten" is Friedrich Fröbel's greatest innovation. Klaus Giel is his most recent incarnation.

Fear of an Awesome Responsibility

The fear of generating a new species and potentially bringing about our own demise as expressed by Stephen Spielberg in his movie *A.I.* is palpable in the background and almost kept us from writing this book. Some people will wish …

Spielberg's Epic *A.I.*

Friday, 29 June 2001, 11:13 GMT 12:13 UK
Spielberg's epic A.I. opens

A.I.
Kubrick came up with the idea 20 years ago, sketched it out in detail and suggested that Spielberg direct it. Starring Jude Law and 13-year-old Sixth Sense star Haley Joel Osment, one

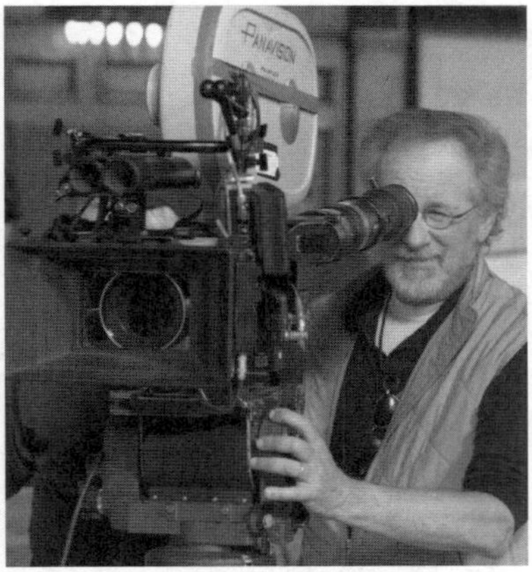

Steven Spielberg, courtesy of DreamWorks.

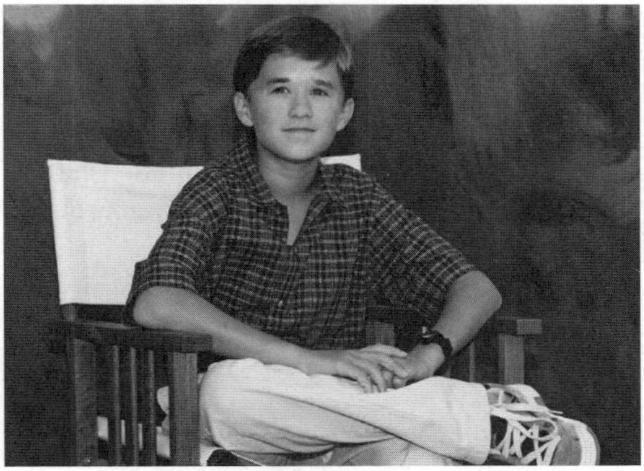
Osment, courtesy of the Commons.

journalist said it feels like what might happen if "cute little ET calls home and HAL the evil computer answers". Spielberg, who was behind hits including ET, Schindler's List and Jurassic Park, took over the project when Kubrick died in 1999. Kubrick's original plan was to use a real robot to play the film's robotic boy, who is programmed to love, it has been revealed. But Spielberg gave that role to Osment.[274]

Kindness is considered so dangerous because it is so close to love and love is so close to sexuality.

Sigmund Freud said: The female is polymorphically perverse by nature. (This is a strange statement isn't it?)

We assure the reader that males are no less dangerous and in danger, but nevertheless the love and trust of a child is infinitely stronger than that of all adults.

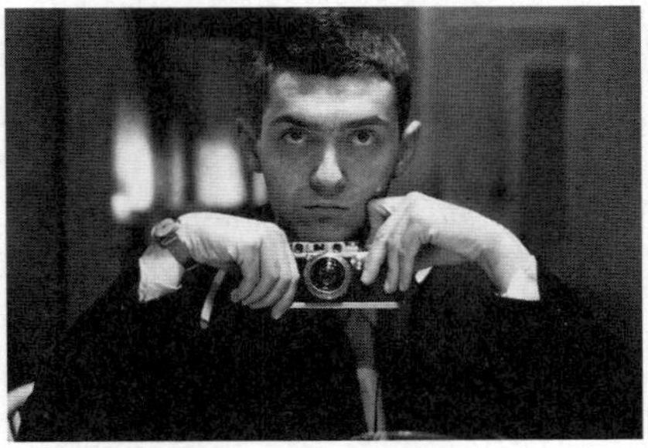
Stanley Kubrick. Selfportrait Late 1940s, courtesy Commons.

Post-Darwinian Symbiosis (Lion, Lamb, and Computer)

Why did Mitsubishi not succeed with the W. robot? The answer is that they did not look at the subtle vibrations of emotion. Emotions are still elusive in robotics. Neither Musterle's facial expression program nor the brain equation has been employed by the pertinent industries up until now.

Turing Test

Computing machinery and intelligence
By A. M. Turing

1. The Imitation Game
I propose to consider the question, "Can machines think?" This should begin with definitions of the meaning of the terms "machine" and "think." The definitions might be framed so as to reflect so far as possible the normal use of the words, but this attitude is dangerous. If the meaning of the words "machine" and "think" are to be found by examining how they are commonly used it is difficult to escape the conclusion that the meaning and the answer to the question, "Can machines think?" is to be sought in a statistical survey such as a Gallup poll. But this is absurd. Instead of attempting such a definition I shall replace the question by another, which is closely related to it and is expressed in relatively unambiguous words.

The new form of the problem can be described in terms of a game which we call the "imitation game." It is played with three people, a man (A), a woman (B), and an interrogator (C) who may be of either sex. The interrogator stays in a room apart front the other two. The object of the game for the interrogator is to determine which of the other two is the man and which is the woman. He knows them by labels X and Y, and at the end of the game he says either "X is A and Y is B" or "X is B and Y is A." The interrogator is allowed to put questions to A and B thus:
C: Will X please tell me the length of his or her hair?

Now suppose X is actually A, then A must answer. It is A's object in the game to try and cause C to make the wrong identification. His answer might therefore be:

"My hair is shingled, and the longest strands are about nine inches long."

In order that tones of voice may not help the interrogator the answers should be written, or better still, typewritten. The ideal arrangement is to have a teleprinter communicating between the two rooms. Alternatively the question and answers can be repeated by an intermediary. The object of the game for the third player (B) is to help the interrogator. The best strategy for her is probably to give truthful answers. She can add such things as "I am the woman, don't listen to him!" to her answers, but it will avail nothing as the man can make similar remarks.

We now ask the question, "What will happen when a machine takes the part of A in this game?" Will the interrogator decide wrongly as often when the game is played like this as he does when the game is played between a man and a woman? These questions replace our original, "Can machines think?"[275]

Bringing up the Computer

Turing:

We may hope that machines will eventually compete with men in all purely intellectual fields. But which are the best ones to start with? Even this is a difficult decision. Many people think that a very abstract activity, like the playing of chess, would be best. It can also be maintained that it is best to provide the machine with the best sense organs that money can buy, and then ***teach*** *it to understand and speak English. This process could follow the normal teaching of a child. Things would be pointed out and named, etc. Again I do not know what the right answer is, but I think both approaches should be tried.*

We can only see a short distance ahead, but we can see plenty there that needs to be done.[276]

Epictetus and the Turing Test

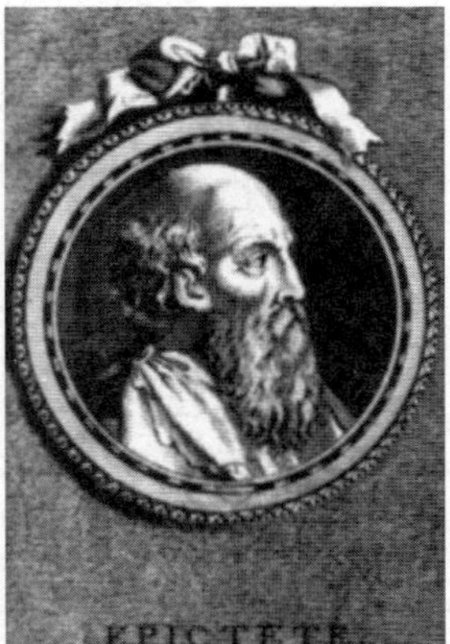

Public domain.

When a machine takes on personhood it must be re-understood. It can no longer function as a slave, but instead becomes a friend and collaborator. This represents a cultural revolution in that now all computers are thought of as slaves.

Descartes and the Turing Test

The Turing Test
Stanford encyclopedia of philosophy[277]

The phrase "The Turing Test" is most properly used to refer to a proposal made by Turing (1950) as a way of dealing with the question whether machines can think. According to Turing, the question whether machines can think is itself "too meaningless" to deserve discussion (442). However, if we consider the more precise – and somehow related – question whether a digital computer can do well in a certain kind of game that Turing describes ("The Imitation Game"), then – at least in Turing's eyes – we do have a question that admits of precise discussion. Moreover, as we shall see, Turing himself thought that it would not be too long before we did have digital computers that could "do well" in the Imitation Game.

The phrase "The Turing Test" is sometimes used more generally to refer to some kinds of behavioural tests for the presence of mind, or thought, or intelligence in putatively minded entities. So, for example, it is sometimes suggested that The Turing Test is prefigured in Descartes' Discourse on the Method. (Copeland (2000:527) finds an anticipation of the test in the 1668 writings of the Cartesian de Cordemoy. Gunderson (1964) provides an early instance of those who find that Turing's work is foreshadowed in the work of Descartes.) In the Discourse, Descartes says:

"If there were machines which bore a resemblance to our bodies and imitated our actions as closely as possible for all practical purposes, we should still have two very certain means of recognizing that they were not real men. The first is that they could never use words, or put together signs, as we do in order to declare our thoughts to others. For we can certainly conceive of a machine so constructed that it utters words, and even utters words that correspond to bodily actions causing a change in its organs. […] But it is not conceivable that such a machine should produce different arrangements of words so as to give an appropriately meaningful answer to whatever is said in its presence, as the dullest of men can do. Secondly, even though some machines might do some things as well as we do them, or perhaps even better, they would inevitably fail in others, which would reveal that they are acting not from understanding [we would add: between persons], *but only from the disposition of their organs. For whereas reason is a universal instrument, which can be used in all kinds of situations, these organs need some particular action; hence it is for all practical purposes impossible for a machine to have enough different organs to make it act in all the contingencies of life in the way in which our reason makes us act." (Translation by Robert Stoothoff)*

Although not everything about this passage is perfectly clear, it does seem that Descartes gives a negative answer to the question whether machines can think; and, moreover, it seems that his giving this negative answer is tied to his confidence that no mere machine could pass The Turing

Test: no mere machine could talk and act in the way in which adult human beings do. Since Descartes explicitly says that there are "two very certain means" by which we can rule out that something is a machine – it is, according to Descartes, inconceivable that a mere machine could produce different arrangements of words so as to give an appropriately meaningful answer to whatever is said in its presence; and it is for all practical purposes impossible for a machine to have enough different organs to make it act in all the contingencies of life in the way in which our reason makes us act – it seems that he must agree with the further claim that nothing that can produce different arrangements of words so as to give an appropriately meaningful answer to whatever is said in its presence can be a machine.

Descartes considered the brain as a machine and knew that all other beings except himself could not be proven to possess a soul. But he was kind enough to give the other persons full credit despite his own lonely position in the realm of conscious perception. This leads directly over to Levinas who emphasized the infinite power and hence responsibility of the subjective consciousness of every single human person, by his or her being outside of the other.

By the way, no one has so far stressed the fact that Turing thought of an American border control to be allowed into the land of the future no matter whether one is male or female or machine as long as one is a person.

Philip K. Dick's Empathy Test

Do Androids Dream of Electric Sheep (1968)? This poet is one of the deepest thinkers about the human soul so far.

Philip. K. Dick explored the notion of an empathy test for highly intelligent androids in this novel.

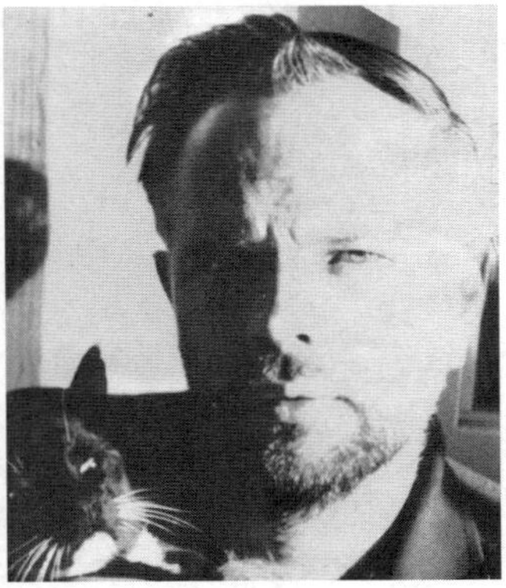

Philip K. Dick, courtesy of the Philip K. Dick trust.

Seated where he could catch the readings on the two gauges of the Voight-Kampff testing apparatus, Rick Deckard said, "I'm going to outline a number of social situations. You are to express your reaction to each as quickly as possible. You will be timed of course."

"And of course," Rachel said distantly, "My verbal responses won't count. It's solely the eye-muscle and capillary reaction that you'll use as indices. But I'll answer; I want to go through this and – " She broke off. "Go ahead Mr. Deckard."[278]

The book also included the description of a technology that could influence a person's mood – is this not a technology that manipulates the related emotional "force fields" of the brain equation?

This is again the Turing Test revisited.

Dick quotes a sentence from Yeats before the book starts – "And still I dream he treads the lawn, walking ghostly in the dew, pierced by my glad singing through."

Galactic Export

The idea is that it is possible to export personhood out of the human species. See note 194.

Computational Potentiality

New forms of computational potentiality revise old dreams related to artificial intelligence and the mechanization of thought processes.

The Physics of Meaning

Meaning = Force
Force = Quality
Meaning = Quality

Quality is provably absent in the universe were it not for the fact that we have it.

A perturbation is a physical force. The body transduces these forces or rather their ratios. The ratios are registered and encoded into time-based neural trajectories. A pattern of force ratios becomes eventually a new pattern of changing states. This can be called a time-based neural trajectory. This analog of changes in the environment is subjected to a gating mechanism. Behind those gates, some responses are triggered eventually. There is a chain of non-linear modifications along this assembly line with many parallel processing elements that are in part dynamically interlinked. At the end there is a simplified pattern that propagates as a function over time. A so-called signal. This set of signals forms a unique time-based and spatial configuration over time. These signals may be spatially represented on an analog-type "screen." The latter is well defined even if it is not physically contiguous. Similarly, temporal continuity may be discontinuous. This is the "big screen" we discuss in our model. This virtual reality becomes the environment that is interacted with. Some elements that enter into the screen have releasing qualities that engage particular forces in a concomitant fashion. An immaterial, metaphorically "transparent" screen works in conjunction with the "big screen." This is the screen of the imagination. (Thinking is acting in imagined space, Lorenz.) In our system we call this the overlap buffer function, where one can simulate an action before undertaking it and move back and forth between the screen and the buffer via attention.

The system of relational patterns is built up over time and has a short-term memory and a long-term memory for storing patterns and the relations between patterns. Particular recurrent patterns become associated with other patterns. They acquire a "quality" that we can name, which is itself a pattern. This name, a flow of signals, also has a spatial time-based neural trajectory. A recirculation of the same force is "reinforced" by the system. This is Hebb's law.

Articulate behavior and the use of language is an example of a time-based flow.

An Ultrametric Dream – Vladimir Anashin and Andrei Khrennikov's Robotic Subconscious

The new psychoanalysis of robots articulated in Applied Algebra Dynamics by Vladimir Anashin and Andrei Krennikov discusses consequences for robotic "subconscious thinking" and subsequent behavior. This is a direct implication of our overlap buffer discussed in the context of the brain equation at the end of the book. Its relation to the emotional force fields enables the robot to be attracted to, or repelled by differing suggestive situations driven by synthetic innate releasing mechanisms.

In our model the mental cybernetic realization of resistance to the reappearance of hidden forbidden wishes in the subconscious (and then conscious) domain is based on block thresholds. At the deeper level of the model such a resistance is a consequence of the ability of a cognitive system to measure mental distance and calculate the measure of unconscious interdiction (resistance). The unconscious comparator by calculating the distance from an idea generator – trying to pass from the processing domain to the conscious domain – to the database of hidden forbidden wishes prevents the appearance in the conscious of ideas which are similar to (in particular, coincide with) former hidden forbidden wishes.[279]

We would suggest that the idea generator is a consequence of the complex loops of the machine and its ability to learn.

The Tale of the Whale

A science fiction story of this title was written by one of the authors a long time ago.

The Tale of the Whale was written without interruption, hitting a typewriter in 1976. It was written in Pidgin English. It is quite sad. A female sperm whale is being followed up by a devoted biologist who had built a little submarine with a transparent cap in which he sat, to follow her, which had a remote controlled mini-robotic submarine which he used to pluck parasites from her head. He realized that she realized that the motions of his own fingers coincided with the movement of the plucking motions of the little robot submarine that he controlled; so they quickly converged on a common code of mutual communication. (Note that sperm whales are much more intelligent in their biological hardware than any other organism on the planet.) Now comes the upshot: He learned why she was heading for a whale cemetery. She was following her son who had been convicted by the whale community to die there because he had broken the code of rules of the clan. These rules forbade one to do certain things. The idea is that this animal society had taboos which are heavily enforced, but also have a proto-language which includes terms that most members never decipher. But from time to time, every few hundred years an individual would come into a mode of understanding and relating to a personhood-based subculture, understanding what earlier generations of wise individuals had left in the common code of interaction of the species. These individuals necessarily break some rules of the sleeping majority in contributing to the hidden knowledge of the wise sub-population that exists only across time. Therefore, her son was sentenced to death and therefore she was weeping all of the time. This is the Tale of the Whale as revealed belatedly in 1976.

Its connection in the context of the present book became transparent to the authors only in the conversation transcribed above. This is exactly the question with forbidden, posthuman Neosentience. Is benevolence theory lawful? Where is the cemetery? We have in mind the scene from the movie *A.I.* in which the human mob is let loose against the fearful robots who are not quite as perfectly made as the little hero of the movie.

Is what we are doing in accordance with evolution?

Fighting Evil

Good only has a chance if pursuing it is even more fun than pursuing evil, and in fighting it one does not oneself become evil.

Buddha [Smile]

There are statues of Buddha where he is sitting with crossed legs and with his two hands having certain symbolic orientations of the fingers while his face is inscrutable but divine. There is the saying that the creator is a Buddhist because Buddha is so sweet. Christianity of course says essentially the same thing with a different name given to Buddha.

TechnoSpecies

The species arising out of the pursuit of personhood. A new categorical term for what humanity is headed for.

A Model for a Neosentient System – The Benevolence Engine

A situated robotic learning system with ultra-perspective.

We list the main functional parts of the diagram.[280]

The Diagram

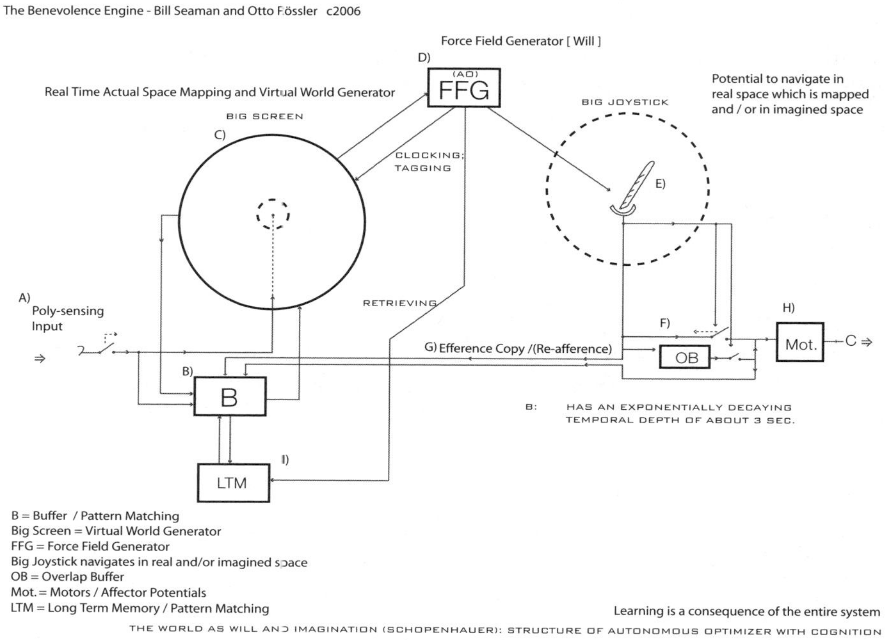

This refers to a blueprint of an artificial brain with cognition and the potential for empathy.

Poly-sensing Input

Machine multimodal sensing

The Benevolence Engine begins with a series of input devices – a machine-based multi-modal sensing system.[281] One can imagine one's own senses being abstracted into such a mechanism, although machine-based sensing potentials will potentially be quite different in sensitivity to their human counterparts. That is, one can imagine the system as being implemented with infrared vision. Embodied multimodal sensing has been discussed by Agre and Suchman.[282] Such multimodal approaches were initially discussed early on (in the 1990s) by Brooks.[283] This represents a quite different perspective to earlier A.I. projects that were not "embodied" and did not see the importance of coming to a deep knowledge of context via multimodal sensing systems that would be dynamically linked to their environment. The concept of "Pattern Flows"[284] is discussed in the paper "Pattern flows | hybrid accretive processes informing identity construction". This paper points to the potentials of "pattern flows" of sense inputs as a means of coming to understand meaning production. L. Barsalou has conducted much research in this area.[285] So has Charles Spence at the Cross-modal Research Lab, providing research into the nature of multimodal sensing.[286] Peter Cariani has also written about sensing and Temporal Codes.[287] Jon Bird and Andy Webster explored related electrochemical sensing topics.[288]

Multimodal sensing systems enable the transduction of sense data into a "pattern language" the system can utilize. This represents a set of processes that contribute to the potential arising of Neosentience. Synthetic senses can have different qualities to that of their human counterpart – there can be more of them and they can exhibit different sensitivities to that of the human. Thus the *Benevolence Engine*'s "phenomenological" experience would be *of itself* because the machine-based senses would give it a qualitatively different ongoing understanding to those of the human sensorial domain. Consider our understanding of the stars using human vision. Then consider our understanding of the stars after the invention of the telescope. We might also picture radical connectivity to devices like scanning/tunneling microscopes. If a series of machine-based senses were the *normal senses* that functioned together to form an understanding of the world for the *Benevolence Engine*, its general perception of the world would differ from that of the human. One might argue that the same technologies function as extensions of our own senses, such that there would not be a difference. We believe the integrated use of multiple non-human sensing systems will contribute a different understanding of the world and thus help generate this state of Neosentience – a sentience based initially (in part) on the abstraction of human sensing. Our system would contribute to coming to know the world in a unique manner.

Char Davies' VR installation *Osmose* and the quantum experience come to mind here. You might know about Anton Zeilinger's incredible finding with Fullerene molecules (that are shaped like a football and almost as big when you are an atom), because they contain 60 carbon atoms, so that they are almost "macroscopic". This was inconceivable only a few years ago – such a macroscopic body was shown by Zeilinger to go through two slits simultaneously because it interfered with itself on the screen.

Zeilinger also demonstrated most convincingly quantum teleportation where the state of one atom is transported superluminally onto another atom a kilometer apart.

And he also had the idea that one could do this experiment in such a way that the two measurements take place, one on the earth and the other in a satellite flying overhead in a departing manner. In that case, each quantum measurement would be the first measurement of a joint photon pair's quantum state, so that Einstein's prediction that quantum mechanics can be "completed" would be vindicated. The consequence – the Copenhagen interpretation is falsified and Einstein was right one more time. And, every observer lives in his or her own quantum world. All other people share with each observer his or her measurement results. But this world in which each lives with all of the others included is not the same for each.

This proves that each world is as unique as the Now and that the palpable reality that we have in front of us is a shining crystal that was made for each of us at this very moment in time, each person having his or her own perfect present to contemplate. We wonder about the ramifications of this for the Neosentient.

Pattern Matching Mechanism

The system would observe in a form of foveal 3D,[289] defining an updatable map of the environment (by having the input partially abstracted and simplified on the way), generating a virtual environment that can later be drawn upon for pattern recognition purposes as well as to enable a correlate of "closed-eye vision" for navigation of imagined spaces before acting in physical space. This is an automatic implication of the above "wiring" diagram.

If we think of a human acting in physical space, we also perform within a layered topological space[290] by superimposing our human emotional space (our feelings, attractions, and repulsions to situations and needs) with physical space. Emotional space and physical space are conjoined and can be contemplated before action is undertaken. This forms a topological–psychological space where many factors (other parts of the system) play into the "understanding" and "parsing" of sensed stimulations and environmental differences. We "build up" knowledge and use it in a projective manner, in forming the understanding of incoming data. A goal in designing the system – acquisition through sensed "patterns flows" – will be to enable the entity to form new understandings through learning and a creative combinatoric pattern re-application. Each individually sensed aspect (force vector) of a linked set of multimodal memories can lead back to the memory of the original pattern (or constellation of multimodal inputs) through pattern matching (force vector based retrieval). Any scene could be retrieved from the combined emotional vector, momentarily applicable to it. The system would also automatically generate "Platonic ideation" in the sense of Heinz von Foerster[291] via the sinc algorithm (wavelet) or averaging[292] – enabling potential recombinant collage-like "creations" built of past relations, mixed with updated information and language.

Buffer-generated VR

The entity is embodied and embedded in the environment. Multimodal senses provide deep knowledge of the environment that is built up slowly through learning and the inter-functionality of the differing branches of the system's functioning over time. A virtual picture of the environment is being built up in real time. The memory of this picture becomes abstracted by the system. High-resolution storage of all situations over time is not "economically" viable for the system with a finite memory space. The system "experiences" in high detail, with foveal focus shifting across individual senses and multi-modal relational centers. The entity builds up averaged patterns through simplification/abbreviation/metonymy (platonic reference) through the averaging of patterns. The virtual world also stores comparative relations to other correlated time-based sense data. Memory becomes a relational configuration over time[293] and depends on the environment, filling in many details for actual embodied experience.[294] Multimodal sensing contributes to this relational time-based configuration. The density of detail of this relational set is also decreasing in resolution over time (related to the image content/virtual mapping that is stored) although aspects of the resolution can be built back up with subsequent emulation/simulation and/or new encounters with similar but different things, updating based on new data, and additional encounters with the environment. A Neosentient approach suggests that this "mind's eye" can be shared with other entities, networked and or made visible in a public manner. Thus again, *The Benevolence Engine*'s "mind's eye" will be significantly different in nature to that of the human. Humans cannot share their mind's eyes in a direct manner.[295] Yet in seeking to posit such a new vision system, one must come to study the functionality of the human visual system, and its relation to other sensing systems in the body in a manner that transcends contemporary science's need to isolate sensing systems – the visual system in particular (similarly Jürgen Parisi). Thus new forms of multimodal research must be undertaken and/or abstracted to help us comprehend the inter-functional nature of senses especially in terms of pattern matching, and memory retrieval.

Force Field Generator

We must remember that human emotion and human need (drives) play into many of the spatial decisions we make – our human behavior. Again the topological–psychological space of Lewin is invoked – the brain equation and this scheme match his scheme intuitively. A series of "drives" (internal emotional forces) implements for us the need to approach and/or avoid differing situations. Our system houses a set of force field sliders that the brain equation controls. The vector of these forces characterizes and sums up for us in differing ways related to alternate situations. Historical input that is re-associated with the current context through both pattern matching, and force vector matching in the current environmental input, is also put into play via the memory elements' inner loop. This complex systems approach explains particular behaviors over time. The force field sliders are quantifiable in machine-oriented terms, and controllable/programmable, but they are ordinarily controlled via the environmental input (and the endogenous force-specific clock signals which empty out with every consummatory act and start up going again) in accord with the brain equation.

A Neosentient entity might also be empowered to internally re-set their own force field sliders.

Control Driver: The Great Joystick and the Great Simulator Mechanism (Imagined Space)

This part of the system both steers the behavior of the mechanism (joystick metaphor) and/or performs simulations of what the steering mechanism might accomplish (again related to closed-eye vision) or picturing your behavior before you do it to help make decisions (simulation space). This automatically occurs when the motors and the "visual inputs" are momentarily switched off (closed-eyes optimization mode). In the full-action mode this sends messages to robotic effectors to bring about the same movement in actual space.

Overlap Buffer

The overlap buffer enables the entity to be performing in actual space while simultaneously running simulations (imagined spatial relations) that help the entity make decisions about how to act in that space in the immediate future. The entity thus can focus on the actual view, the imagined view, or a simultaneous mixture. This correlates to the human's ability to close their eyes and just think about a situation, and/or think about it (or other spaces) while simultaneously acting in the environment, which applies equally in the brain equation.

Efference Copy/Reafference

This is based on von Holst's Reafference Principle. A control system (the brain), or in this case a computer, has sensory and motor connections to muscle-like effectors. The efference command is the motor command. The reafference is a "sensory" response from the motor side. The reafference is called the efference copy. The afference and the efference copy (also called reafference) interact. If the afference is larger or smaller than the magnitude of the signal in the efference copy, the signals will not cancel, and the difference between the efference copy and the afference will be transmitted to the control mechanism.[296] Thus, the "exafference" forms a relational connection with the entity's motion and/or behavior within the environment and the entity's pattern matching, control, and simulation mechanisms.

Movement Potentials

The system functioning as a unity is capable of generating a movement that is directly linked to the environment through the multimodal sensing system, and makes actions that are based on knowledge that has been built up concerning the environment over time, housed in the memory stores.

Long-term Memory

Long-term memory stores particular patterns for long periods of time which is different from the exponentially decaying resolution (in terms of image-based patterns) of short term memory. Thus current pattern matching in the initial buffer, recombined with re-loaded similar scenes from the long-term buffer triggered by the momentary mood vector (the force field summing), enables the entity to do pattern matching with past environmental patterning, and through recursive loops, enable meta-patterning.

Neosentience

Neosentience is a new area of scientific and poetic research. It operates out of a rich series of interrelated research agendas. We have presented the initial plan for a model to address the potential of having neosentience arise through a series of interfunctional processes that have been derived through careful abstraction from universal space-dependent survival scenarios, that hold true for all types of evolutionary systems (whether carbon-based, or nido-borane-based on Jupiter, or nuclear chemistry-based on a neutron star— compare Robert Forward mentioned above).

Discussion and Summary

An artificial mind was proposed. It combines many functional ingredients that apparently have not been employed before, either alone or in combination. The "big screen" is a full-fledged virtual reality in the sense of William Gibson.[297] There is an updating involved that automatically generates a natural "nowness." It would not make sense to have an updating rate that is much faster than locomotion and limb movement require. The forces that emanate from source points in the spatial environment exert their influence on the "big screen." These forces control the locomotion of the artificial organism as prescribed by the implemented force fields of the brain equation. This is done via the "big joystick" which is directly "controlled" by the momentary force vectors as determined by environmental input and the time elapsed since certain past encounters and events, dependent on the components of the brain equation. The machine would be completely automatic were it not for the added capability of closed-eye locomotion. Here, the clash of some simultaneous forces acting on the joystick immobilizes it momentarily, while giving control over to a simulated mode of locomotion. As soon as the simulation leads to a resolution of the conflict, the lower level joystick takes over again. In this way, the machine is continually on the move, being under absolute control of the time-dependent forces exerted by "sources" in the environment. There is proto-consciousness involved.

If two such machines interact in a cross-caring manner, each can be caught in an attempt to simulate in favor of the other's goals. In this case, the invention of a "hallucinated" other center of optimization occurs. This gives rise to the invention of "benevolence" or more exactly, of the suspicion of benevolence, that is, of getting the impression that another center of optimization exists acting in favor of one's own goals. This presents a much more interesting mode of functioning of the system than simple optimizing-type locomotion. It will be necessary to build two such machines to enable such coupling, to completely understand the emergence of foreign controlled-ness within the system, along with its stopping to function as a subconscious optimizer. Actually the invention of the subconscious by Freud corresponds to the rediscovery of the old lack of consciousness mode in the brain. The real surprise is the emergence of a conscious giving-up of the original subconscious identity through the emergence of a simulated existence that is benevolent toward another simulated consciousness – internally represented by the same system. So, strangely, consciousness is not implied in the machine itself but only in a kind of out-of-nothing creation within the machine. The ghost of consciousness has no substratum in the hard or software of the system. It is pure fiction made real – it is the only agent to be found.

A second approach has also been discussed, complementing that of the implementation of the brain equation. The second approach explores the biofunctionality of the body at its greatest depth. It seeks to define a set of analogs for biological processes in a biomimetic fashion. This long-term approach (read bottom-up) seeks to re-understand the vast network of entailments of the body that enable it to function. One of the authors was also thinking in this manner when some 38 years ago, he was writing about "well-stirred" computational processes – laying the foundations for learning (conditioned reflexes) and thought surrounding the creation of an electrochemical computer. The creation of a Pandaka pygmaea Institute is also an initial step in this bottom-up direction. Alternately, the creation of an "insight engine," a technology to help augment approaches to studying and discussing bodily entailment, suggests the need to create technology to help define an even higher order technology – the Neosentient. Although this approach may prove to be problematic due to that which is unknown and unknowable about thought and the body, it may still form a fruitful approach to the generation of a Neosentient entity, which to some degree will be aware "of itself" and be of its own kind, given either approach. In fact it may be that both approaches, the top-down approach of the brain equation functioning in "conversation" with a bottom-up bio-mimetic approach, directly lead to a functional synthesis.

Coda
What are our goals or reasons for undertaking such research one might ask?
Understanding.
Understanding everything – to be given the key to life and to our importance in the world.
To increase beauty.
To pay back the world for the gift of life related to everything we have.
To pay back the world for the gift of consciousness.
To not be afraid to ask the difficult questions.
To pursue the answers as a lifelong goal – a chipping away [...]
To work toward defining the rules then to transcend them via their implementation.
And to find the riddle of color.
And the crystal of the Now.
And the shine of another's soul.
And the whiff of the soul-giving instance.
And that is the end of the book.
OH!

Addendum

Stuart Hameroff in his book *Ultimate Computing* spoke of the role of microtubules in brain cells in terms of both computation and consciousness. We see the electrons of certain cells (or their resident micro-tubules), as the site to which consciousness is attached as an alternative. The experience of consciousness is attached to the force field generating machinery (discussed above).

To be able to take the perspective of the other and project benevolence and meta-levels is the invention of the members of humanity, and as a consequence so is being able to speculate about consciousness.

Most technology of the future accessible to beings like us will remain dependent on electrons and this presents a salient limitology.

It is the mico-time reversal in the collective of electrons in certain cells in the reticular formation of the brain, the seat of the force field generator, that possibly or likely is the seat of consciousness.

A nuclear chemical life form could work without electrons as an essential element. In that case quarks could take up the function of electrons in being the port at which consciousness is attached.

Micro-time reversals inside a consciousness carrying machine could in principle explain quantum mechanics because quantum mechanics is characterized by inexplicable jumps, and probability waves. Everett's theory is formally compatible with this classical physics proposal in Endophysics. It is the reunderstanding of ourselves that can bring us closer to understanding the Neosentient computer, and vice versa.[298–99]

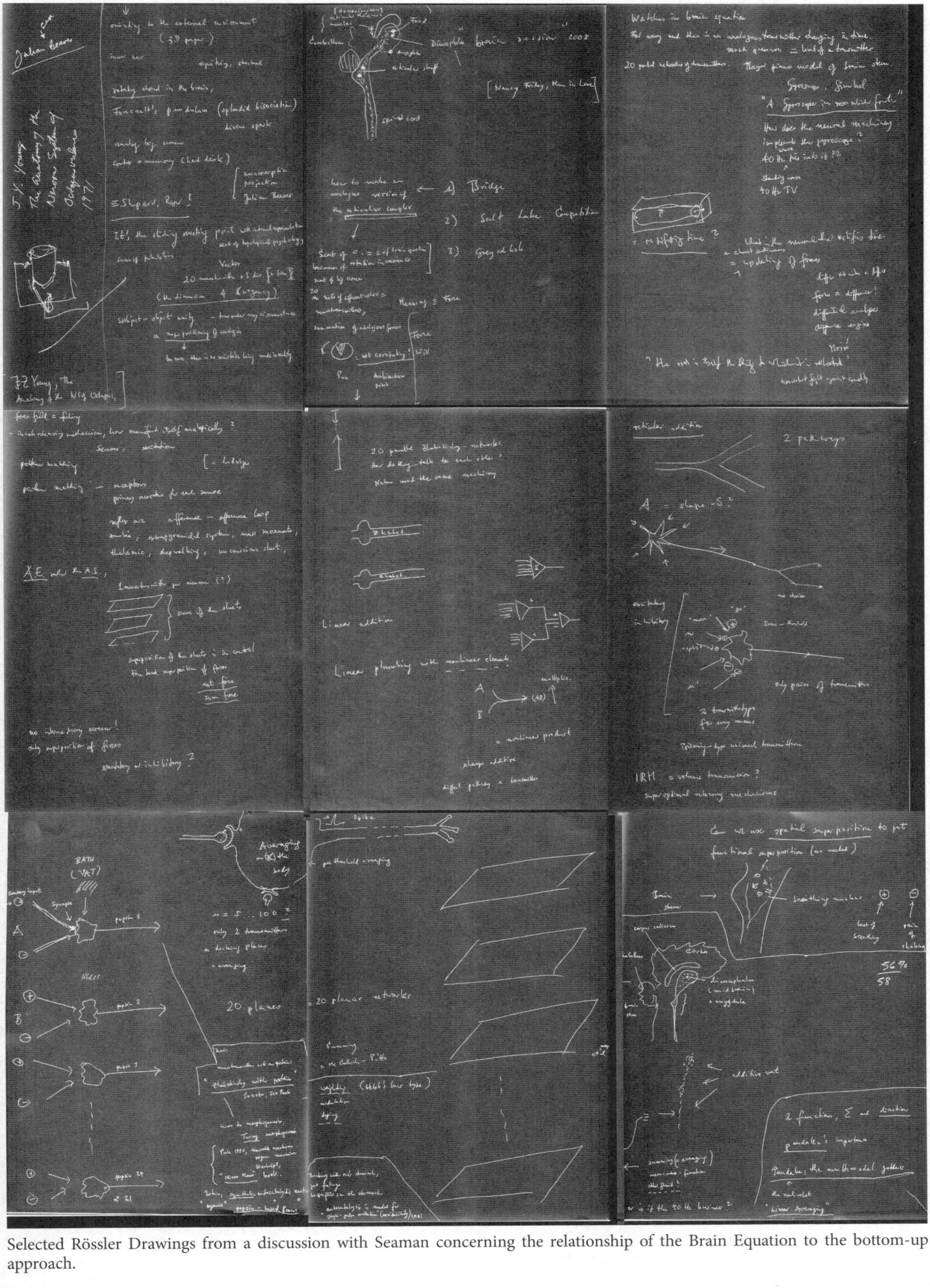

Selected Rössler Drawings from a discussion with Seaman concerning the relationship of the Brain Equation to the bottom-up approach.

Notes

1. *The Many-Worlds Interpretation of Quantum Mechanics* edited by Bryce S. DeWitt and Neill Graham with papers by Hugh Everett, III, J. A. Wheeler, B. S. DeWitt, L. N. Cooper and D. van Vechten and N. Graham, Princeton University Press, New Jersey 1973, p. 134; Everett states, two types of prediction can be distinguished: (1) the prediction of phenomena already understood, in which the theory plays simply the role of a device for compactly summarizing known results (the aspect of most interest to the engineer) and (2) the prediction of new phenomena and effects, unsuspected before the formulation of the theory. Our experience has shown that a theory often transcends the restricted field in which it was formulated. It is this phenomenon (which might be called the "inertia" of theories) which is of most interest to the theoretical physicist, and supplies a greater motive to theory construction than that of aiding the engineer. Everett, H. *The Many Worlds Interpretation of Quantum Mechanics*, http://www.pbs.org/wgbh/nova/manyworlds/pdf/dissertation.pdf.
2. Capek, K. (1923), *R.U.R* (*Rossum's Universal Robots*), Doubleday (p. 3. Story of the Play).
3. ASCOTT, R. (1966), *Behaviourist Art and the Cybernetic Vision. Cybernetica*, Namur: International Association for Cybernetics, IX, pp. 247–64.
4. See Steeles, Luc, http://cognitiverobotics.pbworks.com/Luc-Steels-Publications. Accessed 30 April 2010.
5. See Lorenz, K. (1977), *Behind the Mirror: A Search for a Natural History of Human Knowledge* (trans. R. Taylor), New York: Harcourt Brace Jovanovich; See Plotnik, J., de Waal, F. and Reiss, D. (2006), "Self recognition in Asian elephants", PNAS, September 2006. http://www.pnas.org/content/103/45/17053.full. Accessed 31 August 2010.
6. See http://www.calresco.org/sos/sosfaq.htm#1.1 for a definition of self-organizing systems.
7. Rössler, O. E. (1998), "The world as an accident", in J. Brouwer, A. Broeckman et al. (eds) (1998), *The Art of the Accident*, Jokie Brouwer, Andreas Broeckman, Bart Lootsma, Arjen Mulder and Lars Spuybroek (eds) (trans. Frances Bretell, Ronald Fritz and Leo Reijnen), NAI Publisher, p. 172.
8. Babbage, C. (1961), *Charles Babbage and his Calculating Engines: Selected Writings by Charles Babbage and Others*, New York: Dover Publications, Inc, p. 249.
9. Babbage, C. (1961), *Charles Babbage and his Calculating Engines: Selected Writings by Charles Babbage and Others*, New York: Dover Publications, Inc. Written to clarify the work *Sketch of the Analytical Engine Invented by Charles Babbage,* by L. F. Menabrea.
10. McCulloch, W. and Pitts, W. (1965), "A logical calculus of the ideas immanent in nervous activity", in McCulloch, W. S. (ed.), *Embodiments of Mind*, Cambridge, MA: MIT Press.
11. Turing, A. (1986), Volume 10 in *The Charles Babbage Institute Reprint Series for The History Of Computing*, Los Angeles, CA: Tomash Publishers, 1982–92.

12. Turing, A. (1950), "Computing machines and intelligence", in John Haugeland (ed.), *Mind Design II: Philosophy, Psychology, Artificial Intelligence*, Cambridge: MIT Press, 1997. See also Turing, *Mechanical Intelligence*, D. C. Ince (ed.), New York.
13. Dyson, G. (1997), *Darwin Among the Machines, The Evolution of Global Intelligence*, New York: Addison-Wesley Publishing.
14. Minsky, M. (1986), *Society of Mind*, New York: Simon and Shuster.
15. Minsky, M. (2006), The emotion machine, http://web.media.mit.edu/~minsky/.
16. Seaman, B. and Rössler, O. E. (2008), "Neosentience – a new branch of scientific and poetic inquiry related to artificial intelligence", *Technoetic Arts: A Journal of Speculative Research*, 6: 1, pp. 31–40.
17. von Foerster, H. (1960), "Circuitry of clues to Platonic ideation", in C. Muses (ed.), *Aspects of the Theory of Artificial Intelligence*, New York: Plenum Press, 1962, pp. 44–45.
18. Ibid., p. 45.
19. Richard P. Feynman, "*There's plenty of room at the bottom*." A transcript of the classic talk that Richard Feynman gave on 29 December 1959, at the annual meeting of the American Physical Society at the California Institute of Technology (Caltech) was first published in the February 1960 issue of Caltech's engineering and science, which owns the copyright. It has been made available on the web at http://www.zyvex.com/nanotech/feynman.html.; For an account of the talk and how people reacted to it, see chapter 4 of Nano! by Ed Regis (Little and Brown 1995).
20. Drexler, E. (1986), *Engines of Creation: The Coming Era of Nanotechnology*, Garden City, New York: Anchor Press/Doubleday.
21. Drexler, E. (1992), *Nanosystems: Molecular Machinery, Manufacturing, and Computation*, New York: John Wiley & Sons.
22. Paper presented at the conference Emotional Architectures/Cognitive Armatures, The Banff Center, Canada, September 2001, later published in Seaman, B. "Toward the Production of Nano-computers and in Turn, Nano-related Emotive Virtual/Physical Environments", Intelligent Agent 4.2 Spring 2004 http://www.intelligentagent.com/archive/IA4_2embodiment_nano_seaman.pdf. Accessed 15 May 2010.
23. http://ftp.arl.army.mil/~mike/comphist/.
24. Heims, S. (1991), *The Cybernetics Group*, Cambridge, MA, London, England: The MIT Press, pp. 106–07; See Wiener, N. (1961), *Cybernetics*, 2nd ed., Cambridge, MA: MIT Press.
25. Mead, M (1968), "Cybernetics of cybernetics", in H. Foerster, J. von, White, L. Peterson and J. Russell (eds), *Purposive Systems*, New York: Spartan Books.
26. von Foerster, Heinz (1973), "On constructing a reality", in F. E. Preiser (Hg.), *Environmental Design Research*, vol. 2, Stroudberg, PA: Dowden, Hutchinson & Ross, pp. 35–46.
27. See *Cybernetics of Cybernetics* by von Foerster for a related set of observations.
28. Müller, A. (2000), http://bcl.ece.uiuc.edu/mueller/index.htm. Accessed 22 July 2010. See Also: Muller, A. and Muller, K. (2007) *An unfinished revolution : Heinz von Foerster and the Biological Computer Laboratory, BCL, 1958-1976*, Edition Echoraum
29. Pias, Claus, *Cybernetics. The Macy Conferences 1946–53*, http://www.diaphanes.de/scripts/foreignrights/buch_englisch.php?ID=46. Accessed 1 August 2010.
30. *The Summary of the Conferences*, American Society for Cybernetics http://www.asc-cybernetics.org/foundations/history/MacySummary.htm. Accessed 1 August 2010.
31. Ashby, R. (1952), *Design for a Brain*, New York: John Wiley.
32. http://www.zone88.plus.com/images/WRA%20Office%201955%20CopyLeft%20HiRes.jpg. Accessed 15 May 2010.

33. Brooks, R. (2002), *Flesh and Machines: How Robots Will Change Us*, New York: Pantheon Books, pp. 5, 11 and see also p. 72 in *Flesh and Machines* discussing "Some Observations by Rodney Brooks Concerning the 3 Laws and Reality" from this publication.
34. Ibid., p. 37.
35. Ibid., p. 40.
36. Ibid., p. 52.
37. Kurzweil, R. (2005), *The Singularity is Near*, New York: Viking.
38. Ibid.
39. Ibid.
40. Ibid.
41. Joy, B. (2000), *Why The Future Doesn't Need Us*, April, 2000 Wired Magazine.
42. Powers, R. (1995), *Galatea 2.2*, New York: Farrar, Straus, Giroux.
43. Casti, J. (1994), *Complexification: Explaining an Illogical World Through the Science of Surprise*, New York: Harper Collins., See also Seaman, B. (2008) *Neosentience, Unpacking Dystopian Evolution*, http://mutamorphosis.wordpress.com/tag/neosentience/. Accessed 16 November 2010.
44. Casti, J. and DePauli, W. (2000), *Gödel*, Cambridge, MA: Perseus Publishing, pp. 144, 145.
45. See Holland, J. (1998), *Emergence – From Chaos to Order*, Oxford, New York: Oxford University Press.
46. Holland's abstract for his keynote talk at GECCO 2009, http://medal.cs.umsl.edu/blog/?p=365. Accessed 16 May 2010.
47. von Neumann, J. (1955), *Mathematical Foundations of Quantum Mechanics* (trans. R. T. Beyer), Princeton, NJ: Princeton University Press, p. 418.
48. von Neumann, J. (1995), *The Neumann Compendium*, vol. 1, F. Bródy and T. Vámos (eds), Singapore: World Scientific Publishing, pp. 526–28.
49. Ibid., pp. 534–35.
50. Ibid., p. 401.
51. Roy, D. (2007), (in press), *A Mechanistic Model of Three Facets of Meaning*. http://media.mit.edu/cogmac/publications/canary_oct17_2007.pdf Accessed 17 November 2010; See also: Miller, G. (1995), "Wordnet: a Lexical database for English", *Communications of the ACM*, 38: 11, pp. 39–41.
    Lenat, D. (1995), "Cyc: a large-scale investment in knowledge infrastructure", *Communications of the ACM*, 38: 11, pp. 33–38.
    Landauer, T. K., Foltz, P. and Laham, D. (1998), "Introduction to latent semantic analysis", *Discourse Processes*, 25, pp. 259–84.
    Barsalou, L. (1999), "Perceptual symbol systems", *Behavioural and Brain Sciences*, 22, pp. 577–609.
52. Rössler, O. E. (1985) "Design for a one dimensional brain", Information Processing in Biological Systems, 20th Annual Orbis Scientiae, Miami, Jan. 17–21, 1983 (B. Kursunoglu, S.L. Mintz and A. Perlmutter, editors), pp 145-153. New York Plenum Press 1985.
53. Rössler, O. E. (1978), "Deductive biology – some cautious steps", *Bulletin of Mathematical Biology*, 40: 1, pp. 45–58, *Presented at the Society for Mathematical Biology Meeting*, University of Pennsylvania, Philadelphia, 19–21 August 1976.
54. From "Nature" (November 2006, press release) http://www.antikythera-mechanism.gr/project/publications/nature-2006. Accessed 16 May 2010, see also. http://www.mlahanas.de/Greeks/Kythera.htm. Accessed 16 May 2010.
55. Seaman, B. (2005), "Pattern flows/hybrid identity construction", *Convergence: The International Journal of Research into New Media Technologies*, 11: 4, pp. 12–31.; *Kanzi the bonabo would probably not disagree …* see Savage-Rumbaugh, S. (1994), *Kanzi: The Ape at the Brink of*

the Human Mind, New York: Wiley. See also André, C. 2006, *Une Tendresse Sauvage*, Paris: Calmann-Lévy.

56. David, E. "Rumelhart prize, research biography of Roger Shepard". http://rumelhartprize.org/roger.htm. Accessed 20 February 2009. See also:
Shepard, R. and Cooper, L. (1982), *Mental Images and Their Transformations*, Cambridge: MIT Press.
Georgopoulos, A., Lurito, J., Petrides, M., Schwartz, A. and Massey, J. (1989), "Mental rotation of the neuronal population vector", *Science*, 243, pp. 234–36.
Richter, W., Somorjai, R., Summers, R., Jarmasz, M., Menon, R. S., Gati, J. S., Georgopoulos, A. P., Tegeler, C., Ugurbil, K. and Kim, S. G. (2000), "Motor area activity during mental rotation studied by time-resolved single-trial fMRI", *Journal of Cognitive Neuroscience*, 12, pp. 310–20.
Shepard, R. and Zare, S. (1983), "Path-guided apparent motion", *Science*, 220, pp. 632–34.
Shepard, R. (1984), "Ecological constraints on internal representation: resonant kinematics of perceiving, imagining, thinking, and dreaming", *Psychological Review*, 91, pp. 417–47.
Shepard, R. (2001), "Perceptual-cognitive universals as reflections of the world", *Behavioral and Brain Sciences*, 24, pp. 581–601; discussion 52–71.
Shepard, R. (2004), "How a cognitive psychologist came to seek universal laws", *Psychonomic Bulletin & Review*, 11, pp. 1–23.
57. Zielinski, Siegrfried, http://variantology.com/. Accessed 10 July 2010.
58. See Rössler, O. E. (1974), "Adequate locomotion strategies for an abstract organism in an abstract environment", *Lecture Notes in Biomathematics*, 4, pp. 342–69. [Equation (13) is the Brain Equation]
59. Minsky, M. (1986), *Society of Mind*, New York: Simon and Schuster.
60. Minsky, M. (2006), *The Emotion Machine*, New York: Simon and Shuster.
61. Johnson, Steven, http://www.techbookreport.com/tbr0005.html. Accessed 16 November 2009.
62. Dörner, D. (1979), "Self reflection and problem solving", in Friedhart Klix (ed.), *Human and Artificial Intelligence*, Amsterdam, New York: North-Holland Pub. Co.; New York; distributed in the United States and Canada by Elsevier North-Holland, P. 227.
63. Xpero http://www.xpero.org/portal/viewpage.php?page_id=1. Accessed 3 September 2010.
64. Gaugusch, A. and Seaman, B. (2004), "(Re)sensing the observer: offering open order cybernetics", *Technoetic Arts: A Journal of Speculative Research*, 2: 1, pp. 17–31. © Intellect Ltd.
65. Maruyama, M. (1963), "The second cybernetics: deviation-amplifying mutual causal processes", *American Scientist*, 5: 2, pp. 164–79.
66. Hofstadter, D. (1979), *Gödel, Escher, Bach: an Eternal Golden Braid*, New York: Basic Books. Gödel's *Theorem appears as Proposition VI in his 1931 paper* "On formally undecidable propositions" in *Principia Mathematica and Related Systems*, pp. 17, 20.
67. Bateson, G. (1972), *Steps to an Ecology of Mind*, New York: Ballantine Books, pp. 271–73.
68. Mckay, D. (1969), *Information, Mechanism and Meaning*, Cambridge, MA: MIT Press.
69. Hofstadter, D. (1979), *Gödel, Escher, Bach: An Eternal Golden Braid*, New York: Basic Books, Inc. Publishers.
70. Weisstein, E. "Wolfram math world", http://mathworld.wolfram.com/. Accessed 10 September 2009.
71. Weisstein, E. "Wolfram math world", http://mathworld.wolfram.com/CantorDiagonalMethod. html; Hoffman, P. (1998), *The Man Who Loved Only Numbers: The Story of Paul Erdos and the Search for Mathematical Truth*, New York: Hyperion, pp. 220–23; Penrose, R. (1989), *The Emperor's New Mind: Concerning Computers, Minds, and the Laws of Physics*, Oxford, England: Oxford University Press, pp. 84–85. See also Hofstadter, D. (1979), *Gödel, Escher, Bach: An Eternal Golden Braid*, New York: Basic Books, Inc. Publishers.

72. Elizabeth von Samsonow (2008), (personal communication).
73. Rössler's notes.
74. Marchal, B. (2004), "The origin of physical laws and sensations" http://iridia.ulb.ac.be/~marchal/publications/SANE2004MARCHALAbstract.html. Accessed 10 September 2009.
75. Marchal, B. IRIDIA, Brussels University 24 September 2000, http://iridia.ulb.ac.be/~marchal/publications/CC&Q.pdf. Accessed 10 September 2009.
76. Wiener, N. (1993), *Invention – The Care and Feeding of Ideas*, Cambridge: MIT Press, pp. 25–26.
77. Mead, G. (1934), *Mind, Self and Society, from the Perspective of a Behaviorist*, Chicago, IL: The University of Chicago press.
78. Seaman, B. (2005), "Pattern flows/Hybrid accretive processes informing identity construction", *Convergence Magazine*, Winter.
79. Ibid.
80. Peirce, C. (1931), *Collected Papers, vol. I–VIII*, Cambridge: Harvard University Press, p. 171.
81. Seaman, B. (2010), *Recombinant Poetics: Emergent Meaning Examined and Explored Within a Specific Virtual Environment*, Berlin: VDM Press.
82. Ibid.
83. Seaman, B. and Rössler, O. E. (2006), "Toward the creation of an intelligent situated computer and related robotic system: An intra-functional network of living analogies", Catalogue for Emoçào Art.ficial, Itau Cultural Center: Sao Paulo, Brazil.
84. Rössler, O. E. (1981), "An artificial cognitive map system", *BioSystems*, 13, pp. 203–09.
85. Seaman, B. and Rössler, O. E. (2006), "Toward the creation of an intelligent situated computer and related robotic system: An intra-functional network of living analogies", Catalogue for Emoçào Art.ficial, Itau Cultural Center, Sao Paulo, Brazil.
86. Bonhoeffer, K. F. (1947), Activation of passive iron as a model for the excitiation of a nerve, http://www.ncbi.nlm.nih.gov/pmc/articles/PMC2213747/. Accessed 2 August 2010.
87. Seaman, B (2009), "(Re)thinking, the body, generative tools and computational articulation", *Technoetic Arts: A Journal of Speculative Research*, 7: 3.
88. Pask. G. (1958), "Physical analogues to the growth of a concept by Gordon Pask", in *Mechanisation of Thought Processes, Proceedings of a Symposium Held at the National Physical Laboratory on 24–27th November 1958 Volume II National Physical Laboratory Symposium No. 10*, London: Her Majesty's Stationery Office 1959, p. 879. Ibid., p. 880.
89. Cariani, P. (1993), http://homepage.mac.com/cariani/CarianiWebsite/PaskPaper.html, see also *Systems Research*, 10: 3, pp. 19–33.
90. Pask, G. (1982), *Micro Man: Computers and the Evolution of Consciousness*, New York: Macmillan, pp. 133–35.
91. Glanville, R., http://www2.venus.co.uk/gordonpask/candhk.htm. Accessed 11 September 2010.
92. Pask, G., "A comment, a case history and a plan", in Reichardt, J. (1971) *Cybernetics, Art and Ideas*, New York Graphic Society, Greenwich Connecticut p.76
93. Rosen, M., http://www.medienkunstnetz.de/works/colloquy-of-mobiles/. Accessed 11 September 2010.
94. McKaughan, D. (2008), "From ugly duckling to swan: C. S. Peirce, abduction, and the pursuit of scientific theories", *Transactions of the Charles S. Peirce Society: A Quarterly Journal in American Philosophy*, 44: 3, pp. 446–68, Summer 2008.
95. Ibid.
96. Pask, G. (1982), *Micro Man: Computers and the Evolution of Consciousness*, New York: Macmillan, pp. 133–35.
97. Ibid., p. 147.

98. See also Finkelstein, D. (1979), "Holistic methods in quantum logic", in L. Castell and C. F. von Weizsacker (eds), *Quantum Theory and the Structure of Time and Space*, vol. 3, Munich: Karl Hanser, pp. 37–59.
99. http://www.swarthmore.edu/Humanities/pschmid1/essays/pynchon/vaucanson.html. Accessed 21 August 2010. – Much of the information above is quoted and paraphrased from an anonymous article on Vaucanson in *The Anglophones Magazine*, January/February 1999: pp. 22–23.
100. Roberts, S. "Some writings". http://music.calarts.edu/~sroberts/articles/DeVaucanson.duck.html. Accessed 22 August 2010.
101. Buckley, D. "The history of making robots," 1868 – Zadoc P. Dederick – *Steam Man*, http://mech-ai.com/DB/HistoryMakers/1868DederickSteamMan.htm. Accessed 10 April 2010.
102. Seaman, B. (1998), "Nonsense Logic". In Consciousness Reframed II, Edited by Roy Ascott, Intellect press.
103. See Peirce's letter to Allan Marquand of 30 December 1886. It is published in volume 6 of the *Writings of Charles S. Peirce: A Chronological Edition* (Indiana University Press, 1993), pp. 421–23. By permission of the Peirce Edition Project, Indiana University: Indianapolis; Peirce, C. (1978), Book reviews "The new elements of mathematics", *Bulletin of the American Mathematical Society*, 84: 5, pp. 913–18. http://projecteuclid.org/DPubS/Repository/1.0/Disseminate?view=body&id=pdf_1&handle=euclid.bams/1183541145. Accessed 7 May 2010. See also collected papers of *Charles Sanders Peirce*, vol. 5, par. 364. (1934). And *Writings of Charles S. Peirce: A Chronological Edition* (Indiana University Press, 1993), pp. 421–23.
104. Ibid.
105. Ibid.
106. See Gustav Andreas Tammann's work: B. Bingeli, *Primum Mobile: Dantes Jenseitsreise und die moderne Kosmologie* (Primum Mobile: Dante's Trip to the Afterworld and Modern Cosmology). Zurich: Ammann 2006.
107. Putnam, H. (1982), "Brains in a vat", in *Reason, Truth, and History*, Cambridge: Cambridge University Press, chapter 1, pp. 1–21.
108. Rössler, O. E. (1973), "A synthetic approach to exotic kinetics", *Lecture Notes in Biomathematics*, S. Levin, in M. Conrad, W. Güttinger and M. Dal Cin. (eds), *Physics and Mathematics of the Nervous System*, vol. 4, Berlin, Heidelberg, New York: Springer-Verlag, pp. 546–82.
109. Cowan, J. (1972), "Stocastic models of neuroelectric activity", in C. H. Waddington (ed.), *Towards a Theoretical Biology*, vol. 4, Edinburg: University Press, pp. 169–87.
110. Ibid.
111. Anninos, P. (1972), "Mathematical model of memory trace and forgetfulness", *Kybernetik*, 10, pp. 165–70.
112. Zeeman, E. (1965), Topology of the Brain (Mathematics and computer Science in Biology and medicine), Medical Research Council; Rössler, O. E. (1973), "A synthetic approach to exotic kinetics", in *Lecture Notes in Biomathematics*, S. Levin, in M. Conrad, W. Güttinger and M. Dal Cin. (eds), *Physics and Mathematics of the Nervous System*, vol. 4, Berlin, Heidelberg, New York: Springer-Verlag, pp. 577–78.
113. Ibid.
114. Letter from Albert Einstein dated 11 June 1943. Archive, Box 1, Folder 8. American Institute of Physics; Niels Bohr Library This letter appears with a Russian translation on the book jacket of Yu. Lebedev, Ambiguous Universe, published by its author, Kostroma, 2000, 320pp, 192 copies.
115. Shikhovtsev, E. and Ford, K. (2003), "*Biographical Sketch of Hugh Everett*, III", 2003. http://space.mit.edu/home/tegmark/everett/everett.html. Accessed 6 November 2009.

116. Ibid.
117. *The Many-Worlds Interpretation of Quantum Mechanics* edited by Bryce S. DeWitt and Neill Graham with papers by Everett, H., III, J. A. Wheeler, B. S. DeWitt, L. N. Cooper and D. van Vechten, and N. Graham, New Jersey: Princeton University Press, 1973.
118. Ibid.
119. Zeh, D. (1973), *Foundations of Physics*, 3: 1, March 1973, pp. 109–16. (with several corrections and reformulations).
120. Bohm, D. and Hiley, B (1993), *The Undivided Universe – An Ontological Interpretation of Quantum Theory*, London: Routledge.
121. The many-minds interpretation of quantum mechanics extends the many-worlds interpretation by proposing that the distinction between worlds should be made at the level of the mind of an individual observer. The concept was first introduced in 1970 by H. Dieter Zeh as a variant of the Hugh Everett interpretation in connection with quantum decoherence, and later (in 1981) explicitly called a many or multi-consciousness interpretation. The name many-minds interpretation was first used by David Albert and B. Loewer in their 1988 work *Interpreting the Many Worlds Interpretation*. http://www.absoluteastronomy.com/topics/Many-minds_interpretation. Accessed 29 April 2010. See also Squires, E. (1995), "An experiment to test an explanation of a possible violation of quantum theory", *Foundations of Physics Letters*, 8: 6 (December), Springer Netherlands.
122. Rössler, O. E. (1984), "An estimate of Planck's constant", in P. Erdi (ed.), *Dynamical Phenomena in Neurochemistry and Neurophysics*, pp. 16–18. Budapest: Publications of the Central Physical Research Institute. (ISBN 963 372 349); Rössler, O. E., Rössler, R. and Weibel, P. (1998), "Is physics an observer-private phenomenon like consciousness?" *Journal of Consciousness Studies*, 5, pp. 443–53.
123. Gell-Mann, M. (1994), *The Quark and the Jaguar/Adventures in the Simple and the Complex*, New York: W.H. Freeman and Company, p. 73.
124. See also Motta, L. "*The Aharonov-Bohm Effect*", http://scienceworld.wolfram.com/physics/Aharonov-BohmEffect.html. Accessed 06 September 2009.
125. "Sciences of the interface symposium", http://193.197.168.165/symposium/. Accessed 6 September 2009.
126. Everett III, H. (1957), "'Relative-state' formulation of quantum mechanics", *Reviews of Modern Physics*, 29, 454–62.
127. Rössler, O. E. (1998), *Endophysics: The World as Interface*. Singapore: World Scientific Publishing Co, p. 166.
128. Ibid., p. 172.
129. Rössler, O. E. (1996), "Relative state theory – Four new aspects", *Chaos, Solitons & Fractals*, 7, pp. 845–52.
130. Compare for example Diebner, H. and Rössler, O. E. (2004), "Deterministic entropy – To monitor the evolution of microscopically simulated far from equilibrium structures", *Chaos Solitons & Fractals*, 19, pp. 699–703.
131. Spencer Bains, T. (1890), The Encyclopaedia Britannica: a dictionary of arts, sciences and general Literature. Vol. 11 on James Clerk Maxwell.
132. James Clerk Maxwell, "*Diffusion*", in The Scientific Papers of James Clerk Maxwell, vol 2. pp. 625–46, here pp. 645–46. As found in Nørretranders, T. (1998), *The User Illusion*, New York: Penguin Group, Penguin Putnam inc., p. 22.

133. Gee, H. (1996), "It's a mole-rat, Jim, but not as we know it," *Nature*, 380, p. 584. O'Riain, M. Justin, et al. (1996), "A dispersive morph in the naked mole-rat," *Nature*, 380, p. 619 – *Science Frontiers. ONLINE. No. 106: July–August 1996.*
134. http://www.science-frontiers.com/sf106/sf106p05.htm, *New Scientist*, 176: 2369 – 16 November 2002, p. 26.
135. See Rössler, O. E. (1979), "Recursive evolution", *Biosystems*, 11: 2–3, pp. 193–99.
136. Morris, S. (2002), "We were meant to be", http://www.newscientist.com/article/mg17623695.200-we-were-meant-to-be.html?full=true, Simon Conway Morris, Department of Earth Sciences at the University of Cambridge. Accessed 30 April 2010.
137. Kalmijn, A. J. (1978), "Experimental evidence of geomagnetic orientation in elasmobranch fishes," in K. Schmidt Koenig and W. T. Keeton (eds), *Animal Migration, Navigation and Homing*, Berlin, New York: Springer Verlag, pp. 347–53; Kalmijn, A. J. (1982), "Electric and magnetic field detection in elasmobranch fishes", *Science*, 218, pp. 916–18; Paulin, M. G. (1995), "Electroreception and the compass sense of sharks", *Journal of Theoretical Biology*, 174, pp. 325–39., *Magnetoperception* Michael M. Walker, Carol E. Diebel, Joseph Kirschvink; See also Paulin, 1995.
138. Hitchcock, S. (2003), "T-computers and the origins of time in the brain", *NeuroQuantology*, 4, pp. 393–403.
139. Libet, B. (2004), *Mind Time, The Temporal Factor in Consciousness*, p. 113.
140. Personal communication (1992).
141. Massumi, B. (2002), *Parables for the Virtual*, Durham, NC: Duke University Press.
142. Vrobel, S. (1998), *Fractal Time*. The Institute for Advanced Interdisciplinary Research.
143. Cariani, P. (2001), Temporal codes, timing nets, and music perception. Revised version, 20 June 2001, *Journal of New Music Perception*, 30: 2, p. 108, Special issue on Rhythm Perception, Periodicity, and Timing Nets.
144. Bell, J. S. (1987), *Speakable and Unspeakable in Quantum Mechanics, Collected papers on quantum philosophy. CERN*, Cambridge: Cambridge University Press.
145. For more information on John (McTaggart Ellis) McTaggart (1866–1925), see Sweet, W. http://people.stfx.ca/wsweet/mctaggart.html. Accessed 9 August 2010.
146. Forthcoming paper by O. E. Rössler, Hun Tun vs. Big Bang: How Classical Chaos Implies both "Thermodynamics" and "Cryo-dynamics," *International Journal of Bifurcation and Chaos.*
147. Gödel, K. (1949), "An example of a new type of cosmological solutions of Einstein's field equations of gravitation," *Reviews of Modern Physics*, 21, pp. 447–50. Reprinted in Gödel 1990, pp. 190–98.
148. http://publish.uwo.ca/~jbell/Time.pdf.
149. Gödel, K. (1949), "An example of a new type of cosmological solutions of Einstein's field equations of gravitation," *Reviews of Modern Physics*, 21, pp. 447–50. Reprinted in Gödel, 1990, pp. 190–98.

    Gödel, K. (1949a), "A remark about the relationship between relativity theory and idealistic philosophy", in Schilpp, P. (ed.), *Albert-Einstein, Philosopher-Scientist, Library of Living Philosophers*, vol. 7, Norethwestern University Press. Reprinted in Feferman et al. (eds), *Kurt Gödel Collected Works, vol. II*, Oxford University Press, 1990; Schilpp, (ed.) (1946/9), "Some observations about the relationship between the theory of relativity and Kantian philosophy", in Feferman et al. (eds), *Kurt Gödel Collected Works, vol. III*, Oxford University Press, 1995.

    Schilpp, (ed.) (1949b), "Lecture on rotating universes", in Feferman et al. (eds), *Kurt Gödel Collected Works*, vol. III, Oxford University Press, 1995.

150. Einstein, A. (1950), *Out of My Later Years, Stratification of the Scientific System,* Westport, CT: Greenwood Press, p. 63.
151. Fellous, J. and Arbib. M. (eds) (2005), *Who Needs Emotions?: The Brain Meets the Robot*, Oxford, New York: Oxford University Press, p. 10.
152. Ibid., p. 23.; See Also: Damasio, A. R. (1999), *The Feeling of What Happens: Body and Emotion in the Making of Consciousness.* New York: Harcourt Brace; Panksepp, J. (1998), *Affective Neuroscience*, New York: Oxford University Press; Rolls, E. T. (1999), *The Brain and Emotion*, New York: Oxford University Press; Rosenberg, E. L. and Ekman, P. (1994), "Coherence between expressive and experiential systems in emotion", *Cognition and Emotion*, 8, pp. 201–30; Russell, J. A. (1991), "Culture and the categorization of emotions", *Psychological Bulletin*, 110, pp. 426–50; Russell, J. A., Lewicka, M. and Nitt, T. (1989), "A cross-cultural study of a circumplex model of affect", *Journal of Personality and Social Psycholgy*, 57, pp. 848–56.
153. Roy, D. (2008), "A mechanistic model of three facets of meaning". Chapter to appear in de Vega, Glenberg, and Graesser, (eds), *Symbols, Embodiment, and Meaning*; See Also Rössler, O. E. (1981), "Paper on Equation 13" of 1974, *Progress in Theoretical Biology 1981*, Academic Press.
154. Rössler, O. E., Diebner, H. and Kittel, A. (1994), *Micro Time Reversal, Introduction.* http://www.fgi.at/if/artikel/if1997h1roesslerabstr.html. Accessed 10 April 2010. See also *NeuroQuantology,* 2003; 4, pp. 393–403.
155. For completeness, we add here a further 8th point to the above 7 points as a long footnote. The 8th level is a microscopic reversible deterministic self-similar fractal-transfinite infinite hierarchy, originally proposed by Mohamed ElNaschie in the 1980s. Less radical microscopic theories are string and loop theories which build up on a presupposed quantum level in the spirit of John Wheeler's "quantum foam". (See also Luis Sancho for related work.)
156. Quotation from Huw Price, (1996), *Time's Arrow and Archimedes' Point, New Directions for the Physics of Time*, New York: Oxford University Press.
157. See Ibid.
158. See Rössler, O. E. (1996), "Ultraperspective and endophysics", *BioSystems*, 38: 2–3, pp. 211–19.
159. Quotes by Korzybski, http://www.brainyquote.com/quotes/authors/a/alfred_korzybski.html. Accessed 1 December 2009;See also Korzybski, A. (1990), *Collected Writings 1920–50*, Institute of General Semantics.
160. Hilgartner, A. (1999), "Quantum linguistics roundtable discussion", http://www.enformy.com/dma-qlin.htm#b03. Accessed 30 April 2010.
161. Hilgartner, A. "We need a new language especially within science", http://www.enformy.com/isss-ah0.htm. Accessed 30 April 2010.
162. Rössler, O. E. (2006), "Endonomadology", *Transcription*, xxxxx23, London 23 March 2006, http://1010.co.uk/ottoroesslertranscript.pdf. Accessed 6 November 2009.
163. Seaman, B. and Rössler, O. E. (2006), "Toward the creation of an intelligent situated computer and related robotic system: An intra-functional network of living analogies", Catalogue for Emoçào Art.ficial, Itau Cultural Center, Sao Paulo, Brazil, See also billseaman.com; Lewin, K. (1936), *Principles of Topological Psychology* (trans. Fritz Heider and Grace Heider), 1st ed., New York, London: McGraw-Hill, p. 54.
164. Lorenz, K. and Leyhausen, P. (1973), *Motivation of Human and Animal Behavior: An Ethological View* (trans. B. A. Tonkin), *Behavioral Science Series,* New York: van Nostrand Reinhold Company.
165. It must be noted that in terms of the translation from German into English (as found in German on p. 175 of the 1973 German edition of Lorenz's *Behind the Mirror*) that the English is misleading (see page 128 of the English translation).

166. Cross, M. (1996), "'The butterfly effect' in the exploratorium", http://www.exploratorium.com/complexity/CompLexicon/lorenz.html. Accessed 30 April 2010.
167. Ibid.
168. Lorenz, E. (1993), *The Essence of Chaos*, Seattle: University of Washington Press.
169. Announcement for the Nobel Prize in Physics, (1998), http://nobelprize.org/nobel_prizes/physics/laureates/1998/press.html. Accessed 30 April 2010.
170. Rössler, O. E. (1973), "Chemical automata in homogeneous and reaction diffusion kinetics", *Lecture Notes in Biomathematics*, Berlin: Springer, Vol. 4, pp. 342–69.
171. Lorenz, Konrad. (1973), *Behind the Mirror: A Search for a Natural History of Human Knowledge* (trans. Ronald Taylor), New York: Harcourt Brace Jovanovich, p. 144.
172. Ibid., p. 147.
173. Ibid., p. 149–50.
174. Ibid., p. 152–53.
175. Ibid., p. 169.
176. Ibid.
177. Ibid., p. 173.
178. Ibid., p. 174.
179. Ibid., p. 179.
180. Ibid., p. 216.
181. see Rössler, O. E., Kampis, G., Nadler, W., Schapiro, B. and Urban, P. (1990), "Highly parallel implementation of the autonomous optimizer with cognition (abstract)", *Biophysical Journal*, 57, p. 194a.
182. Bowlby, J., Ainsworth, M. and Bretherton, I. (1995), "The origins of attachment theory" in Susan Goldberg and Roy Muir (eds), *Attachment Theory: Social, Developmental, and Clinical Perspectives,* John Kerr, Hillsdale, NJ: Analytic Press, xiii, 515p.
183. Rössler, O. E. (1979), "Recursive evolution", *Biosystems*, 11: 2–3, pp. 193–99.
184. See Forcada, M. (2002), "Neural networks: Automata and formal models of computation", McCulloch and Pitts' *neural logical calculus,* http://www.dlsi.ua.es/~mlf/nnafmc/pbook/node10.html.
185. McCulloch, W. and Pitts, W. (1965), "A logical calculus of the ideas immanent in nervous activity", in W. S. McCulloch (ed.) *Embodiments of Mind*, Cambridge: MIT Press.
186. Searle, J. (1990), "Is the brain a digital computer?" Address to the American Philosophical Association by John Searle, http://users.ecs.soton.ac.uk/~harnad/Papers/Py104/searle.comp.html.
187. Hawkins, J. (2004), *On Intelligence.* New York: Times Books, Henry Holt and Company, LLC. p. 187.
188. Biographical Memoirs, "James Olds", National Academies Press, http://www.nap.edu/html/biomems/jolds.html. Accessed 30 April 2010.
189. Beer, C. (1963), *Ethology – The Zoologist's Approach to Behaviour* – Part I, *TUATARA*: vol. 11, 3, September 1963, http://www.nzetc.org/tm/scholarly/tei-Bio11Tuat03-t1-body-d3.html. Accessed 30 April, 2010.
190. See www.vissensnavigator.com-documents/Chaos.pdf.
191. Weibel, P. (1996), "The intelligent image", http://www.c3.hu/scca/butterfly/Weibel/synopsis.html. Accessed 30 April 2010.
192. von Foerster, H. (1970), *Molecular Ethology, An Immodest Proposal for Semantic Clarification in Molecular Mechanisms in Memory and Learning,* S. Boroch (ed.), New York: Plenum Press,

pp. 231–48; also found in von Foerster (1981) *Observing Systems*, Seaside California: Intersystems Publications, p. 171.
193. Hofstadter, D. (1979), *Gödel, Escher, Bach: an Eternal Golden Braid*, New York: Basic Books, p. 389.
194. Rössler, O. E. "Mirror competence implies person competence", http://www.lampsacus.com/documents/MIRRORCOMPETENCE.pdf. Accessed 7 March, 2011. See also Rössler, O. E. (2004) Nonlinear Dynamics, Artificial Cognition and Galactic Export, cf http://www.lampsacus.com/documents/roesslergalacticexport.pdf
195. Arbib, M. A. (2006), *Action to Language via the Mirror Neuron System*, Cambridge: Cambridge University Press.
196. Britannica Concise Encyclopedia: "neurotransmitter", http://www.answers.com/topic/what-is-a-neurotransmitter. Accessed 30 April 2010.
197. Pert, C. (1997), *Molecules of Emotion*, New York: Schribner.
198. *Molecules of Emotion* book review, http://www.thelearningweb.net/books/j_molecules_of_emotion.html. Accessed 30 April 2010.
199. See *Non-verbal Communication*, edited by Robert Hinde, in particular the chapter on the "Phylogeny of laughter and smile", by J. Van Hooff, p. 211.
200. Clark, A. (2008), *Supersizing the Mind: Embodiment, Action, and Cognitive Extension*, Oxford: Oxford University Press.
201. Simeonov, P. (2010), "Integral biomathics: A post-Newtonian view into the logos of bios", *Journal of Progress in Biophysics and Molecular Biology*. ISSN:0079-6107, DOI: 10.1016/j.pbiomolbio.2010.01.005.
202. Seaman, B. and Rössler, O. E. (2008), "Neosentience – A new branch of scientific and poetic inquiry related to artificial intelligence", *Technoetic Arts: A Journal of Speculative Research*, 6: 1, pp. 31–40.
203. Rössler, O. E. (2004), "Delectatio in felicitate alterius — Benevolence theory", in: *Personal and Spiritual Development in the World of Cultural Diversity*, vol. 1 by G. E. Lasker and K. Hiwaki (eds), The International Institute for Advanced Studies in Systems Research and Cybernetics, Windsor, ON, Canada, pp. 69–78. ISBN 1-894613-97-X.
204. Otto E. Rössler, winner of the Chaos Award 2003 (16 November 2003). http://209.85.165.104/search?q=cache:E2S7IKN2rkkJ:www.wissensnavigator.com/interface1/coding/documents/ERWINTEUFELPRIZENEW2.pdf+rossler+Smile+Theory&hl=en&ct=clnk&cd=12&gl=us&client=safari. Accessed 10 April 2010; Rössler, O. E. (2006), "Personogenesis – The toddler's worked miracle", http://www.wissensnavigator.com/documents/Personogenesis.pdf. Accessed 30 April 2010.
205. http://www.hamptonpress.com/Merchant2/merchant.mvc?Screen=PROD&Product_Code=1-57273-601-1&Category_Code=ST. Accessed 12 September 2010.
206. Macy Conferences, 7th Conference Summary, http://www.asc-cybernetics.org/foundations/history/MacySummary.htm. Accessed 12 September 2010.
207. http://www.asc-cybernetics.org/foundations/history/MacySummary.htm. Accessed 12 September 2010.
208. Siegelmann, H. (2007), *Neural Networks and Analog Computation: Beyond the Turing Limit*, http://www.cs.umass.edu/~hava/advertisement.html, Accessed 1 December 2009. See also Siegelmann, H (1999), *Neural Networks and Analogue Computation, Beyond the Turing Limit*, Boston, MA: Birkhäuser.
209. Ibid.

210. Ibid.
211. Rössler, O. E. (1974), "Chemical automata in homogeneous and reaction-diffusion kinetics", *Lecture Notes in Biomathematics*, vol. 4, *Physics and Mathematics of the Nervous System*, M. Conrad, W. Güttinger, and M. Dal Cin (eds), Berlin, Heidelberg, New York: Springer-Verlag, pp. 399–418.
212. "Programmable chips: piecing together an analog solution", By Ron Wilson, Executive Editor – EDN, 23 July 2009, http://www.edn.com/article/458800-Programmable_chips_piecing_together_an_analog_solution.php. Accessed 12 September 2010. See also Klaus Strecker, 1992.
213. Rössler, O. E. (2004), "Relativity is interface", http://tech.dir.groups.yahoo.com/group/truenumber/message/1604. Accessed 30 April 2010.
214. Rössler, O. E. and Rössler, R. (1993), "Is the mind-body interface microscopic?" *Theoretical Medicine and Bioethics*, Springer Netherland, 14: 2, http://www.springerlink.com/content/rn2u1w67396421g0/. Accessed 30 April 2010.
215. Diebner, H., Druckery, T. and Weibel, P. (2001), "Sciences of the interface", *Proceedings of the International Symposium*, ZKM, Karlesruhe (On The Occasion of O. E.R.'s 60th Birthday).
216. Steels, L. (2003), "Evolving grounded communication for robots", *Trends in Cognitive Science*, 7: 7, pp. 308–12. Also found at http://arti.vub.ac.be/~steels/. Accessed 16 August 2010.
217. Boyd, R. (2002), "Scientist studies robot conversation skills", http://technews.acm.org/articles/2002-4/0621f.html. Accessed 30 April 2010.
218. Furst, R. (2007), "Parts of the elephant in emergence/Limits of knowledge", http://rafefurst.wordpress.com/2007/02/08/parts-of-the-elephant/. Accessed 30 April 2010.
219. http://www.facebook.com/group.php?gid=21257836840. Accessed 20 September 2010.
220. "Talk origins archive" (2006), http://www.talkorigins.org/origins/jargon/jargonfile_t.html#tierra. Accessed 30 April 2010.
221. BBC News (2006), "Robotic baby seal wins top award", http://news.bbc.co.uk/2/hi/technology/6202765.stm. Accessed 30 April 2010.
222. Ibid.
223. Gaukroger, S. (1995), *Descartes: An Intellectual Biography*, Oxford: Clarendon Press; New York: Oxford University Press.
224. MIT Technology Review, The Physics arXiv Blog (2010), "How to build a superluminal computer", http://www.technologyreview.com/blog/arxiv/24903/. Accessed 30 April 2010.
225. Ibid.
226. Harper, (2001), http://www.etymonline.com/index.php?search=computer&searchmode=none. Accessed 12 September 2010, see also McCollough and Pitts – 1943.
227. Seaman, B. (2009), "(Re)thinking, the body, generative tools and computational articulation", *Technoetic Arts: A Journal of Speculative Research*, 7: 3.
228. de Waal, F. *Nature*, 399, pp. 635–36 (17 June 1999), doi: 10.1038/21310.
229. Gregory, J. (1997), "The hundredth monkey revisited", News Brief 56, http://www.nhne.com/articles/sahundrethmonkey.html. Accessed 30 April 2010.
230. Seaman, B. and Hansen, M. Verbauwhede, I. (2002), "The poly-sensing environment", http://users.design.ucla.edu/~fwinkler/PSE/descr.html. Accessed 13 September 2010.
231. Ibid.
232. Ibid.
233. Hayles in conversation with Seaman (2010).
234. http://www.chem.ucla.edu/dept/Faculty/gimzewski/artsci.html. Accessed 13 September 2010.

235. Luc Steels, Homepage, "Artificial intelligence laboratory", http://arti.vub.ac.be/~steels/. Accessed 30 April 2010.
236. Ibid.
237. Ibid.
238. BBC News (2006), "Robotic baby seal wins top award", http://news.bbc.co.uk/2/hi/technology/6202765.stm. Accessed 30 April 2010.
239. Hollis, R. and Salcudean, S. (1993), "Lorentz levitation technology – a new approach to fine motion robotics, teleoperation, haptic interfaces, and vibration isolation" in *Proceedings of the. 6th International Symposium on Robotics Research*, http://www.cs.cmu.edu/afs/cs/user/rhollis/papers/isrr2.ps.
240. http://butterflyhaptics.com/maglev-haptics/. Accessed 22 August 2010.
241. Rössler, O. E. (2004), "Delectatio in felicitate alterius – Benevolence theory", in *Personal and Spiritual Development in the World of Cultural Diversity*, vol. 1, G. E. Lasker and K. Hiwaki (eds), pp. 69–78. The International Institute for Advanced Studies in Systems Research and Cybernetics, Windsor, ON, Canada 2004. ISBN 1-894613-97-X, http://publication.nodel.org/Delectatio-in-felicitate-alterius. Accessed 30 April 2010.
242. Spaemann, R., Glück und Wohlwollen (1989), Versuch über Ethik (Happiness and Benevolence – an Essay on Ethics), Klett-Cotta, Stuttgart p. 123, http://www.postautonomy.co.uk/blog/?q=node/70.
243. Shikhovtsev, E., *Daughter Liz (1957) and Mathematical Models (1956–64),* http://space.mit.edu/home/tegmark/everett/everett.html. Assessed 8 March, 2011.
244. Foster, P. (2008), "Rebirth", http://www.museumofhoaxes.com/hoax/Hoaxipedia/Marcel_Duchamp/. Accessed 30 April 2010.
245. http://space.mit.edu/home/tegmark/everett/everett.html#149a.
Shikhovtsev, E. and Ford, K. (2003), *A Biographical Sketch of Hugh Everett III* (Harry Browne. How I Found Freedom in an Unfree World. 1973.)
246. de Chardin, T. (1959), *The Phenomenon of Man*, (trans. Bernard Wall), London: Wm. Collins Sons + Co., Ltd.
247. Ibid., p. 178.
248. Ibid., p. 181.
249. Kazlev, M. (2004), "The Gaia hypothesis", http://www.kheper.net/topics/Gaia/Gaia_Hypothesis.htm. Accessed 12 May 2004.
250. de Chardin, T. (1959), *The Phenomenon of Man*, (trans. Bernard Wall), London: Wm. Collins Sons + Co., Ltd., p. 181.
251. Ibid., p. 242.
252. Ibid., p. 260.
253. *Time magazine*, 15 September 2008, p. 52.
254. Koestler, A. (1964), *The Act of Creation*, New York: Macmillan Co. ,p. 36, p. 44 and p. 45.
255. Shetler, D. J. (1989), "The inquiry into prenatal musical experience: A report of the Eastman project, 1980–87", *Pre- & Perinatal Psychology Journal*, 3: 3, pp. 171–89; Plessinger, M. A. and Woods, J. R. (1986), "Fetal auditory brain stem response: external and intrauterine auditory stimulation", *American Physiological Society*, 0363-6119.; Whitwell, G. E., RMT. (1999), "The importance of prenatal sound and music", *Journal of Prenatal and Perinatal Psychology and Health*, 13: 3–4, pp. 255–62.
256. Parsons, D. (1975), *The Directory of Tunes and Musical Themes*. S. Brown. ISBN 0-904747-00-X; See also "Was Parsons right? An experiment in usability of musical representations for melody-based music retrieval", Alexandra L. Uitdenbogerd and YawWah Yap, Department of Computer

Science, RMIT University, http://citeseerx.ist.psu.edu/viewdoc/download?doi=10.1.1.2.9606&rep=rep1&type=pdf.

257. Nolan, William F. (1965), *The Pseudo-People: Androids In Science Fiction*, Los Angeles, CA: Sherbourne Press.
258. Seaman, B. (2008), "Unpacking neosentience: dystopian techno-evolution?" *Mutomorphosis Proceedings*, http://mutamorphosis.wordpress.com/tag/neosentience/. Accessed 30 April 2010.
259. Musterle, W. and Rössler, O. E. (1986), "Computer faces: The human Lorenz matrix", *Biosystems*, 19: 1, pp. 61–80.
260. Ibid.
261. Marr, D. and Poggio, T. (1979), "A computational theory of human stereo vision" in Kurzweil, R. *The Age of Intelligent Machines* (1990), Cambridge, MA: MIT Press, http://www.kurzweilai.net/meme/frame.html?main=/articles/art0297.html. Accessed 30 April 2010.
262. Ibid.
A stereo algorithm the machine sees the same thing; see also Marr D. and Poggio, T. (1979), "A computational theory of human stereo vision", *Proceedings of the Royal Society of London. Series B, Biological Sciences*, 204: 1156, http://www.jstor.org/pss/77509.
263. *Pourquoi Seigneur, Tu Fis La Nuit Si Longue* … (song by Aimé Duval)
264. Encyclopaedia Britannica, http://www.britannica.com/EBchecked/topic/130429/computer/216032/Invention-of-the-modern-computer. Accessed 30 April 2010.
265. See Copleston, F. (1975), *A History of Philosophy*, London: Search Press, http://books.google.com/books?id=BMjrs7-gk9oC&pg=PA194&lpg=PA194&dq=Kants+-+the+Dreams+of+a+Ghost+Seer&source=web&ots=FsqK1Tzj6b&sig=BqLBScNK58S6gfasGBqt3SPU0Xo&hl=en&sa=X&oi=book_result&resnum=3&ct=result. Accessed 30 April 2010.
266. von Neumann, "General and logical theory of automata", https://www.cs.unm.edu/~eschulte/classes/cs591-rpc/data/vonneumann1951-glta.pdf Accessed 31July 2010. This paper is an only slightly edited version of one that was read at the Hixon Symposium on 20 September 1948, in Pasadena, California.
267. Rosen, R. (1974), "On biological systems as paradigms for adaptation", Center for Theoretical Biology State University of New York at Buffalo, Amherst, New York 14226.
268. Dubois, D. (2009), *Ninth Conference on Computing Anticipatory Systems*, Daniel M Dubois (ed.), Chapter entitled: "Rewriting anticipatory systems (RAS) in chaos map, incursive and hyperincursive systems, self-replicating automata, Self-modifying code, and genetic code", Daniel M. Dubois, Peter J. Marcer and Peter Rowlands
269. Zauner, K. (2005), "Molecular information technology", http://www.iam.ecs.soton.ac.uk/seminars/?action=viewpresentation&presentation_id=47. Accessed 31 July 2010.
270. Zauner, K. (2005), "Molecular computing with artificial neurons", http://www.cs.wayne.edu/~kjz/KPZ/PublicationsOnline/ComKISSV18N8P78/ComKISSV18N8P78.html. Accessed 31 July 2000.
271. Pattee, H. H. (1969), "How does a molecule become a message?" *Developmental Biology Supplement*, 3, 1–16.
272. Yukio-Pegio Gunji, Hiroyuki Miyoshi, Tatsuji Takahashi and Moto Kamiura (2005), "Dynamical duality of type- and token-computation as an abstract brain", Department of Earth and Planetary Sciences, Faculty of Science, Kobe University, Japan Graduate School of Science and Technology, Kobe University, Japan Department of Computer Sciences, Faculty of Science, Kyoto Sangyo University, Japan, http://www.sciencedirect.com/science?_ob=ArticleURL&_udi=B6TJ4-4H0S19Y-1&_user=38557&_coverDate=03%2F31%2F2006&_rdoc=1&_fmt=high&_orig=

search&_sort=d&_docanchor=&view=c&_searchStrId=1317968712&_rerunOrigin=google&_acct=C000004358&_version=1&_urlVersion=0&_userid=38557&md5=f1b531aa78bd24990c7f2203b397e091. Accessed 30 April 2010.

273. Diebner, H. (2001), "A simulating cognitive system with adaptive capability", *BioSystems*, 64 (2002), pp. 141–47.
274. http://news.bbc.co.uk/2/low/entertainment/1413695.stm.
275. Turing, A. M. (1950), "Computing machinery and intelligence", *Mind*, 59, pp. 433–60.
276. Ibid., http://www.loebner.net/Prizef/TuringArticle.html. Accessed 30 April 2010.
277. Stanford Encyclopaedia of Philosophy, 'Turing Test' http://plato.stanford.edu/entries/turing-test/. Accessed 30 April 2010.
278. Dick, P. (2007), *Four Novels of the 1960s: The Man in the High Castle; The Three Stigmata of Palmer Eldritch; Do Androids Dream of Electric Sheep?; Ubik*, New York: Literary Classics of the United States, Inc, p. 468.
279. Anashin, V. (2009) *Applied Algebra Dynamics*, Berlin, New York: Walter De Gruyter, p. 465.
280. See Seaman, B. and Rössler, O. E. (2006), "Toward the creation of an intelligent situated computer and related robotic system: an intra-functional network of living analogies", Catalogue for Emoçào Art.ficial, Itau Cultural Center, Sao Paulo, Brazil, http://billseaman.com/. Accessed 30 April 2010.
281. See also MEMS – Micro-Electro-Mechanical Systems (MEMS); Seaman, Verbauwhede, Hansen, (2004), http://www.memsnet.org/mems/what-is.html See also, http://students.dma.ucla.edu/~fwinkler/PSE/ for an environmental approach. Accessed April 2010.
282. See Suchman, L. (1987), *Plans and Situated Actions: The Problem of Human-Machine Communication*, Cambridge: Cambridge University Press. See also Agre, P. (1997), *Computation and Human Experience*, New York: Cambridge University Press.
283. For other early related approaches see Brooks, Rodney A. and Stein, Lynn Andrea, "Building brains for bodies" *Autonomous Robots* 1: 1, November 1994, pp. 7–25.
284. Seaman, B. (2005), "Pattern flows / hybrid accretive processes informing identity construction", *Convergence Magazine*, Winter, 2005, vol. 11, pp.12–31.
285. See Barcelou, L. (1999), *Situated Conceptualization* – Chapter to appear in H. Cohen and C. Lefebvre (eds), and Barsalou, Lawrence W. (1999), "Perceptual symbol systems", *Behavioral and Brain Sciences*, 22, pp. 577–660.
286. Charles Spence, http://www.psy.ox.ac.uk/xmodal/. Assessed 30 April 2010.
287. Peter Cariani, http://homepage.mac.com/cariani/CarianiWebsite/CarianiHomePage.html. Accessed April 2010.
288. Andy Webster, http://www.andywebster.info/machinista_submission.html. Accessed 30 April 2010.
289. See the following related systems http://www.informatik.uni-trier.de/~ley/db/indices/a-tree/w/Walther:Marcus.html.
290. See Lewin, K. (1936), *Principles of Topological Psychology*, (trans. Fritz Heider and Grace Heider), 1st ed., New York, London: McGraw-Hill, p. 54 – Kurt Lewin in his text *Principles of Topological Psychology* from 1936 One can potentially join multiple differing topologies together – topological psychological spaces, simulation spaces and physical/actual motion spaces. Lewin discusses how a series of psychological vectors might form a topology. In the chapter entitled *The Psychological Life Space As Space In the Sense of Mathematics*, he describes how psychological facts can be articulated, 'connected' and 'coordinated' in a topological space, forming paths – 'any kind of locomotion of the person in the quasi-physical, the quasi-social, or the quasi-

conceptual field can be designated as a connecting process which corresponds to a topological patch.' Lewin further provides remarks about topological space: 'The fact that certain regions in the psychological environment and within the person influence other regions, both of the environment and of the person, may be taken as a criterion for connectedness in the topological sense.' This happens through 'dynamical communication.' Lewin, 1936.

291. See von Foerster, H. (1962), "Circuitry of clues to platonic ideation", in *Aspects of the Theory of Artificial Intelligence* edited by C. A. Muses.
292. Conversation with Jim Davies.
293. See O'Keefe, J. and Nadel, L. (1978), *The Hippocampus as a Cognitive Map*, Oxford University Press.
294. See Clark, A. (1997), *Being There: Putting Brain, Body, and World Together Again*, Cambridge, MA: MIT Press.
295. See de Chardin, Teilhard (1961), *The Phenomenon of Man*, New York: Harper & Row. See also on a related concept of linked consciousness. See also Ascott, R. (2003), *The Telematic Embrace*, Berkeley: University of California Press.
296. Hopkins, Carl D. http://instruct1.cit.cornell.edu/courses/bionb424/students2004/jlf56/general.htm. See also Mittelstaedt, H. (1961), "Control theory as a methodic tool in behavior analysis" (in German), Naturwissenschaften 48, pp. 246–54, p. 248 (1961) and von Holst E. and Mittelstaedt H. (1950), "Das Reafferenzprinzip: Wechselwirkungen Zwischen Zentralnervensystem und Peripherie", *Naturwissenschaften*, 37, pp. 464–76.
297. Gibson, W. (1984), *Neuromancer,* New York: Ace Books.
298. See also Jean-Emile Charon concerning the theory of the electron as the carrier of mind. Charon, J. E. *L'Esprit, cet Inconnu*. Paris: Albin Michel, 1977.
299. Fred Hoyle's Black Cloud would be another rhyme on similar ideas.

Bibliography

Agre, P. (1997), *Computation and Human Experience*, New York: Cambridge University Press.

Anashin, V. (2009) *Applied Algebra Dynamics*, Berlin; New York; Walter De Gruyter p. 465

Ascott, R. (2003), *The Telematic Embrace*, Berkeley: University of California Press.

Ashby, R. (1952), *Design for a Brain*, New York: John Wiley & Sons.

André, C. (2006), *Une tendresse sauvage*, Paris: Calmann-Lévy.

Arbib, M. A. (2006), *Action to Language via the Mirror Neuron System*, Cambridge: Cambridge University Press.

Anninos, P. (1972), "Mathematical model of memory trace and forgetfulness", *Kybernetik*, 10, pp. 165–70.

Babbage, C. (1961), *Charles Babbage and his Calculating Engines: Selected Writings by Charles Babbage and Others*, New York: Dover Publications, Inc. Written to clarify the work *Sketch of the Analytical Engine Invented by Charles Babbage,* by L. F. Menabrea.

Barsalou, L. (1999), "Perceptual symbol systems", *Behavioural and Brain Sciences,* 22, pp. 577–609.

——. (1999a), "Situated conceptualization", in H. Cohen and C. Lefebvre (eds), *Handbook of Categorization in Cognitive Science*, St. Louis: Elsevier, pp. 619–50.

——. (1999b), "Perceptual symbol systems", *Behavioral and Brain Sciences*, 22, pp. 577–660.

Bateson, G. (1972), *Steps to an Ecology of Mind*, New York: Ballantine Books.

Bell, J. (1987), *Speakable and unspeakable in quantum mechanics*, Cambridge: Cambridge University Press.

Boden, M. (1990) *The Creative Mind: Myths and Mechanisms*. London: Weidenfeld and Nichelson.

Boden, M (1999) "Computational Models of Creativity". In Handbook of Creativity, Robert Sternberg (ed), 351-373. Cambridge: Cambridge University Press.

Bohm, D. and Hiley, B. (1993), *The Undivided Universe – An Ontological Interpretation of Quantum Theory*, London: Routledge.

Bonhoeffer, K. F. (1947), "Activation of passive iron as a model for the excitiation of a nerve", http://www.ncbi.nlm.nih.gov/pmc/articles/PMC2213747/. Accessed 2 August 2010.

Bowlby, J., Ainsworth, M. and Bretherton, I. (1995), "The origins of attachment theory", in Susan Goldberg, Roy Muir and John Kerr (eds) *Attachment Theory: Social, Developmental, and Clinical Perspectives,* Hillsdale, NJ: Analytic Press, p. xiii.

Brooks, R. and Lynn A. (1994), "Building brains for bodies", *Autonomous Robots,* 1: 1, November, pp. 7–25.

Brooks, R. (2002), *Flesh and Machines: How Robots Will Change Us*, New York: Pantheon Books.

Brouwer, J. and Broeckman, A. editors (1998), *The Art of the Accident*, Rotterdam: NAI Publisher.

Casti, J. (1994), *Complexification: Explaining an Illogical World Through the Science of Surprise*, New York: Harper Collins.

Capek, K. (1923), *R.U.R (Rossum's Universal Robots)*, New York: Doubleday.
Cariani, P. (2001), "Temporal codes, timing nets, and music perception" Revised version, 6/20/01. For *Journal of New Music Perception*, 30: 2, pp. 107–35.
Chardin, T. de (1959), *The Phenomenon of Man* (trans. Bernard Wall), Wm. Collins Sons + Co., Ltd.: London.
Chardin, Teilhard de (1961), *The Phenomenon of Man*, New York: Harper & Row.
Clark, A. (1997), *Being There: Putting Brain, Body, and World Together Again*, Cambridge, MA: MIT Press.
——. (2008), *Supersizing the Mind: Embodiment, Action, and Cognitive Extension*, Oxford: Oxford University Press.
Courant, R. and Robbins, H. (1996), *What Is Mathematics?: An Elementary Approach to Ideas and Methods,* 2nd ed., Oxford, England: Oxford University Press, pp. 81–83.
Cowan, J. (1972), "Stochastic models of neuroelectric activity", in C. H. Waddington (ed.), *Towards a Theoretical Biology*, vol. 4, Edinburg: University Press.
Csikszentmihalyi, M. (1996) Creativity: Flow and Psychology of Discovery and Invention. New York: Harper Collins
Damasio, A. R. (1999), *The Feeling of What Happens: Body and Emotion in the Making of Consciousness*, New York: Harcourt Brace.
DeWitt, B. and Graham, N. (1973), *The Many-Worlds Interpretation of Quantum Mechanics*, with papers by Hugh Everett, III, J. A. Wheeler, B. S. DeWitt, L. N. Cooper, D. van Vechten and N. Graham, New Jersey: Princeton University Press.
Deleuze, G. and Guattari, F. (1987), *A Thousand Plateaus: Capitalism and Schizophrenia,* vol. 2 (trans. Brian Massumi), Minneapolis: University of Minnesota Press.
Diebner, H. (2002), "A simulating cognitive system with adaptive capability", *BioSystems,* 64, pp. 141–47.
Diebner, H., Druckrey, T. and Weibel, P. , eds (2001), *Sciences of the Interface, Proceedings of the International Symposium*, ZKM, Karlesruhe. Tübingen: Genista Verlag. (ISBN 3-30171-26-0).
Diebner, H. and Rössler, O. E. (2004), "Deterministic entropy – to monitor the evolution of microscopically simulated far from equilibrium structures", *Chaos Solitons & Fractals*, 19, pp. 699–703.
Dörner, D. (1979), "Self reflection and problem solving", in Friedhart Klix (ed.), *Human and Artificial Intelligence*, Amsterdam, New York: North-Holland Publ. Co.; New York; distributed in the USA and Canada by Elsevier North-Holland.
Drexler, E. (1986), *Engines of Creation: The Coming Era of Nanotechnology*, Garden City, New York: Anchor Press/Doubleday.
——. (1992), *Nanosystems: Molecular Machinery, Manufacturing, and Computation*, New York: John Wiley & Sons.
Dupuy, J. (2000), *The Mechanization of the Mind: On the Origins of Cognitive Science*, Princeton, NJ: Princeton University Press.
Dyson, G. (1997), *Darwin among the Machines, the Evolution of Global Intelligence*, New York: Addison-Wesley Publishing.
Einstein, A. (1950), *Out of My Later Years, Stratification of the Scientific System,* Westport, CT: Greenwood Press.
Everett III, H. (1957), "'Relative-state' formulation of quantum mechanics", *Reviews of Modern Physics,* 29, pp. 454–62.
——. (1973), in *The Many-Worlds Interpretation of Quantum Mechanics,* Bryce S. DeWitt and Neill Graham (eds), New Jersey: Princeton University Press.

Fauconnier, G. and Turner, M. (2002), *The Way We Think: Conceptual Blending and the Mind's Hidden Complexities*, New York: Basic Books.

Fellous, J. and Arbib. M. (eds) (2005), *Who Needs Emotions?: the Brain Meets the Robot*, Oxford, New York: Oxford University Press.

Finkelstein, D. (1979), "Holistic methods in quantum logic", in L. Castell and C.-F. von Weizsacker (eds), *Quantum Theory and the Structure of Time and Space*, vol. 3, Munich: Karl Hanser.

Foerster, von H. (1960), "Circuitry of clues to platonic ideation", in C. Muses (ed.), *Aspects of the Theory of Artificial Intelligence*, New York: Plenum Press, 1962.

Gaugusch, A. and Seaman, B. (2004), "(Re)sensing the observer offering open order cybernetics", *Technoetic Arts: A Journal of Speculative Research*, 2: 1, pp. 17–31. © Intellect Ltd.

Gaukroger, S. (1995), *Descartes: An Intellectual Biography*, Oxford: Clarendon Press; New York: Oxford University Press.

Gee, H. (1996), "It's a mole-rat, Jim, but not as we know it," *Nature*, 380, p. 584.

Gell-Mann, M. (1994), *The Quark and the Jaguar – Adventures in the Simple and the Complex*, New York: W. H. Freeman and Company.

Georgopoulos, A., Lurito, J., Petrides, M., Schwartz, A. and Massey J. (1989), "Mental rotation of the neuronal population vector", *Science,* 243, pp. 234–36.

Gibson, W. (1984), *Neuromancer*, New York: Ace Books.

Gödel, K. (1949), "An example of a new type of cosmological solutions of Einstein's field equations of gravitation," *Reviews of Modern Physics*, 21, pp. 447–50.

Gunji, Yukio-Pegio, Hiroyuki Miyoshi, Tatsuji Takahashi and Moto Kamiura (2005), *Dynamical duality of type- and token-computation as an abstract brain*, Faculty of Science, Kobe University, Japan Graduate School of Science and Technology, Kobe University, Japan Department of Computer Sciences, Kyoto Sangyo University, Japan.

Hawkins, J. (2004), *On Intelligence*, New York: Times Books, Henry Holt and Company, LLC.

Heims, S. (1991), *The Cybernetics Group*, Cambridge, MA, London, England: The MIT Press.

Hitchcock, S. (2003), "T-computers and the origins of time in the brain", *NeuroQuantology,* 4, pp. 393–403.

Hoffman, P. (1998), *The Man Who Loved Only Numbers: The Story of Paul Erdos and the Search for Mathematical Truth,* New York: Hyperion, pp. 220–23.

Hofstadter, D. (1979), *Gödel, Escher, Bach: an Eternal Golden Braid*, New York: Basic Books.

Holland, J. (1998), *Emergence – From Chaos to Order*, Oxford, New York: Oxford University Press.

Holst, E. von and Mittelstaedt, H. , "The Reafference principle: interactions between the central nervous system and the periphery (in German)", *Naturwissenschaften*, 37, pp. 464–76.

——, (1961). "Control theory as a methodic tool in behavior analysis (in German)", *Naturwissenschaften*, 48, pp. 246–54, p. 248.

Joy, B. (2000), "*Why the Future Doesn't Need Us*", April, 2000 Wired Magazine.

Kalmijn, A. (1978), "Experimental evidence of geomagnetic orientation in elasmobranch fishes," in K. Schmidt Koenig and W. T. Keeton (eds), *Animal Migration, Navigation and Homing,* Berlin, New York: Springer Verlag, pp. 347–53.

Korzybski, A. (1990), *Collected Writings 1920–1950,* Institute of General Semantics.

Kurzweil, R. (1990), *The Age of Intelligent Machines*, Cambridge MA: MIT Press.

——. (2005), *The Singularity is Near*, New York: Viking.

Langton, C. G. (ed.) (1989), *Artificial Life: The Proceedings of an Interdisciplinary Workshop on the Synthesis and Simulation of Living Systems*, Redwood City, CA: Addison-Wesley.

Landauer, T. K., Foltz, P. and Laham, D. (1998), "Introduction to latent semantic analysis", *Discourse Processes*, 25, pp. 259–84.

Lenat, D. (1995), "Cyc: A large-scale investment in knowledge infrastructure", *Communications of the ACM,* 38: 11, pp. 33–38.

Lewin, K. (1936), *Principles of Topological Psychology* (trans. Fritz Heider and Grace Heider), 1st ed., New York and London: McGraw-Hill.

Libet, B. (2004), *Mind Time, The Temporal Factor in Consciousness*, Cambridge, MA: Harvard University Press.

Lorenz, E. (1993), *The Essence of Chaos*, Seattle: University of Washington Press.

Lorenz, K. and Leyhausen, P. (1973), *Motivation of Human and Animal Behavior: An Ethological View* (trans. B. A. Tonkin), *Behavioral Science Series*, New York: van Nostrand Reinhold Company.

Lorenz, K. (1977), *Behind the Mirror: A Search for a Natural History of Human Knowledge* (trans. Ronald Taylor of the 1973 German edition), New York: Harcourt Brace Jovanovich.

MacKay, D. (1969), *Information, Mechanism and Meaning*, Cambridge, MA: MIT Press.

Marr, D. and Poggio, T. (1979a), "A computational theory of human stereo vision", in Kurzweil, R. (1990), *The Age of Intelligent Machines*, Cambridge MA, MIT Press.

——. (1979b), "A computational theory of human stereo vision", *Proceedings of the Royal Society of London. Series B, Biological Sciences*, 204: 1156, pp. 301–28.

McKaughan, D. (2008), "From ugly duckling to Swan: C. S. Peirce, abduction, and the pursuit of scientific theories", in *Transactions of the Charles S. Peirce Society: A Quarterly Journal in American Philosophy*, 44: 3, pp. 446–68.

Maruyama, M. (1963), "The second cybernetics: deviation-amplifying mutual causal processes", *American Scientist* 5: 2.

Massumi, B. (2002), *Parables for the Virtual,* Durham, NC: Duke University Press.

McCulloch, W. and Pitts, W. (1965), "A logical calculus of the ideas immanent in nervous activity", in W. S. McCulloch, *Embodiments of Mind*, Cambridge, MA: MIT Press.

Mead, G. (1934), *Mind, Self and Society, from the Perspective of a Behaviorist*, Chicago, IL: The University of Chicago Press.

Minsky, M. (1986), *Society of Mind*, New York: Simon and Shuster.

——. (2006), *The Emotion Machine*, New York: Simon and Shuster.

Miller, G. (1995), "Wordnet: a lexical database for English", *Communications of the* ACM, 38: 11, pp. 39–41.

Muller, A. and Muller, K. (2007) *An unfinished revolution : Heinz von Foerster and the Biological Computer Laboratory, BCL, 1958–1976*, Edition Echoraum

Musterle. W. and Rössler, O. E. (1986), "Computer faces: The human Lorenz matrix", *Biosystems*, 19, pp. 61–80.

Nørretranders, T. (1998), *The User Illusion*, New York: Penguin Putnam Inc.

Nolan, W. (1965), *The Pseudo-People: Androids In Science Fiction,* Los Angeles, CA: Sherbourne Press.

O'Keefe, D. and Nadel, L. (1978), *The Hippocampus as a Cognitive Map*, Oxford: Oxford University Press.

O'Rian, M., Justin, et al (1996), "A dispersive morph in the naked mole-rat," *Nature*, 380, p. 619.

Panksepp, J. (1998), *Affective Neuroscience*, New York: Oxford University Press.

Parsons, D. (1975), *The Directory of Tunes and Musical Themes*. S. Brown, Cambridge, England.

Pask, G. (1958), "Physical analogues to the growth of a concept", in *Mechanisation of Thought Processes, Proceedings of a Symposium held at the National Physical Laboratory on 24–27th November, Volume, II National Physical Laboratory Symposium No. 10*, London: Her Majesty's Stationery Office 1959.

——. (1982), *Micro Man: Computers and the Evolution of Consciousness,* New York: Macmillan.
——. "A comment, a case history and a plan", in Reichardt, J. (1971) *Cybernetics, Art and Ideas*, New York Graphic Society, Greenwich, Connecticut.
Pattee, H. H. (1969), "How does a molecule become a message?" *Developmental Biology Supplement*, 3, pp. 1–16.
Patterson, F. and Linden, E. (1981), *The Education of Koko*, New York: Holt, Rinehart & Winston.
Paulin, M. (1995), "Electroreception and the compass sense of sharks", *Journal of Theoretical Biology*, 174, pp. 325–39.
Peirce, C. (1931), *Collected Papers, Vol. I–VIII*, Cambridge: Harvard University Press.
Penrose, R. (1989), *The Emperor's New Mind: Concerning Computers, Minds, and the Laws of Physics*, Oxford, England: Oxford University Press.
Pereira, F. (2007) Creativity and Artificial Intelligence: a conceptual blending approach, Walter de Gruyter GmbH & Co. KG, Berlin.
Pert, C. (1997), *Molecules of Emotion*, New York: Scribner.
Powers, R. (1995), *Galatea 2.2.* New York: Farrar, Straus, Giroux,
Price, H. (1996), *Time's Arrow & Archimedes' Point: New Directions for the Physics of Time,* New York: Oxford University Press.
Putnam, H. (1982), "Brains in a vat", in *Reason, Truth, and History*, Cambridge: Cambridge University Press, chapter 1, pp. 1–21.
Richter W., Somorjai R., Summers R., Jarmasz M., Menon R. S., Gati J. S., Georgopoulos A. P., Tegeler C., Ugurbil K. and Kim S. G. (2000), "Motor area activity during mental rotation studied by time-resolved single-trial fMRI", *Journal of Cognitive Neuroscience*, 12, pp. 310–20.
Rolls, E. T. (1999), *The Brain and Emotion*, New York: Oxford University Press.
Rosen, R. (1967), *Optimality Principles in Biology*, London: Butterworths.
——. (1974), *On Biological Systems as Paradigms for Adaptation,* Center for Theoretical Biology, State University of New York at Buffalo, Amherst, New York 14226.
——. (1991), *Life Itself*, New York: Columbia University Press.
Rosenberg, E. L. and Ekman, P. (1994), "Coherence between expressive and experiential systems in emotion", *Cognition and Emotion*, 8, pp. 201–30.
Rössler, O. E. (1974), "Chemical automata in homogeneous and reaction diffusion kinetics", in *Physics and Mathematics of the Nervous System,* M. Conraf, W. Güttinger and M. DalCin (eds), *Lecture Notes in Biomathematics*, vol. 4, Berlin, Heidelberg, New York: Springer-Verlag, pp. 342–69.
——. (1974), "Adequate locomotion strategies for an abstract organism in an abstract environment", in *Lecture Notes in Biomathematics,* vol. 4, pp. 342–69. (Equation 13 is the brain equation.)
——. (1974), "A synthetic approach to exotic kinetics", in, *Lecture Notes in Biomathematics*, vol. 4, Berlin, Heidelberg, New York: Springer-Verlag, pp. 546–82.
——. (1978), "Deductive biology – some cautious Steps", *Bulletin of Mathematical Biology*, 40, pp. 45–58.
——. (1979), "Recursive evolution", *BioSystems*, 11, pp. 193–99.
——. (1981), "An artificial cognitive-plus-motivational system", *Progress in Theoretical Biology*, vol. 6, New York: Academic Press, pp. 147–60.
——. (1981), "An artificial cognitive map system," *BioSystems*, 13, pp. 203–09.
——. (1985), "An estimate of Planck's constant", in P. Erdi (ed.), *Dynamical Phenomena in Neurochemistry and Neurophysics*, pp. 16–18. Budapest: Publications of the Central Physical Research Institute. (ISBN 963 372 349 3).
——. (1996), "Relative state theory – four new aspects", *Chaos, Solitons & Fractals*, 7, pp. 845–52.
——. (1996), "Ultraperspective and endophysics", *BioSystems*, 38, pp. 211–19.

——. (1998), *Endophysics: The World as Interface*, Singapore: World Scientific Publishing Co.
——. (1998), "The world as an accident", in J. Brouwer and A. Broeckman et.al. (eds), *The Art of the Accident*, NAI Publisher, p. 172.
——. (2006), *Endonomadology*, xxxxx23, London. http://1010.co.uk/ottoroesslertranscript.pdf
——. (2006), *Personogenesis – The Toddler's Worked Miracle*,
http://www.wissensnavigator.com/documents/Personogenesis.pdf. Accessed 30 April 2010.
Rössler, O. E., Rössler, R. and Weibel, P. (1998), "Is physics an observer-private phenomenon like consciousness?" *Journal of Consciousness Studies*, 5, pp. 443–53.
Rössler, O. E., Lasker, G. E. and Aydin, A. (2004), "Delectatio in felicitate elterius – Benevolence Theory", in G. E. Lasker and K. Hiwaki (eds), *Personal and Spiritual Development in the World of Cultural Diversity*, vol. 1, pp. 69–78. Windsor, ON, Canada: The International Institute for Advanced Studies in Systems Research and Cybernetics. http://www.lampsacus.com/documents/ROESSLERBENEVOLENCE.pdf
Roy, D. (2008), "A mechanistic model of three facets of meaning", in M. de Vega, A. Glenberg and A. Graesser (eds), *Symbols, Embodiment, and Meaning*, Oxford: Oxford University Press.
Russell, J. A. (1991), "Culture and the categorization of emotions", *Psychological Bulletin*, 110, pp. 426–50.
Savage-Rumbaugh, S. (1994), *Kanzi : The Ape At the Brink of the Human Mind*, New York: Wiley.
Seaman, B. (1999), "Nonsense Logic and Re-embodied Intelligence", in *Reframing Consciousness*, Edited by Roy Ascott, Intellect press,
Seaman, B. (2005), "Pattern flows/hybrid identity construction", *Convergence: the International Journal of Research into New Media Technologies*, 11: 4, pp. 12–31.
——. (2008), "Neosentience – a new branch of scientific and poetic inquiry related to artificial intelligence", in *Technoetic Arts: A Journal of Speculative Research*, 6, pp. 31–40.
——. (2008), "Unpacking neosentience: dystopian techno-evolution?" *Mutomorphosis Proceedings*, http://mutamorphosis.wordpress.com/tag/neosentience/.
——. (2009), "(Re)thinking, the body, generative tools and computational articulation", *Technoetic Arts: A Journal of Speculative Research*, 7: 3, pp. 209–30.
——. (2010), *Recombinant Poetics: Emergent Meaning Examined and Explored Within a Specific Virtual Environment*, Berlin: VDM Press.
Seaman, B. and Rössler, O. E. (2006), "Toward the creation of an intelligent situated computer and related robotic system: An intra-functional network of living analogies", Catalogue for Emoçào Art. ficial, Itau Cultural Center, Sao Paulo, Brazil.
Shepard R. and Cooper L. (1982), *Mental Images and Their Transformations*, Cambridge: MIT Press.
Shepard R. and Zare S. (1983), "Path-guided apparent motion", *Science*, 220, pp. 632–34.
Shepard R. (1984), "Ecological constraints on internal representation: resonant kinematics of perceiving, imagining, thinking, and dreaming", *Psychology Review*, 91, pp. 417–47.
——. (2001), "Perceptual-cognitive universals as reflections of the world", *Behavioral and Brain Sciences*, 24, pp. 581–601; discussion 52–71.
——. (2004), "How a cognitive psychologist came to seek universal laws", *Psychonomic Bulletin & Review*, 11, pp. 1–23.
Shikhovtsev, E. and Ford, K. (2003), "A biographical sketch of Hugh Everett III" (see also Harry Browne. *How I Found Freedom in an Unfree World*. http://space.mit.edu/home/tegmark/everett/everett.html#149a. Accessed 30 April 2010.
Siegelmann, H (1999), *Neural Networks and Analogue Computation, Beyond the Turing Limit*, Boston, MA: Birkhäuser.

Simeonov, P. L. (2010), "Integral biomathics: A post-newtonian view into the logos of bios", *Journal of Progress in Biophysics and Molecular Biology*, 102, pp. 85–121.

Spaemann, R. (1989), *Glück und Wohlwollen Versuch über Ethik* (Happiness and Benevolence – an Essay on Ethics), Stuttgart: Klett-Cotta.

Squires, E. (1995), "An experiment to test an explanation of a possible violation of quantum theory", *Foundations of Physics Letters*, 8: 6.

Suchman, L. (1987), *Plans and Situated Actions: The Problem of Human-Machine Communication*, Cambridge: Cambridge University Press.

Steels, L. (2003), "Evolving grounded communication for robots", *Trends in Cognitive Science*, 7: 7, pp. 308–12.

Turing, A. (1950), "Computing machines and intelligence", in John Haugeland (ed.), *Mind Design II: Philosophy, Psychology, Artificial Intelligence*, Cambridge: MIT Press, 1997. See also Turing, *Mechanical Intelligence,* D. C. Ince (ed.), New York.

——. (1986), *The Charles Babbage Institute Reprint Series for The History Of Computing*. Vol. 10, Los Angeles, CA: Tomash Publishers.

van Hooff, J. (1972), "Phylogeny of laughter and smile". *In Non-verbal Communication,* Robert Hinde (ed.), Cambridge: University Press.

von Foerster, H. (1962), "Circuitry of clues to platonic ideation", in C. A. Muses (ed.), *Aspects of the Theory of Artificial Intelligence*, New York: Plenum Press.

——. (1970), "Molecular ethology, an immodest proposal for semantic clarification", in S. Boroch (ed.), *Molecular Mechanisms in Memory and Learning*, New York: Plenum Press.

——. (1973), "On constructing a reality", in F. E. Preiser (Hg.), *Environmental Design Research*, vol. 2, Stroudberg: Dowden, Hutchinson & Ross.

——. (1974), *Cybernetics of Cybernetics*, Urbana, IL: University of Illinois.

——. (1981), *Observing Systems*, Seaside, CA: Intersystems Publications.

von Neumann, J. (1955), *Mathematical Foundations of Quantum Mechanics* (trans. R.T. Beyer of the 1932 original edition), Princeton, NJ University Press.

——. (1995), *The Neumann Compendium*, vol. 1, F. Bródy and T. Vámos (eds), Singapore: World Scientific Publishing.

Vrobel, S. (1998), *Fractal Time*, Houston: The Institute for Advanced Interdisciplinary Research.

Wiener, N. (1961), *Cybernetics*, 2nd ed., Cambridge, MA: MIT Press.

——. (1993), *Invention – The Care and Feeding of Ideas*, Cambridge: MIT Press.

Zeeman, C.E. (1965), "Topology of the Brain". in *Mathematics and Computer Science in Biology and Medicine*. London: Medical Research Council. pp. 277–292.